Reforming Schools

Also available from Continuum:

Mike Bottery, *Education, Policy and Ethics*
Linda Evans, *Managing to Motivate*
Peter Gronn, *The Making of Educational Leaders*
Garry Hornby, *Improving Parental Involvement*
Maureen O'Connor *et al., Hackney Downs*

REFORMING SCHOOLS

Kimberly Kinsler
and Mae Gamble

CONTINUUM
London and New York

Continuum
The Tower Building, 11 York Road, London SE1 7NX
370 Lexington Avenue, New York, NY 10017-6503

www.continuumbooks.com

First published 2001

British Library Cataloguing-in-Publication Data
A catalogue record for this book is available from the British Library.

ISBN 0-8264-4801-1 (hardback)
     0-8264-4817-8 (paperback)

Typeset by CentraServe Ltd, Saffron Walden, Essex
Printed and bound by Creative Print and Design, Ebbw Vale, Wales

Contents

Preface

Improving public schools is a topic worthy of study unto itself. It has a history with recurrent themes; an ample literature; and differing schools of thought on the goals of public schooling; on the best practice for instruction; and on how best to go about the change process. It is also a topic whose time has come. As our own country and other technologically developed nations face the necessity of educating ever-larger numbers of students who are poor and from ethnic groups other than the dominant population, dissatisfaction with and interest in changing the outcomes of public schooling for these students have grown. Amidst a plethora of conflicting explanations and cure-alls, many nations and school systems seem to be stymied in their efforts to reform or significantly change the schooling process.

It is not that educators and many individuals interested in school improvement do not know what works. We have known for quite some time the essential components of effective schools. Rather, the issues are problems of politics, economics, scale, intent, personal understanding, and the daily realities encountered in the institutional innovation process. These are not simple matters.

This book is an effort to bring some order and to make some sense of this truly complex issue. Our goal is to provide an integrated resource for information on school reform. Toward this end, we have set several objectives for this book. They are: (1) to provide a realistic picture of the state of school reform in the United States today; (2) to facilitate readers' understanding of why the nation's public schools are as they are from both a historical and a cultural perspective; (3) to begin to explain why school systems are so difficult to change and why reform efforts so often lead to failure; (4) to review the major proposals currently being offered to improve the nation's public schools;

and (5) to illuminate paths along which the school reform process may proceed in the future.

While these goals may seem all encompassing, in reality, we feel the book barely scratches the surface. Embedded, as public schools are, in the larger society and responsive to its political systems, the complexity that results renders it nearly impossible for any one book to do justice to the full range of factors – even if we were to presume to know them all. From the broad spectrum of known factors, we have chosen to discuss issues that we have that found to be significant, based not only on the literature, but also on our actual work in the field of school reform. In trying to integrate the literature with our own practical understanding of the reform process, we too came to a new level of understanding of the topic. This further confirmed for us the need to bring these pieces together for others. We make no claims that what we say is new. This book is a synthesis, a "pulling together," of what has been written by others, what has been found from research in related fields, and what we have concluded in working with troubled schools.

This book is targeted at education professionals and others interested in the school reform process. It is written primarily with education professionals in mind, i.e., researchers on school change and the schooling process, educational program developers, school administrators, teachers, and baccalaureate and masters degree candidates in related programs. We hope this book will provide a resource for these individuals as they contemplate or actually engage in school improvement efforts. We also target legislators truly interested in changing the public schools, concerned parents and the public. We sincerely hope that for these individuals the book will help them better to reason through the accusations and panacean claims, and come to a more real understanding of the realities of the school change process. For individuals in this latter group, i.e., those who are unfamiliar with the education literature, we suggest that the book be read in an order different from that for academics in the field. Instead of starting with the history, theory, and culture of school reform (Part I), we suggest the reader reverse the placement of Parts I and III, i.e., that they read Part III first, then Part II, followed by Part I, and finally, read Part IV. In this way, the novice to educational theory is introduced to the key issues and concepts in a meaningful way before they are discussed as entities.

Throughout this book, we have made every effort to make the

writing as free of jargon and technical language as possible. We have also tried to make this book interesting, although of necessity we fear that some chapters may seem full of theory. We, nonetheless, hope that the presentation is clear enough that those without an extensive background in or knowledge of pedagogy and the operation of schools will find the book comprehensible and informative.

Philosophy

Teaching and schooling are areas in which there have historically been philosophical, theoretical and political differences of opinion. While we may adhere to one or another of these views, we feel it essential that a book of this nature seeks to maintain an eclectic, or middle-of-the-road position. We, therefore, have made a concerted effort throughout the writing of this text not to advocate for or against any one political or theoretical position. Rather, where space permits, we seek to offer as clear and unbiased a rendering of these positions as possible, as well as to give a balanced critique of these views. In some cases this position is easier to maintain than in others. For example, we do not feel that any one theoretical perspective regarding the various approaches to instructional methodology, leadership, and organizations, is best. Rather, we strongly believe that some combination is usually the wisest. This is consistent with our belief that educational theory and its various products, e.g., classroom strategies, leadership styles, and organizational perspectives, are best viewed as tools in toolkit, as a means to some end. Educators must be well versed with each tool, its operation, its strength and limitations, and the implications of its use; and as the needs and the aims of the user change, so too should the tool. On the other hand, we blatantly advocate for the academic success of children who have historically been underserved by the public schools. The book reflects a very definite concern with issues of equity in the outcomes of the schooling process. Long dismayed at the way the system perpetuates existing socio-economic and ethnic stratifications, we maintain that the nation's current push for excellence in the system's outcomes cannot be attained without equity. This view is heightened by the nation's rapidly changing demographics, where more and more states and cities find that the majority of students in their public schools are students from former "minority" ethnic groups. If our nation is to prosper, our public schools can no longer continue to under-educate these children without dire consequences to the larger society as a whole.

We present the book as a product of our accumulated life experiences and knowledge, i.e., as two professors of education with over 45 combined years of experience actively working to improve public education. Both of us, as young adults, were teachers in public elementary schools. Both of us have coordinated major teacher preparation programs and actively worked, periodically, to revise a number of educator preparation programs for Hunter College's School of Education. In addition, the first author worked for several years as a program evaluator for the New York City Board of Education, and in turn worked as a facilitator and school improvement coach for two of the major comprehensive reform models mentioned in Chapter 4. The second author, long an activist for school improvement, in the 1960s worked to form one of the first alternative elementary schools in New York City and in the 1990s was instrumental in bringing one of the major comprehensive models discussed in Chapter 4 to public schools in that city. For the last 15 years, our work in the field has been primarily with schools identified as at-risk by the New York State Department of Education or the New York City Board of Education. All these experiences have provided us with a range of theoretical and practical knowledge about the realities and needs of educator preparation programs and the school innovation process. Most significantly, these experiences have shown us the difficulties of translating educational theories and school improvement models into practice, as well as how the politics and culture of schooling manifest themselves to maintain the status quo.

In our effort to give as real a picture as possible of the complexity of school change, we have purposely tried not to "sugar coat" the material. As our own experience and the literature reveal, many if not most school innovations end in failure or abandonment. We attempt to shed light on why. In doing so, we want readers to "see" the possible obstacles that may present themselves and their operation in context. We, therefore, use a three-year case study of a school innovation effort that failed as an illustrative example. To some, this may be controversial. But, we feel that the literature, which almost exclusively focuses on reform successes, paints a deceptively simple picture that may not prepare schools, reform agents, parents and legislators for the gargantuan nature of the undertaking. It is important to note from the beginning that it is not our intent to blame any stakeholder group for the problems of the public schools. Rather, we seek to uncover the belief systems, associated behaviors, and institutional policies and practices that work against school improvement and the equitable outcomes of the schooling process. While the book at times may seem less than hopeful, we do believe that change is possible. The first step is in knowing and embracing the challenges. We cannot say that we have succeeded in all our efforts in this book. That is for the reader to judge.

The Organization of the Book

This text is divided into four broad Parts. The first Part orients the reader and sets the stage, progressing from the past to the present. Chapter 1 gives a brief 100-year history of previous school reform efforts. Chapter 2 discusses the politics of the school reform process, i.e., societal goals for public education, the stakeholders, and their roles in the change process. Chapter 3 brings us to the schoolhouse door with a discussion of the culture of the school and why it has become the target of current innovation efforts.

In the second Part we explore the substance and process of school reform. In Chapter 4, we introduce several of the major programs and proposals currently being advocated to improve the schools. We explore these change recommendations not from the perspective of advocacy, but rather from the perspective of the often hidden challenges to and assumptions underlying these proposals. Our purpose here is to provide a critical resource for educators about to make decisions as to which innovation to bring to their schools. In Chapter 5 we explore the school reform process by unpacking it in terms of its basic phases. We also discuss how new conceptions of schools as organizations have altered thinking about this process.

In the third Part we both illustrate and discuss some of the many problems that may pose obstacles to school innovation. Using an actual three-year longitudinal case study, we try to convey the realities of the process. Each of the three chapters in this Part is divided into two sections. The first section of each chapter recounts the events of one year in an effort to improve the academic performance of students at one inner-city junior high school using one of the comprehensive reform models discussed earlier. The second section is an analysis of the obstacles encountered.

In the fourth, and final Part, titled Reforming School Reform, we discuss how the school improvement process may be altered to make it more effective. We adopt a conception of schools as the center of a series of ever-widening concentric circles composed of educational institutions, governmental agencies and the larger society. We envision effective school reform as necessitating change not only in the schools themselves (Chapter 9), but in the organizations and programs that prepare teachers and administrators (Chapter 10), as well as in the surrounding agencies and the larger society that support the schools (Chapter 11). Ultimately, we believe that it truly takes the entire village to educate all its children.

Pedagogical Features

Each chapter of this book begins with a set of framing questions that starts the reader thinking about the content of the chapter to come. They often ask the reader to consider their own conceptions of the content in advance of the discussion. In this way readers hopefully are made aware of the ways in which the chapter content informs, builds upon or challenges these ideas.

In some chapters are boxes, some of which contain school examples of the content being discussed, several of which are taken from our own experiences working with schools. Some chapters contain query boxes, which ask readers to consider common dilemmas encountered in the school improvement process. There are no right or wrong answers to questions posed in these boxes, as the issues have not yet been resolved among practitioners in the field. We pose these problems for consideration, as readers who are in a school setting may very well be faced with these same questions when implementing innovations.

Each chapter ends with a set of questions. These questions not only review the content of the chapter, but frequently ask the reader to use material learned in previous chapters to answer questions or solve problems posed in the current chapter.

The aim of these features is to have the reader, as much as possible, imagine themselves as problem solvers in the school innovation process. In this fashion, it is hoped, the reader will begin to understand the complexity of the situation, and comprehend the many any varied forces that affect the outcomes of any change effort.

Acknowledgements

This book took several years to write, and many individuals and institutions aided us in a number of ways. Here we can only acknowledge the most significant, but in our hearts silently recognize the many others who assisted us in our work with school improvement and the writing of this book. Regrettably, space limitations prevent us from listing them all.

We first wish to acknowledge and thank those agencies and institutions that financed our work in school improvement and made it possible for us to work in the schools. We are indebted to the New York State Education Department's Office of Professional Opportunity Programs and the Office of School Improvement, which over the years have been instrumental in supporting our efforts. We are especially grateful to Alysan Slighter from the Professional Opportunity Programs and Pierre Hinton from the School Improvement Office for their intelligent responses to our requests and their faith in our abilities. We also wish to acknowledge the help of two project directors from private foundations, i.e., Norman Fruchter, with the Aaron Diamond Foundation for many years and Gilda Wray from the Charles Haydn Foundation. Both these individuals gave us encouragement and the opportunity to test various reform strategies at a time when we were truly novices in the school improvement world.

Our home college, Hunter College of the City University of New York, and especially the former Dean of the School of Education, Hugh J. Scott, must be recognized and thanked for many years of in-kind support. Dean Scott allowed us to use College facilities for project activities and generally assisted us in overcoming college bureaucracy, freeing us to work in nonconventional ways to achieve our goals. We also thank Hunter College faculty and staff, who gave us moral support and encouragement, most notably Sue Marsa, who gave us continuous feedback, and Carol Hope, who assisted with the technical aspects of getting the manuscript onto the computer.

For showing us "the ropes" in working with schools, we thank Henry Levin, Professor of Education at Teachers College Columbia University; Pilar Soler, the Accelerated Schools Center Director at Teachers College; James Comer, at the Yale Child Study Center; and Ed Joyner from the School Development Project at Yale. These two reform models gave us a framework that assisted in our work and continues to provide us with benchmarks that we still use in our quest for improvement. We also value the work done by Michael Fullan and Ruth S. Johnson. Fullan helped us understand the change process and consequently to accept conflict and complexity, while Ruth Johnson advanced our understanding of how inquiry and data can be used to attain equity in education.

The people from whom we learned the most are the administrators, teachers, and parents of Community School District Four in New York City. These people dedicate their lives everyday to providing the best learning environment possible to the 14,000 children who attend their schools. We thank the Superintendent, Evelyn Castro, for allowing us into her schools and supporting our efforts in every way she could. We thank Bob Gyles, Deputy Superintendent, for always being available when problems arose and being able to come up with intelligent solutions. Hilda Sanchez, Director of Funded Programs, met with us regularly to plan ways to work with schools, generously providing of her time, resources, and expertise. Her support and that of Marty Wolpoff have been critical to our ongoing efforts. We are also greatly indebted to the principals of the many schools in which we worked. They agreed to work with untried ways, relying on their personal faith in us, absent proof that what we were proposing would bring about improvements in the learning experiences of the children attending their schools. They invited us to meet with their teachers on a regular basis, worked with us in planning activities for professional development, and taught us a great deal about the difficulties and frustrations of achieving the higher standards currently being mandated for all public school systems, including those that have historically been underfinanced and over-regulated, frequently to the detriment of children. In this regard, we specifically wish to acknowledge Migdalia Maldonado-Torres, for being the first principal to invite us into her school and for teaching us so much about what makes a superb leader. Sally Bell, for being the second principal to allow us to experiment in her school, and for staying with us even when we made blunders; Adrienne Lake, for her commitment to children and her stick-to-it-ness in the face of obstacles and difficulty; Eileen Reiter, for her enthusiastic support of our efforts and her ability to engender cooperation and excitement among her staff; Nydia Sancho, for her warm heart and constant efforts to support all her teachers; and Victor Lopez, for showing us that leaders can be open to change with miraculous results.

We must also thank the hundreds of teachers who volunteered time and expertise trying to learn and adopt new ways of working together and doing research collaboratively on their school problems, somehow overcoming the constraints of their time schedules, conflicting goals and multiple top-down mandates. Some of them have developed into teacher leaders in their schools and now continue the process by mentoring less experienced staff in the new ways of working. We especially acknowledge Gryssele Machicote, for her skill in human relations, meeting management, and group process; Dawn Pimentel, for her wisdom about children and their learning; Tracey Wright, for her ability to motivate people by her sincerity and hard work; Carol Stern Schulze, for her skill in coaching teachers to become the very best they can be, Linda Abarbanell, for her assistance in editing and proofreading; and Cindy Brozen, for her valuable input as a research assistant and as a draft reader, providing valuable feedback at each step of the process.

Last, but by no means least, we are greatly indebted to our families, who encouraged, sacrificed, listened and patiently tolerated us as we worked under the simultaneous pressures of writing the book, performing our school improvement work, and for the first author, being a full-time professor. They helped reduce our stress levels when our responsibilities exceeded our capability for fulfillment. We particularly thank Will Gamble for his committed involvement in writing and editing parts of the book, and Kwaku Adeigbola for rescuing lost text from our computer's black hole at the twelfth hour. Finally, we wish to dedicate this book to our families for their unwavering love and faith in us.

Part I

Setting the Stage for School Reform

As we enter the new millennium, school reform is very much the topic of the day. From a plethora of "reliable sources" in government and business, the media report widespread societal dissatisfaction with the poor quality and products of our nation's public school systems. Fueled most recently by national reports decrying the inability of our public schools to prepare our youth enough to keep apace with other major world nations (Beaton *et al.*, 1996) or to assume entry level positions in the world of work, representatives of government and the media have besieged these systems with myriad recommendations and mandates for changing public education. As some have asserted, the decision is not whether to change our public school systems, but rather how and in what direction to guide their evolution.

What to make of the claims and accusations? If true, how have the nation's public schools come to be in this plight? This book is written to bring together and to consider the key points in this debate.

Part I sets the scene by familiarizing educators and students of school reform with the key themes and players in the current debate. Its purpose is to construct a framework to contextualize these criticisms and the various proposals for change discussed later on. The part is organized developmentally, i.e., it starts by considering the nation's history of past school reform efforts and progresses to the present target of complaint. Chapter 1 provides a brief, recent history of school reform efforts in the United States. Focused almost exclusively on reforms of the past century, its purpose is to reveal the antecedents of the current debate and to identify the key issues and recurrent themes that have continually re-emerged, each time cloaked in new vestments. Chapter 2, the politics of education, extends this picture by providing readers with some early insight into the process of school reform, particularly from the perspective of change initiation. Political rather than pedagogic in nature, this process of change initiation provides some clues as to why public schooling has so long been an area of considerable public contestation and little real change. In this chapter we review the major stakeholders and the means through which they seek to influence and "improve" the schools. Chapter 3, the last chapter of this Part, brings us to the schoolhouse door. It paints a picture of the traditional culture of schools, which have become the target of most recent school reform efforts, the means through which this culture is transmitted to novices, as well as changing conceptualizations of the school as an organization and of school leadership. The chapter concludes with a discussion of the role of students on school culture.

Taken together, these opening chapters provide an orientation to and some background information for the material presented in the chapters that follow. They are intended to provide the reader with a still rudimentary, but adequate knowledge of the basic issues and players sufficient to begin the process of unpacking and analyzing the current clamor for school reform.

Reference

Beaton, M., Mullis, I., Martin, M., Gonzalez, E., Kelly, D. and Smith, T. (1996) *Mathematics Achievement in the Middle School Years: The 3rd International Mathematics and Science Study*. Boston: Center for the Study for Testing and Evaluation and Educational Policy.

1

Putting School Reform in Context

Innovation is not new to our nation's public school systems; in the past 100 years, there have been numerous efforts to reform public schooling. Yet despite the many waves of change that have repeatedly washed over their shores, the structure of our schools as well as the schooling process appear to have remained remarkably intact. This presents a paradox, in light of these seemingly constant calls for their change. Is it, as some have asserted (e.g., Tyack and Cuban, 1995), that the vast majority of these reform efforts have been no more than a mere "tinkering around the edges" or have the structure and process of schooling become so entrenched in the minds of educators and the larger society that they are relatively immutable, recreating itself like a phoenix from its ashes?

At the start of the new millennium, the public schools again find themselves at the epicenter of a somewhat prolonged tempest calling for their change. Amid accusations from government and business asserting the inability of our schools to prepare the nation's youth adequately to keep apace with other major world nations (Beaton *et al.*, 1996) or to assume entry level positions in the world of work, the schools have again been besieged with myriad recommendations and mandates seeking to reshape or transform the schooling process. Consistent with the adage that those who ignore history are doomed to repeat it, some of the most trumpeted of the current proposals would have the nation pursue actions that recapitulate, with little deviation, previously failed and incomplete efforts. If the nation and its public schools are not to repeat the past, then knowledge of what has been tried before, and of the factors associated with their failure is crucial. Our first step, therefore, is to look backward.

Accordingly, in this chapter we briefly review the history of public school reform in the United States. As no condition or problem exists within a vacuum, knowledge of its genesis, its socio-history, if you will, can provide a valuable context with which to make sense of the current debate. Through exploring the public school's reform history, the reader may discern similarities between past and present initiatives, critical turning points, as well as insight and "wisdom" useful to the task ahead. In preparation for reading this chapter, consider the following questions to orient this exploration:

1. What are the major problems with the schools today, either as portrayed by the media or as perceived by society at large?
2. Can you recall, from your own personal experience, readings or word of mouth, earlier reforms that were in any way similar to those currently being advocated?
3. What do you think, historically, have been the primary or most common forces motivating changes in our nation's public schools?
4. What might the expression "those who ignore history are bound to repeat it" mean in this context?

A Century of School Reform

Since their inception, public schools have been the focus of individuals and interest groups seeking to influence the lives of Americans in future generations. In fact, the annals on public school reform in the United States are figuratively strewn with the detritus from successive reform campaigns. So much so that almost any adult observer or participant of one of these school systems can recall one, if not a succession, of educational "innovations" that have come and gone, e.g., the "New Math," "Distar," back to basics, "Open Education," Programmed Instruction and whole language, to name only a very few. Moving into the new millennium, society's collective memory accumulated from these struggles has become these systems' baggage, for good or bad. The question now arises, how should this luggage be handled? As something of great value, the repository of rich lessons for generations to come or as something better left than carried, a burden to be lifted so as to start anew? To make this determination, we must know their contents and evaluate each piece for its usefulness in the days ahead.

The short history provided below paints in very broad strokes the major school reform efforts of the twentieth century. Noted are those campaigns which led to relatively significant changes in the public school systems or trends in school reform that have cyclically reoccurred. Also noted are the key forces or interest groups that sparked these change efforts.

1900 to 1950: the administrative progressive era

The two adjectives best describing American education throughout most of the 1800s are diversity – in its nature and curriculum, and contrasts – in its organizational structures. Schools came in many forms, e.g., charity schools, town-sponsored ventures, church-sponsored systems, and quasi-public academies that were open to all free individuals (i.e. exclusive of slaves and Native Americans). The curriculum exposed students to a common belief system, combining Protestantism and nonpartisan patriotism; instruction in standard American English; an elementary familiarity with basic arithmetic; bits and pieces of literature, history, and geography; norms of punctuality, achievement, competitiveness, fair play, merit, and respect for adult authority. These schools also exposed students to processes of reasoning, argument, and criticism. While not necessarily at a high and cultivated level, the curriculum still eased students' way into the world of work and made possible various uses of printed materials. Beyond the common schools and academies were the colleges, universities, and other "seminaries" of learning for the nation's elite (Cremin, 1977).

Organizationally, public schools were similarly disparate, broadly characterized as either rural schools with decentralized administrations or as urban schools with centralized administrations. As the USA was then mostly a rural nation, the vast majority of public schools were dispersed across broad stretches of farmland, where instruction was predominantly conducted in one-room schools. Control of these community school networks, with few exceptions, was usually vested in local school districts. Numbering upwards of 100,000, leadership of these districts was highly decentralized and democratic (Cuban, 1990). Typically administered by local school trustees and citizens, these local boards strongly resisted government centralization in any form. According to Tyack:

> There was "school-based management" and community con-
> trol to a degree unimaginable in today's schools. Local
> trustees and parents selected the teachers, supervised their
> work, and sometimes boarded them in their homes . . . In
> the nineteenth century, educational leaders often wanted to
> consolidate one-room district schools and to turn them into
> graded schools . . . but they did not succeed in large-scale
> consolidation until well into the twentieth century. (1990:
> 176)

In marked contrast stood the city public schools, situated in the
nation's burgeoning industrial centers that had grown rapidly in
the latter half of the nineteenth century. These schools were
populated by the children of immigrants, attracted by the prospect of jobs and wealth. With denser student populations, urban
schools were generally hierarchically organized and graded, and
in them routines and instruction were tightly controlled, orderly
and standardized – very much resembling the exam-driven, centralized instruction characteristic of many schools today (Tyack,
1990: 176). Unlike their rural counterparts, urban schools were
managed by area superintendents who sought to buffer them
from their communities' demands and disparate interest groups.

As early as 1893, reform sentiment was much afoot, when,
empowered by the National Education Association, a committee
of prominent educators advocated for a more standardized and
academic curriculum for all students in the nation's high schools.
This so-called Committee of Ten, chaired by Charles W. Eliot,
then president of Harvard, argued that the primary task of
secondary education should be to develop and discipline students'
minds through the teaching of academic subject matter.
Acknowledging that only a small percentage of high school
students were bound for college-level instruction, the panel nonetheless urged that:

> every subject which is taught at the secondary school should
> be taught in the same way and to the same extent to every
> pupil so long as he pursues it, no matter what the probable
> destination of the pupil may be or at what point his edu-
> cation is to cease.

Lofty in their intent, these recommendations were not fated for
enactment. For while college-bound and workforce-bound students could then attend the same "comprehensive" high school, a

trade-off was in the planning. Within a decade, conditions combined to create a new educational outlook, one that increasingly viewed the role of public schools in nonacademic terms (Toch, 1991: 442).

In the early 1900s, a managerial *Zeitgeist* emerged from the nation's industrial revolution of the late 1800s that was pushed by a group of the educational and business elite to be reflected in the nation's public schools. These "progressive" school reformers, who could count among their numbers prominent leaders in government and in industry, were driven by the belief that progress in the future would best be made through use of the principles of scientific management. Their "Social Efficiency" approach to education equated progress with school systems that were more efficient, accountable, and a site for their personal conceptions of expertise. Having the wherewithal to advance their views, they lobbied for the elimination of one-room schools, the consolidation of small rural districts into larger ones, and the centralization of power in the hands of smaller, more efficient school boards that would hire trained professionals to run the schools (Tyack, 1989; Cuban, 1990). To handle the growing numbers of immigrant children and newly freed slaves, they advocated for the public schools to be used to socialize and to train these children to meet the needs of the new industrial economy. As these "administrative progressives" increasingly came to dominate the nation's educational leadership, they created hierarchies of curriculum experts and middle-level supervisors to prescribe the what and the how of teaching to the predominantly female instructional force. Opportunistically using the timely threat of Germany's growing industrial potential and the need to make the nation more competitive economically, they sought ostensibly to make the schools more rational, scientifically based and orderly organizations through the introduction of models and theories taken from the worlds of science and business. The most influential among them being Taylor's "time and motion" studies from the fields of business and management, and the work of Thorndike, from the Behaviorist (mechanistic) school of psychology.

> Like manufacturing industries, schools were developed as specialized organizations run by carefully prescribed procedures engineered to yield standard products. Based on faith in rationalistic management, in the power of rules to

direct human behavior, and in the ability of administrators to discover and implement common procedures to produce desired outcomes, twentieth-century education policy has assumed that continually improving the design specifications for schoolwork – required courses, textbooks, testing instruments, and management systems – will lead to student learning. (Darling-Hammond, 1997: 16)

During this time, there was a profound change in public high schools that significantly figured in this reform debate. Prior to 1875, fewer than 25,000 students were enrolled in these schools, nationwide, as attendance was voluntary. Most adolescents who were engaged in some form of secondary education attended private academies. However, from the late 1880s to 1920, laws on compulsory school attendance steadily grew for individuals under 20 years of age until by 1918 all states had them. By 1920, 2,382,542 students attended public high school, and by 1978, attendance in public and private secondary schools had risen to over 15.5 million. Similarly, the percentage of 14–17 year olds who were attending school grew from 6.7 to 94.1. This rapid growth necessitated that some structure for the high school be put in place and that debates be resolved regarding the purpose of secondary education. As previously, the early academies taught not only academic subjects but also vocational skills, educational administrators had to decide on four troubling issues: (a) whether schools would teach classical or modern subjects, (b) whether all schools would prepare students to meet college entrance requirements, (c) whether students should study subjects that would prepare them for life, as opposed to traditional subjects, and (d) whether all students should pursue the same course of study or whether the course of study should be determined by the interest and abilities of the students (James and Tyack, 1983; Sadovnik *et al.*, 1994: 78).

In keeping with the principles of "Social Efficiency," the administrative progressives called for the differentiation of the curriculum in accordance with the life destinies and abilities of different sectors of society. The schools would include vocational programs; the use of IQ tests – "scientifically" designed to sort and label students on the basis of their supposed "intellectual" potential; the creation of educational "tracks" matched to these groupings; and the development of standardized achievement tests to measure learning. Fortuitously, the rapid industrialization of the

nation's economy itself spurred the expansion of vocational studies, as businesses and unions urged public education to play a
significant role in meeting the "voracious manpower demands" of
the new economic juggernaut. The growth of this utilitarianism
approach to public education culminated in 1918 with the publication of one of the most influential educational statements in
the nation's history: *The Cardinal Principles of Secondary Education*. Written by the National Commission on the Reorganization of Secondary Education, it flatly rejected the earlier
contention of the Committee of Ten that the purpose of secondary education should be to develop students' intellectual powers
through instruction in academics. They conversely asserted that:
"The character of the secondary-school population has been
modified by the entrance of large numbers of pupils of widely
varying capacities, aptitudes, social heredity and destinies in
life . . ." To meet their needs, subject matter and teaching methods "must be treated in terms of the laws of learning and the
application of knowledge to the activities of life, rather than
primarily in terms of the demands of any subject as a logically
organized science." The value of education, in the Commission's
view, corresponded directly to the extent to which students could
put their education immediately to use in the conduct of their
daily lives. The main objectives of secondary education, the
Commission declared, should be: "1) health; 2) command of
fundamental processes; 3) worthy home-membership; 4) voca-
tion; 5) citizenship; 6) worthy use of leisure; and 7) ethical
character" (Hofstadter, 1970, quoted in Toch, 1991: 47–48). In
its final report, the Commission implied that "fundamental processes" were nothing more than rudimentary skills in the three
Rs, and argued that mastery of them was "not an end in itself."
The *Cardinal Principles* became the pedagogical *corpus juris* of
school systems nationwide. With the start, during this era, of
social promotion, by the early 1930s high school students could
do well in school without succeeding in their courses, and the
school was thus able to enrol, retain and graduate students
without succeeding in educating them (Powell *et al.*, 1985, in
Toch, 1991: 49).

These views were not unchallenged. Concurrent with this
school reform movement, a group of "soft" progressives sought to
involve the schools in the "democratization" of American life and
society. The most prominent among them was John Dewey.
Calling his view Developmental Democracy, Dewey and his

supporters promulgated a more child-centered approach to education that would give primary regard and consideration to developing the whole child and to their day-to-day experiences. Accordingly, Deweyans advocated for the creation and introduction into the public schools of curricula based on the needs and interests of individual children; the introduction of the child's emotions into the learning equation, and the participation of all citizens, including students, in decision-making processes as a means to develop rational thought and problem-solving ability. Many public educators interpreted Dewey's views as a rationale for teaching a new, nonacademic curriculum to the students whom they strongly believed to be intellectually inferior. Cremin (1964: 220), however, asserts that Dewey's goal had been to develop a curriculum "that would begin with the experience of the learners" but "culminate with the organized subjects that represented the cumulative experience of the race." Dewey's message was lost, however, on the relative few who thought themselves his disciples (Toch, 1991: 51), and on the many who adhered to the anti-intellectualism of the era.

The anti-intellectual sentiment both within the nation and in public education came to a temporary and dramatic halt with the launching of Sputnik in 1956. This foreign achievement led to a new wave of school reformers who severely criticized the flabbiness of the high school's academic curricula and the excessive number of practical courses that seldom stretched students' minds (Cuban, 1997: 24). Threatened by the Soviets' aggressive program of political expansion, the Federal Government, through the National Science Foundation, began a massive investment in defense-oriented school reform and the institution of a "core curriculum" in math, science and foreign languages (Tozer et al., 1998). Critics of the public schools further demanded the tougher selection and training of teachers, greater regimentation in the classroom, attention to patriotism and fewer frills (Tyack and Cuban, 1995).

Looking back on the first half of the twentieth century, the stage had been set for all future conflicts and reform efforts that were to come in the next half century. The administrative progressives had established a rational, linear and mechanistic approach to organizations as the basic model for our public schools that persists to this day (Tyack, 1990; Tozer et al., 1998). Vying for prominence as best practice were the teacher-centered approach and the more child-centered views of Dewey. Although

Dewey's teachings had spread rapidly to small pockets of liberal educators across the country, social efficiency advocates had been the most successful in transforming the public schools of the late 1800s and early 1900s. Doing largely what they set out to do, the administrative progressives reorganized public schools into far more centralized and mechanistically functioning organizations. In their promise to lift education "above politics" and to make the system more publicly accountable (not by assessing the results of instruction but by demonstrating conformity to scientifically based organizational structures and processes) they had firmly staked out the sides.

The 1960s: human relations and the previously disenfranchised

In this early transformation of the system, many people were left behind. According to Tyack and Cuban (1995: 22):

> [There were] major disparities in educational opportunities. These inequalities stemmed from differences in place of residence, family occupation and income, race, and gender, and from physical and mental handicaps. At mid-century American public education was not a seamless system of roughly similar common schools but instead a diverse and unequal set of institutions that reflected deeply embedded economic and social inequities.

In efforts to address these inequities, beginning in the mid-1950s and growing in intensity throughout the 1960s, groups that previously had little voice in the old system began to challenge several of the basic practices established during the reorganization era and the assumptions upon which they were based. Challenging the class and ethnic stratifications institutionalized in the sorting practices of the former era, the civil rights movement pushed for school desegregation while challenging the validity of IQ tests as the sole basis for tracking a disproportionate number of Black, Latino and poor children into the lowest sectors of the nation's schools. Militants in the 1960s called for the decentralization of educational decisions and community control of schools in urban areas heavily populated by minority students. Finding local school systems resistant to their demands, they turned to higher levels of government – to state and federal legislatures and to the courts – for redress. In support, friends of the civil rights movement concurrently advocated for the inclusion of human relations programs in the schools as a means to achieve greater understanding among the various ethnic groups (see Taba and Van Til, 1945; Taba and Wilson, 1946). Teachers, too, began to demand greater control over their work, splitting with organizations that had previously joined them with administrators (e.g., the National Education Association) to create new unions that would better pursue their separate interests (Tyack, 1990).

In combination, these reform movements of the 1960s led to several significant changes in the nation's school systems. One result was the increased influence of federal and state governments in school policies, practices, and decisions. Federal and state legislatures created dozens of new categorical programs (e.g., Title I, and later Chapter I, for needy students and Public Law 94–142 for the handicapped). In the process, school bureaucracies grew at a rate never before equaled, as mid-level managers were hired to link local bureaucrats to state and federal officials. At the same time, decentralization re-emerged, exemplified by the creation of community school boards in New York City. But unlike the decentralization of the nineteenth century, this new era created what Meyer (1980) termed "fragmented centralization," i.e., "everybody and nobody was in charge of public schooling." During and consistent with this era, there was also a resurgence in Deweyan progressive thinking, manifest this time in greater curricular choice, open classrooms, flexible scheduling, and the creation of middle and alternative schools. Accountability evolved into accounting, variously meaning responsiveness to the many protest groups demanding attention to their agendas; compliance to the legal mandates resulting from the expansion of litigation in education; conformity to the sometimes contradictory governmental mandates and categorical programs; and the broadening of students' choices, as in electives or alternative schools (Cuban, 1990; Tyack, 1990). However, as the school system made progress in regards to equity, i.e., the poor and people of color gained greater access to more equal schooling, social scientists started to question the value of these educational reforms. Were these changes indicative of progress or a form of regression? (Tyack and Cuban, 1995: 29).

The 1980s: the new "First Wave"

The Reagan era of the 1980s spurred by a number of critical national reports that warned of a major crisis in public education strongly reasserted conservative thinking as the dominant view in the nation and in its schools. The key treatise – *A Nation at Risk* (National Commission on Excellence in Education, 1983) – proclaimed the existence of a precipitous decline in the educational achievements of the nation's students that threatened America's competitiveness with other technological nations. Based on both national and international comparisons of students' test scores, these reports claimed that the general knowledge base of students educated in the United States was not only failing to keep pace with the needs of business and with technological advances, but was rapidly declining. Blame was placed on a weakening of standards and curricular rigor condoned during the Humanists' era, a deterioration in the overall quality of the nation's teaching force, and in the teacher training programs that prepared them. Conservative reformers called for a shift from the 1960s' focus on equity to one on excellence. Uncharacteristically, presidential attention also turned to education as Reagan campaigned on the failures of education and later, George Bush – declaring himself the "Education President" – sought the re-examination and redesign of public schools through the America 2000 project (Bell, 1993). In the context of the declining economy of the early 1980s, "commonsense remedies" that required little or no additional expenditure of money were opportunistically sought, e.g., cultural literacy, accountability through testing, new tougher graduation and teacher certification requirements, the use of vouchers and schools of choice (House, 1998).

State policies in general mirrored the federal agenda and reinforced federal preferences. State governors and legislators under the slogan of "back to basics" began to legislate and to implement a series of sweeping changes to public education, sometimes called the (new) "first wave" of report-based reforms. Seeking to purge their systems of *laissez-faire* and Humanistically oriented approaches to curriculum and testing, State Departments of Education set "standards" which increased academic requirements in English, mathematics and science for high school graduation as well as for college admission. They also reduced or eliminated electives (especially "soft" subjects) and increased the number of statewide tests (Sergiovanni, 1989; Tyack, 1990). To improve the quality of the teaching force, several states mandated that teacher candidates meet minimum college grade point average requirements and began to require tests for teacher certification. States also began to develop guidelines and requirements for evaluating teachers. These efforts by reformists to restore the traditional academic side of instruction and learning resulted in the imposition of new "top-down" requirements for local school systems, universities, teachers and students; greater monitoring, inspecting, and enforcing standards, and moved public education back toward greater centralization. In this era of reform, accountability became synonymous with exposing students to an increasingly standardized curriculum and their demonstration of its acquisition on standardized tests (Tyack, 1990).

The 1990s: the second (and third?) wave(s) of school reform

Only a few years later, educators in the late 1980s and early 1990s began to realize that the student achievement goals intended from these state-mandated initiatives were not generally being realized – despite the implementation of many of the regulations. According to Ravitch and Finn (1987), the states' tactic of attempting to reform the system "primarily by yanking and shoving and regulating and tempting the people and the institutions that compose it to operate differently" may not be the best way to bring about the sorts of change needed in the schools. The primary barrier to change, asserted Lieberman and Rosenholtz (1987), was the culture of the school itself, i.e., its organization and the "regularities" that govern the way things happen. From this perspective, the way to bring about improvement and change in the system must be through the same culture. A similar conclusion was reached by the Policy Analysis for California Education (PACE) group (Passow, 1989: 18). This body concluded that:

> In order to achieve full and effective implementation of the goals of reform – "better curriculum, improved teaching, successful schools, and rising student knowledge and ability to think – requires changes in teachers' attitudes and skills, in administrators' expertise, and in school organization and culture, all of which are difficult, time consuming to produce, and dependent upon local enthusiasm, commitment and effort." In sum, PACE argued that if change were to take place, the locus of action and responsibility must now shift from the state level to the local level. PACE observed that although the state could "initiate and nurture these processes, it cannot mandate their outcomes . . . the state

now depends upon the action of those at the local level, persons who actually manage and deliver educational services to students, to implement the hopes of educational reform and improvement."

Findings of this sort precipitated what Passow (1989) termed a "second wave" of reform reports, the most significant of which were the Holmes Group's *Tomorrow's Teachers* (1986) and *A Nation Prepared: Teachers for the 21st Century* (Carnegie Forum on Education and the Economy, 1986). Both these reports proposed more sweeping changes, including greater empowerment of teachers, giving teachers greater control over the teaching-learning process, yet holding them more accountable for student achievement. Both reports argued that a shift was needed from the approach of the "first wave," which focused on state legislation, regulation, and mandates to be implemented at the district and local levels, to one that focused on changing the very structure and nature of teaching as the keystone in this new wave reform. Passow concluded:

> There can be little question that the first wave of reform of the 1980s has resulted in greater state control of education and the enactment of the kinds of changes PACE described as "structural changes" in the school. How much and what kind of improvements have occurred as a consequence of these reform efforts is uncertain. While the nature and substance of a "second wave of reform" are perceived differently by different groups, the recognition that a second wave is currently underway suggests that the goals of the reformers have not been fully attained and that if school reforms are to be realized, reform by legislation, regulation, and mandate are not sufficient. (1989: 26)

Some assert that we have now moved into a third wave of reform (e.g., Goodman, 1995), characterized by the use of the latest advancements in organizational development, systems design or systems analysis. Advocates call for an even greater reliance on new business-based programs and use of electronic, resource-based delivery systems (e.g., integrated learning systems and self-instruction modules) which can effect cost savings by substituting for human-based delivery (ibid.: 12). As yet this new view is not adequately distinct unto itself, as several of the major changes proposed under Deming's business management model, Total

Quality Management, e.g., flattening the ˙system's hierarchy, empowerment with accountability, increased collaboration and professional development are surprisingly consistent with the second wave of reform. With the close of the twentieth century and the start of a new millennium, the common view is that the nation's best bet for improving our schools lies not with fine-tuning state reforms (although some of these reforms are also necessary) but rather with stimulating individual schools to change and providing them with appropriate assistance. According to Louis (1986), under the right circumstances, change orchestrated at the school level would have a significant chance of making a difference.

Change and Stability in Public Education

Key issues in school reform

In the past century, recurrent oppositional forces have sought to determine the organization and substance of the nation's public schools. Although shifting from era to era, key stakeholders and interest groups have organized and vied with other interest groups to express their values and to secure their agenda in the public schools (Tyack and Cuban, 1995). Alternating in the relative success of their efforts, their periodic skirmishes have produced seemingly pendular swings in our nation's public schools relative to their concerns. Thus, with each reform wave, the same general themes recur, but with each reappearance they are updated, reclothed in vestments reflecting the current economy, techno-logical advances, world events and views on race and class. What are these recurrent themes that continually emerge in the push and pull over the nation's school system? And how have these reform battles altered the nature of public education to date?

Control of the schools

Of all the themes, who should control these systems is probably the most contentious. By the start of the twentieth century, forces for centralization vied with those for decentralization in its myriad forms. Constitutionally, the matter is quite clear. As public education is mentioned nowhere in the Constitution, by default, each state's government has ultimate authority over its public schools. States can determine curriculum, set standards for graduation, and establish the educational criteria for the credentialing of various professions. The more states exercise this prerogative and the federal government intercedes in these regards, the greater the centralization of power at the top of the educational hierarchy and the more removed is decision-making from the local school sites and the communities they serve. At odds with this trend are populist forces, which seek to vest control of the schools in parents served by the school and in the local educational communities. When these forces move to assert their "natural" authority over their children's and students' education, greater decentralization results as these efforts disperse, or bring authority back down to individuals situated at the base of the system's power pyramid (e.g., to teachers, parents, and to boards staffed by elected community officials). With each reform wave, the power pendulum has shifted from one pole to the other, mutating with each swing.

The philosophy and methodology of instruction

A perennial quest among educational methodologists is for "best practice." Two broad philosophical positions have vied for this honor, each advocating contrasting views on the nature of the child and the learning process. On one hand, there are mechanistic and behavioral approaches, which characterized thinking during the Progressive Administrative era. On the other, is the progressive, or constructivist, approach reminiscent of Dewey's beliefs in that same era. At the time the public schools were constituted in their current form, mechanistic and behavioral views were popular and became the bases for the schools' structures and culture. The behavioral view portrayed the child as passive and learning as a passive process of linking actions and information together, based upon their frequent association in time or the receipt of rewards. The mechanistic view was embodied in the work of Taylor, whose time and motion studies in the early 1900s were the bases for successfully increasing the productivity and efficiency of the nation's factories. Taylor's work strongly supported the practice of segmenting work and the rigid sequencing of tasks such that "all possible brainwork is removed from the implementer and centered with upper level planners. . . . The task specifies not only what is to be done but how it is to be done and the exact time allowed for doing it"

(Braverman, 1974). When these views are adapted to the classroom, instructional content is similarly segmented and sequenced in small linear steps, which is then delivered to students in the most concise and economical fashion possible (i.e., through direct instruction). Learning is subsequently reinforced through drill and practice, praise, or some other form of reward. The strength of this approach is that large amounts of (preferably factual) information can be disseminated in a relatively short amount of time. As an approach to instruction, its advocates have traditionally been concerned with the amount of information students acquire, as well as their acquisition of literacy basics.

In contrast, constructivist approaches regard the child as active, and learning is described as a process of construction in which learners build upon their previous, or pre-existing, knowledge and seek meaningfulness in these constructions. Based upon the works of Dewey and the theories of Jean Piaget and Lev Vygotsky, advocates for this approach state that children should be given the time and opportunity to manipulate and experiment with objects, as well as to converse with others, to facilitate their spontaneous "discovery" of principles, problems, solutions and acquire an in-depth understanding of topics. Instruction works best when the material to be learned is meaningful, i.e., connected to the learners' existing knowledge and to their lives in the real world outside the classroom. This approach has been found to be most appropriate for content that is conceptual in nature, involving higher order thinking and problem solving. Consistent with Dewey, advocates for this approach urge concern for the learner-as-person and with the qualitative aspect of the instructional environments.

Historically, pedagogical skirmishes between these two philosophical approaches to instruction have been framed in terms of breadth versus depth, product versus process, and teacher-centered versus child-centered instruction.

Teaching as a profession

In terms of sociological definitions, teaching is not now regarded as a true profession. Characteristically, using medicine and law as their models, sociologists have variously listed as defining criteria: (a) the existence of a body of knowledge (without which the practitioner is unable to ply the trade); (b) government certification and licensure (Tozer et al., 1998); (c) a code of ethics that guides the actions of practitioners in the field in the service of the public (Vollmer and Mills, 1996); (d) board review by a panel of peers which seek to guarantee quality in both the qualifications and practice of its practitioners; (e) a large degree of uncertainty in terms of both the problems posed by clients and the possible solutions to these problems (Bacharach and Conley, 1989); and (f) an extensive supervised internship or apprenticeship (Bennett and LeCompte, 1990). (See Box 1.1.) Teaching, as a field, appears to be wanting in almost all regards.

Part of the problem rests with the field's inauspicious beginnings, for historically, teaching, as a field, required little if any formal training until the mid-1800s and the advent of "normal" schools. Housed in high schools, the curriculum for these preparatory schools coalesced a body of knowledge that laid the groundwork for the professionalization of teaching, but still fell far short of that for traditional professions. The reform wave of the early 1900s, which severely criticized this curriculum as being ill-defined and lacking rigor, aimed at raising these standards. As a result, teacher preparation was moved from two-year normal schools to a more rigorous academic setting – the four-year college or university, where teacher candidates could receive higher level instruction in the newly emerging psychological research on learning and, in the process, earn a baccalaureate degree.

Despite these modifications in their preparation programs, teachers, their training, and their status as professionals continue to be challenged. In looking for scapegoats for the system's woes, dissatisfaction with the schools and student learning often is translated into blame of those closest to the learner, i.e., teachers. At such times, the public and press tend to question, if not challenge, the ability of public school teachers to dispense quality instruction. Often, these challenges are framed in terms of whether teachers have adequate (minimum) preparatory requirements, and how much or what kinds of control should teachers have over the schooling process. In this debate, there tend to be two, generally opposing positions, i.e., those who favor "deskilling" teachers and "teacher-proofing" instruction, i.e., taking away any significant decision-making capacity versus those who favor increasing teachers' autonomy and decision-making. With successive reform waves, policies and practices consistent with both positions have been in evidence.

Box 1.1

Is teaching a true profession?

One of the most comprehensive category system is that of Bacharach and Conley (1989). They focus on whether management and administrative entities assume a bureaucratic or professional attitude toward the subordinate's duties and responsibilities in three key regards:

1. The nature of job-related knowledge: a bureaucratic attitude toward job-related knowledge assumes that the knowledge of subordinates can be specified, delineated and totally objectified. Alternatively, a professional attitude assumes that line personnel bring with them a unique body of knowledge, derived from experience as much as from textbooks. Creative interpretation is a significant feature of the work of the professional and is a function of unique and individual skill.
2. Control: the bureaucratic orientation asserts that management can control not only administrative knowledge but substantive knowledge as well, e.g., pedagogical knowledge. The professional orientation, on the other hand, suggests that while management may understand the broad parameters of substantive knowledge, the primary control of the knowledge should be left to line professionals.
3. The work of the professional: the bureaucratic position regards the tasks of the subordinate as repetitious and routine. The professional stance is that there is a high degree of uncertainty and great variation in the work.

Decisions made concerning where teaching falls on these issues will result in different characterizations of teaching as a profession. Thus, for example, teachers may be regarded as "appendages to bureaucracy," concerned with predictability and regulation; technicians, requiring the "teacher-proofing" of their autonomous decision-making; craftspersons, where failure is attributable to a lack of skill; or as professionals, where teachers are given a high degree of discretion and assistance in developing their repertoire of skills and knowledge (see Figure. 1.1).

		Variations in problems encountered	
		Low	High
Number of possible solutions	Few	Teachers as bureaucrats	Teachers as technicians
	Many	Teachers as crafts persons	Teachers as professionals

Figure 1.1   Two dimensions of uncertainty as a basis for classifying the work of teachers

Source: Bacharach and Conley (1989)

Institutional accountability

Accountability refers to the relationship between an individual who dispenses a service and the recipient or patron of that service. The patron has certain expectations concerning the work, e.g., that it will be done in an ethical, informed, responsive, and responsible manner to achieve certain outcomes, and has the power to reward, punish, or replace the provider if these expectations are not met (Kirst, 1990; Seyfarth, 1999), for example, in education, teachers are expected to choose materials and methods that enable children to learn new content. They are expected to administer tests and other forms of assessment to gauge students' progress and to give parents timely and accurate feedback on their children's performance. Historically, the customers, or patrons, of public education have sought to reward, punish or replace agents viewed as responsible for dispensing these services in a number of ways. One popular conceptualization identifies five distinct types of accountability, i.e., political, legal, bureaucratic, professional, and market means. Seyfarth (1999), summarizing the work of Darling-Hammond and Snyder (1992), describes them as follows:

- *Political accountability* uses voting to indicate approval or disapproval of a candidate or ballot initiative. Elected officials who fail to carry out the actions to which they committed themselves during a campaign may find themselves held accountable by voters who remove them from office in the next election. School board elections are an example of political accountability applied to schools.

- *Legal accountability* relies on the courts to enforce legal mandates related to schools. This form of accountability was prominent in the 1960s and early 1970s as previously disenfranchised groups brought suits against the school system and states for noncompliance with federal equity laws.
- *Bureaucratic accountability* is achieved by assigning responsibility for oversight of subordinates to those who hold supervisory positions in bureaucratic organizations. The superintendent of a district oversees the work of school personnel at lower levels of the school hierarchy, and principals supervise the work of teachers, counselors, aides, secretaries and others.
- *Professional accountability* depends on members of professional groups to protect the public interest. It requires that educators be well informed about the research, show knowledge of which instructional practices lead to the greatest gains in student learning and under what conditions learning is most likely to occur. It depends on the exercise of informed judgment by teachers and administrators and rejects reliance on rules mandating specific actions that are typical of the bureaucratic approach to accountability.
- *Market accountability* is achieved by allowing individual consumers to choose the provider of a service. In a market, consumers have the right to choose the schools their children will attend. If a school is not able to provide the services desired, it should be unable to attract students, and theoretically, it should cease to operate. This form of accountability is currently being proposed for the public schools today and is described more fully in Chapter 4.

In the end, accountability has three main functions: to inform, to reorient action, and to justify what is done. In the first regard, it serves to transmit information to the public or to authorities about what is being accomplished or to transmit information back to the provider about what stakeholders want so as to improve program designs and better operations. This informative function is non-threatening and, theoretically, is intended to help schools and sponsors understand each other. In regards to its reorientation function, accountability serves to help schools and legislatures to improve on certain tasks and programs. Legislatures wanting to achieve particular results may, thus, give additional resources or set penalties to move organizations in a particular direction or to achieve compliance. As a means of justification, it can become a protective strategy. When systems create accountability procedures that set norms or formalize outcomes that the system is already evidencing, it becomes a means of justifying itself and maintaining the status quo, e.g., IQ testing and tracking (Benveniste, 1985). At this point in the history of our public schools, all types have been used or are currently being tried in some form or other.

Change amidst stability

As both our brief history of school reform and our topic-specific review show, debate and contestation have been fairly constant in the field of public schooling. The results of these various reform efforts have been both significant change as well as surprising stability. That is, while various public school systems have implemented or adopted many of the recommended changes, the basic features of the schooling process have changed little. In explaining the school's remarkable ability to change in the midst of stability, distinctions have been made in the types of innovations made to and by these systems. Several researchers make the distinction between surface, or superficial, change and deep, or structural, change. Romberg and Price (1983) make the distinction between ameliorative and radical reforms. Ameliorative change is the process of making ongoing practices more efficient and effective. Basic values and power relationships within the institution are not examined as part of the effort. Cuban (1990: 73) makes a similar distinction between first- and second-order changes:

> First order changes try to make what already exists more efficient and more effective, without disturbing the basic organizational features, without substantially altering the ways in which adults and children perform their roles . . . Second-order changes seek to alter the fundamental ways in which organizations are put together . . . [and] introduce new goals, structures and roles that transform familiar ways of doing things into new ways of solving persistent problems.

An example of ameliorative or second-order change may be found in changes in the school's instructional procedures. Here the school's basic organization and culture remain intact. In contrast, radical school reform projects are those that confront and seek to alter the basic cultural traditions and beliefs that underlie current practices and organizational arrangements, e.g., current proposals that seek to detrack students or have teachers and parents collaborate in school governance. These theorists agree that the types of change previously made to the system as a result of the progressive era were essentially "tinkering" (Tyack and Cuban, 1995) and have failed to alter the basic organizational structures and cultural beliefs upon which the system is based.

First-order or ameliorative change has been rather pervasive throughout our nation's recent history of school reform, yet second-order or radical change has been much more elusive. There are many contributory factors, not least of which may be that public schools are designed to continue to fulfill their mission despite societal change. Thus, in the face of changing world events and fluctuations in societal consensus – all of which tend to precipitate school reform efforts – our schools not only continue to function, but seem to absorb the proposed changes – at least temporarily. Like a tree in a storm, schools bend but are neither broken nor transformed considerably. In the next chapter, we explore the politics of the school's responsiveness to change efforts in the context of the mission of public education.

Study Questions

1. What were the socio-historical forces that influenced educational change and policy in each era?
2. Compare and contrast centralized and decentralized control of the public schools. What are the pros and cons of each? In your opinion, which is preferable, centralized or decentralized and why?
3. What external factors have affected the locus of power in the schools?
4. Compare and contrast the mechanistic, or behavioral approach with the progressive, or constructivist approach. What are the pros and cons of each?
5. Which approach is more compatible with the centralization of power and why? Which is more compatible

with decentralization and why? Is it possible for the two philosophical approaches to co-exist? Explain.

6. Under which model (centralization or decentralization, progressive or mechanistic) would teaching be regarded as more of a profession? Why?

7. How have educators' views of teachers as professionals shifted from one era to the next?

8. In your opinion, what changes need to be made in teaching to make it a true profession?

9. In the schools today, there are increasingly more "teacher-proof" materials and curricula while simultaneously greater demands for participation in administrative decision-making. Are these two conflicting trends compatible? Explain.

10. How has the nature of accountability changed from one era to the next?

11. Explain the difference between first- and second-order change. In your opinion, which is achievable and why?

References

Bacharach, S. G. and Conley, S. C. (1989) Uncertainty and decision making in teaching: implications for managing line professionals. In T. Sergiovanni and J. H. Moore (eds) *School for Tomorrow: Directing Reform to Issues that Count*. Boston: Allyn and Bacon.

Beaton, M., Mullis, I., Martin, M., Gonzalez, E., Kelly, D. and Smith, T. (1996) *Mathematics Achievement in the Middle School Years: The 3rd International Mathematics and Science Study*. Boston: Center for the Study for Testing and Evaluation and Educational Policy.

Bell, T. (1993) Reflections one decade after *A Nation at Risk*. *Phi Delta Kappan*, April, pp. 592–597.

Bennett, K. P. and LeCompte, M. D. (1990) *How Schools Work: A Sociological Analysis of Education*. New York: Longman.

Benveniste, G. (1985) The design of school accountability systems. *Educational Evaluation and Policy Analysis*, Fall, vol. 7, no. 3, pp. 261–279.

Braverman, H. (1974) *Labor and Monopoly Capital*. New York: Monthly Review Press.

Carnegie Foundation on Education and the Economy, Task Force on Teaching as a Profession (1986) *A Nation Prepared: Teachers for the 21st Century: The Report of the Task Force on Teaching as a Profession*. New York: Carnegie Corporation of New York.

Cremin, L. (1964) *The Transformation of the School: Progressivism in American Education, 1876–1957.* New York: Vintage Books.

Cremin, L. (1977) *Traditions of American Education.* New York: Basic Books, Inc.

Cuban, L. (1990) Reforming again, again, and again. *Educational Researcher*, January–February, vol. 19, no. 1, pp. 3–13.

Cuban, L. (1997) School reform: the riddle of change and stability. In B. Kagan (ed.) *Common Schools, Uncommon Futures: A Working Consensus for School Renewal.* New York: Teachers College Press, pp. 14–32.

Darling-Hammond, L. (1997) *The Right to Learn: A Blueprint for Creating Schools that Work.* San Francisco: Jossey-Bass.

Goodman, J. (1995) Change without difference: school restructuring in historical perspective. *Harvard Educational Review*, vol. 65, no. 1, pp. 1–29.

House, E. (1998) *Schools for Sale: Why Free Market Policies Won't Improve America's Schools and What Will.* New York: Teachers College Press, Columbia University.

James, T. and Tyack, D. (1983) Learning from past efforts to reform the high school. *Phi Delta Kappan*, February, pp. 400–407.

Kirst, M. W. (1990) *Accountability: Implications for State and Local Policy Makers.* Washington, DC: Office of Educational Research and Improvement, US Department of Education.

Lieberman, A. and Rosenholtz, S. (1987) The road to school improvement: barriers and bridges. In J. Goodlad (ed.) *The Ecology of School Renewal.* Chicago: University of Chicago Press

Meyer, J. W. (1980) *The Impact of the Centralization of Educational Funding and Control of State and Local Educational Governance.* Stanford: Institute for Research on Educational Finance and Government, Stanford University.

National Commission on Excellence in Education (1983) *A Nation at Risk: The Imperative for Educational Reform.* Washington, DC: US Department of Education.

Passow, H. A. (1989) Present and future directions in school reform. In T. Sergiovanni and J. H. Moore (eds) *School for Tomorrow: Directing Reform to Issues that Count.* Boston: Allyn and Bacon.

Powell, A. G., Farrar, E. and Cohen, D. (1985) *The Shopping Mall High School: Winners and Losers in the Educational Marketplace.* Boston: Houghton Mifflin.

Ravitch, D. and Finn, C. (1987) *What Do our 17-year-olds Know? A Report on the First National Assessment of History and Literature.* New York: Harper and Row.

Sadovnik, A. R., Cookson, P. W., and Semel, S. (1994) *Exploring Education: An Introduction to the Foundation of Education.* Boston: Allyn and Bacon.

Sergiovanni, T. J. (1989) What really counts in improving schools? In T. J. Sergiovanni and J. H. Moore (eds) *School for Tomorrow: Directing Reform to Issues that Count.* Boston: Allyn and Bacon.

Seyfarth, J. T. (1999) *The Principal: New Leadership for New Challenges.* Upper Saddle River, NJ: Merrill.

Taba, H. and Van Til, W. (eds) (1945) *Democratic Human Relations* (16th Handbook). Washington, DC: National Council for the Social Studies.

Taba, H. and Wilson, H. (1946) Intergroup education through the school curriculum. *Annals of the American Academy of Political and Social Science*, vol. 244, pp. 19–25.

Toch, T. (1991) *In the Name of Excellence: The Struggle to Reform the Nation's Schools, Why it's Failing and What Should Be Done.* New York: Oxford University Press.

Tozer, S. E., Violese, P. C. and Senese, G. (1998), *School and Society.* 3rd edn. New York: McGraw-Hill.

Tyack, D. (1990) "Restructuring" in historical perspective: tinkering toward utopia. *Teachers College Record.* Winter, vol. 92, no. 2, pp. 170–191.

Tyack, D. and Cuban, L. (1995) *Tinkering Toward Utopia: A Century of Public School Reform.* Cambridge, MA: Harvard University Press.

Vollmer, H. and Mills, D. (1966) *Professionalization: Reading in Occupational Change.* Englewood Cliffs, NJ: Prentice-Hall.

2

The Politics of Schooling

> School criticism . . . is nothing new. Behind any criticism, however, are assumptions about what schools should and can do, and criticisms have shifted as assumptions about the goals and potentialities of schools have changed. (Ravitch, 1985)

Is our public school system so bad? Despite the media blitz and national reports attesting to the woeful state of affairs in our schools today, scrutiny of these criticisms casts serious doubt on their validity. International comparisons, in which we fare so poorly, may be misleading. For, in reality, our public schools are educating a larger total proportion and a more diverse population of students, for longer periods of time than most other nations, or our own nation's history (Kirst, 1987; Berliner and Biddle, 1995). Still, as one, all parties critical of the failure of our educational system cry that we must do better. As one, they say their aim is to improve our schools. But are they truly as one? Calm and closer inspection would quickly reveal that among them there are many different conceptions of this ideal, many different agendas and interests to be furthered, and many different paths toward "improvement."

Why have our public schools become the focal point of such a prolonged and contentious debate? Why do so many place such intense importance on this institution? And why unlike other large institutions and enterprises do so many feel they have the right, the knowledge, and the authority to prescribe remedies for its perceived ills? Addressing these questions is the aim of this chapter. Before exploring the politics of education, the reader is asked to consider the following framing questions:

1. What are or should be the goals of public schooling? How would you prioritize these goals; and what would you do where the goals conflict?

2. What are the varied interests, or stakeholders, that influence educational policy?
3. How, most typically, is educational policy made and/or changed?
4. Why is public schooling so important? Why is everyone so concerned with it?

The Goals of Education

There are many who think that schools exist or should exist for the primary, if not the sole, purpose of instilling in future generations knowledge of the three Rs, i.e., "reading," "ritin'," and "'rithmetic." However, schools exist in every society for varied reasons; not all of which relate to education. For example, in countries where the government is inseparable from the nation's religious doctrine, transmission of the national religion would be a primary goal of the school system and might even take precedence over the teaching of "scientific knowledge." In Western countries, there are differing views on the role of education. The two most common, theoretical perspectives are functionalist and conflict theories.

The functionalist perspective

Functionalists frequently compare society to an organism and its institutions to a body's organs. Like body organs, institutions are said to have specialized functions, or tasks, needed for the survival of the society and of its members. Accordingly, the task of the public schools is the intergenerational transmission of appropriate societal knowledge. Moreover, as schools assertedly provide an equal opportunity to all children to access this knowledge, they are also said to further societal integration by giving youths access to information unknown to their parents, allowing them to rise above their families' economic station. Through education, children can develop their skills to their fullest and obtain well-paid jobs. It is up to each student to take advantage of what the school has to offer (Farris, 1999: 36). The functionalist perspective assumes that change tends to occur through outside forces rather than through internal conflict or contradiction. Thus, the natural state of a social system, and the one that it seeks, is equilibrium.

According to this view, there are four specific goals, or purposes, of schooling. Sadovnik *et al.* (1994: 22–23) describe them in terms of their intellectual, political, social and economic roles within society.

1. The intellectual purposes of schooling are to teach basic cognitive skills such as reading, writing, and mathematics; to transmit specific knowledge (e.g., in literature, history, the sciences, etc.); and to help students acquire higher-order thinking skills such as analysis, evaluation and synthesis.

2. Its political purposes are to inculcate allegiance to the existing political order (patriotism); to prepare citizens who will participate in this political order; to help assimilate diverse cultural groups into a common political order; and to teach children the basic laws of society.

3. The social purposes of the schooling process are to help solve social problems; to function as one of many institutions, such as the family and the church (or synagogue) to ensure social cohesion; and to socialize children into the various roles, behaviors, and values of society. This process, referred to as socialization, is the key ingredient to the stability of any society.

4. Its economic purposes are to prepare students for their later occupational roles and to select, train, and allocate individuals into the division of labor. Toward these ends, schools should teach students the attitudes, technical skills and social behaviors appropriate to the workplace. They also act as sorting machines, categorizing students by their perceived ability and stratifying them into tracks specific to the diverse roles and careers required by a complex modern industrial workforce. In so doing, the schools are said to create a "meritocracy" (Bennett and LeCompte, 1990: 10).The importance of education in preparing individuals to earn a living has grown throughout the twentieth century. Today, individuals without an education are qualified for fewer than 10 percent of all jobs (Darling-Hammond and Snyder, 1992).

These goals at times conflict. For example, to develop all students to their fullest intellectually may be to over-skill them for jobs, leading to societal discontent.

Conflict theories on the goals of schooling

Conflict theories use the same general systems analysis, as does functionalism, but differ in their emphasis. Asserting that equilibrium is not natural, they focus on conflict, change and inequality, which are viewed as inherent in social systems. There are two major views consistent with this perspective: class and interest group conflict models.

Class conflict theory

Rooted in Marxist theory, supporters of this position believe that society is divided into various groups, or classes, based on the possession and control of wealth and capital. Capitalists, who own businesses and industry, are said to be in constant opposition to the working class, which provides the labor needed to make the products and services offered by businesses and industries. Capitalists seek to maintain their wealth by the perpetuation of the working class as a cheap source of labor through reinforcing traditional class, ethnic and gender inequalities. While differing among themselves on particular points of emphasis, in the final moment they concur that the primary objective of the school is the production and reproduction of existing class stratifications, either through the differential transmission of capitalist ideology or economically needed skills and attitudes. Mirroring inequalities in the larger society, schools teach children their later work roles through an explicit curriculum of skills and attitudes (e.g., advancing the ideal of equal opportunity) and a hidden curriculum of values, beliefs and behaviors (e.g., individualism and survival of the fittest) (Bennett and LeCompte, 1990; Farris, 1999). The school becomes a site of struggle when subordinate groups resist capitalist values and domination (Dougherty and Hammack, 1990).

Interest group conflict theory

Rooted in the theory of Max Weber, this perspective, while not rejecting Marxist views, expanded on this class analysis to include the maintenance of dominant religious, party, and cultural group interests. Conflict theorists assert that, as leaders of social, governmental, religious, or other groups and organizations achieve status and increasing power, they seek to meet the needs of constituents within their group, resulting in friction with other groups. Schools may be used in this struggle in two significant ways. First, they can maintain the cohesion of dominant groups by transmitting and reinforcing their culture and values. And, second, schools can be used to restrict the holding of educational credentials common among the dominant status group as a means of denying access to powerful and well-paid jobs. In this way, schools not only help interest groups compete with other groups for wealth, prestige and power, they, in turn, are shaped and modified by the desires of these groups or as a result of interest group conflicts (Dougherty and Hammack, 1990).

The central point is that there is, in fact, no commonly agreed upon goal or set of goals for public schooling. There are differing views, and even within the same view, i.e., the functionalist perspective, individuals and groups may differ on the priority to be given to the various sub-goals. This poses problems for educators and for public schools, for this uncertainty leaves them vulnerable to criticism from all fronts. Any one or any combination of these goals may be opportunistically held up as the rightful objective and the schools found to be wanting.

The Politics of School Reform

Amidst this uncertainty, a range of forces and interest groups have sought to direct, change, and (re)focus the public school system. The overwhelming majority of these change initiatives come not from within the educational system itself, but from outside the field. Two of the most dominant forces spurring change efforts are political perspectives and interest group politics. In this subsection, we outline the key characteristics of the three major political perspectives and the major interest sectors that have tended to take central roles in school reform efforts.

Political perspectives

The names of the major political perspectives are familiar to all of us, although their positions are more complex than most realize. Precisely for these reasons, one of the problems in using common labels or typologies is that there are often differences of opinion as to what constitutes the basic principles of any particular perspective. Moreover, the meanings and principles of the various perspectives have shifted somewhat over time. Based on Sadovnik, Cookson, and Semel (1994), we offer the following contemporary positions advocated by the three major political perspectives, i.e., the conservative perspective, the liberal perspective, and the radical perspective.

The conservative perspective

Conservatism has its origins in nineteenth-century social Darwinist thought, which applied the evolutionary theories of Charles Darwin to the analysis of societies. Accordingly, social evolution is viewed as a process that enables the strongest individuals and/ or groups to survive, and looks at human and social evolution as adaptations to changes in the environment. A second feature of the conservative viewpoint is the belief that the free market or market economy of capitalism is the most economically productive system as well as the most respectful of human needs (e.g., for competition and freedom). Conservatives argue that free market capitalism allows for the maximization of economic growth and individual liberty, with competition ensuring that potential abuses can be minimized. The conservative view of social problems places primary emphasis on the individual who is said to have the capacity to earn or not to earn their place within a market economy; and solutions to problems should be addressed at the individual level.

The liberal perspective

This view has its origins in the twentieth-century work of John Dewey and the progressive era of US politics from the 1880s to the 1930s. The liberal perspective, although accepting the conservative belief in a capitalist market economy, believes that the free market, if left unregulated, is prone to significant abuses, particularly of those groups who are disadvantaged economically and politically. It insists that government involvement in the economic, political, and social arenas is necessary to ensure fair treatment of all citizens to produce a healthy economy. The liberal perspective, then, is concerned with balancing the economic productivity of capitalism with the social and economic needs of the majority of people in the United States. Liberals place a heavy emphasis on equality issues, especially equality of opportunity, as they believe that the capitalist system often gives unfair advantages to those with wealth and power. Liberals assert that the role of the government is to ensure the fair treatment of all citizens, to ensure that equality of opportunity exists, and to minimize the vast differences in the life chances and life outcomes of the country's richest and poorest citizens. Individual effort alone, they assert, is sometimes insufficient and the government must sometimes intercede on behalf of those in need (Sadovnik *et al.*, 1994: 25).

The radical perspective

The radical perspective, in contrast, opposes the belief that free market capitalism is the best form of economic organization, favoring in its stead democratic socialism. Based on the writings of Karl Marx, advocates of this perspective suggest that the capitalist system produces fundamental contradictions that ultimately will lead to its transformation into socialism. The analysis of these contradictions is complex and beyond the needs of this text. Suffice it to say that the central contradiction pointed out by radicals is between the laws of the accumulation of wealth (e.g., that it is controlled privately) and the general social welfare of the public. Society should ensure a minimally acceptable standard of living, including food and shelter, for all its citizens. Radicals, thus, believe that a socialist economy that builds on the democratic political system (and retains its political freedoms) would more adequately provide all citizens with a decent standard of living. Essential to this perspective is the belief that social problems such as poverty and the educational problems of the poorest citizens are endemic to capitalism and cannot be solved under the present economic system (Sadovnik *et al.*, 1994: 25–26).

Stakeholder groups in school reform politics

As our brief history showed, the public schools and public schooling have long been arenas for struggles among advocates of these varied political perspectives. The reason for this, according to Fullan, is that the schools are a means to influence and socialize future generations consistent with one's particular interest and ideologies:

Innovations are still means by which some people organize
and control the lives of other people and their children
according to their conceptions as to what is preferable. It
disguises the reality that some people helped to plan the
changes; that some benefited from them while others did
not, and that some consequences were intended while others
were not. (Fullan, 1982)

Agencies or groups vary in their ability to influence the schools
directly depending, to a large degree, on their distance from the
local site level. As one moves further from the local school and
school district, influence and control tend to be increasingly
regulatory and indirect (Bennett and LeCompte, 1990). In the
next subsection, we briefly outline the interest groups and the
mechanisms through which they effect change, and illustrate
some of their major initiatives.

The federal government

Until, and for much of, the first half of the twentieth century,
the US federal government was not heavily involved in guiding
the schools, as aegis over the public schools rests with the states.
This pattern began to change in the 1950s, when civil and human
rights groups appealed to the government, through the courts,
for more equitable treatment in all aspects of society, including
the public schools. In the liberal atmosphere of President Johnson's Great Society, Congress passed the Elementary and Secondary School Act (ESEA) of 1965 and its various Titles. The Act
was designed to stimulate innovation, to strengthen the states, to
link research with the schools, and to make the problems of the
poor the nation's number one educational priority. In short,
ESEA was the first step toward translating this spirit of reform
into educational practice (Murphy, 1971). While its central thrust
was to eliminate poverty, embodied in the Act's first and most
important Title, it is important to understand that this reform
was not a response to public pressure. As far as the educational
associations in Washington were concerned, their primary interest
was general support for ongoing public school activities and
breaking barriers to federal aid, on the ground that this would be
a major step toward general support at a later date. Its objective
was a law, not a reform.

The precedent that had been set by the Supreme Court's civil rights decisions and ESEA continued throughout the 1970s with additional legislation and federal grant-in-aid programs that required the creation of regulatory agencies to monitor their implementation. Although the federal government's contribution to the schools accounted for only about 10 percent of their budgets, federal regulations on schools and servicing requirements exploded. Not only were schools being controlled by the rules and regulations tied to ESEA's various Titles, Congress passed additional laws, e.g., the Education for All Handicapped Children Act (P. L. 94–142) and the Bi-lingual Education Act, that required monitoring to ensure that federally mandated services for children with special needs were being provided. Although some researchers found that the federal laws and regulations were not burdensome (Moore *et al.*, 1991), schools and school systems complained that they had little flexibility in implementing programs and that the needs of all children were not being met.

In the late 1970s and early 1980s, as the government shifted its political perspective from liberal to conservative, the nature of federal influence also shifted. Abandoning a concern with equity, the government now sought to focus the nation's and the schools' attention on excellence. Using the weight of the Presidency and the Federal Government to support the 1983 release of *A Nation at Risk* (National Commission on Excellence in Education, 1983), conservative forces sought to agitate and elicit critical interest in the schools through alarmist phrases that proclaimed "a rising tide of mediocrity" and "an act of war" to describe the present state of public education (Toch, 1991: 27). Reasons for the schools' plight were attributed to the fragmented policy system with too much dispersed power and too little alignment between goals and actions. For the USA to regain economic competitiveness, there was a need to forge curricular standards and to push for the use of standardized tests to monitor the schools' progress – all to be achieved as cheaply as possible in an era of huge federal budget deficits (Cuban, 1997: 17). These beliefs became mainstream policy wisdom in the mid-1990s, embedded in the Goals 2000 legislation, which, while initiated by a Republican President, was signed into law by a Democrat. In turn, these views became the bases for state legislation and federally sponsored grants for the initiation of local level reforms.

In these events, what is clear is that the role of the federal government in public education has changed significantly. While conservative and liberal politicians in federal government may continue to disagree on specifics, both of the major political parties now regard education as a significant issue worthy of and requiring national attention.

State departments of education

The primary functions of State Education Agencies (SEAs) in regard to the schools have been the administration of federal programs and monitoring local compliance with state regulations. The organization of SEAs reflects federal policy priorities and a good deal of their operating budgets comes from federal funds (Cohen, 1990: 273). SEAs have two domains under their supervision, i.e., the accreditation of schools and the licensing of teachers. Within these domains, SEAs have the ability to determine the scope of educational funding, to establish minimum curriculum requirements and the minimum time allocations for school subjects. They also set minimum standards for the promotion and graduation of students, describe the rights of and set minimum competencies of teachers, define the characteristics of administrative structures, and create rules for the physical safety of school inhabitants (Wirt and Kirst, 1974). Some states also govern the adoption of specific sets of approved textbooks.

As with the federal government, state involvement in education was relatively limited until the mid-1960s (Bennett and LeCompte, 1990). However, with the passage of ESEA, state involvement increased, as the activities funded by this Act's Titles greatly expanded the state bureaucracy needed for program monitoring, review, technical assistance, data collection and evaluation (Moore *et al.*, 1983). This brought an important shift in the locus of power and control in school systems. While national educational agencies still had little influence over day-to-day behavior in the classroom, there was a shift toward greater SEA authority over school districts and the emergence of a more legalistic relationship between the two levels (Moore, Goertz and Hartle, 1983; Bennett and LeCompte, 1990: 62).

State involvement has continued to increase as states and governors have become progressively involved in advancing the bureaucratic changes that were part of the "new" first wave of reform efforts. As a result, an estimated 3,000 separate reform measures were enacted in the states during the mid-1980s. A plethora of state reform task forces were also assembled, in addition to those appointed by governors, State Boards of Education, state legislatures, and state commissioners of education. A sizable number of reform commissions were formed by independent organizations. Nationwide, no fewer than 54 state-level education reform commissions were established in 1983, and by January 1985 there were well over one hundred (Toch, 1991: 33–36). State reform initiatives have led to almost all states adopting standards in the core academic subjects for schools at the high school level, and only 11 states do not use standardized tests in order to assess progress in their achievement (*Education Week*, 1999a: 110; 1999b: 114). Similarly, for schools at the elementary level, over 70 percent of the states have established standards in the areas of math and science, and 50 percent have established standards in English/language arts. Schools that do not reach these standards are frequently put on published lists of low-performing schools. And while some states view these lists as an end in themselves, in others they are merely the first step on a "shape up or ship out" approach to failing schools. Although most states provide assistance to schools on these lists as a first step, continued failure to improve can result in loss of accreditation with loss of state funding, and outright closure and "reconstitution" of schools have been tried, with varying degrees of success (White, 1999: 38).

State initiatives have also been extended to efforts to upgrade the quality of the teaching profession. Starting in the 1980s, many states began requiring teachers to pass national teachers examinations in order to be licensed. Since then, all but eight states require some sort of examination of candidates' basic knowledge for certification, and 28 states require tests of candidates' professional knowledge as well. Additional mandates variously instituted by the states include mentoring for new teachers, liberal arts majors for all teacher candidates, more field experience (especially in urban areas), and extended student teaching experience among other initiatives (Bradley, 1999: 47).

In accordance with the second wave of reform efforts, during the 1990s, many of the states began to mandate second-order changes. In addition to heightening first-wave bureaucratic initiatives, many states also mandated the creation of school leadership teams to bring about greater participatory governance at the local school level. Some states began to incorporate mandated portfolio assessment of students' work and/or to require that standardized tests include items requiring demonstrations of higher order and critical thinking. By the end of the twentieth century, states found themselves participating in school reform as never before.

Central boards of education

At the local, i.e., city or district level, school boards establish overall policy, ratify the budget, set overall curricular and instructional directions, and oversee the hiring of personnel. The bureaucratic structure at this level parallels that of the states. At the top there is a chief officer or superintendent, an elected or appointed board of education, and an executive branch or agency, which carries out the activities of the department (Bennett and LeCompte, 1990). There are about 15,000 central school boards, or local education agencies (LEAs) governing over 90,000 schools across the nation. One-third of the boards are located in five states: California, Texas, Illinois, Nebraska, and New York. School boards are elected to represent the community and to set educational policy for that district. However, according to Bennett and LeCompte (1990), the politics of school boards tend to reflect prevailing business ideology. Business and professional people dominate central school boards all over the country, constituting more than three-fifths of their members. Housewives, usually middle- and upper-class wives of professionals account for 7.2 percent, and skilled and unskilled workers account for 9.4 percent. In 1987, women made up 26.5 percent and blacks 2.4 percent of all elected school board officials in the country (Bennett and LeCompte, 1990: 59). As most boards lack expert knowledge about educational issues, in many districts and cities, real power may rest with the superintendents hired by these boards and the professional staff in the central office. This structure, in part, may account for the perception that boards have made little progress in reforming schools. The "ambiguous structure of authority" (Wong, 1995: 571) engendered by its representational nature and the position of the superintendent relative to the board itself makes much of their activity combative and contentious, and much depends upon the political ability of individual superintendents to muster and maintain a consensus (Bennett and LeCompte, 1990: 59).

Since the 1960s, school reform has progressively reduced the power of central boards of education, redistributing their authority to the state or local site levels. Impatient with the lack of progress made at the city level (Smith and Scoll, 1995), states began to assume greater responsibility for the curriculum, through the setting of standards and standardized testing, and to shift greater decision-making power over budgets and staffing to local schools. In many states, school-based management teams (SBMTs) or councils now make budget decisions, determine professional development, and hire school staff. Most school boards are now limited to appointing the superintendent, distributing funds, and evaluating students (Wong, 1995). In extreme cases, SEAs have taken control of chronically low-performing city school systems from city boards of education. For example, in 1997, the State Department of Education in New Jersey took over the Newark school system, hired a new superintendent, and pushed aside the local school board as the governing body (Hall, 1998). It is questionable how long boards will continue to exist, as more schools develop SBMTs, and the federal and state governments exercise greater and more direct control as oversight agencies.

Professional organizations and their constituents

Among the various interest groups involved with school reform, the most powerful may be the professional unions. The first teachers' organization was the National Teacher Association, founded in 1857. Its merger in 1870 with the National Association of School Superintendents and the American Normal School Association created the National Education Association (NEA). It also set the precedent for dominance of the NEA by supervisory personnel and college professors, rather than teachers, creating "a collection of warlike tribes who fail to serve well the interests of any of the participants" (Bennett and LeCompte, 1990: 66). Despite heavy recruiting, the NEA never attracted the allegiance of a majority of teachers (Brenton, 1974: 82), many of whom belong to the American Federation of Teachers (AFT). The teachers' union became more militant and reversed the power relationship between unions and school management in the 1960s, first by a successful strike by the United Federation of Teachers, a local AFT affiliate in New York City, to win raises and prevent retaliation, and second, in alliance with the conservative school administrators union, the UFT fought off attempts to give control over the hiring and firing of teachers to decentralized local community boards (Scimecca, 1980). By the early 1990s, over 3 million teachers belonged either to the NEA or the AFT, who with their affiliates act as collective bargaining agents for teachers and administrators. An indicator of the strength of the NEA's national political network is that its members have been the single largest block of delegates at every Democratic Convention since 1980 (Toch, 1991: 153–154)!

On the issues contained in school reform initiatives of the last half century, the unions' position has been largely adversarial. Until recently, the NEA record on civil rights minorities, and the rights of women – who numerically dominated it – was weak. With the majority of its affiliates, the NEA has opposed virtually all the major teacher reforms, especially those that would raise standards and reward performance, steps that reformers have argued are crucial to improve the status of teaching as a profession (ibid., pp. 155–156). As the teachers' unions were more militant, particularly in regards to their welfare, civil rights, and academic freedoms, they were perceived as presenting major stumbling blocks to school reform.

However, during the late 1980s and early 1990s, the position of the AFT, under the leadership of Al Shanker, began to take a different stand from that of the NEA. Increasingly, they have embraced, in principle, many of the reforms of the first and second waves. Shanker spoke critically of due process procedures that were "excessively long and expensive" and the traditional legalistic system used to dismiss teachers (Toch, 1991: 143). He asserted that changes in union policy and attitude were necessary to further professionalize the field of teaching. This message has been somewhat slow to filter down to teachers at the grass-roots level, although not falling on totally deaf ears. According to Johnson (1983: 325):

> One of the most frequently voiced dissatisfactions of both active and inactive union members was that unions, in meeting their obligation to fairly represent all teachers, overly protect poor teachers. One metropolis respondent argued this way: "They no longer should have to defend the riff-raff. When they first organized, it was important for teachers to see that the Federation was strong and that they would defend people. But now they're plenty large. They could police their own instead of defending some teachers who can't teach himself [sic] out of a paper bag."

The AFT and its affiliate are now trying reform experiments in various parts of the country and some change in these regards may be in the offing.

In most states, any new school regulations involving teachers frequently have the input of the unions' collective bargaining agents in the planning and institutionalization stages. As a result, the unions have become a major player in the reform agreement process.

Parent and community groups

These can be a significant force for change to school systems. When these groups become concerned and organize around issues in their local schools, they can put pressure on district administrators (either directly or through school boards) to "do something" about a problem or oppose certain potential adoptions. Their power to bring about change, and the contestation of control over the schools by various groups were clearly illustrated in the dispute referred to above involving the New York City teachers' union. Civil rights organizations had rallied and organized to bring about the creation of decentralized local community school boards. They then fought with the professional unions over whether these boards would have the power to hire and fire teachers. In other communities across the nation, parent and community groups have variously fought for the removal, institution, or modification of particular curricula and literature, staff changes, extracurricular activities, the amount of homework assigned by schools, methodological practices, and the assigning of children to particular schools through zoning and forced bussing, to name just a few. Among the findings on the process and patterns of community control, Fullan (with Steigelbauer, 1991: 57–58) lists:

1. More highly educated communities seem to put general pressure on their schools to adopt high-quality, academic-oriented changes. They also can react strongly and effectively against proposed changes that they do not like.
2. Less well-educated communities are less likely to initiate change or put effective pressure on educators to initiate changes on their behalf. They are also less likely to become activated against changes because of lack of knowledge, but once activated they too can become effective.

Fullan concludes that there is a very powerful message implicit in these findings:

> In relatively stable or continuous communities there is a tendency for innovations favoring the least advantaged not to be proposed (the bias of neglect) and there is a greater likelihood that educators can introduce innovations (which they believe in) unbeknownst to the community. (Fullan and Steigelbauer, 1991: 58)

Recognizing the importance of parental and community support, and cognizant of the fact that when parents are involved with their children's learning, students do better in schools, reformers at all levels are calling for supportive parent involvement. So much so that all the stakeholder groups listed above have variously suggested, requested, or even mandated parent input in the hiring of staff, the allocation of budgets, school policy, discipline procedures, and the like (Epstein, 1997: 256). In addition to traditional forms of support, e.g., fund raising, attendance at local school/community events and volunteer work, parents are now being asked to participate in school governance and decision-making through membership of site-based management teams and action-based research committees. For example, in Illinois, to reform the governance of Chicago schools, the state mandated in 1988 that all its 600 district schools have local site councils composed of parents and teachers that hire and fire principals and make curricular and instructional decisions (Bryk and Rollow, 1992).

Business interests

Historically, business, business interests and many of the major organizational movements have profoundly influenced the schooling process. In fact, the schools' ability to prepare the nation's youth for their roles and careers in the world of work has been a primary concern of these interests, as well as of adults and parents seeking to ensure their own and their children's economic viability. National pride concerning US industrial viability and supremacy relative to other world powers has constituted a major factor influencing calls for change in the schools. As a motivating force behind the current first and second reform waves, North Americans have been repeatedly warned of their slipping world pre-eminence, both industrially and economically, which was blamed on the failure of the public schools. In making this argument, business and the media most frequently cited the following conditions: (1) the decline of manufacturing as the economic base of the United States and the concurrent rise of information processing, service industries, and high technology; (2) businesses' declining ability to compete in world markets, with the result that the United States has gone from being a major lending nation to perhaps the world's leading debtor nation; and (3) the apparent decline in the academic skills of American students, whether measured against past American performance or against that of students from other industrialized nations (Tozer *et al.*, 1998: 449). Conservative political forces have advantageously used societal alarm in these regards to push school reform legislation that would increase the setting of standards and standardized tests, the privatization of the schools and/ or their various operations, the opening of the schooling process to free market forces, the elimination of middle-management positions, increased accountability, and pay-for-performance clauses in administrator contracts (Bradley, 1993; Capper and Jamison, 1993; Harp, 1992; Rothman, 1993). According to Apple (1990: 158), the political right in the USA has been very successful in mobilizing support against the educational system, often exporting the crisis in the economy to the schools. In the process, the value of education has been reduced to economic utility.

Business also influences our schools in the transposition of business models to public educational systems. Twentieth-century Administrative Progressives used the "social efficiency" model as the basis for restructuring the public schools. Twenty-first-century business models now constitute the basis for much of the current restructuring effort.

Foundations

Private funding institutions, while having far less money to dispense than the federal, state or local governments, nonetheless, have been very influential in their ability to affect the school reform agenda – at both the national and local levels. At the national level, foundations, historically, have influenced the school process through the establishment of commissions and the issuing of major reports on education. For example, the Carnegie Foundation made a major impact on the teaching profession, as a whole, with the release of their 1986 report on teachers, *A Nation Prepared: Teachers for the 21st Century*. Warning that able and ambitious people would not be drawn to teaching or stay in the field unless school systems made major changes, the report made sweeping recommendations regarding the "restructuring" of schools to permit greater teacher decision-making, the establishment of a hierarchy of teaching positions (just as there is in the medical profession) and differential staffing and salary schedules (Tozer *et al.*, 1998: 294). The Carnegie Corporation of New York in conjunction with the Rockefeller Foundation similarly funded the work of a blue-ribbon commission, the National Commission on Teaching and America's Future, in 1994, which including prominent teacher educators, college presidents, two governors, NEA and AFT leaders, legislators, and key business people. Its purpose was to "provide an action agenda for meeting America's educational challenges, connecting the quest for higher student achievement with the need for teachers who are knowledgeable, skillful, and committed to meeting the needs of all students." They produced a report, *What Matters Most: Teaching for America's Future* (National Commission on Teaching and America's Future, 1996), which was widely distributed and embraced by educators at all levels.

Locally, foundations affect reform through their ability to fund research initiatives and reform projects at local school sites that are consistent with their agenda. A few very large private research foundations, such as the Rockefeller, Ford, and the Spencer Foundations, have a pervasive effect not only on the topics of investigation and the methods by which they are carried out, but upon the use of research data. Other foundations, like the De Witt Wallace-Readers Digest, the Annenberg, and the Lowenstein Foundations have funded a variety of reform measures including school restructuring, the creation of small schools, professional development laboratories, the return of the arts to many schools' curricula, and the use of alternative assessment, among others. In addition, recipients of awards from these agencies form an elite network of intellectual opinion leaders and referees whose judgment is sought on educational matters in both the public and private sectors (LeCompte, 1972).

Scholars and the academic elite

Academics can also influence the schools primarily through their research and other writing related to the teaching/learning process, the politics of education, school culture and organizations, and other related matters. Professional researchers, based largely at colleges and universities across the country, continually conduct studies to understand better how humans learn and how to improve the delivery and acquisition of knowledge. This work creates a constant flow of articles, books and other publications that seek to inform the public and academic communities of their findings, encourage their translation and adoption by instructional institutions, as well as their advocacy by philanthropic foundations and governmental agencies. Thus, instructional, methodological and organizational innovations, often with unproven efficacy and applicability to major public school systems, have been able to spark the interest of public and private educational funding sources. Agencies favorably disposed to these innovations' initial results or based on a belief in their superiority as approaches, may seek larger tests of their efficacy by offering funds to public schools or school systems willing to test and hopefully adopt them. Scholars whose writing becomes particularly respected in the field constitute an elite group of educational authorities, such that their opinions and advice are sought on pivotal matters related to the schools.

Thus, with so many perspectives, stakeholders, and means through which to change the schools, how is it that in so many regards, so little seems to change? According to Cuban (1997: 27), educational administrators, politicians and interest groups, past and present, "talk, trade ideas, and latch onto what they believe will fly politically every election year." This rhetoric of reform matters because it often gets translated into laws and new funded programs that are driven by an electoral clock. As conditions change, as elections tick tock by, these laws have then to be translated into action at the school level. Reformers do not teach in classrooms or run schools. Implementation, the putting of ideas into practice, is not their bailiwick; that is for practitioners. For most practitioners, policy talk about ideas and political timetables seldom shape their daily routines. As we will see in Chapter 5, translating laws into school practice is scarcely begun by the close of a political term by the time new election promises are made, or before new reform laws are passed.

School Politics in Action

So far, we have discussed a number of themes around which the politics of education have been played out. We close this chapter focusing on one last current issue, around which surprising little reform has been generated: school funding.

School funding

While public education may be a right, fairness and equity in the financing of public schools are not. While reason should dictate that if disparities exist, a disproportionate amount of funding be invested in those schools, students, and areas that are most needy of additional pedagogic services, in the USA the exact opposite is true. According to Berliner and Biddle (1995: 264):

> Within the worst states (Texas for example) schools in a rich community may receive more than five times as much per-student funding as schools in a poor community. In a recent article, Ronald Ferguson reports that the 1986 per-student support for Texas public school districts ranged from an abysmal low of $2,042 to a munificent high of $11,082. Or, if you prefer a single metropolitan area, Jonathan Kozol indicates that the 1986 per-student support in the New York City area ranged from $5,585 in New York City itself to more than $11,000 each in the suburban school districts of Manhasset, Jericho, and Great Neck.

Despite periodic outcries as to the unfairness of the system that perpetuates it, the politics of education keeps these disparities firmly in place. According to Darling-Hammond (1997: 261):

> The plain truth is that school-funding policies in the United States do not begin to ensure that all students will have access to the teachers, materials, or ideas they need to learn. Although some U.S. schools have adequate resources that could be much more effectively spent, many others lack even the basic levels of funding needed to support the curriculum and teaching to which students should be entitled.

The reasons for this inequality can be traced to the mechanisms used by the state and federal governments to maintain public education and the historical spread of public education in the mid-nineteenth century. There are two primary mechanisms for funding education, the direct channeling of federal and state aid to local districts and the granting of authority to local school districts (LEAs) to tax real property for this purpose. The direct channeling of funds may be accomplished in three general ways, i.e., general, categorical, and block grant programs. General financial aid flows from federal and state governments to LEAs with few limitations. In contrast, categorical aid links grants to specific objectives and targeted areas and populations specified by the government providing the aid. Block grants define a middle ground, whereby LEAs are allowed variously to fund a range of services within a broad set of government purposes (Swanson and King, 1995: 192–193). The portion of LEA budgets coming directly from the state, and to a much lesser degree the federal government, varies not only among states but with changing political sentiments. More conservative national and state governments, typically characterized by a strong belief in the decentralization of power, tend to assume less responsibility for educational funding, instead shifting greater responsibility to local authorities.

In the past century, as the extent and weight of the responsibility for public education increased, states, in turn, ceded more and more direct responsibility for running and funding the public schools to local school boards. In the process, these boards were granted the power to levy property taxes, in part, to finance these efforts. Thus, by the 1970s, local taxes produced half of public education revenues. This practice and the decentralization of authority over the schools have resulted in huge funding disparities among states, as well as among areas within states. In general, poor states (e.g., with a paucity of profitable industry) and localities with large populations of the poor are unable to raise tax levy funds adequate to support their schools, while conversely, wealthier states and communities with large populations of the upper middle-class and professionals tend to have well-funded and well-endowed schools. Even within districts, inequalities exist between schools servicing richer and poorer neighborhoods, as wealthier parents are able to subsidize the resources of their local school. According to Wise and Gendler (1989: 12):

> While children from advantaged families are more likely to attend clean, well-appointed schools staffed by adequate numbers of qualified teachers and supplied with up-to-date

books and technological aids, children from disadvantaged families are more likely to attend class in dilapidated school buildings staffed by less-than-fully qualified teachers, supplied with outdated textbook, and few, if any, technological aids.

As is to be imagined, the funding of schools in working-class communities is usually somewhere in between. With this latter group in particular, as well as for elderly property owners with no children, high taxation for schools is a burden.

By the 1960s, efforts had been made by the federal government to achieve greater equity in funding and educational practices among states and school communities. ESEA with its various Titles, particularly Title I, provided school communities with categorical funds specifically targeted to address the educational needs of economically disadvantaged and other special needs students. These monies were low, relative to the needs of schools in disadvantaged communities, and were categorical in nature (i.e., they had to be used for specific purposes). There, thus, was no flexibility in how they could be spent. As such, they provided no tax relief for the working class. Local school costs, nonetheless, had continued to rise (e.g., per-pupil expenditures had *tripled* since 1950) largely as a result of mandated educational services for students who were disabled (Lankford and Wyckoff, 1995: 196).

As taxpayers began to see their incomes diminishing, due to inflation and the loss of manufacturing jobs in the country, the school finance reform movement arose within the various states to bring about greater equalization in school funding. Actual and threatened legal action produced substantially revised or altogether new systems of school finance in more than 35 states (Barton et al., 1991: 17). For example, some states instituted the use of foundation state aid programs as one means of ensuring that all districts received a minimum standard of funding. States would give more aid to poorer districts up to a minimum level as a means of achieving greater parity among the districts. This method, however, was no remedy, for huge disparities among communities could continue to exist, as local communities could still raise funds for their schools in excess of the foundation amounts. Moreover, it did not address the issue of unequal needs. Even if per-student funds were made equal among states and communities, inequality would still exist as schools and school children in decaying urban centers have far greater needs. According to Berliner and Biddle (1995: 266):

> Many of America's urban schools now . . . are burdened by efforts to provide extra health, recreational, and social services for students and other citizens. Thus, if we truly wanted to fund schools based on need, we would not provide support on a per-student basis. Instead, *extra* funding would be provided for schools in impoverished communities where needs are greater.

In general, the courts while damning the inequalities, supported the continued use of property taxes as a valid revenue source. For example, the California Supreme Court, in *Serrano v. Priest* (1971), ruled that the system of unequal school financing between wealthy and poor districts was unconstitutional, but did not declare the use of property taxes for school funding illegal. Five other state courts (in Arizona, Minnesota, New Jersey, Texas, and Wyoming) rendered similar rulings within the next year. And in 1973, the US Supreme Court in *San Antonio (Texas) Independent School District v. Rodriquez* ruled, in a 5–4 opinion, that this method of funding, although unjust, was not unconstitutional (Sadovnik *et al.*, 1994: 451). The state courts' choosing to uphold the existing systems of finance tacitly condoned state legislatures' lack of receptivity to commit new resources or reallocate existing funds. And states in which the courts struck down the finance system had considerable difficulty implementing the decisions (Vandersall, 1998: 17).

With the onset of the conservative Republican administration of Reagan in the early 1980s and the subsequent excellence movement in the late 1980s and early 1990s, actions were taken to reverse the policies of the earlier liberal era by further devolving responsibility for education to state and local units and by budget reductions for education. Efforts were made to dissolve the Department of Education, and federal funding for elementary and secondary education was decreased by 17 percent, after adjusting for inflation (House, 1998: 20). In 1981, Congress passed the Education Consolidation and Improvement Act (ECIA), as a way to streamline Title 1/Chapter 1, to devolve further authority to the states and cut costs. It also created Chapter 2, which combined a number of categorical programs into a single grant block to each state that, in effect, further reduced funds for education (Elmore and McLaughlin, 1988).

Although Chapter 2 removed many of the onerous restrictions and monitoring requirements and allowed states considerable latitude in how these funds were spent, it also allowed states to shift funds away from large urban areas toward suburban and rural areas (Henderson, 1986).

A number of local tax initiatives arose hostile to the public schools. Proposition 13 in California (1978), Proposition 2½ in Massachusetts (1980) and many lesser-known tax limitation measures were adopted by referendum to sharply curtail the increasingly burdensome taxes levied by local districts to fund the schools. The resultant school revenue crunch led to salary freezes, layoffs, program cuts, and, in a few extreme cases, to bankrupt school districts (Toch, 1991: 5).

Concomitant with this change in federal policy, state funding for education increased. Across the states, as a whole, real revenues per pupil rose 31 percent between 1980 and 1988, although this increase varied tremendously from state to state (House, 1998). Governors became more active in state educational politics, interested primarily in the link between education and their states' ability to attract industry. Their thrust, however, was still conservative, and in general mirrored the federal agenda. State funds, therefore, did not alter the schools' funding patterns, nor fix the disparities among communities caused by the use of land taxes to finance the public schools.

Despite the strong gains in property wealth that have filled local and state coffers during the late 1980s, some states and their officials continue to staunchly defend these funding practices, and are quick to cite studies asserting that funding makes little difference to students' academic performance. For example, the former Governor of New Jersey, Christine Todd Whitman, faced with a court order to equalize spending between rich and poor public school districts, is quoted in the *New York Times* (May 16, 1997: B2) as expressing concerns that troubled urban districts are so understaffed and overwhelmed with problems that they will not use extra funds wisely. "What I don't think does anybody any good," she said at a news conference, "is throwing money at a system that can't absorb it well." After several needy communities sued their states to bring greater parity among localities, some states, e.g., Wisconsin and Rhode Island, passed legislation to dramatically reduce the burden on property taxes and shift to broader-based sales or income taxes, yet other states, e.g., Colorado, Nebraska, and New Hampshire, have rejected such legislation

(Swanson and King, 1991: 152). With the close of the last decade of the twentieth century, the "savage inequalities" in education funding and school resources persist (Kozol, 1991), and the words of Wise and Gendler (1989: 17) ring as true as ever:

> It is reassuring to know that schools can overcome, to some extent, the handicaps of dilapidated classrooms, textbook shortages, high student to teacher ratios and limited library facilities, but that does not justify such conditions. Nor has any research been able to show that a school with high expectations and no German teacher will produce students who speak German, or that a school with orderly classrooms and no laboratory facilities will train its students to be good scientists.

In summary, the nation's public school system historically has been and continues to be a political arena. As schools are the means through which the society prepares its youth for future generations, the system may be perceived as the primary vehicle for ensuring societal growth, upward mobility, and the creation of a responsible citizenry, or as the machinery for furthering class stratification and the perpetuation of an unequal status quo depending upon one's political and theoretical perspective. The ways in which governments, interest groups, and individuals seek to change the public schools are very dependent upon the change agent's particular conception of the role of public schooling and how well the system has fulfilled this task. As schools cannot be everything to everybody, there will always be individuals and groups dissatisfied with the current state of affairs, who will seek to alter the schools better to fit their views of the world and the schools' functioning. When the public clamor for change becomes strong enough, as at present, politicians and elected officials will seek to respond by passing legislation consistent with these changing images and views of public schooling.

Study Questions

1. Which of the theories on the goals of public education best fits your own view? Explain.
2. Of the various functionalist goals of education, how do you think society at large would prioritize them? How, if at all, would you prioritize them differently? Why?

3. What are the benefits and problems associated with the system's responsiveness to interest group politics?

4. In what ways has the intervention of the federal government been advantageous to the public school system? In what ways has it been disadvantageous?

5. Trace the pendular political swings from conservative to liberal and/or radical perspectives in the history of school reform, particularly in regard to control and instructional methodology.

6. With the current reform trend simultaneously toward centralization and decentralization, LEAs have less and less of a role. How can LEAs continue to ensure a role for themselves in the politics of education and how might they be changed to accommodate the changing times?

7. Teachers' unions and administrators' unions have historically been conservative forces in school reform. Explain why this might have been so. How might they take a more proactive role in the politics of reform, at the same time advancing the interests of their constituents?

8. Give two instances where community group pressure has led to changes to your local school system. In what way was this achieved?

9. Would you shift the funding of public schooling from its reliance on property taxes? Explain. What would be a good alternate funding source and why?

10. Do you think the system's responsiveness to interest group politics makes the system more conservative and less likely to change or volatile and trendy? Explain your response.

References

Apple, M. W. (1990) What reform talk does: creating new inequalities in education. In S. Bacharach (ed.) *Educational Reform: Making Sense of it All.* Boston: Allyn and Bacon.

Barton, P. E., Coley, R. J. and Goertz, M. E. (1991) *The State of Inequality.* Princeton, NJ: Educational Testing Service Policy Information Center.

Bennett, K. P. and LeCompte, M. D. (1990) *How Schools Work: A Sociological Analysis of Education.* New York: Longman.

Berliner, D. C. and Biddle, B. J. (1995) *The Manufactured Crisis: Myths, Fraud and the Attack on America's Public Schools.* New York: Longman.

Bradley, A. (1993) The business of reforming Cincinnati's schools. *Education Week,* vol. 19, May, pp. 16–17.

Bradley, A. (1999) Zeroing in on teachers: an essential element in high performing schools. *Education Week. Quality Counts: Rewarding Results, Punishing Failure,* vol. xviii, no. 17, January 11.

Brenton, M. (1974) Teachers organizations: the new militancy. In E. A. Useem and M. Useem (eds) *The Education Establishment.* Englewood Cliffs, NJ: Prentice-Hall.

Bryk, A. and Rollow, S. (1992) The Chicago experiment: enhanced democratic participation as a level for school improvement. *Issues in Restructuring Schools,* Fall, vol. 3, pp. 3–8.

Capper, C. A. and Jamison, M. T. (1993) Let the buyer beware: total quality management and educational research and practice. *Educational Researcher,* November 22, vol. 8, pp. 25–30.

Carnegie Foundation on Education and the Economy. Task Force on Teaching as a Profession (1986) *A Nation Prepared: Teachers for the 21st Century: The Report of the Task Force on Teaching as a Profession.* New York: Carnegie Corporation of New York.

Cohen, M. (1990) Key issues confronting state policy makers. In R.F. Elmore and Associates (eds) *Restructuring Schools: The Next Generation of Educational Reform.* San Francisco: Jossey-Bass, pp. 251–288.

Cuban, L. (1997) School reform: the riddle of change and stability. In B. Kagan (ed.) *Common Schools, Uncommon Futures: A Working Consensus for School Renewal.* New York: Teachers College Press, pp. 14–32.

Darling-Hammond, L. (1997) *The Right to Learn: A Blueprint for Creating Schools that Work.* San Francisco: Jossey-Bass.

Darling-Hammond, L. and Snyder, J. (1992) Reframing accountability: creating learner-centered schools. In A. Lieberman (ed.) *The Changing Contexts of Teaching.* Chicago: University of Chicago Press, pp. 11–36.

Dougherty, K. and Hammack, F. M. (1990) *Education and Society.* New York: Harcourt, Brace and Jovanovich.

Education Week (1999a) All students achieving at high standards. *Quality Counts: Rewarding Results, Punishing Failure,* vol. xviii, no. 17, January 11.

Education Week (1999b) Academic standards, assessment and accountability. *Quality Counts: Rewarding Results, Punishing Failure,* vol. xviii, no. 17, January 11.

Elmore, R. F. and McLaughlin, M. W. (1988) *Steady Work: Policy, Practice and the Reform of American Education.* Santa Monica, CA: Rand.

Epstein, J. L. (1997) School/family/community partnerships: caring for the children we share. In M. Fullan (ed.) *The Challenge of School Change.* Arlington Heights, ILL: Skylight, pp. 255–284.

Farris, P. J. (1999) *Teaching: Bearing the Torch*, New York: McGraw-Hill.

Fullan, M. (1982) *The Meaning of Educational Change*. New York: Teachers College Press, Columbia University.

Fullan, M. with Steigelbauer, S. (1991) *The New Meaning of Educational Change*. New York: Teachers College Press, Columbia University.

Hall, B. (1998) State intervention in the Newark public schools. *Educational Policy Conversations*. Institute for Educational and Social Policy, Occasional Papers 1997–1998. New York: New York University.

Harp, L. (1992) Group dissects education "industry" with eye to improving productivity. *Education Week*, vol. 18, November 12, no. 1, p. 3.

Henderson, A. T. (1986) For better or worse? *Phi Delta Kappan*, vol. 67, no. 1, pp. 597–602.

Holmes, S. A. (2000) After standing up to be counted, Americans number 281,421,906. *New York Times*, December 29.

House, E. (1998) *Schools for Sale: Why Free Market Policies won't Improve America's Schools and What Will*. New York: Teachers College Press, Columbia University.

Johnson, S. M. (1983) Schoolwork and its reform. In J. Hannaway and R. Crowson (eds) *The Politics of Reforming School Administration*. New York: Falmer Press, pp. 95–112.

Kirst, M. (1987) How well do U.S. schools perform? In M. Kirst (ed.), *Evaluating State Education Reforms: A Special Legislative Report*. Palo Alto, CA: Stanford University, pp. 83–101.

Kozol, J. (1991) *Savage Inequalities: Children in America's Schools*. New York: Crown.

Lankford, H. and Wykoff, J. (1995) Where has the money gone? An analysis of school district spending in New York. *Educational Evaluation and Policy Analysis*, vol. 17, no. 2, Summer, p. 196

LeCompte, M. D. (1972) The uneasy alliance between community and action research. *School Review*, vol. 79, no. 1, pp. 123–132.

Murphy, J. (1971) Title I of ESEA: the politics of implementing federal education reform. *Harvard Educational Review*, vol. 41, no. 1, pp. 35–63.

Moore, M. T., Goertz, M. E. and Hartle, T. W. (1983) Interaction of state and federal programs. In A. R. Odden (ed.) *Education Policy Implementation*. New York: State University of New York Press.

National Commission on Excellence in Education (1983) *A Nation at Risk*. Washington, DC: US Department of Education.

National Commission on Teaching and America's Future (1996) *What Matters Most: Teaching for America's Future*. New York: Carnegie Corporation.

Oakes, J. (1985) *Keeping Track: How Schools Structure Inequality*. New Haven, CT: Yale University Press.

Olson, L. (1999) Rating the standard: looking for consensus in three separate rankings of state standards. *Education Week. Quality Counts:*

Rewarding Results, Punishing Failure, vol. xviii, no. 17, January 11, pp. 106–109.

Ravitch, D. (1985) Forgetting the questions: the problem of educational reform. In D. Ravitch (ed.) *The Schools We Deserve*. New York: Basic Books.

Rothman, R. (1993) Taking account: states move from "inputs" to "outcomes" in efforts to regulate the schools. *Education Week*, vol. 12, no. 25, pp. 9–13.

Sadovnik, A. R., Cookson, P. W., and Semel, S. (1994) *Exploring Education: An Introduction to the Foundation of Education*. Boston: Allyn and Bacon.

Scimecca, J. A. (1980) *Education and Society*. New York: Holt, Rinehart and Winston.

Shannon, T. (1984) Adopt a public relations action plan. *American School Board Journal*, July, vol. 171, no. 1, pp. 38, 43.

Smith, M. S. and Scoll, B. W. (1995) The Clinton human capital agenda. *Teacher College Record*, Spring, vol. 96, no. 3, p. 390.

Swanson, A. D. and King, R. A. (1991) *School Finance: Its Economics and Politics*. 2nd edn. New York: Longman Publishers.

Toch, T. (1991) *In the Name of Excellence: The Struggle to Reform the Nation's Schools, Why It's Failing and What Should be Done*. New York: Oxford University Press.

Tozer, S. E., Violese, P. C. and Senese, G. (1998) *School and Society*. 3rd edn. New York: McGraw-Hill.

Vandersall, K. (1998) Post-Brown school finance reform. In M. J. Gittell (ed.) *Strategies for School Equity*. New Haven, CT: Yale University Press, pp. 11–23.

White, K. A. (1999) What to do when all else fails: dealing with low performing schools. *Education Week, Quality Counts: Rewarding Results, Punishing Failure*, vol. xviii, no. 17, January 11, pp. 37–40.

Wirt, F. M. and Kirst, M. W. (1974) State politics of education. In E. L. Useem and M. Useem (eds) *The Education Establishment*, Englewood Cliffs, NJ: Prentice-Hall, pp. 69–86.

Wise, A. E. and Gendler, T. (1989) Rich schools, poor schools, the persistence of unequal education. *College Board Review*, no. 151, Spring, pp. 12–17, 36–37.

Wong, K. K. (1995) Governing public schools: new times, new requirements. *Teachers College Record*, Spring, vol. 96, no. 3, pp. 569–576.

3

The Culture of Schools

Culture as a concept has had a long and checkered history. It has been used by the layperson as a word to indicate sophistication, as when we say that someone is very "cultured." It has been used by anthropologists to refer to the customs and rituals that societies develop over the course of their history. In the last decade or so it has been used by some organizational researchers and managers to indicate the climate and practices that organizations develop around their handling of people or to refer to the espoused values and credo of an organization. (Schein, 1997: 3)

When most people think of or picture the schooling process, they tend to recall images of teachers dispensing information in front of their charges, who, seated at desks, listen intently and raise their hands intermittently to respond to right-answer-oriented questions or to gain attention for some pressing need. So common and pervasive may be this image that there seems to be something natural and proper about this formula for schooling. Increasingly, however, pedagogical research indicates that these very character-istics of the schooling process are anachronistic and contrary to the goals of many current reform efforts. Other aspects of trad-itional school culture have also been labeled counter-productive, as, for example, the hierarchical nature of its organizational structure; the compartmentalized way in which instruction is divided into classes, grades, departments and tracks; and the sink or swim mentality by which many teachers are indoctrinated into the system and students fail year after year. More and more, school reformers are calling for "second-order change," i.e., modi-fication of the culture, or "deep structure" of the school. What is school culture, what is its role in the schooling process, and why has it become the current focus of such intense reform efforts?

In preparation for our discussion of school culture, its role in current reform efforts and the role of teachers, principals and students in establishing and maintaining school culture, consider first your own views in regard to the following issues:

1. Think of yourself as a member of your particular gender, ethnic, political or religious group. What are the outward manifestations, the espoused beliefs and the underlying assumptions of group members? What is the process by which new group members acquire this knowledge?
2. What does membership in these groups offer you? What life questions does it answer for you? And how does it make functioning in the world easier or more difficult?
3. Think of a cultural group with which you are familiar that has multiple leaders. How and in what ways do these leaders vary one from the other? In what ways do these differences affect their following? How might variations in group membership, e.g., ethnic composition, affect attitudes of group members as well as those outside the group toward the group?
4. And, finally, think about what it would be like to be told that a cultural group of which you are a member and whose beliefs you hold dear is wrong, and as a result that you must abandon these beliefs and practices. How would you feel?

Culture

Groups and organizations, more and more, are being characterized by their culture, i.e., those behavioral, emotional and cognitive elements that are held in common by its members. In unpacking culture, Schein (1997: 8–9) lists the following as elements: observed behavioral regularities of interpersonal interaction; embedded skills; climate; espoused and implicit values; broad policies and ideological principles that guide a group's actions toward stakeholders; and root metaphors, or the ideas, feelings and images groups develop to characterize themselves. These elements combine to form an integrated, stable paradigm or gestalt for the purpose of solving the internal and external problems facing the organization and its members. In the creation of culture, member and group patterns that prove successful are identified, rendered right and good, and passed not only from one member to another, but inter-generationally. In so doing, they become "institutionalized," i.e., taken for granted as the appropriate way to function, to think about group matters and to feel – eliciting neither question nor debate. Once internalized by group members, these paradigms begin to operate outside of awareness, emerging as defining properties of the group, permitting the group to differentiate itself from other groups in terms of them.

While theorists commonly accept the multidimensional nature of cultures, they often disagree on how best to organize descriptions of culture. For example, Hargreaves (1994) uses a two-part system, distinguishing the *form* from the *content* of cultures. Schein (1997), on the other hand, distinguishes three levels: the level of artifacts, that of espoused values, and the level of assumption. In our discussion of school culture, we use Schein's taxonomy as delineated below, as we believe there are common beliefs and assumptions associated with the schooling process that inherently undermine the success of many students and teachers as well.

Schein's first level, the *artifactual*, contains the most visible aspects of a culture. It includes all the phenomena that one sees and hears when one encounters the group, e.g., its organizational structures, the overt characteristics of the physical environment, its language, its style as embodied in clothing and in manners of address, its observable rituals and ceremonies, and the myths and stories told and published about the organization. Analysis at this level can provide some information about the basic functioning of an organization. However, to interpret these observances, one must usually look to the next two levels. At the level of an organization's *espoused values* are those beliefs that have been socially validated through shared social experiences, and which promise members who adopt them relative comfort and freedom from anxiety in meeting the day-to-day traumas they typically face. Values at this conscious level will predict much of the behavior that can be observed at the artifactual level, but not all. When discrepancies are found between what group members say or espouse and what they actually do, it is at a still deeper level that explanations may be found. At the third level, the level of assumptions, reside the organization's true "theories in use," i.e., those beliefs and values that actually guide behavior, that tell group members how to perceive, think about, and feel about

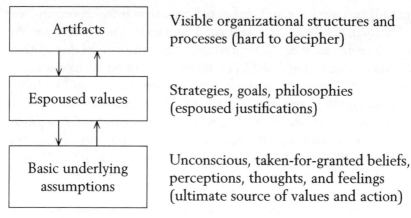

| Artifacts | Visible organizational structures and processes (hard to decipher) |

| Espoused values | Strategies, goals, philosophies (espoused justifications) |

| Basic underlying assumptions | Unconscious, taken-for-granted beliefs, perceptions, thoughts, and feelings (ultimate source of values and action) |

Figure 3.1   Levels of culture
Source: Schein (1997)

things (Argyris, 1976; Schein, 1997: 21). So deep-rooted is this level of culture, that its content is seldom, if ever, confronted or debated, and hence is extremely difficult to change.

The Culture of Public Schooling

Most descriptions in the literature of school culture, particularly in the context of reform, are of what might best be termed traditional school culture. As with any stereotype, wide variations from these norms may be found, both among schools, as well as within particular organizations (Little, 1990; Myers and Goldstein, 1997). We use this stereotype picture of schooling in our discussion below as these characterizations serve well to describe those things that have become the target of the most current reform wave.

The artifactual level

For many Americans, the schooling process has become synonymous with its artifacts, e.g., those things briefly described in the second paragraph of this chapter, along with other very visible features of traditional public education. So taken for granted are these common elements that Americans vary little in their views of desirable and appropriate educational experiences for young people. Moreover, having been pupils themselves, most adults have developed a notion of what a "real school" (Metz, 1989) should be like. This notion typically includes the school's hierarchical organization, its stratification and compartmentalization, and the solitary nature of learning and instruction.

Hierarchical organization

The school system is essentially organized as a pyramid. At its base, where the vast majority of its members are located, organizational power and authority are minimal. With each ascending level, power and authority increase, with ultimate power vested in the very few located at the top. As indicated in Chapter 2, at the base of the pyramid are local schools. Moving upward are local educational authorities (LEAs) in the form of county and city boards. And at the top of the pyramid are state agencies of education (SEAs) where ultimate power rests. Within each level are a plethora of substrata, departments and compartments, each with its own hierarchical organization. Most well known is the organization at the lowest level, i.e., at the local school site. Moving from the top down, the greatest authority within local schools and colleges rests with their top administrators, the highest being the principal or president, with penultimate authority assigned to its assistant principal, vice president or provost. From this point, authority diminishes rapidly as one moves to the levels of Dean and department heads (or head teachers at the elementary school levels). Still lower are various educational specialists and classroom teachers. At the lowest levels of the power pyramid are a school's semi- and non-professional support personnel and its students.

The lower on the power pyramid, the more constrained and prescribed are the activities and responsibilities of individuals. For example, the activities of teachers, located near the bottom of the professional hierarchy, are heavily prescribed. They, characteristically, teach a predetermined curriculum, using books often chosen by centralized committees, toward their students' attainment of pre-specified, grade appropriate learning objectives.

Stratification and compartmentalization

The schools' student body and the knowledge they receive are also partitioned and stratified. Age and amount of previous schooling are used initially to divide students into three broad instructional subdivisions: primary or elementary school; secondary-level schools; and post-secondary education. These same criteria are used again to further subdivide students, within each level, into grade or class cohorts. To facilitate the delivery of information, students may be yet further subdivided at the elementary through secondary school levels into ostensible ability-determined tracks, i.e., special education, regular education and gifted education students, and at the secondary school level until the late 1960s (Lucas, 1999), into interest tracks, i.e., academic, vocational or general courses of study. The curriculum is similarly stratified into grade-appropriate content, and at the secondary and post-secondary school levels into subject area disciplines.

Isolationism

To most expeditiously instruct students in their assigned seg-mented content, teaching takes place in isolated classrooms, partitioned one from the other by walls. Here, usually a lone adult authoritatively ministers to a group of 15–35 students. As students cannot be left unsupervised, teachers typically spend the vast majority of their workday in the company of children, and when their doors are shut, become the lone authorities in these isolated domains. Separated from other adults by this "egg-crate structure of schooling" (Lortie, 1975), teachers have little free time to talk with peers either informally or in scheduled, formal settings. Save for monthly grade-level or subject-area meetings, which are often devoted to school business, there is scarce opportunity or time for joint instructional planning, problem-solving and professional reflection.

Among schools, the degree of teacher isolation may vary and Hargreaves (1991; 1992; 1994) has categorized teacher cultures along this continuum into four broad types: individualistic, bal-kanized, contrived collegial and collaborative. Hopkins *et al.* (1994) summarize these four types as follows:

1. *Fragmented individualism* occurs where the teacher is isol-ated, is protected from outside interference, and at times takes refuge behind the "sanctity of the classroom door." This form reinforces uncertainty and insulates the teacher from positive feedback and support.
2. *Balkanization* describes a teacher culture "made up of sep-arate and sometimes competing groups jockeying for

    position and supremacy like loosely connected independent city states . . ." The existence of such groups often reflects and reinforces very different group outlooks on learning, teaching styles, discipline and curriculum.

3. *Contrived collegiality* occurs where administrators, not teachers, determine the forms of collaboration. As a result they are usually "regulated, compulsory, implementation orientated, fixed in time and space and predictable." As this form of collaboration is imposed from above, it discourages true collegiality through the desire for power.

4. *Collaborative cultures* facilitate teacher development through mutual support, joint work and a broad agreement on educational values. Within schools that possess a collaborative culture "the individual and the group are inherently and simultaneously valued."

These artifactual characteristics of schools have a number of ramifications that now are regarded as detrimental to the schooling process. On the one hand, the school's hierarchical organization makes it extremely difficult for supervisory personnel to know at first hand the activities of their subordinates. As various parts of the system can be dispersed over large geographic areas, e.g., across cities, counties and states, they typically are held together by policies, rules, and paperwork, where compliance is monitored by disproportionately few, overworked individuals. Such "loose *coupling*," i.e., where components have their own identity and a certain amount of autonomy, yet are connected to and responsive to each other (Tye, 2000: 71), makes it difficult for central agencies to control and directly supervise the tasks of large numbers of subordinates located at the local sites. Further exacerbating these structural features is the "anatomy of the closed door" (Lortie, 1969), i.e., as administrators at all levels can seldom visit the workplaces of subordinates, subordinates may simply close their doors as a successful means to avoid surveillance and close monitoring, and do largely as they see fit. This also includes compliance with innovation efforts, as we will see later.

    What is more, as all significant roles and functions are strictly defined, particularly at the lower levels, there are few differentiated functions within the role of teacher. Thus, save for salary increments, the tasks and rewards for entry-level teachers are the same as those for veterans with decades of experience. Teachers who desire career advancement must leave the classroom, either by attaining the credentials sufficient to enter the administrative ranks or by becoming staff or curriculum developers in particular subject areas. In both cases the result is the same, their departure from the school site to be centrally "housed" at district, city or county agencies. This has led in the profession to the expression that there is nowhere to go but out.

And, finally, many school reformers now regard as a detriment the long-standing isolation of teachers. According to Hargreaves and Fullan (1996: 6), teachers' professional isolation limits their access to new ideas and better solutions, drives stress inward to fester and accumulate, fails to recognize and praise success, and permits incompetence to exist and persist to the detriment of students, colleagues and the teachers themselves. Isolation allows, even if it does not always produce, conservatism and resistance to innovation (Lortie, 1975). While some researchers feel these conditions may facilitate the development of a sense of professional autonomy, allowing teachers to teach what and how they wish, and avoid conformity to administrative dictates (Bennett and LeCompte, 1990; Lortie, 1969), others believe this isolation makes collective action difficult as it inhibits communication and interaction. In contrast, research increasingly indicates that collaborative cultures are the most desirable; although this form of teacher interaction is both rare and difficult to sustain over time because it "goes right against the grain of all the pressures and constraints that normally come with teachers' work" (Hargreaves, 1992: 227).

The level of espoused values

The espoused values that underlie these practices are those most valued by the larger society and by Western culture, i.e., rugged individualism, competition, and advancement based on merit (Firestone and Seashore Louis, 1999). Consistent with these beliefs, students have for generations been taught seated at individual desks, which until very recently were separated one from the other. Learning tasks are performed largely on an individual basis, as knowledge is something possessed and acquired by individuals rather than by groups. Periodically, students are tested, not only as a means of informing parents of their children's relative attainments, but to rank, promote, and to sort learners based on their differential success in acquiring the canon. With all students ostensibly provided with an equal opportunity to acquire knowledge, those who study the hardest and are most able, should be and are acknowledged by the system with high grades and other forms of institutional recognition. In this way, children are socialized to regard and to value individual hard work and effort as guiding principles for their lives ahead.

To a lesser, but no less significant extent, these same values underlie the work of many teachers and system administrators. Despite consistent findings indicating that social relations in schools, particularly working relationships among teachers and administrators, are crucial factors not only in promoting teachers' own professional learning (Lieberman and Miller, 1984; Lortie, 1975) but in advancing student learning (Purkey and Smith, 1983; Rosenholtz, 1989), a significant number of new educators as well as veteran teachers face these tasks relatively alone. In many schools, teachers must learn "to cut the mustard" independently. Laboring under a code of self-sufficiency and independent trial and error as the principal route to competence (Little, 1990: 513), new teachers privately learn the ropes of gaining class control, student respect, and the mechanics and art of instruction (Grimmet and Crehan, 1992; Lieberman and Miller, 1984). So pervasive are these values, that when asked what they would do if more time could be made available, teachers gave priority to individualistic tasks (McTaggart, 1989). Similarly, Lortie (1975), in his classic study on the sociology of teaching, found that teacher preferences were not for collective reflection on practice, but for work which kept them isolated from their colleagues. Focusing on the more negative aspects of privacy, Grimmet and Crehan (1992: 62) note that:

> Such [individualistic] control over one's workplace is essential to any professional endeavor but the value accompanying this belief frequently confounds teachers' need for autonomy with their idiosyncratic wish for privacy . . . a surrogate for teacher seclusion and secrecy. This preference for privacy over responsible autonomy breeds norms of reticence and isolationism.

The consequence of the system's individualistic orientation, combined with teachers' commitment to privacy, extends beyond the structural realities of their workplace conditions (McTaggart, 1989: 347). Characteristically, it leads to the creation of psychological boundaries that separate teachers and interfere with acts of collegial sharing, help and problem solving.

> Teachers carefully preserve the boundary between offering advice when asked and interfering in unwarranted ways in another teacher's work. Most teachers expect to supply advice when asked – and only when asked . . . Teachers with many years' experience armed with well-formulated and well-grounded views on effective teaching, nonetheless refrain from advocating specific approaches even to beginning teachers. (Little, 1990: 515–516)

Thus, while teachers generally identify one another among their most valuable sources of on-the-job learning (Smylie, 1989), McTaggart (1989) found teachers in her study reluctant to inform colleagues about innovative changes they had made in their classrooms. For example, in one school district, even though a set of teachers had been commissioned to conduct demonstration workshops on their innovations in other district schools, they were reluctant to do so at their home schools. With their colleagues, there was an apparent moral commitment to keep ideas about teaching private, except under very special conditions. Privacy was recognized as a commitment for oneself, and as a virtue and right for others. In this sense, privatism appeared to be an ethic of teaching (ibid.: 347).

Researchers attempting to account for this culture of privacy among teachers have proffered a number of contributing factors including uncertainty (Lortie, 1975), apprehension (Hargreaves, 1980), and elective individualism for personal care and solitude (Hargreaves, 1994: 173). Little (1990) interestingly suggests that questions asked by one teacher of another are interpreted as requests for help, which become difficult to separate from judgments of teacher competence. "Understandably, teachers may show little inclination to engage with peers around matters of curriculum and instruction if doing so can only be managed in ways that may jeopardize self esteem and professional standing." Along similar lines, Hargreaves (1994: 164) suggests that offering and asking for help may be viewed as forms of "substantive heresy," i.e., acts which threaten particular parts of belief systems and particular doctrines which the faithful hold dear. Thus, teachers' reticence to provide feedback to one another, their tendency to act as "gatekeepers" to their isolated "kingdoms" rather than as professional colleagues may be due more to a regard of advice seeking and giving as contrary to larger societal norms of privacy and independence. This aspect of school culture, i.e., the exalted value of independent learning and its sink or swim ramifications for both teachers and students present a contradiction for an institution where learning, by whatever legitimate means, should be the ultimate goal. Schein would assert that the answer to this apparent dilemma is to be found at the deeper level of assumption.

The level of basic assumption

Consistent with Schein, at this level are a culture's deep-seated assumptions about success and failure, so profound that they virtually "go without saying." According to Tye (2000: 21), the underlying assumptions of both the system's and this country's espoused beliefs in rugged individualism, competition and advancement based on merit is the conservative belief in social *Darwinism*. Support for this belief as an underlying motive for teachers' extreme privatism are alluded to in Lortie's (1975) explanation of uncertainty, Hargreaves' (1980) factor of apprehension, and Little's (1990) notion of competence. It is only a small step from Little's statement that "teachers may show little inclination to engage with peers if doing so can only be managed in ways that may jeopardize self esteem and professional standing," to state that they may fear being regarded or regarding others as less worthy.

This assumption also underlies perceptions about students' academic performance as well. Despite historical exhortations concerning the egalitarian nature of US society and of its school systems, espoused beliefs about upward mobility, and current, mantra-like proclamations that all children can learn, the outcomes of the schooling process have been marked by the persistent failure of large portions of its poor and minority students to acquire the knowledge and cultural capital needed to prepare them to lead productive future lives. If these exhortations are to be believed, how, then, to account for the system's perpetuation in the face of this apparent failure? How do those outside, as well as inside, the schools perceive, think about, and explain these occurrences so as to tolerate, if not condone, their continuation generation after generation? Consistent with social Darwinism as an underlying assumption, the American school systems and US culture as a whole have long subscribed to *deficit theories* as causal explanations of between-group differences in cognitive performance.

Thus, up and until the mid-1900s, the seemingly intractable disparities in academic and professional performance between members of the dominant culture, i.e., middle- and upper-class Anglo-Protestants (and subsequently, European Americans) and that of minority cultures (initially immigrant European-American, and subsequently economically disadvantaged African, Native, and Latino-Americans) were explained first by the existence of a *genetic deficit*. This view posited that the gene pools of these latter groups of individuals were inferior, rendering them biologically less fit and worthy. As such, they just lacked the intellectual ability to do well in school and in the larger society.

This view was seriously challenged when biological evidence could not be found to support the notion of a "gene for intelligence" (Gould, 1981), and in its stead, *cultural deficit theory* was advanced in the mid-1900s. Based on findings of large between-group differences in the homes and culture of these communities, it was asserted that the early experiences of children from marginalized groups so lacked the cultural and academic supports needed to do well in school (e.g., print and language-rich environments, educational games and trips) that children from these groups enter school severely retarded in their ability to do well academically. So much so, in fact, that the schools cannot be expected to offset or compensate for these circumstances, particularly if the handicapping conditions continue to exist.

As a belief system, deficit thinking constitutes a severe impediment to both rigorous efforts at teaching poorly performing minority and majority group students, as well as to pedagogic reforms that have the academic excellence of these children as their goal. As these deficits are regarded are quite immutable – for schools can neither alter students' genetic make-up nor provide them with middle-class homes and parents – adherents believe that little can be done to bring these students up to levels of academic excellence. Thus, many adherents, in fact, condone current strategies, which either sort such students into groups or tracks, where the curriculum tends to be watered down (Oakes, 1985), or seek to "save them" by solicitous treatment. Both techniques, however, tend to doom these students to academic failure. For not only do they fail to provide these students with the academic work needed to "catch up," they convey strong implied messages about their incompetence. According to Bempechat (1998: 110), as early as second grade, poorly performing students are fully aware of the occasions when teachers ask less of them than of others and at a very young age are able to discern that they are not getting the challenging assignments because teachers probably think they are dumb. Similarly:

> any intervention or policy whose goal is to save individuals is bound to fail, for in the very act of saving, we communicate our belief that those whom we perceive to be in need are incapable of problem solving and limited in their ability to save themselves. As Bernard Weiner (1994) has argued, this has a tendency to foster feelings of incompetence, which may lead to learned helplessness. (Bempachat, 1998: 15)

Both genetic and cultural deficit theories in advance negate the public schools' responsibility for these children's poor academic achievement. According to Delpit (1995: 171):

> Teacher education usually focuses on research that links failure and socioeconomic status, failure and cultural difference, failure and single parent households. It is hard to believe that these children can possibly be successful after their teachers have been so thoroughly exposed to so much negative indoctrination. When teachers receive that kind of education, there is a tendency to assume deficits in students rather than to locate and teach to strengths.

As a consequence, educators who embrace deficit thinking feel neither guilt for nor ownership of the resultant condition, as they believe that they have done nothing to cause the situation, and that save for providing social services that might ameliorate some aspects of these children's plight, there is basically nothing that can be done. Where teachers and school administrators regard the existing patterns of underachievement as consistent with a natural ordering of ability levels or due to unalterable circumstances, they will resist altering their goals for these students' education and changing their methods of teaching. Adherents of this belief system can, with true conviction assert: "It's not me, my teaching, nor anything that the school is doing that is wrong. Nothing needs changing, except the children themselves!"

How pervasive is deficit thinking among teachers and other educators in our public elementary and secondary schools? It is very difficult to say, but according to Doyle (1993):

[S]o many defenders of the public schools have begun to assert that the problems of the public schools are the problems of their clients. Indeed, the assertion is so often made that schools cannot deal with "these" children that it is a commonplace. That it is usually offered as a rationale for school failure is too often overlooked. So close to "blaming the victim" is this assertion that one wonders if it is a distinction without a difference.

Thus, despite contrary evidence indicating that poor and minority children can be brought to advanced levels of academic functioning irrespective of their home environments, many educators tenaciously adhere to deficit thinking.

A second assumption, closely associated with the first is the taken-for-granted use of middle-class, European-American culture and codes as the basis against which to judge all student behavior. Why this is the case may be found in Schein's (1997: 54) notion of the latent function of organizations. To reveal these functions, one needs to understand the intentions of an organization's founders and leaders relative to their definitions of the situation. In regards to the schools, Vallance (1994: 84) states:

[T]he reformers of the mid-century period were not at all sure that the national character could withstand the onslaught of cultural diversity. It was clear to the Common School crusaders that the national character was basically "AngloAmerican;" the problem facing the character was now one of self-preservation. "To sustain an extended republic like our own," wrote Calvin Stowe in 1836, "there must be a national feeling, a national assimilation . . . It is altogether essential to our national strength and peace that the foreigners should cease to be Europeans and become Americans. Let them be like grafts which become branches of the parent stock."

Not coincidentally, these standards and codes are those of both the nation's and the schools' dominant adult populations. According to Feiman-Nemser and Remillard (1996), staff of most public schools are disproportionately white, female and middle class. They come from small towns and suburbs, go to local colleges and institutions, and are not strong academically. These demographic characteristics are accompanied by a distinctive mindset, or orientation to teaching, in which they expect, if not desire, for their students to be much like themselves (Firestone and Seashore Louis, 1999). They view their primary responsibility as the evaluation of students "along a single continuum of achievement." Acting as "an agent of adult society," they make broad-based judgments of the students' capability to act in accordance with society's values (Parsons, 1959). Students' adoption and demonstration of these values and behaviors, therefore, become gatekeeping criteria for many of society's rewards, as well as the criteria for placement into regular and upper-level education tracks.

These aspects of school culture, despite the many problems they engender, have proven extremely resistant to change. Significant to an understanding of current efforts to change school culture and the resistance with which it may be met is an understanding of how these beliefs are transmitted within the organization and of the life stages in teachers' careers.

Teacher Acculturation and Career Stages

To what degree new teachers embrace these values is dependent on many factors not least of which are the cultural characteristics of their workplace. Individual schools vary, of course, in the extent to which they conform to the stereotypes of traditional school culture, and there may be more than one culture and set of associated beliefs within a given institution – depending on its history, generational experiences, orientations and commitments. Nonetheless, culture forms the glue that holds loosely coupled systems together (Sikes, 1992), forming the framework for occupational learning. It is through cultures of teaching that teachers learn what it means to teach, and what kind of teachers they want to be within their school, their departments or other professional communities. It affects how both teachers and administrators approach and define their work, how they respond to change, and how much power they feel they have. Where you teach and how the work of teaching is organized in that place will, thus, significantly influence the kind of teacher you will become (Hargreaves, 1997; 1980).

Teacher acculturation

To greater or lesser degree, a school's culture is passed on to new generations of group members. In schools where strong, shared assumptions are not held, new members' interactions with old members will be a more creative process of building a culture. Where shared assumptions exist, the culture survives through teaching them to newcomers. As in the larger society, much of this transference of knowledge in done informally. Granted that the minds of novice teachers are not a *tabula rasa*, they assimilate the culture of their particular school through observations and opportunistic conversations with administrators and colleagues.

Little (1990) sorts the mechanisms by which collegial collaboration and learning occur into four types: storytelling and scanning; aid and assistance; sharing; and joint work:

- *Storytelling and scanning* is mostly found in schools characterized by loose cultural ties, where teachers act or regard themselves as independent contractors. Contacts among teachers are opportunistic; and teachers gain information and assurance in the quick exchanges of stories. As powerful occupational norms suppress more instrumental forms of help seeking, novices learn that teacher autonomy is highly valued and rests on freedom from scrutiny. They also learn to acknowledge and to tolerate the individual styles and preferences of others, and that independent trial and error serves as the principal route to competence. Storytelling, where the dominant or exclusive mode of teacher interaction, tends to sustain rather than alter patterns of independent practice.
- *Aid and assistance* is characterized by the ready availability of mutual aid and one-on-one interactions among peers. Yet despite the giving of help and advice when asked, this form of collegiality still preserves the boundary between offering advice when asked and interfering in unwarranted ways in another teacher's work. The choices teachers make to solicit aid or to accept assistance are determined in large part by teachers' assessment of the psychological and social costs.
- *Sharing* involves the routine or the open exchange of materials, methods, ideas and opinions. Sharing may vary widely in form and consequence. Teachers may reveal little or much of themselves, for they guard preciously their

painstakingly accumulated individual stores of resources, which may be diminished, depleted, or compromised when revealed to others.

- *Joint work* rests on shared responsibility for the work of teaching (interdependence), collective conceptions of autonomy, support for teacher initiatives and leadership, and group affiliations grounded in professional work. Collegiality as joint work anticipates truly collective action. Teachers are motivated to participate with one another to the degree that they require each other's contribution in order to succeed in their own work.

The forms of collaboration and culture transference characteristic of any particular school are issues or problems of external adaptation and survival. While culture becomes the mechanism of social control and can be the basis of explicitly manipulating members into perceiving, thinking, and behaving in ways consistent with a school's traditional culture, members' attitudes toward and their willingness to participate in cultural change may be affected by a host of factors, not least of which is their stage in the life cycle of the teaching profession.

The life stages of teachers' career development

Despite its characterization as a flat or monochromatic career, researchers have found identifiable stages in the life cycle of teachers (see Ball and Goodson, 1985; Huberman, 1988; Miller *et al.*, 1982). Teachers of similar age and sex have been found to share similar experiences, perceptions, attitudes, satisfactions, frustrations and concerns, and the nature of their motivation and commitment tend to alter in a predictable pattern, as they get older. While there are obviously variations among teachers related to their ethnic group and such differentiating characteristics as the type and location of their school, subject area, and managerial regimes, however, common professional sentiments may be found among teachers working in different educational systems in different countries at different times, suggestive of a life cycle. Summarizing the work of key researchers in the field, Leithwood (1992) outlines five general stages in the development of professional expertise and life cycle changes.

The first phase, the development of survival skills, is divided into "easy beginnings" and "painful beginnings." Easy beginnings involve positive relationships with pupils, manageable pupils, the sense of pedagogical mastery, and enthusiasm. In contrast, painful beginnings are characterized by role overload and anxiety, difficult pupils, heavy time investment, close monitoring by teacher-education staff, and isolation inside the school (Huberman, 1988).

The second phase, stabilization, or becoming competent in the basic skills of instruction, is noteworthy as two pivotal events occur. Teachers gain a sense of mastery and a feeling of being at ease with their work. They also decide to commit themselves to the field, embodied in their receipt of a permanent contract and tenure. Each feature is a staple in the life-cycle literature (Huberman, 1988: 124).

The third stage is one is which teachers expand their instructional flexibility and expertise, and may take several forms. On the one hand, teachers, who are usually between the ages of 30 and 40, indicate that once a level of classroom mastery is achieved, there is a need for refinement and diversity. A second route may dispose teachers to assume greater responsibility in administrative roles and key panels or commissions. Consistent throughout these alternatives is the thread of "affirming oneself" or "emancipation," "new challenges, new concerns." Having attained tenure, teachers now feel free to follow their own leads and to "integrate into a group of peers." Some teachers may take a third route that is less upbeat, and upon receipt of tenure, some teachers tended to reduce their professional commitment (Sikes et al., 1985).

In the fourth stage, teachers reach a professional plateau, usually between the ages of 40 and 50–55. In this stage, it usually becomes apparent if the work, begun in their twenties and thirties of establishing an occupational career, family and a personal identity has been successful (Huberman, 1988; Sikes et al., 1985: 50). Teachers in this stage may stop striving for promotion and simply enjoy teaching. In search for modes of expression and fulfillment, teachers may re-order their priorities and make new starts in various areas of their lives. They may seek to build careers outside the school. Or, now usually well established by virtue of their seniority, they enjoy a renewed commitment to school improvement. Often forming the largest group in the school, they can exert considerable influence on younger, junior teachers, and upon teacher cultures and the ethos/atmosphere of the school. Those, on the other hand, who stagnate at this stage may become bitter, cynical and cease to be interested in further professional growth.

Depending of which of these two routes is taken, teachers prepare for retirement, the fifth stage, in different ways. According to Huberman (1988), teachers may engage in "positive focusing," becoming more interested in their grade level, subject matter or a group of students. Those who stagnated in the previous stage now engage in "defensive focusing," which is characterized by less optimism and generosity toward their past experiences with change, their students and their colleagues. Huberman (1988) identified a third and final group pattern that he termed "disenchanted." These teachers are bitter about past experiences with change and the administrators associated with them.

In addition, some research suggests that many patterns once attributed to age-related influences are in fact as much or more the result of "cohort" or "period" influences, which means that historical or sociological factors need to be given more weight (Huberman, 1988). What is known about cohort effects is that different generations of teachers come into contact with different ideas, which can be expected to have some influence on their ideologies and approaches to teaching, as well as on their expectations of what a teaching career involves and their expectations and attitudes toward reform. This is not to say that teachers get stuck in a time warp, as, like anyone else, they can and do change their thinking if it seems appropriate and beneficial. It depends on how change is perceived in the context of teachers' life experiences, which in turn, is associated with the particular life-cycle stage they have reached.

In this light, it is significant that the external constraints which shape teachers' lives have never been more oppressive. With resources for education diminishing, public disregard for schools increasing, and the demands upon the profession burgeoning, teachers are feeling more beleaguered and chronically dissatisfied with their work. These problems and the relatively poor salaries make it an increasingly unattractive profession, particularly for high achieving and ambitious college graduates. These trends have major implications for existing teacher potential to reform themselves and their schools.

School Culture and School Leadership

Principals play an important role in establishing and maintaining the culture of a school. It once was believed that principals played the most important role in these regards. However, with changing conceptions on the nature of organizations, as well as on the nature of the principalship, opinions of how school leaders should best fulfill their functions have also changed.

Changing conceptions of schools as organizations

The structuralist-functionalist view

In the first half of the twentieth century, a *structural-functionalist* perspective prevailed, based largely on conceptions of bureaucratic leadership that were guided by Taylor's organizational theory. This view of organizations regarded them as closed hierarchical systems, i.e., sealed from the irrationality of societal forces and governed by logic and reason for the purpose of maintaining equilibrium in accomplishing their goals or purposes (Heck and Hallinger, 1999). Rules and regulations are instituted as a means to promote efficiency, regularity, predictability, and fairness in making decisions, as well as to minimize the influence of subjectivity, human idiosyncrasy, and personal relationships. This perspective also emphasized empiricism, i.e., objective assessment and data analysis, as well as positivism, i.e., the "factual" explanation of anomalies arising in and from these data in solving organizational problems.

Authority and influence are allocated to formal positions in proportion to the status of those positions in the organizational hierarchy. Some advocates in the field treat leadership and management as distinct and to some extent as competing concepts. Management involves the responsibility for policy implementation, maintaining organizational stability, and ensuring that routine organizational tasks are done right. Leadership, in contrast, is assigned the challenges of policy-making, organizational change and making sure the "right things are done." The task of the leader is, ultimately, to enhance the functioning of the organization by developing formal structures, e.g., path-goal analysis, and accordingly, "managing" the plant and its personnel.

The most popular current application of this business perspective to education is Deming's Total Quality Management model, an outgrowth of statistical process control. Described as an attitude or state of mind, reformists advocating its extension to the schools seek to flatten the authority hierarchy, to create natural work groups and/or quality teams, to grant these teams empowerment coupled with accountability and an attention to consumer preferences (Bradley, 1993, quoted in Seyfarth, 1999). The focus, in general, is on an ongoing effort to improve the product. It is reasoned, however, that once freed from excessive supervisory oversight, teachers will become more creative and willing to accept responsibility for student learning.

The transformational view

In the 1960s and 1970s, the *transformational* perspective arose. Consistent with human relations theories prevalent at that time organizations were regarded as more "open," i.e., influenced by and responsive to world and interest group conflicts. Advocates emphasize consideration of the complexity and variability of the system's component parts and the "looseness" in the coupling of the connections between them. Structure and managerial orientations are de-emphasized in favor of organizational process (Campbell *et al.*, 1987). Consistent with this view of organizations, effective leaders are those who can take an organization in a new direction by persuading the staff to accept and work toward goals that serve institutional interests even though they may not be fully compatible with the immediate self-interest of employees (Burns, 1978, quoted in Seyfarth, 1999: 85). Variously written about as charismatic, visionary, cultural, and empowering and transformational leaders, the focus is on heightening the commitments and capacities of organizational members, assuming the result will be extra effort and greater productivity. This model conceptualizes such leadership along seven dimensions:

1. building school vision, establishing school goals;
2. providing intellectual stimulation;
3. offering individualized support;
4. modeling best practices and important organizational values;
5. demonstrating high performance expectations;

    6. creating a productive school culture;

    7. developing structures to foster participation in school decisions. (Leithwood, 1992)

This entails not only a change in the purpose and resources of those involved in the leader-follower relationship, but an elevation of both.

The most prominent current application of this organizational model is strategic planning. As an approach to changing organizations, five key steps are listed to guide the transformation process:

    1. Develop a mission statement.
    2. Conduct assessments and identify critical trends.
    3. Set priorities and develop long-range goals.
    4. Identify strategies and construct action plans.
    5. Determine outcomes and evaluate.

The effective schools movement, promulgated by Ron Edmunds in the USA and Rutter *et al.* (1979) in the UK, is by far the best example of this approach. This research produced a set of correlates associated with effective schools that was consistent to a great degree with those outlined above (see also Box 4.1). Schools, now conceived of as learning organizations and principals as proactive (see Reynolds and Cuttance, 1992), were advised to follow these correlates. In this process, leaders were strongly encouraged to grant their staff and students greater participatory involvement in the governance of their schools and to assume greater responsibility over the instructional and cultural aspects of the organization. As their schools' transformational leaders, it was their task to develop and nurture the conditions in their school for improvement and reform.

Radical perspectives

In the last quarter of the twentieth century a spurt of new organizational theories arose, rooted variously in Neo-Marxist, constructivist, and postmodernist perspectives. All strenuously opposed the dehumanizing aspects of scientific management, its empiricist/positivist orientation, its structural-functionalism, and control-oriented, managerial views of leadership. Of these perspectives, *chaos* or *complexity theory* has become widely embraced by many educational reformists. This view focuses on the extreme openness and nonrational nature of organizational systems, denying the existence of basic truths, objective realities or transferable principles that can be used to guide and advise the leadership process. Stressing the fact that the nature of school life is, more often than not, spontaneous, simultaneous, multidimensional and unpredictable, it should not be expected to conform to logical and linear organizational analyses. This conception of organizations is well captured in Senge's (1992) notion of dynamic complexity, in which "cause and effect" are not close in time or space, and interventions do not produce expected outcomes because other "unplanned" factors dynamically interfere. Complexity, dynamism, and unpredictability are not merely things that get in the way; they are normal! Problems, therefore, cannot be "solved," because behavior is predictable only "within certain tolerances." What we can do is to explore the issues from which problems are created and how tasks, processes and events are and are not conceptualized as problematic (Gunter, 1997).

Other models, similarly eschewing the rationalist/empiricist approach are *political conflict* and *organizational constructivist theories*. Starting with the assumption that leadership does not necessarily reside in a school's administrator, these organizational views seek sources of initiative, improvement, and reform outside of the school's formal system (i.e. goals, authority, rules and plans). Conflict theories place emphasis on exploring how competing interest groups within the school and its community negotiate for power. Exemplified by the work of Greenfield (1975) and Bates (1982) political negotiation is stressed as the heart of leadership. Constructivist theories, similarly, stress the constructed nature of meaning in their concept of "sense-making." This approach examines how leaders and others in the organization create shared understandings about their roles and their participation in the life of the school. The role of the leader is to help others create meaning and make sense of their work (Heck and Hallinger, 1999). In general, both these views advocate the leader's responsibility to develop educational organizations whose fundamental purposes are to nurture not only equity among stakeholders but also the freedom and autonomy of their individual members (Bates, 1993; Foster, 1986; Ortiz and Marshall, 1988; Smyth, 1989). Part of leaders' ethical commitment is to advocate principles of democracy, respect for others, social justice and equality.

Consistent with these views, principals are urged to adopt moral or contingent leadership approaches. Moral leaders are those who focus on the values and ethics of an issue. Authority and influence are to be derived from defensible conceptions of what is right or good. Leaders are urged to choose higher, or transrational, values over lower level values when confronted with value conflicts and to eschew "subrational" values, which encompass self-justifying preferences. Having a metaphysical grounding, these higher values take the form of ethical codes, injunctions, or commandments. The contingent leadership approach, on the other hand, assumes that there are wide variations in the contexts for and styles of leadership, and that to be effective these concepts and contexts require different leadership responses. Also assumed is that individuals providing leadership are capable of mastering a large repertoire of leadership practices. The literature on problem solving focuses on the internal cognitive and affective processes engaged in by leaders as they ponder the challenges facing them and decide how best to act. From this perspective there is a virtually unlimited universe of leadership practices.

As the contingent approach to leadership infers, there is a plethora of other perspectives to leadership, claiming its assumption as the best route to achieving the school goals. The leadership style and organizational views adopted by a school's administrators play a significant role in setting the tone and influencing critical aspects of its culture. For example, administrators who adopt the traditional view of organizations and leadership will tend to foster those structural aspects of the school that have become the targets of second-order change. Conversely, administrators who embrace a more transformational or moral view will seek to nurture more collaborative and collegial school cultures.

Students and the Culture of School

Considerations of school culture are incomplete without consideration of students. The characteristics of a school's student body have a significant influence on the culture of the school, the school's perceived status both inside and outside the schoolhouse doors, and the ease with which teachers can perform their tasks.

Students' demographic characteristics and school culture

A significant component of a school's culture is the status attributed to the school by the teachers, students, parents, and the larger society. The primary factor in determining the status of a school, interestingly, is not academic achievement, but rather, the social-economic status of the children who attend. Mirroring the values of the larger societal culture, schools that contain a high proportion of students from elite SES (social economic status) backgrounds, who come to school possessing large amounts of cultural capital, who do well on standardized tests, and have relatively few problems of truancy, violence, and other rule infractions are given high status. Even within schools, classes that contain a high proportion of such students are, similarly, highly regarded. Many teachers, therefore, aspire to and are rewarded by assignment to such schools and classes.

Conversely, schools and classes that contain a high proportion of students from low SES and ethnic minority backgrounds, where students come to school with little cultural capital, do poorly on standardized tests, and have high incidences of truancy, violence and role infraction are given low status. Such schools and classes are frequently labeled "disadvantaged," and the current euphemism, "at-risk." These schools tend to be plagued by low morale and lack of optimism on the part of teachers, for consistent with the literature and beliefs associated with deficit theory, these characteristics in students are synonymous with their inability or profound difficulty to achieve academically. Teachers do not optimally aspire to teach in such situations, as evidenced by the high faculty turnover rates and the lower incidence of certified teachers at these schools (National Commission on Teaching and America's Future, 1996). Principals, similarly, seldom aspire to lead such institutions.

These perceptions of students and, in turn, of schools, invariably impact on school culture and their teachers' and administrators' sense of efficacy (Teddlie and Stringfield, 1993). Where teachers, administrators and students are pleased and feel proud to be a part of a particular school environment, morale is high and the culture is supportive and reinforcing. Conversely, where stakeholders feel relatively helpless to effect change, or displeased or reluctant to be in a situation, school morale tends to be low, and the culture of the school suffers, e.g., teachers disassociate themselves from responsibility for or commitment to their students' outcomes.

Student motivation and school culture

Another significant contributor to school morale and culture is student motivation, i.e., the extent to which students are energized or willing to participate in the activity of schooling. Fullan (with Stiegelbauer, 1991: 183) asserts, that students will participate to the extent that they understand and are motivated to try what is expected. Increasingly teachers indicate, however, that students across all SES levels tend to be less responsive and attentive, and are more confused about school than previous generations. Teachers report that they must take time from academic activities to motivate and build esteem in children who have negative feelings about school and about themselves (Wagner, 1993, quoted in Seyfarth, 1999: 126).

Research on motivation identifies three factors that influence or predict school performance: (1) high expectations on the part of parents and other significant adults; (2) a demanding curriculum; and (3) peer support of learning. By the sixth grade, students have firm and stable beliefs in their intellectual abilities (Nicholls, 1978). Schools play a significant role in the establishment of these beliefs. However, despite the system's assertion that we want children to believe that hard work and effort are the determining factors, the school's real message is that success is primarily based on innate ability. Teachers convey this message in subtle ways. Interestingly, if teachers get angry, evidence frustration or disappointment with students for doing poorly, students take this to mean that their teachers have high expectations for them and believe they aren't working hard enough. If, on the other hand, teachers convey an attitude of resignation or pity, or give a great deal more support to one student than another, students take this to mean that the teacher believes they are dumb (Bempechat, 1998: 53). Similarly, where schools and teachers offer students challenging curricula, students infer that they expect that they can acquire the knowledge. Where, as a result of such messages from both home and school, students believe that success is beyond their ability, they will exert less effort, because no one wants to try and still fail (Bempechat, 1998; Tomlinson, 1992). In our system, even "bright" children don't want to be seen as making too much effort, as it implies that you're not innately bright, but must work hard at it.

Peer groups also exert an influence on students' motivation to work hard in the context of school and may actually define the stance most older students take toward academic achievement (Tomlinson, 1992). Nowadays, most students who work hard risk being considered excessively ambitious, "uncool" or of limited ability by their peers, all of which they regard as embarrassing. To avoid unpopular labels, many students adopt an attitude of indifference to hard work, a demeanor that conveys both confidence in their ability and casual regard for academic success. This phenomenon is qualified by ethnicity and immigrant status, with the peer culture of African Americans tending to exert a greater force away from trust and pursuit of formal academic achievement (Fordham and Ogbu, 1986) than other ethnic groups. And while students who are members of certain Asian populations tend as a culture to espouse hard work as a virtue, these students too would rather their peers regard them as smart.

Finally, the strong public connection between school achievement and economic viability may also pose a problem for students and the schooling process. House (1998: 5) asserts: "It is not that education creates jobs, but also that jobs create education. People will undertake education when they see a payoff. If good jobs are not there, then education will suffer." Many children, particularly middle-class children, are motivated to attend school primarily as a means to obtain "good" jobs. Increasingly, there is confusion concerning the nation's future job market. Despite public declarations of the need for more highly skilled workers and higher-level thinkers, currently, one out of every five college graduates has a job that does not require a college degree (Kuttner, 1993). Moreover, data indicate that the areas providing the biggest demand for new workers will arise in dead-end jobs, like janitors, nurses aides and fast-food workers (House, 1998; Tyack and Cuban, 1995). It, thus, may be that the "dirty little secret" known by generations of poor and working-class students, but only recently peeked by those in the middle class is that there may be no room for them at the top. To the extent that students have internalized the purpose of their schooling as job-related, and this seems to be progressively the case for all sectors, students will be less motivated to engage in the often boring tasks that this process involves. According to House (1998: 48), the lack of jobs for the educated calls into question the legitimacy of the entire social system, and the purposefulness of schooling in particular.

In schools where the majority of students are apathetic or hostile about learning, and assume a passive or resistant attitude toward academic achievement, their cultures will mirror these sentiments. As students increasingly see diligent people who never seem to get ahead economically and others, particularly in the fields of entertainment and sports, who win big money with very little effort (Wagner, 1993), they will reject the assertion that hard work guarantees success, and with it much of the mission of public schooling itself. Without this motivation, these students, by definition, become at-risk. And historically our schools have not been very effective in reaching at-risk and apathetic students. As these tendencies become more pervasive, school culture will be correspondingly affected.

In conclusion, schools and school culture are open systems, influenced by the espoused values and deep assumptions of the society that they serve. This larger culture in which schools are embedded has been characterized as largely conservative, and grounded in notions of rugged individualism and social Darwinism. These values of the larger culture have traditionally been manifest in teacher isolationism, and the sink or swim nature of teachers' induction process. Students are socialized into the culture of the larger society partly through school culture; teacher expectations regarding who succeeds and why; and the use of ostensible ability tracks into which students are sorted. Students' demographic characteristics and their general motivation to learn will, reciprocally, affect the culture of their schools. Principals may influence and shape a school's culture, but the degree to which this will occur depends on their organizational views and leadership styles. Increasingly, these culturally based beliefs and organizational patterns have been identified as contributory factors to many of the negative outcomes associated with the schooling process, and, thus, have become the targets of the second reform wave.

Study Questions

1. Do you think the traditional image of the culture of schooling is an accurate one? Explain. How does it differ from your own image of school culture?
2. Do you agree with the chapter's assertions about the assumptions underlying the culture of schooling? Explain. If you disagree, what other assumptions would you propose?
3. List and describe additional artifacts, espoused values,

and assumptions of the culture of schooling that were not discussed in this chapter.

4. How well and in what ways does your school conform to the stereotypic characterization of the culture of schooling? In what ways does it differ, and why do you think it differs in these ways?

5. How would you characterize the mechanisms or transmission patterns that exist in your school (relative to Little's typology) for socializing novice teachers? Explain.

6. Do you feel that the school is a closed or open system? Justify your answer.

7. What are the implications of the validity of open systems and chaos theory relative to the role of teaching as a profession?

8. Which of Little's collaboration and culture transmission types most characterizes social interactions at your school and why? In what ways does the type chosen differ, or not apply to your school?

9. In your mind, which of the various organizational leadership models is the most accurate and optimal relative to the principalship and why?

10. The highly segmented nature of the schooling process, both in terms of students and content, may remind you of latter-day factories. This is no coincidence, as it is at this artifactual level that the legacy of Taylor's system of scientific management is most evident. It served as the model for much of the essential design changes made to the schools between 1915 and 1930. According to Bennett and LeCompte (1990), here the bureaucratic layering of middle-level managers, the credentialing of professional staff, and the instituting of uniform rules, record keeping, curricula and time allocations for instruction were begun. How many ways can you think of in which the schools are like factories?

References

Argyris, C. (1976) *Increasing Leadership Effectiveness*. New York: Wiley Interscience.

Ball, S. and Goodson, I. (eds) (1985) *Teachers' Lives and Careers.* Lewes: Falmer Press.

Bates, R. (1982) Toward a critical practice of educational adminis- tration. Paper presented at the annual meeting of the American Educational Association, New York.

Bates, R. (1993) On knowing: cultural and critical approaches to educational administration. *Educational Management and Adminis- tration,* vol. 21, no. 3, pp. 171–176.

Bempechat, J. (1998) *Against the Odds: How At Risk Students Exceed Expectations.* San Francisco: Jossey-Bass.

Bennett, K. P. and LeCompte, M. D. (1990) *How It Works: A Sociologi- cal Analysis of Education.* New York: Longman.

Bradley, L. (1993) *Total Quality Management.* Lancaster, PA: Technomic.

Burns, J. (1978) *Leadership.* New York: Harper and Row.

Campbell, R. E., Fleming, T., Newell, L. J. and Bennion, J. W. (1987) *A History of Thought and Practice in Educational Administration.* New York: Teachers College Press.

Carlson, R. V. (1996) *Refraining and Reform: Perspectives in Organiza- tional Leadership and School Change.* New York: Longman Publishers.

Chapman, J. D., Sackney, L. E. and Aspin, D. N. (1999) Internationali- zation in educational administration: policy and practice, theory and research. In J. Murphy and K. Seashore Louis (eds) *Handbook of Research in Educational Administration.* 2nd edn. San Francisco: Jossey-Bass, pp. 73–98.

Delpit, L. (1995) *Other People's Children.* New York: The New Press.

Doyle, D. P. (1993) The white house and the school house. *Phi Delta Kappan,* vol. 74, no. 2, p. 129.

Firestone, W. and Seashore Louis, K. (1999) Schools as culture. In J. Murphy and K. Seashore Louis (eds) *Handbook of Research in Educational Administration.* 2nd edn. San Francisco: Jossey-Bass, pp. 297–322.

Fordham, S. and Ogbu, J. (1986) Black students' school success: coping with the "burden of acting white." *The Urban Review,* vol. 18. no. 3. pp. 176–206.

Foster, W. (1986) *Paradigms and Promises: New Approaches to Educa- tional Administration.* Buffalo, NY: Prometheus.

Fullan, M., with Stiegelbauer, S. (1991) *The New Meaning of Educational Change.* 2nd edn. New York: Teachers College Press, Columbia University.

Fullan, M. and Hargreaves, A. (1996) *What's Worth Fighting for in your School.* New York: Teachers College Press.

Gould, S. J. (1981) *The Mismeasure of Man.* New York: W. W. Norton.

Greenfield, T. (1975) Theory about organization: a new perspective and its implications for schools. In M. Huges (ed.), *Administering Edu- cation: International Challenge.* London: Athlone.

Grimmett, P. P. and Crehan, E. P. (1992) The nature of collegiality in teacher development. In M. Fullan and A. Hargreaves (eds) *Teacher Development and Educational Change*. London: Falmer Press, pp. 56–85.

Gunter, H. (1997) Chaotic reflexivity. In M. Fullan (ed.) *The Challenge of School Change*. Arlington Hts, ILL: Skylight.

Hargreaves, A. (1992a) Cultures of teaching. In M. Fullan and A. Hargreaves (eds) *Teacher Development and Educational Change*. London: Falmer Press.

Hargreaves, A. (1992b) Teacher development and instructional mastery. In M. Fullan and A. Hargreaves (eds) *Teacher Development and Educational Change*. London: Falmer Press.

Hargreaves, A. (1994) *Changing Teachers, Changing Times: Teachers' Work and Culture in the Postmodern Age*. London: Cassell.

Hargreaves, A. (1997) Introduction. In A. Hargreaves (ed.) *Rethinking Educational Change with Heart and Mind*. Alexandria, VA: ASCD, pp. 1–26.

Heck, R. H. and Hallinger, P. (1999) Next generation methods for the study of leadership and school improvement. In J. Murphy and K. Seashore Louis (eds) *Handbook of Research in Educational Administration*. 2nd edn. San Francisco: Jossey-Bass, pp. 141–162.

Hodgkinson, C. (1978) *Toward a Philosophy of Administration*. Oxford: Basil Blackwell.

Hopkins, D., Ainscow, M. and West, W. (1994) *School Improvement in an Era of Change*. London: Cassell.

House, E. R. (1998) *Schools for Sale: Why Free Market Policies won't Improve America's Schools, and What Will*. New York: Teachers College Press

Huberman, M. (1988) Teacher careers and school improvement. *Journal of Curriculum Studies*, vol. 20, no. 2, pp. 119–132.

Kuttner, R. (1993) Training programs alone can't produce $20-an-hour workers. *Business Week*, March 18, p. 16.

Leithwood, K. A. (1992) The principal's role in teacher development. In M. Fullan and A. Hargreaves (eds) *Teacher Development and Change*. London: Falmer Press, pp. 86–103.

Lieberman, A. and Miller, L. (1984) *Teachers, Their World, and Their Work: Implications for School Improvement*. Alexandria, VA: ASCD.

Little, J. W. (1990) The persistence of privacy: autonomy and initiative in teachers' professional relations. *Teachers College Record*, vol. 91, no. 4, Summer, pp. 509–536.

Lortie, D. (1969) The balance of control and autonomy in elementary school teaching. In A. Etzioni (ed.), *The Semi-professionals and their Oganization: Teachers, Nurses, Social Workers*. New York: The Free Press, pp. 1–53.

Lortie, D. (1975) *School Teacher: A Sociological Study*. Chicago: University of Chicago Press.

Lucas, S. R. (1999) *Tracking Inequality: Stratification and Mobility in*

American High Schools. New York: Teachers College Press, Columbia University.

McTaggart, R. (1989) Bureaucratic rationality and the self-educating profession: the problem of teacher privatism. *Curriculum Studies*, vol. 21, no. 4, pp. 345–361.

Merriam-Webster (1998) *Collegiate Dictionary*. 10th edn. Springfield, MA: Merriam-Webster, Inc.

Metz, M. H. (1989) Real school: a universal drama amid desparate experience. In D. E. Mitchell and M. E. Loetz (eds) *Educational Politics of the New Child*. The Twentieth Anniversary Yearbook of the Politics of Education Association. New York: Falmer Press, pp. 75–91.

Miller, J. P., Taylor, G. and Walder, K. (1982) *Teachers in Transition: Study of an Aging Teaching Force*. Occasional Series 44. Ontario, OISE.

Murphy, J. and Hallinger, P. (1992) The principalship in an era of transformation. *Journal of Educational Administration*, vol. 30, no. 3, pp. 77–88.

Myers, K. and Goldstein, H. (1997) Failing schools or failing systems. In A. Hargreaves (ed.) *Rethinking Educational Change with Heart and Mind*. Alexandria, VA: ASCD.

National Commission on Teaching and America's Future (1996) *What Matters Most: Teaching for America's Future*. New York: Carnegie Corporation of New York.

Nicholls, J. (1978) The development of the conceptions of effort and ability, perception of academic attainment, and the understanding that difficult tasks require more ability. *Child Development*, vol. 49, pp. 800–814.

Oakes, J. (1985) *Keeping Track: How Schools Structure Inequality*. New Haven, CT: Yale University Press.

Ortiz, F. and Marshall, C. (1988) Women in educational administration. In N. Boyan (ed.) *Handbook of Research in Educational Administration*. New York: Longman, pp. 123–141.

Parsons, T. (1959) The school class as a social system: some of its functions in American society. *Harvard Educational Review*, vol. 29, pp. 297–313.

Purkey, S. C. and Smith, M. S. (1983) Effective schools: a review. *Elementary School Journal*, vol. 83, pp. 427–453.

Reynolds, D. and Cuttance, P. (1992) *School Effectiveness: Research Policy and Practice*. London: Cassell.

Rosenholtz, S. J. (1989) *Teachers' Workplace: The Social Organization of Schools*. New York: Longman.

Rutter, M. J., Maughan, B., Mortimore, P. and Ouston, J. (1979) *Fifteen Thousand Hours: Secondary Schools and their Effect on Children*. Cambridge, MA: Harvard University Press.

Schein, E. H. (1997) *Organizational Culture and Leadership*. 2nd edn. San Francisco: Jossey-Bass Publishers.

Schrag, F. (1978) The principal as a moral actor. In D. Erickson and T. Reller (eds) *The Principal in Metropolitan Schools*. Berkeley, CA: McCutchan, pp. 208–232.

Senge, P. (1992) Building learning organizations. *Journal for Quality and Participation*, vol. 15, no. 2, pp. 20–38.

Seyfarth, J. T. (1999) *The Principal: New Leadership for New Challenges*. Upper Saddle River, NJ: Prentice-Hall.

Sikes, P. (1992) Imposed change and the experienced teacher. In M. Fullan and A. Hargreaves (eds) *Teacher Development and Educational Change*. London: Falmer Press, pp. 36–55.

Sikes, P. J., Measor, L. and Woods, P. (1985) *Teacher Careers: Crises and Continuities*. Lewes: Falmer Press.

Smylie, M. A. (1989) Teachers' views of the effectiveness of sources of learning to teach. *Elementary School Journal*, vol. 89, pp. 543–558.

Smyth, J. (1989) A "pedagogical" and "educative" view of leadership. In J. Smyth (ed.) *Critical Perspectives on Educational Leadership*. London: Falmer Press, pp. 179–204.

Sykes, G. (1990) Fostering teacher professionalism in schools. In R. Elmore and associates (eds) *Restructuring Schools. The Next Generation of Educational Reform*. San Francisco: Jossey-Bass.

Teddlie, C. and Stringfield, S. (1993) *Schools Make a Difference: Lessons from a 10 Year Study of School Effects*. New York: Teachers College Press, Columbia University.

Tomlinson, T. (1992) *Hard Work and High Expectations: Motivating Students to Learn*. Issues in Education. Office of Educational Research and Improvement. Washington, DC: US Department of Education.

Tyack, D. and Cuban, L. (1995) *Tinkering Toward Utopia: A Century of Public School Reform*. Cambridge, MA: Harvard University Press.

Tye, B. B. (2000) *Hard Truths: Uncovering the Deep Structure of Schooling*. New York: Teachers College Press.

Vallance, E. (1994) Hiding the curriculum: an interpretation of the language of justification in 19th century education reform. In H. S. Shapiro and S. Harden (eds) *The Institution of Education*. 3rd edn. New York: Simon and Schuster, pp. 79–102.

Wagner, T. (1993) Ignorance in educational research: or how can you not know that? *Educational Researcher*, vol. 22, no. 5, pp. 15–23.

Wagner, T. (1994) *How Schools Change: Lessons from Three Communities*. Boston: Beacon.

Waller, W. (1965) *The Sociology of Teaching*. New York: John Wiley and Sons.

Weiner, B. (1994) Integrating social and personal theories of achievement striving. *Review of Educational Research*, vol. 64, pp. 557–573.

Wheatley, M. J. (1994) *Leadership and the New Science*. San Francisco: Bennett Koehler.

Part II

The Substance and Process
of School Reform

In this second Part we unpack both the current reform agenda and the process of school reform in general. A plethora of programs for reforming the schools are currently afloat, varying one from the other in a myriad of ways. Probably, as never before, has there been such an array of proposals; there is literally something for everyone or every interest group. Each promises to be the panacea for the schools' ills. As is characteristic, advocates push their strengths conveniently omitting their assumptions, weaknesses and negative implications. The media, the public, politicians, as well as educators and school administrators embrace varied proposals often ignorant of this knowledge and of the realities of the innovation process at the local site level. Ignorance in some instances can be bliss, but in these regards ignorance can be a major contributor to the high failure rate of innovations.

In an effort to address this problem Chapter 4 specifically focuses on the often hidden assumptions and requirements that can and have led to inappropriate adoption, inadequate implementation, and overload by school staff. We admit, in advance, that the innovations discussed do not constitute anywhere near an exhaustive list of all those that are being promulgated. Nor do we attempt to describe in any depth or detail the specifics of even those addressed. To do either of these things would require a lengthy volume in itself. Rather, here we can only briefly describe broad types of plans and mention their most glaring and often omitted assumptions and requirements. At times, the text may seem pessimistic and inordinately focused on the negative aspects of these innovations. However, we believe reformers and their advocates do a great job of touting their strengths and accomplishments, and this information can be handily obtained. More difficult to obtain is one central source where challenges to the major innovations can be accessed. It is hoped that in this process, specific reform advocates will not feel unduly criticized and reform adopters will understand the underlying principle of this endeavor and will make similar efforts on their own when selecting or facilitating the selection of innovations for schools.

Chapter 5 focuses on the innovation process. Characteristically divided into three stages: initiation, implementation and adoption/abandonment, we unpack each stage to reveal the constituent parts, time requirements and factors associated with the facilitation or the hindrances to each. In the last half of this chapter, we discuss more recent conceptualizations of the innovation process. This second Part is the heart of this text, revealing the realities of this era in school reform as best we can.

4

___

New Promises, Old Pitfalls

The current reform slate offers educators, politicians and the general public a virtual potpourri of possibilities for changing the public schools. Starting with the (new) first wave of reform of the 1980s, states legislated an array of bureaucratic procedures to improve the schools, including the setting of standards, greater standardized testing and increasing the requirements for public school graduation and teacher certification. Business and other interest groups also floated plans to privatize the schools and to allow parents various forms of school choice. As the decade and the schools hobbled along, governmental agencies, increasingly recognizing the relative failure of this "first wave" of "top-down" reform mandates, began to shift their attention to the local schools as the unit of change. Using as a model the literature on the practices of successful schools, they began to mandate a series of "bottom-up" reforms in the hope that these processes would be embraced by school staffs, thereby leading to these schools' improvement. Not abandoning their earlier "top-down" legislative approach to school reform, states simply extended their list of mandates to include these "bottom-up" efforts. As a result, schools now find themselves awash in a sea of mandates and options, many conflicting, one with the other, in their philosophies and underlying assumptions.

Forced, often hastily, to choose from a virtual shopping list of possible plans and models, staffs at underperforming schools and districts are making adoption decisions often blind to the underlying assumptions, hidden requirements, and implications of these reform models.

This chapter seeks to unpack the most significant of these plans for the wary consumer. We focus, specifically, on the often hidden assumptions and requirements that can and have led to inappropriate adoption, inadequate implementation, and overload of school staff. We admit, in advance, that there are glaring omissions in this chapter. We do not assume to know or to discuss anywhere near the totality of proposals that are being promulgated. We also do not attempt to describe in any detail the specifics of even those addressed. Nor do we report the strengths or successes of the various models. To include these omissions would require a lengthy volume in itself. Rather here, we only briefly describe broad types of plans and mention their most glaring and often omitted assumptions, work requirements and challenges. In so doing, we hope to provide some central source where challenges to the major innovations can be accessed and to reveal not so readily attainable information about these plans to facilitate their more knowledgeable selection and/or advocacy. For while most innovators assert that their products can be adapted to the specifics of any school site, we have found it a myth in working with truly troubled schools that "one size fits all."

Before reading this chapter, please consider the following framing questions:

1. Based on the previous chapter on school culture as well your own practical knowledge of how schools function, list the characteristics, or elements, that you think are integral to a successful school – particularly one with a large population of underachieving students.
2. What are the reforms that you feel would most expeditiously facilitate the creation or the adoption of these characteristics by underperforming schools?
3. On what, if any, assumptions are these characteristics and reforms based? And what would be the effects of attempting to institute these reforms where these assumptions do not apply?

Elements of Success

Schools and schooling do have an effect upon children's academic and social development. Despite fatalistic research in the 1960s and 1970s in both the United States (Coleman *et al.*, 1966; Jencks *et al.*, 1971) and in Britain (Department of Education and Science, 1967) proclaiming to the contrary, with the development of more sophisticated research tools, subsequent studies in the late 1970s and the 1980s in both countries showed that school attendance had an independent influence upon children's levels of academic attainment and behavior patterns (Fogelman, 1978, 1983; Levine and Lezotte, 1990). These latter studies further revealed that there were substantial variations between schools in their ability to educate traditionally underperforming students (Reynolds, 1992). While key factors associated with SES differences among students remain the major determinants accounting for group differences in achievement, a flurry of research in these and other countries sought to discern school characteristics associated with the successful education of under-achieving students.

This body of research, generally labeled the "effective schools" or "school effectiveness" literature, produced lists of variables that differentiated features of effective schools from ineffective schools. Although the lists differed somewhat among the various countries in the factors discerned, a number of striking similarities were found (Levine, 1992; Reynolds and Cuttance, 1992). So much so that school reformers can say with some assurance that there exists substantiated general knowledge on the components for school success. Among the lists, that compiled by Levine and Lezotte (1990), shown in Box 4.1, is probably the most detailed and based on the most extensive body of research (Reynolds and Cuttance, 1992). Although some of this research, like most other large research bodies in the social sciences, has some flaws, e.g., variation in the measures used to assess academic success, the need to control better for SES, ethnic and gender differences among subject populations, and the need to focus on higher order learning tasks and the upper (elementary) grade levels (Levine, 1992; Reynolds, 1992), the findings clearly show that the characteristics most associated with school success are weighted heavily on the side of factors associated with the school's culture and with pedagogic instructional.

These components, or elements, of school success formed the bases for much of the second wave of school reform, focused as it is on transforming school culture. Along with the various top-down mandates promulgated during the first wave of school reform, they have been variously packaged to constitute a combined slate of reform projects and programs from which schools are variously asked to choose or are mandated to adopt. In order for schools best to implement any one or some combination of these plans, a number of assumptions and requirements, ideally,

---

Box 4.1

Characteristics of Unusually Effective Schools

Productive school climate and culture

Focus on student acquisition of central learning skills

Appropriate monitoring of student progress

Practice-oriented staff development at the school site

Outstanding leadership

Salient parent involvement

Effective instructional arrangements and implementation

Highly operationalized expectations and requirements for students

Source: Levine and Lezotte (1990)

---

must be met. Moreover, some plans have hidden ramifications of which adopters and advocates should be aware.

Unpacking the Components of Reform

While almost all innovations, at least on the surface, proclaim as their ultimate end the increased academic performance of schools and students, their immediate aims, their paths and their scope vary. For example, some innovations advocate that control of the schools be transferred to themselves or to others. Other plans advocate that administrative controls be left as they are, but that classroom instruction or the attitudes of staff be altered. Yet other proposals seek to change nothing directly, but to hold individuals at various levels responsible for student outcomes.

Plans may also vary in their range, or scope. Some plans propose to change only one feature of the school, most often instruction in a specific subject area, while other plans seek to bring to the school an integrated set of strategies designed simultaneously to alter the school's governance structure, teachers' instructional techniques, as well as their values and beliefs. These plans are called comprehensive plans.

Below, we examine the components of these reform efforts. We look at the assumptions of each component and, where such research exists, their implementation outcomes independent of other components. We do this fully aware that for some plans, including the effective schools literature, the belief is that for success to be achieved, all parts must come together to form their own unique gestalt. We pursue this tactic for the sake of economy and to avoid the inference of criticizing or recommending any specific commercial reform package. Below we discuss the major school reform efforts in four broad categories: (1) plans related to altering the control or organization of the schools; (2) those related to reform pedagogy; (3) plans that seek to address the attitudes and values of school staff; and (4) other.

Control, governance and organization

The control and organization of the public schools have been recurrent themes throughout the nation's history. This reform era is no exception, as advocates of particular plans seek variously to alter either the governance of the schools and/or its size and structure. Governance proposals seek to invert the power pyramid by giving greater control over the schools to those traditionally located at its bottom, i.e., parents or to committees comprised of teachers, parents and sometimes students. A prominent feature of second wave reform is the formation of broad-based councils, sometimes called Site-Based Management/Shared Decision-Making Teams (SBM/SDMTs). Consistent with first wave reform, there is an array of plans that open the public schools to market forces, thereby shifting control to parents through their freedom to choose their children's schools. Finally, there are plans that seek to alter the structure of the school through deconstructing large schools, particularly those at the high school level, and transforming them into smaller schools, or "houses." Each strategy is discussed below.

Site-based management/shared decision-making

Within the field of public education, probably the most well known of the governance proposals is site-based management/ shared decision-making (SBM/SDM). Under site-based management, particular bureaucratic regulatory functions traditionally held by the district superintendent, the school board and the principal devolve to local site level professionals in exchange for staff assuming responsibility for results (Cohen, 1988; Lindquist and Mauriel, 1989). Three areas of responsibility are specifically targeted for transfer to the schools: budget, curriculum and personnel (Clune and White, 1988). Consistent with this plan, schools receive either a lump-sum budget or some portion of their budget to manage, usually for equipment, materials, supplies and sometimes other categories such as staff development. With shared decision-making, site level teams or councils consisting of teachers, parents and, where feasible, students are created to make these decisions. The rationale behind the institution of these teams is that (1) local schools should be the primary decision-making unit, i.e., decisions should be made at the lowest possible level; (2) change requires ownership that comes from the opportunity to participate in defining change and in the flexibility to adapt to one's individual circumstances (David, 1989); and (3) successfully communicating and supportive teams facilitate change implementation (Fullan, 1991).

SBM/SDMTs are found in many, if not most effective schools. There are, however, a number of hidden requirements and assumptions associated with their successful operation.

The assumption of ownership As has been alluded to, staff at many underperforming schools are often mandated by their states or central education offices to form these teams. As a result, many teachers feel little or no initial ownership of these bodies. Moreover, as sometimes happens, a small "in-group" of teachers get elected to or are chosen to serve as members, either because they are "doers" or are regarded by the school administration as leaders. Under these circumstances, this body can engender collegial disfavor and sanctions for violation of school norms that define and govern what is regarded as right and proper relationships with others in the workplace (Malen and Ogawa, 1988; Smylie, 1992). When this occurs, plans emanating from such SBM/SDMTs may be regarded as challenges, and be no better received or "owned" by the rest of the staff than those emanating outside the school.

The assumption of empowerment SBM/SDMTs are intended to empower teachers, parents and students by giving them responsibility for making pivotal decisions relative to the functioning of the school. However, teachers may not want to be "empowered" in this way (Eisner, 1992) or may feel disempowered by being forced to participate either on these teams or on SDMT subcommittees. What is more, where these teams are given only marginal authority, e.g., no budget and hiring decisions, by district and school administrations who often prefer to retain these functions (Lindquist and Mauriel, 1989), their purpose may be subverted. In such instances, SBM/SDMTs may become advisory rather than decision-making bodies (David, 1989; Miles, 1981) or their tasks confined to lower level administrative, school climate and/or curricular matters. Conflicts over power are not uncommon. Schools suffered where principals "worked from their own agenda," were perceived as autocratic, or presented work to the teams as a *"fait accompli,"* asking them merely to "rubber stamp" decisions, and power struggles often erupted (Wohlstetter and Mohrman, 1996). Many teachers also are wary of being asked to devise curriculum or other plans for the school, fearing that they will be overturned at the principal or district levels, and have developed a valid skepticism related to the "genuineness" of promises of teacher authority (Miller, 1995). Finally, research finds that many teachers tend to be disinclined to participate in administrative and managerial decisions where they must challenge traditional patterns of principal authority (Conley, 1991; Malen and Ogawa, 1988).

The assumption of automatic collegiality As part of the second reform wave, SBM/SDMTs are seen as one means to decrease teacher isolationism. Advocates assume that when teachers are brought together in this fashion they will spontaneously form collegial and collaborative working groups. However, merely replicating the form of collaborative problem-solving groups found in effective schools will not necessarily recreate the substance. According to Hargreaves (1994), the result is often "contrived collegiality." To recreate the substance of these teams, participants must take risks. This requires that team members feel a sense of confidence in their own ability to do the work, coupled with a belief that their peers have a similar sense of trust in them. This is not a given in troubled schools, which tend to be highly balkanized or individualistic. In one school in which we worked, members of one SDMT subcommittee were so fearful of criticism by their peers and the possible alienation of students and their parents that they spent all their time attempting to anticipate all possible objections, leading to the psychological paralysis of the group!

The assumption of academic engagement   It is also assumed that these teams, once constituted, will realize that one, if not their most pressing, priority are matters of curriculum and instruction. However, according to Rosenholtz (1989: 41), in collaborative settings, "teachers' willingness to work together in solving instructional problems is not an immutable fact of everyday life." In fact, research has repeatedly found no direct connection between the creation of SBM/SDMTs and curricular and instructional reform (Wohlstetter and Mohrman, 1996). Indications are that these teams characteristically follow a sequential focus pattern. Their first order of business tends to be issues of concern to themselves, i.e., school climate. They then tend to turn their attention to student discipline and parent involvement. Only third in priority are issues related to instructional practice (Berman and Gjelten, 1984; David and Peterson, 1984; Lezotte and Bancroft, 1985; Lezotte and Taylor, 1989). This pattern is fully consistent with cultural assumptions about genetic and demographic responsibility for students' underachievement, which contribute to an initial unwillingness to recognize that a major causal factor could possibly be the quality or inappropriate nature of their instruction. According to Peterson *et al.* (1996), changing instructional practices is primarily a problem of learning, not a problem of organization.

Work and knowledge requirements   Hidden from most descriptions of SBM/SDMTs and their subcommittees is that participation requires a great expenditure of time and effort, e.g., to attend meetings, construct and analyze school surveys, plan implementation strategies, and disseminate information. Many staff find themselves overwhelmed when teamwork is simply layered on top of the press of their regular workday (Wohlstetter and Mohrman, 1996). In one of the schools in which we worked, a teacher commented that he was simply "meetinged-out." What is more, teachers, as well as parents and students, are characteristically unprepared to do the work that SBM/SDMTs require. According to Lindquist and Mauriel (1989: 405):

> council members will probably not enter the council with significant amounts of expertise in educational administration, curriculum, budgeting, or personnel. Developing such expertise may require a significant investment of time and energy. Training, however, can be expensive and needs to be repeated as new members join the site councils. It is possible that the proposed site council system demands too much time and energy from its members.

In summary, SBM/SDMTs are not ends in themselves. As a form of governance, they will not on their own generate improvement in school performance or necessarily break down walls of teacher isolationism. Rather, they are a means through which school-level decision-makers representing their various constituencies can implement various reforms that can improve teaching and learning (Wohlstetter and Mohrman, 1996). According to Eisner (1992: 616–617):

> It is not yet clear just how many teachers are interested in being "empowered." It is not yet clear how many teachers want to do educational research. It is not yet clear how many teachers are interested in assuming larger responsibilities such as the formulation of educational policy. Many teachers gain their deepest satisfaction in their own classrooms.

Choice

The schools of choice concept originated under varied auspices to address a broad variety of problems. Some schools of choice arrangements were to accommodate students not otherwise well served within the system, some were a response to strong parent and teacher preferences, some were developed in the interest of dropout prevention, others were to provide pilot sites for innovation and experiment, and still others were an alternative to forced busing (Raywid, 1990). Current proposals that would devolve control to parents through choice, e.g., charter schools, magnet schools, vouchers and tax credit plans, operate on the theory of a market economy. That is, in an open market, parents will seek out the best education for their children through their placement in schools where student achievement is high. Schools unable to attract students would be forced to improve to stay viable or go out of business. In having to produce what parents want, parents would have their interests more forcefully represented and schools would be forced to respond to their interests as opposed to those of other groups. An additional element in many of these plans, e.g., charter and some magnet schools, privatized and some alternative schools, is relative autonomy or exemption from many state and union regulations. In their stead, states would set minimum criteria for these schools. All schools meeting these goals would receive public money or parents sending children to these schools would be eligible for tax credit. While some choice schools may have entrance requirements, e.g., magnet and alternative schools, student diversity in choice schools would be ensured through the provision of free transportation. Demographic and achievement data on schools would be made available to the public through state information centers (House, 1998; Smrekar and Goldring, 1999).

Assumptions of the open market Equal access to information concerning schools is a basic assumption of this proposal. Research indicates, however, that parents vary in their ability to access information about schools, most typically along SES lines. The pool of resources from which lower income parents can draw may be smaller than that available to higher income families (Smrekar, 1996). This constraint is particularly evident for parents who are not employed, never finished high school or attended college, or live in neighborhoods that are unstable, transient, unsafe and isolated. These parents are less likely to have friends or family members who work in the school system or access to other social networks that can deliver relevant information about options, applications, and deadlines (Smrekar and Goldring, 1999). SES stratification may thus increase as a result of choice. In fact, a study of five choice plans in the USA, including vouchers, open enrollment and independent schools, found that parents who choose schools are "better educated, have higher incomes, and are less likely to be underemployed than nonchoosing parents" (Martinez *et al.*, 1994: 679).

Assumption of autonomy Some advocates of school choice also assume freeing schools from bureaucratic control will increase student achievement (e.g., Chubb and Moe, 1990). They reason that by making schools autonomous, many of the rules that change agents find oppressive would be eliminated. However, there is no reason to believe that merely freeing schools from regulations would lead to increased student achievement. One reason is that freedom from rules does not automatically lead to greater school innovation, e.g., curricular changes and increased use of student-centered approaches, as revealed by several studies in both Britain and the USA (see Smrekar and Goldring, 1999: 82). Second, release from federal and union rules would not make the schools autonomous. They would still be forced, now by the market, to do what parents and the community desire of them. The resultant school power structure might be less objective and certainly less knowledgeable concerning issues of pedagogy, equity and school administration, making the schools more vulnerable to interest group politics. In fact, however onerous are state and union rules, many are intended to ensure equity and fair treatment of students and teachers. The introduction of market forces may result in a weakening of educator effectiveness as it takes decision-making away from educators (House, 1998: 100). If the less than scrupulous practices of many privately owned trade schools are any example of what this might look like, serious second thought on the matter might well be advised. And finally, autonomy can mean isolation for some schools participating in choice plans. When choice schools are located in districts that have no direct authority over them, their uniqueness may become a source of benign neglect or even hostility from other school staffs and district personnel (Sarason, 1998).

The assumption of the freedom to teach   Decentralization plans further assume that teachers, once released from state and union rules, would immediately teach in ways that will enhance student achievement. It is a major question if teachers know how to teach in ways different from their present style without extensive staff development and reculturation. Market reform plans seriously underestimate the investment in skills and knowledge that teachers have made. Their styles of instruction are the products of years of trial and error. What they do is their practical answer to what they believe works best or how they have best adjusted to the demands of the task. It is unlikely that teachers have a cache of other instructional techniques reserved for use in another circumstance. Veteran teachers in choice schools tend to bring with them their cultural expectations and old instructional patterns. Thus, as might be expected, most decentralized schools operate much like other schools, and experiences with decentralization indicates that teachers and administrators do not do things much differently once the rules and regulations are removed (House, 1998: 101–102).

The assumption of resultant academic excellence   These plans also assume that the threat of parent displeasure and resultant student exodus will lead to the attainment and maintenance of high levels of student achievement. However, there is little evidence of this. Parents choose schools for a plethora of reasons, only one of which is academic achievement. Smrekar and Goldring (1999) found that the four primary reasons for parents choosing schools are academic reputation, discipline and safety, religion and social values, and transportation. Those who choose on the basis of a school's academic reputation tend to be higher income parents, many of whom want their children to be with children of the highest social class possible (Metz, 1986). Moreover, school reputation rests far more on the quality of their students than on the quality of their programs. The easiest and most pervasive way to attain high achieving students is to recruit them rather than create them from low achieving students (Natriello *et al.*, 1990: 185). Most parents, particularly lower income parents, do not choose schools so much as they leave schools behind due to dissatisfaction (Smrekar and Goldring, 1999). As a whole, parents have been found to be rather disinclined to leave their zoned, or neighborhood schools. Their children are heavily invested in particular schools, in regards to time and friendships with teachers and peers, and often are reluctant to leave. Parents, too, have feelings about community, preferring the convenience and comfort of sending their children to neighborhood schools to busing. Hence, once children are placed, both parents and students become disinclined to leave. Choice schools, rather than leading to increased excellence for all, tend to result in further stratification along SES lines (House, 1998; Smrekar and Goldring, 1999). In support, a study of New Zealand's market education policy, in existence for several years, found that most students did not change schools at all. The students who went to schools outside their zones tended to be from higher SES backgrounds than others. Across all schools, SES and racial segregation, therefore, increased, the two factors confounded by occurring together (Waslander and Thrupp, 1995).

Small schools

Based on the positive student outcomes of small independent (and often private) schools and decrying the impersonality characteristic of large public schools, another group of reformers have advocated for the deconstruction of large schools and their recreation as smaller schools, e.g., as charter schools, "academies," "houses," or small alternative public schools. The logistics of these schools may vary. Some small schools, e.g., houses and mini schools, tend to be situated on a floor or section of their original building with their own director, but under the general aegis of the building principal. Others forms, e.g., charter schools, usually are independent with their own principal, or head master, and their own board of advisors. Many of these schools are organized around themes, which may influence curricular choices, activities and projects. The general claim is that their smaller size creates a more intimate and personal atmosphere, fostering greater engagement, and a sense of community and belongingness among students, which, in turn, is assumed to increase students' academic performance (Meier, 1997). While research does support some benefits of small school size, e.g., better attendance rates, less violence, and some positive "compensatory" outcomes particularly among students from disadvantaged backgrounds (Cotton, 1996), the findings on student achievement, as a whole are mixed. One prestigious research organization, which conducted a 10-year study in over five states across the nation, found no evidence of better student achievement (Kemple and Snipes, 2000), and an extensive review of the literature by Cotton (1996) revealed that in 14 out of 23 studies, no effect was found.

Assumptions regarding size   While small schools can facilitate many of the positive characteristics associated with effective schools, it should not be assumed that they necessarily lead to them or that this factor can stand alone, independent of the other factors associated with school success. As the research findings above indicate, there are many small schools that have not fulfilled their academic promise and have problems, some typical of larger schools. The reasons, we believe, are several. First, small schools are often begun by visionary parents or leaders, who are able to select and coalesce a group of talented teachers who are similarly drawn to this vision. They constitute a cohesive body of practioners with an intrinsic unity of purpose. Often freed from the most restrictive of rules and regulations, directors can develop creative schedules with built-in time for teachers to meet, engage in joint planning, problem solve and experiment. Not unimportantly, teachers who perform poorly or become alienated can be invited to leave, and generally comply. And last, but certainly not least, as magnet, alternative or private schools they may select and accept children, even from outside the district. In total, the combined presence of these other forces casts serious doubt on small school size as the primary or even the major factor in the success of these schools. Moreover, with the passage of time, many of these unique features tend to disappear. When the charismatic leader and many of the founding teachers leave, the mission or themes of these schools are often lost with their exit, and waived regulations may be reimposed – leaving solely their small size and now hollow themes. As these schools come increasingly to look like traditional schools, students' academic performances fall. Commenting on the imposition of features of the traditional school culture on newly created small alternative schools in New York City, Beth Lief, then president of New Visions for Public Schools, stated:

> Two weeks before the current school year began, over the objections of parents and teachers, [the Chancellor] selected the principal of Buswick High School, a large failing high school in Brooklyn, to take over the ailing Local 1199 school, Ms. Lief said. And she said that Bronx high school officials had been transferring teachers to the school who did not support its programs. While the school had tried to avoid the anonymity and formality of huge city high schools, the transferred teachers created a rigid and traditional atmosphere by, among other things, insisting on ringing bells "every 25 minutes." (Hartocollis, 1997: B33)

Already "ailing," it is doubtful whether under these circumstances, this small school will succeed.

The issue of scale   From the above it should be apparent that knowledge of the basic elements for school success alone is hollow. Recreating these elements on the scale required to educate all our nation's youth is the problem. Fullan (1999) makes the point that within living, dynamic and complex organizational systems are three forms of knowledge: (1) public or scientific; (2) industry-specific; and (3) firm-specific, or tacit knowledge. It is in-house, firm-specific knowledge, i.e., that which resides in the heads and experiences of a successful organization's leaders and members that is the life and essence of its success. Problems in recreating this force is one reason why, asserts Fullan, "the performance of successful organizations cannot be easily duplicated" – for you can't transfer tacit knowledge. It is also why the loss of experienced employees in mergers and other transformations is often irreplaceable – "you can't hire firm-specific knowledge, you must grow it" (ibid.: 17). It is impossible to prescribe, as advocated by some authorities on school leadership (e.g., Sergiovanni, 1994), that principals be charismatic, visionary, and moral leaders. What these models don't say is that they are trying to (re)create a life force.

Curriculum and instruction

Probably, the most direct way to improve students' academic performance is to change the curriculum and the teaching practices used in troubled schools (Darling-Hammond, 1997; Fullan, 1990). Recognition of this fact and based on the notion that our nation's public schools are unfocused, with too many goals, federal and state government have moved to institute a specific set of standards, which now constitute the basis for most of the current curricular reforms. Notwithstanding, public debate continues over which of the two major pedagogical philosophies, i.e., constructivist or behaviorally-oriented programmed approaches, are best to use. Currently constructivist approaches to instruction are being advocated as "best practice" by most second wave reformers. However, there are a number of behavioristically-oriented innovations that have been presented to schools as packaged curricular programs. Each approach is discussed below.

National and state standards

In 1990, President George H. Bush in his State of the Union Address offered the nation his set of educational goals to be achieved by the year 2000. In 1994, President Clinton signed federal legislation establishing Goals 2000, a bold, long-range plan to further the establishment of a set of national education goals (see Box 9.1 on p. 278). Consistent with this thrust, states similarly moved to set a series of corresponding academic object- ives for schools, embodied in the form of content and perform- ance standards. *Content standards* specified desired knowledge, skills, understandings, and habits of mind that students should acquire and be able to demonstrate. Content standards often are described as "what students should know and be able to do." *Performance standards*, on the other hand, specify expectations about how well students must perform on the content standards. They cite established levels of achievement, quality of perform- ance, or degrees of proficiency. Ideally, this clearer specification of expected content and performance objectives gives teachers, students, and parents a target toward which to aim. They know what they are expected to do, and have a vivid image of what high-quality work looks like. Students can assess their own work and determine whether it meets expectations and, if it does not, decide what they need to do to ensure it does. This should drive an internal motivation for students to work hard, because they want to produce high quality work, supporters contend. The setting of national and state standards rests on a set of question- able assumptions and has been challenged in several areas.

The assumption of agreement on national standards Some have asserted that it is a myth that the federal government has attained consensus or a coherent vision regarding national goals and stand- ards for public education (e.g., House, 1998: 35). They cite major obstacles that have yet to be resolved such as the nation's and the schools' long history of interest group politics. Contending that these groups do not want the same things from schools, they assert that achieving any common vision or set of consensus goals is a formidable task because it requires reconciling these conflicts. Hampering this goal at both the federal and state levels would be the need to attain consensus, as compromise and bargaining rather than any uniform vision of change would drive such decisions. The results, House contends, can only be goals, strat- egies and outcomes that are short-term or provide inexpensive solutions. Also unresolved is how excellence should be defined for students of different circumstance, e.g., special education, bilingual education and those attending vocational schools.

School capacity and the opportunity to learn No lesser challenge is the wide variation among states, districts and local schools in their capacity to provide students with the types of instruction and other educational experiences needed to meet these standards. The fact that there are vast differences among schools and districts in their access to and financial ability to acquire the key resources, e.g., qualified teachers, libraries, adequate science and computer laboratories, needed to prepare students is a serious challenge to their successful attainment, and depending upon the actions taken by states and districts as a consequence of some schools' inability to meet the standards may be grievously unfair. For example, research has found that teacher qualification and experience account for the vast majority of the variance in student achievement between black and white students, and among students in grades 3, 6, and 8 (Armour-Thomas *et al.*, 1989; Ferguson, 1991). And characteristically, poor and urban schools and districts, and those serving low income and minority students have the highest rates of uncertified and newly hired teachers – one prime reason being their inability to offer competitive salaries. Their relative under-funding also makes it very difficult for them to provide other curricular and supplemental resources. Lacking the organizational capacity of more advantaged schools, students attending these at-risk schools are not on a level playing field with students from such schools. Without an equal opportunity to learn, they are, therefore, unfairly handicapped in their ability to meet the standards.

The challenge of special needs students These problems are particularly significant for students for whom English is a Second Language (ELLs) and for those who have traditionally been placed into "problem" special education tracks. These students, characteristically, receive a watered-down and slower-paced curriculum than students in regular and gifted or honors tracks. ELLs frequently encounter barriers to access to advanced curriculum because many schools fail to provide courses in such areas as science and mathematics (Minicucci and Olsen, 1992), teach in ways that fail to make the content comprehensible to ELLs who are just beginning to learn English (Lacelle-Peterson and Rivera, 1994), or track ELLs and other "problem" special education students into courses that do not address challenging content (Oakes, 1990). If all students are to be judged against the same standards, all students, including ELLs and most of the students in "problem" special education tracks must have access to the full scope of what is tested or measured (Stevens, 1993).

The assumption of implementation   Even granting a school's adequate possession of qualified and experienced teachers, they may still lack the understanding, skill and motivation needed to translate the standards into appropriate curricular and instructional modifications. Teachers will invariably require extensive training to understand what the standards mean for their own behavior, i.e., how particular standards-based objectives for student learning are best translated into changes in specific instructional practices. Teachers, particularly those in at-risk schools, must also learn new evaluative criteria and be able to bring their students to levels of academic performance seldom evidenced in these instructional settings. This is totally new ground for many. It is questionable whether teachers will or are receiving adequate training in these regards, whether they will and are being allotted the time necessary to plan, and whether they will perceive the necessity of taking these efforts seriously.

The assumption of heightened student achievement   By requiring students and teachers to demonstrate their possession of more advanced forms of knowledge for graduation and certification, respectively, the assumption is that a higher quality of worker is being produced. This may be the case, particularly for average students who were previously performing at moderate levels. It does not address, however, the vast numbers of underserved and grossly underachieving students, who tend to be disproportionately poor and ethnic minorities. Without specific efforts to address their needs, these students would be further disadvantaged, increasing the likelihood of their failure, grade retention, and dropping out of school (Darling-Hammond and Falk, 1997; Natriello *et al.*, 1990).

Constructivist pedagogy

This methodological approach paradigmatically shifts the focus of instruction from the teacher to the student. Emphasis is placed on providing students with "opportunities" to construct their own knowledge. By laying out materials and/or advantageously asking probe questions, teachers are said to empower children by giving them greater responsibility for their own learning. Similarly, students are encouraged to try out hunches, as disconfirmations of their theories is said to contribute to their understanding of the why of phenomena, and to provide the means to discover rules, principles and processes. When pupils become stumped, they are encouraged to problem solve with other children who are more knowledgeable. An emphasis is placed on learning in the context of the real world and the child's real needs, rendering the information authentic and meaningful. The curriculum often is based on themes, teacher and/or student interests; and in collaborative planning sessions, teachers and students determine when, within an agreed upon time frame, learning tasks will be completed. No longer the direct dispenser of information, the teacher now becomes a "facilitator," functioning primarily as a resource and catalyst to the learning process. In its extreme form, teachers minimize direct, whole class instruction and giving children answers. Traditional forms of assessment are also eschewed and in their stead descriptive reports and portfolios consisting of, sometimes self-selected, samples of children's assignments and projects are substituted. At one time, the near-exclusive hallmark of often private, "progressive schools," today, with reform emphasis on excellence and the development of abstract and critical thinking skills, these practices are being advocated as the primary, if not the sole methodological approach in all schools with all students. Current examples of this approach to subject-specific instruction are the whole language approach to reading, the writing process model, and the new math curriculum sometimes called "fuzzy" mathematics.

The assumption of students' existing knowledge Constructivist approaches assume that children come to school with some basic pre-existing knowledge within which to embed and upon which to build new knowledge. One of the most essential is "learning to learn" skills, i.e., when presented with a dilemma, children will pursue the answer through self-directed exploration, the testing of hunches and discussion with others.

While this assumption is very likely to hold true for some children, i.e., the offspring of educators and researchers, students in university labs and private schools, and generally those reared by authoritative parents, it may not hold true for many poor and ethnic minority children, who more often are raised in authoritarian or permissive households. Stereotypically, the children of authoritarian parents tend to be adult-oriented, dependent, less questioning and nonexploratory, while those reared by permissive parents tend to be more independent, but are often lacking a sense of higher authority and emotional self-control (Baumrind,

1967). Both sets of characteristics interfere with optimal learning in learner-centered classrooms. With students raised in authoritarian homes, the teacher's reluctance to provide information may significantly extend the amount of time these children take to find a solution on their own as they futilely wait for teacher direction; and for those raised in permissive homes, the simultaneous freedom and responsibility required for constructing knowledge may frustrate those who have not acquired enough self-control to bring a problem to solution. As a result, these children may initially feel lost and abandoned by the non-directiveness of "facilitative" techniques or driven to disruption by the immense freedom to choose to work alone or with others on projects. In general, where nonfacilitative incompatibilities exist between the home and the school environment, as is the case created by exclusive use of learner-centered strategies in inner-city public schools, learning will likely be hindered (Hale-Benson, 1982; Passow and Elliott, 1968).

Also, many academically underperforming children do not bring to school a great deal of school-relevant factual knowledge, and often are not familiar with much of the world beyond their neighborhood and television. The tenet that all information must be authentic, i.e., related to their existing knowledge and needs, when overzealously applied, may severely limit the range of curricular content introduced or inordinately confine students' exposure to events and processes embedded in these contexts.

The assumption of time By its very nature, constructivist approaches are time-consuming. With children who come to school lacking age-appropriate cultural capital, time spent in pursuit down blind alleys and in waiting for teacher direction is increased. As these children are already behind in their formal academic knowledge, exclusive use of these methods may retard, if not prevent them from catching up. Particularly now, when promotion is increasingly based on the passing of standardized tests, such a loss is one that poor and ethnic minority children can ill afford.

The assumption of methodological generalizability A major methodological assumption is that a curricular approach that works well with one group of students will work equally well with another population, with little or no modification. Similarly, political correctness dictates that it is unfair, if not discriminatory, not to extend approaches that work well with traditional and middle-class children to underachieving children. As principles, the first is naïve while the second is idealistic. This is most strikingly brought out with constructivist approaches to writing, reading, and mathematics, as they assume that students will spontaneously extract factual and relational knowledge from emersion in "deep" and "authentic" collaborative experiences with content materials. Where staunch advocates see little need to give formal instruction in the mechanics or rote aspects of phonics, grammar, sentence structure, and number facts, when and how else will children with little cultural capital acquire this information? Similarly with reading, while some children may be able to develop a large sight vocabulary from an intense emersion in literature, this does not ensure that all, or even most, children can do so; and of those who do, that they will be able to abstract the principles of pronunciation so as to generalize this knowledge to pronounce new but similar words correctly. In support, Sharp and Green (1975) demonstrated how the assumptions of open education worked against lower-class children and the *New York Times* (1997) recently concluded that phonics is necessary for 40 percent of all learners for whom word recognition is difficult. It thus seems that small children do not pick up reading any more naturally than anthropologists learn to decipher hieroglyphics or Marines figure out the Morse code. English is a very idiosyncratic language with many exceptions to any given rule. Finding regularities in this confusion may be difficult for even the brightest child, as correct hunches may be falsely negated by an exception. Addressing the political aspects of the writing process, Delpit (1995: 18) writes:

> writing process advocates often give the impression that they view the direct teaching of skills to be restrictive to the writing process at best, and at worst, politically repressive to students already oppressed by a racist educational system. Black teachers, on the other hand, see the teaching of skills to be essential to their students' survival . . . Progressive white teachers seem to say to their black students, "Let me help you find your voice. I promise not to criticize one note as you search for your song." But the black teachers say, "I've heard your song loud and clear. Now I want to teach you to harmonize with the rest of the world." Their insistence on skill is not a negation of their students' intellect, as

is often suggested by progressive forces, but an acknowledgement of it.

The most unfortunate irony of these assumptions is that, unlike in middle-class homes, the parents of many underperforming children in at-risk schools tend to be relatively undereducated themselves, and therefore are less able to correct their children's mistakes, and to fill in the gaps where found. Nor do most of these parents have the wherewithal to otherwise compensate for their and the schools' lack of instruction in the form of tutors and prep courses. For teachers in the public schools consciously to refrain from giving such children formal instruction in these skills is to doom them to second-class citizenship, as there is characteristically nowhere else for them to gain the valuable literacy skills needed for successful commerce in the dominant society.

The assumption of teacher knowledge   When advocates push for the adoption of methodologies that differ from traditional approaches to instruction, there is an assumption that teachers can implement these practices with little or moderate preparation and training. For example, consistent with the development of abstract and critical thinking skills in children, teachers now are expected routinely to ask higher order questions. This is far more difficult than it seems, for many teachers are not skilled in this questioning technique. Many, therefore, have difficulty spontaneously formulating these types of questions; knowing when, most opportunely, to intersperse them into lessons; and how best to follow up on students' responses. These are not skills, which even if taught in a one-shot workshop, are readily internalized so as to significantly modify teachers' immediate practices.

Even when teachers know what to do, they may not know how to use the practices and simultaneously meet curriculum demands set by their states. For example, if the curriculum is based on themes determined by teacher preference and/or student interest, they may deviate from that prescribed by the state. In and of itself, this may not be bad if the teacher has internalized knowledge of the states' curricular and skill requirements for a grade and is able to meet them through the topics chosen. However, many if not most public schools with large populations of academically underperforming students are plagued by a disproportionate number of new, inexperienced teachers, who tend to have the least amount of professional training and knowledge of these requirements. They are therefore more likely inadvertently to omit skills as well as topical instruction that these students need to pass critical gate-keeping examinations. According to Darling-Hammond (1997: 12), a strong advocate of the constructivist approach:

> Perhaps the single biggest obstacle to maintaining progressive reforms is the extensive skill needed to teach both subjects and students well. In all the previous reform eras practitioners asked to implement reforms like "open education" or the "project method" knew they were supposed to make learning relevant and attend to student needs. However, they often did not know how to fashion work that was rigorous as well as relevant, how to employ variable student-based strategies and also teach for high levels of disciplined understanding in content areas . . . Many teachers lost track of either their students or the curriculum goals as they broke with their previous routines, trying to become more child centered by letting go of subject matter standards or more subject centered by ignoring students while the curriculum march on ahead.

Scripted subject-specific pedagogical programs

At the other end of the methodological spectrum are behaviorally based instructional models, many of which have been permutated into scripted instructional packages. According to Apple (1982), the prepackaging of educational materials began in the 1950s and 1960s when the government became interested in rapidly increasing the number of scientists produced by the schools. Believing that public school teachers lacked the sophistication to translate this goal into instruction for the major curriculum areas "necessitated" the creation of packaged programmed instruction. These packages contained predeveloped curriculum and related materials. To ensure that content was conveyed, as intended, the instruction was "teacher-proofed," i.e., all discourse and all interactions between students and teacher were scripted. These scripts prescribed what teachers say, what questions they ask, acceptable student responses, as well as the pacing and time allotments for each activity. Packages may also include diagnostic and assessment tools for monitoring students' progress and assigning students to learning groups. Early prepackaged materials for reading in the early elementary school grades include Distar and Open Court. More current versions include Success for All and Reading Recovery.

The danger of teacher proofing   Based as they are on the assumption that teachers lack the knowledge or the ability to develop and impart instruction adequately, these strategies remove these responsibilities from the teacher, in effect, "deskilling" the job. According to Apple (1982: 142):

> [deskilling] usually has involved taking relatively complex jobs, . . . jobs that require no small amount of skill and decision making, and breaking them down into specified actions with specified result so that less skilled and costly personnel can be used, so that the control of work pace and outcome is enhanced.

Skills that the teacher used to need, that were deemed essential to the craft of working with children – such as curriculum deliberation and planning, designing teaching and curriculum strategies for specific groups and individuals based on intimate knowledge of these people – are no longer necessary. Packaged instructional materials are so specific as to leave little room not only for error, but for creativity and critical thinking, as well. In fact, with many of these programs, much of the presentation of the materials is done via workbooks, cards or computers, which, while allowing students to control the pacing of their own learning, transforms the teacher into a manager or monitor of students' work.

The illusion of scripted knowledge   Notwithstanding the above criticism, this method has been quite successful in helping students acquire large amounts of concrete and factual information in a relatively short amount of time. However, these are not the forms of knowledge consistent with the goals of the current reform wave. In scripting knowledge, the child's thinking processes are constrained and regimented, leaving little or no room for creativity and critical thinking. It is important, therefore, that just because poor and many ethnic minority children do not come to school with cultural capital, and this is probably the best way to instill this information in an expeditious way, that this way does not become the sole approach to their instruction. It must be only a starting point. These children also need to learn to use inquiry and higher-order thinking skills that are best developed through the constructivist approach.

Attitudes and beliefs

As legislators as well as prominent educational reformers increasingly conclude that the kinds of changes that need to be made in the schools are largely cultural, beliefs and assumptions become the targets of reform. Moreover, for any school reform to work, positive and supportive dispositions are absolutely necessary. A critical mass, if not all, of the major adult stakeholders in schools needs to believe that their students can learn and the improvement effort can work – or at least hold their skepticism in abeyance long enough to give the reform a serious try. The significance of the affective, or emotional, component lies in its ability to energize and propel the change effort forward or, conversely, to impede or derail it. Consequently, many of the major comprehensive reform models include an affective component which lists a series of principles, values and attitudes that stakeholders should adopt when attempting to implement their programs. Among the multitudinous attitudes that teachers are variously asked to adopt are the belief that all children can learn; risk taking; trust; no fault; experimentation; co-operation; collaboration; consensus; and empowerment coupled with responsibility. School stakeholders are typically introduced to a particular model's values through one or more orientation workshops, often followed up by "team building" workshops led by outside facilitators.

The challenge of instituted attitude change

The one major assumption underlying this component is that appropriate beliefs and attitudes can be mandated or instituted as one would any other structural or procedural innovation. We all know, unfortunately, that affect cannot be mandated by laws, introduced like a program, nor instituted like a set of procedures (Fullan, 1993). For while school personnel can be forced to adopt new teaching practices, innovative methods of testing, and novel structural organizations, attitudes and beliefs are personal and constitute part of an individual's sense of self. If pushed, staff can become resentful. For example, one teacher told me in a session on a model's values, that it sounded more like a religion than a school improvement effort. There is no critical mass in the

number of workshops that will lead automatically to teachers'
internalizing the desired dispositions. Nor will repeatedly placing
school personnel in situations in which particular attitudes should
be employed lead spontaneously to their utilization (Hargreaves,
1994). Neither telling nor even showing faculty of their need will
necessarily lead to their adoption.

The assumption of student achievement through teacher affect

It is also erroneous to assume that appropriate affect alone will
lead to increased student achievement. Affect is a necessary
condition, but it is not sufficient unto itself. Teachers, again, must
know how to translate high expectations into appropriate curriculum and instructional practices. At best, appropriate affect may
motivate teachers to pursue the acquisition of appropriate knowledge and to attempt its implementation once the knowledge is
found. However, the "how-to" is a critical intervening step, one
that cannot automatically be assumed, nor instantaneously overcome if absent.

Other major reform plans

Standardized assessment of student achievement

Characteristically, standardized tests are timed, paper and pencil
examinations, which are administrated in the same way and under
the same conditions to large groups of students. These procedures
are to ensure equality among students in the tests' administration
and to facilitate inter-group comparisons among schools, regions
and states on the content tested. Test items have traditionally
been predominantly, if not exclusively, of the multiple-choice
variety. However, to enhance the content validity of these tests
relative to states' content standards, a greater range in the types
of performance assessment is being included.

The assumption of content validity   There are four domains of
pupil achievement that schools should address: knowledge acqui-
sition/expression; knowledge application/problem solving; personal and social skills; and motivation and commitment.
Traditional standardized tests measure only the first two domains,
with differential success. Most characteristically, these tests load
heavily on knowledge consistent with the first domain, i.e.,

knowledge rather than skill; memorization rather than problem solving; speed rather than reflection; and individual rather than group performance. To date, these tests only partially assess the second domain, although efforts are currently being made to extend their loading on items related to problem solving and application. This format, however, may not provide the best conditions for the demonstration of these skills and efforts to develop "alternative assessment" measures have not been very successful. "Authentic assessment" techniques, e.g., portfolios, are cumbersome, of dubious reliability and validity, and are extremely labor-intensive and time-consuming to grade.

The challenge of standardized assessments of special needs students   Of particular concern in this regard are issues related to validity and reliability. A significant intervening variable in the knowledge assessment of English Language Learners (ELLs), is their proficiency in English, which may be relatively unrelated to their knowledge in the subject area being assessed. Research on language learning shows that even though minimal survival skills in English can be achieved fairly quickly, the ability to use English for academic purposes takes longer to develop (Collier, 1992; Cummins, 1989). This, thus, poses a serious challenge to the test-retest reliability of these assessments, for as ELLs gain greater academic proficiency in English, their test scores will improve. Translations also are an issue of concern, as validity and norming should not be assumed, for these processes may not have been repeated for the translated versions (Lacelle-Peterson and Rivera, 1994). Lacelle-Peterson and Rivera also make the point that while equity issues related to the administration of standardized tests to ELLs have a long history of investigation, research and discussion of those related to performance assessment are more rare. Particular concern must be focused on the scoring process for performance assessments as fair and valid ratings of ELLs' performances depend on the background knowledge of the rater (e.g., knowledge of language acquisition processes). These researchers caution against assuming that assessment innovations, which contribute to the success of monolinguals, will also work for ELLs, i.e., that once ELLs know a little English, the new and improved assessments will fit them too.

The fallacy of procedural fairness   Despite standardization in their administration, the fairness of these tests cannot also be assumed, as all students are not coming from a level playing field. The issue has already been made regarding the wide variations in schools' capacity to provide students with the opportunity to learn the content that will be assessed by these examinations. There will, similarly, be wide variations in student familiarity with the testing procedures. Characteristically, students in private schools and those in middle-class neighborhoods are more likely to receive instruction in test-taking techniques. With more public schools instructing students on test-taking procedures, these disparities have been reduced; but where such practice is not provided, students will continue to be severely disadvantaged.

As more and more ELLs and some categories of students in "problem" special education classes are required to take these tests, strict conformity to standardized procedures is a problem. ELLs and Learning Disabled students, obviously, need more time to process the information, and other types of procedural and environmental modifications may be advised for AD/HD students. Some researchers have also raised the issue of the need to make procedural modifications sensitive to students' learning style differences. And issues of gender, SES, and ethnic bias remain points of concern and contention. According to Darling-Hammond (1994: 17):

> Of course, many forms of bias remain, as the choice of items, responses deemed appropriate, and content deemed important are the product of culturally and contextually determined judgments, as well as the privileging of certain ways of knowing and modes of performance over others . . . These forms of bias are equally likely to plague performance-based assessments, as the selection of tasks will rest on cultural and other referents, such as experiences, terms, and exposure to music, art, literature, and social experiences that are differentially accessible to test-takers of different backgrounds.

The issue of teaching to the tests   The system's heavy reliance on standardized tests for a multitude of determinations forces schools and teachers to focus on preparing students for these examinations. This has the effect of transforming the tests into educational goals in and of themselves, subordinating their usefulness in the identification of a school's challenge areas to its use as a guide for instruction. As these tests have tended to focus disproportionately on lower order and factual knowledge, the result has been the consumption of valuable time that could be spent in more rich and varied pedagogy and a lowering in the level of instruction for many schools. This has been a major source of criticism among pedagogues (Darling-Hammond, 1994). In an effort to address these issues, states are including more higher-order skills in both their content standards and test items. While this may pose a problem for more advantaged schools and students, in many of the severely underperforming schools in which we have worked, these changes have led to more rigorous and focused teaching than before. Teachers with low expectations for students are, nonetheless, forced to expose them to higher order content.

The issue of publishing school outcome data   Schools' scores on standardized tests are typically reported to the public in terms of lists, ranking schools relative to students' average attainment in particular subject areas. Although many states have moved from norm to criterion referenced tests, most states still report scores in mean rank order, i.e., taking a school's average score (i.e., for a grade or for all students tested) on a particular test and ranking it relative to the mean scores of all other schools in the reporting area. This method of reporting is deceptive because it fails to take into account the intake characteristics of the pupils in schools, nor does it elucidate the effectiveness of schools in terms of the gains made by pupils (Cuttance, 1992). To assess the extent of the gains made by pupils in each school it is necessary to control for the background characteristics and prior attainment of pupils at the point of entry into the school and at the start of the academic year. This may be done through the "value added method" or comparisons within "bands" of schools with similar student characteristics. The type of student background information that should be disaggregated include indicators of students' content knowledge in the subject areas at entry to the school or the end of the previous academic year, language background and school background (e.g., if the student's schooling was interrupted) and the length of time students have been receiving instruction in English as a second language and English language instruction in the content areas. According to Cuttance (1992: 79–80):

> Clearly, a failure to adjust the measures of effectiveness for
> the characteristics of pupils at the time of their intake to the

school invalidates them as measures of the value added by the school concerned ... An unadjusted (i.e., standards) model of effectiveness provides us with an estimate of the absolute level of the average attainment of pupils in a school, but it cannot indicate the extent of pupil progress within each school.

Accountability

Common to many school reform proposals or actual reform plans is the linking of content and performance standards with accountability systems, based on the theory that schools, teachers, and students will try harder and become more effective in meeting performance goals when the goals are clear, when information on the degree of success is available, and when there are real incentives for attainment or consequences for failure. Newmann *et al.* (1997) have identified six forms of accountability: (1) performance reporting; (2) monitoring and compliance with standards or regulations; (3) incentive systems; (4) reliance on the market; (5) changing the locus of authority or control of schools; and (6) changing professional roles. (Three of these forms, i.e., performance reporting, the market, and locus of control were discussed earlier in this chapter. The remaining three are discussed below.)

The challenge of compliance and failure   Current assessment tools yield often questionable and incomplete data regarding both schools' and students' relative ability to attain content and performance standards. Inseparable from concerns related to issues of equity are those related to what happens to schools and students who are unable to make the grade. Authorities may view the results of these assessments as either an opportunity to strengthen the educational infrastructure or as a means to identify schools and individuals for punitive action. Both responses have their challenges. In the former case, truly at-risk public schools may be provided with "opportunity-to-learn" funds in an effort to acquire needed resources. However, these efforts are often accompanied by strong external accountability demands and heavy prescriptions of these schools' programs and the activities of personnel, all which tend to severely limit their autonomy to craft programs that respond to their unique social contexts (Newmann *et al.*, 1997). This presents a dilemma, for it is difficult to hold schools and teachers accountable for student performance where they lack the decision-making capacity and the authority to use their own judgment in executing their tasks. In the case of punitive action, prolonged periods of low performance may result in school closings and other indignities without care to identify or efforts to correct the problem, e.g., large numbers of uncertified and inexperienced teachers, and/or the lack of laboratories and adequate library facilities. Such actions merely punish the victim.

When, on the other hand, authorities use low assessment scores to push low scoring students into special education, retain students in grade, deny them access to further educational opportunities, or encourage them to drop out, a similar injustice is done. Such consequences tend to do little more than reinforce these students' beliefs in their personal inadequacies (Allington and McGill-Franzen, 1992; Darling-Hammond and Falk, 1997). Research has shown that students in special education invariably fall further behind, while those who are retained actually achieve less than their comparable peers who are allowed to move on through the grades. Both students who are placed in special education or are retained in grade subsequently tend to drop out of school (Darling-Hammond and Falk, 1997; Oakes, 1986; Shepard and Smith, 1988).

The assumption of public disgrace and other sanctions To assume that principals and teachers will be motivated by negative publicity regarding their schools' test scores or threats of take over is to overestimate the degree to which many staff at severely underperforming schools assume ownership for the poor academic achievement of their students. Where teachers regard students' attainment of the standards as an impossibility, based on deficit thinking, they will not be motivated by negative sanctions, for they regard themselves as powerless to effect change. If, as they believe, blame lies not with them, but in these students' homes and genes, they become the victims of unfair persecution, rather than motivated by these acts.

Fortunately, this is not the case in all schools and the threat of disgrace and sanctions can produce changes. However, those most able to change and respond as desired may not be those most in need, i.e., severely at-risk schools. For example, in an effort to unpack differential student achievement within schools, some states will begin to disaggregate test data by ethnicity. Some "highly performing schools" have strenuously objected to this practice, as it may reveal that they are not doing a good job educating their minority students. Notwithstanding, if the stakes are high enough, test data can be manipulated and falsified (Benveniste, 1985: 264; House, 1998).

The assumption of incentives Incentives may come in several forms, e.g., merit pay, differential staffing or career ladders, and recruitment bonuses. Almost all forms have been previously tried with little success. There are several factors that make incentives problematic. In regards to merit pay and bonuses, research shows that monetary incentives must be big enough to motivate individuals (Brandt, 1990). Public education has historically been underfunded; salaries are typically low, and the work conditions difficult. Under these circumstances, it is not likely that the monetary incentives will be large enough to make a difference. With career ladders and differential staffing, which are proposed to address teachers' flat job horizon, reasonable and objective criteria must be established for awarding incentives. This is not easy, for while it is possible to identify incompetent teachers, sorting out the top 10 or 20 percent of teachers who perform above average from colleagues who perform at adequate levels appears to be futile (Kirst, 1990). Current methods of teacher evaluation are grossly insufficient. Teachers and unions have a long history of fears and claims of evaluator bias, halo tendencies, ambiguity of feedback, gender discrimination and the inflation of scores. Moreover, singling out teachers, as these plans do, runs counter to many school and teacher cultures and, as a result, may arouse hostility and feelings of low self-esteem in those who are not recognized. These challenges have led to union resistance to such proposals. If student performance is used as the criterion, there simply are no instruments sophisticated enough to parse out the advancement in students' achievement attributable to individual teachers (House, 1998; Meyers, 1993). Scores can be disaggregated by class; but as we all know, there are between-group differences among classes (e.g., in students' entry level academic skills and behavior problems), even within grades in the same school. For these reasons, some accountability systems have shifted the criteria to attendance or voluntary work, or to schools as the award unit.

The assumptions regarding internal or professional accountability An alternative to external, bureaucratic accountability systems is internal or professional accountability systems. With internal accountability, staff within a school identify clear standards for student performance, collect information to inform themselves about their levels of success, and exert peer pressure within the faculty to meet the goals. Professional accountability, as the name implies, is a system created by a broad, representative team of professionals in the field that establishes quality control. Most typically, quality control over personnel is substituted for quality control over service delivery. Professionals establish standards to assure the competence of neophytes before allowing them to become full-fledged members of the profession (Wise, 1989) and accusations of unprofessional behavior are judged by a committee of peers. With internal accountability, there is no reason to assume that those who have perpetuated traditional school cultures will spontaneously address the previously mentioned problems characteristic of at-risk cultures. With professional accountability, the link between teacher credentials and increased student achievement alone may be inadequate to improve student performance, particularly if teacher preparation programs do not keep abreast of the constantly changing demands on teachers, as has been alleged (Goodlad, 1990).

In summary, there exist a plethora of plans, stratagems, and activity lists all proclaiming to be the panacea for the problems that ail our schools. There is something for every political and theoretical perspective, sincere interest and flight of fantasy. All have their various strengths and challenges. Not one, in and of itself, is a cure-all. It is in the would-be consumers' thorough knowledge and artful combination of these elements, tailored to the unique needs of their schools that these challenges will be addressed and compensated for. Without this knowledge, these hidden challenges can and have doomed the fate of these and other reform efforts. Too hasty an adoption of promised panacean plans runs a high risk of resulting in situations where staff are unable, unprepared, or unwilling to meet the implementation requirements, where students do not meet the underlying assumptions on which the plans were based, and staff lack the knowledge on how to prepare themselves in these regards – even if it were possible. It may also explain why these reforms constantly re-emerge with no clear resolution as to their merits. What is most important is the will to make any one of these plans work. Successful schools have a life force, which these plans try either to recreate by combining the various elements, or circumvent its lack by teacher proofing. Addressing this force ultimately is the challenge of any model of excellence.

Study Questions

1. What do you think is the ideal governance or organizational structure for schools? Justify your answer and state how you would deal with the challenges.

2. Similarly, what do you think is the ideal pedagogical model for schools? Again, justify your answer and state how you would address the challenges inherent in each proposal. How would the model change, if at all, for demographic differences among schools in student populations?

3. If you were to design a comprehensive model for reform, what components would you select and how would you combine them and why?

4. How, if at all, would the above comprehensive model change if the following are your goals?
   a. to fulfill each of the functionalists' goals of schooling in turn;
   b. to fulfill the goals of each of the three major political perspectives.

5. If you were selecting a reform model for your school, what would be the questions you would ask or characteristics you would look for in determining the appropriateness of each component and why?

6. The focus of the current second "wave of reform" is school culture. How specifically would you seek to change school culture using these elements or others not mentioned? Explain and justify your response.

7. Which of the reasons mentioned in this chapter would teachers in your school most likely give for rejecting "empowerment" and why? Are there any other reasons that the faculty in your school might offer? How would you respond to them?

8. If you were a teacher or administrator in a school creating an SBM/SDM team, how might you get team members to address issues of instruction early on?

9. Select several of your state's major curriculum standards. How might they best be achieved using the various
elements outlined in this chapter?
10. What administrative style do you think is needed to
most expeditiously facilitate the school reform changes
currently on the table? Do they vary by reform component? Explain.

References

Allington, R. L. and McGill-Frazen, A. (1992) Unintended effects of
educational reform in New York. *Educational Policy*, vol. 6,
pp. 397–414.

Apple, M. (1982) *Education and Power*. Boston: Ark Paperbacks.

Armour-Thomas, E. *et al.* (1989) *An Outlier Study of Elementary and
Middle Schools in New York City: Final Report*. New York: New York
Board of Education.

Baumrind, D. (1967) Child care practices anteceding three patterns of
preschool behavior. *Genetic Psychology Monographs*, vol. 75,
pp. 43–88.

Benveniste, G. (1985) The design of school accountability systems.
Educational Evaluation and Policy Analysis, Fall, vol. 7, no. 3,
pp. 261–279.

Berman, P. and Gjelten, T. (1984) *Improving School Improvement: A
Policy Evaluation of the California School Improvement Program*, vol. 2:
Findings. Berkeley, CA: Berman, Weiler Associates.

Brandt, R. M. (1990) *Incentive Pay and Career Ladders for Today's
Teachers: A Study of Current Programs and Practices*. New York: State
University of New York Press.

Chubb, J. E. and Moe, T. M. (1990) *Politics, Markets, and America's
Schools*. Washington, DC: Brookings Institute.

Clune, W. and White, D. (1988) *School-based Management: Institutional
Variation, Implementation and Issues for Further Research*. New Bruns-
wick, NJ: Rutgers University, Center for Policy and Research in
Education.

Cohen, M. (1988) *Restructuring the Education System: Agenda for the
1990s*. Washington, DC: National Governors' Association.

Coleman, J. S. *et al.* (1966) *Equality of Educational Opportunity*. Washington, DC: US Government Printing Office.

Collier, V. P. (1992) A synthesis of studies examining long-term
language minority student data on academic achievement. *Bilingual
Education Research Journal*, vol. 16, no. 1–2, pp. 187–221.

Conley, S. C. (1991) Review of research on teacher participation in school decision making. *Review of Research in Education*, vol. 17, pp. 225–266.

Cotton, K. (1996) *School Size, School Climate, and Student Performance*. Northwest Regional Education Laboratory.

Cummins, J. (1989) *Empowering Language Minority Students*. Sacramento, CA: California Association for Bilingual Education.

Cuttance, P. (1992) Evaluating the effectiveness of schools. In D. Reynolds and P. Cuttance (eds) *School Effectiveness: Research, Policy and Practice*. London: Cassell, pp. 71–95

Darling-Hammond, L. (1994) Performance-based assessment and educational equity. *Harvard Educational Review*, vol. 64, no. 1, Spring, pp. 5–30.

Darling-Hammond, L. (1997) *The Right to Learn: A Blueprint for Creating Schools that Work*. San Francisco: Jossey-Bass.

Darling-Hammond, L. and Falk, B. (1997) Using standards and assessments to support student learning. *Phi Delta Kappan*, November, pp. 190–199.

David, J. (1989) Synthesis of research on school-based management. *Educational Leadership*, May, pp. 45–53

David, J. L. and Peterson, S. M. (1984) *Can Schools Improve Themselves?: A Study of School-based Improvement Programs*. Palo Alto, CA: Bay Area Research Group.

Delpit, L. (1995) *Other People's Children*. New York: The New Press.

Department of Education and Science (1967) *Ten Good Schools: A Secondary School Enquiry*. London: DES.

Eisner, E. W. (1992) Educational reform and the ecology of schooling. *Teachers College Record*, vol. 93, no. 4, Summer, pp. 611–627.

Elmore, R. F. and Fuhrman, S. H. (1995) Opportunity to learn standards and the state role in education. *Teachers College Record*, vol. 96, no. 3, pp. 432–457.

Ferguson, R. F. (1991) Paying for public education: new evidence on how and why money matters. *Harvard Journal on Legislation*, Summer, pp. 465–498.

Fogelman, K. (1978) The effectiveness of schooling. In W. H. Armytage and J. Peel (eds) *Perimeters of Repair*. London: Academic Press.

Fogelman, K. (ed.) (1983) *Growing Up in Great Britain*. London: Macmillan.

Fullan, M. (1990) Staff development, innovation and institutional development. In B. Joyce (ed.) *Changing School Culture Through Staff Development*. Alexandria, VA: ASCD, pp. 3–25.

Fullan, M. with Stiegelbauer, S. (1991) *The New Meaning of Educational Change*, 2nd edn. New York: Teachers College Press, Columbia University.

Fullan, M. (1993) *Change Forces: Probing the Depth of Educational Reform*. London: Falmer Press.

Fullan, M. (1999) *Change Forces: The Sequel*. London: Falmer Press.

Goodlad, J. (1990) *Teachers for Our Nation's Schools*. San Francisco: Jossey-Bass.

Hale-Benson, J. (1982) *Black Children: Their Roots, Culture and Learning Styles*. Baltimore, MD: Johns Hopkins University Press.

Hanushek, E. A. (1994) *Making Schools Work: Improving Performance and Controlling Costs*. Washington, DC: Brookings Institute.

Hargreaves, A. (1994) *Changing Teachers, Changing Times: Teachers' Work and Culture in the Postmodern Age*. London: Cassell.

Hartocollis, A. (1997) Small schools conference lands Crew in a dispute. *New York Times*, October 26, p. B33.

House, E. (1998) *Schools for Sale: Why Free Market Policies won't Improve America's Schools, and What Will*. New York: Teachers College Press, Columbia University.

Jencks, C. *et al.* (1971) *Inequality*. London: Allen Lane.

Kemple, J. and Snipes, J. (2000) *Career Academies: Impacts on Student Engagement and Performance in High School*. New York: Manpower Development Research Corporation.

Kirst, M. W. (1990) *Accountability: Implications for State and Local Policymakers*. Washington, DC: Office of Educational Research.

Lacelle-Peterson, M. W. and Rivera, C. (1994) Is it real for all kids? A framework for equitable assessment policies for English Language Learners. *Harvard Educational Review*, vol. 64, no. 1, pp. 55–75.

Leonard, P. (1990) Fatalism and discourse on power. In L. Davies and E. Schragge (eds) *Bureaucracy and Community: Essays on the Politics of Social Work Practice*. Montreal: Black Rose Books.

Levine, D. U. (1992) An interpretive review of US research and practice dealing with unusually effective schools. In D. Reynolds and P. Cuttance (eds) *School Effectiveness: Research, Policy and Practice*. London: Cassell, pp. 25–47.

Levine, D. U. and Lezotte, L. W. (1990) *Unusually Effective Schools: A Review and Analysis of Research and Practice*. Madison, WI: National Center for Effective Schools Research and Development.

Lezotte, L. W. and Bancroft, B. A. (1985) School improvement based on effective schools research: a promising approach for economically disadvantaged and minority students. *Journal of Negro Education*, vol. 54, no. 3, pp. 301–312.

Lezotte, L. W. and Taylor, B. S. (eds) (1989) *Case Studies in Effective Schools Research*. Okemos, MI: National Center for Effective Schools Research and Development.

Lindquist, K. M. and Mauriel, J. J. (1989) School based management: doomed to failure. *Education and Urban Society*, vol. 231, no. 4, August, pp. 403–416.

Malen, B. and Ogawa, R. T. (1988) Professional-patron influence on site-based governance councils: a confounding case study. *Educational Evaluation and Policy Analysis*, vol. 10, pp. 251–270.

Martinez, V., Thomas, K. and Kemerer, F. (1994) Who chooses and why: a look at five schools of choice. *Phi Delta Kappan*, vol. 75, no. 9, pp. 678–681.

Meier, D. (1997) Habits of mind: democratic values and the creation of effective learning communities. In B. Kogan (ed.) *Common Schools, Uncommon Futures: A Working Consensus for School Renewal*. New York: Teachers College, Columbia University, pp. 60–73.

Metz, M. (1986) *Different by Design*. New York: Routledge.

Meyer, R. H. (1993) Can schools be held accountable for good performance? In E. P. Hoffman (ed.) *Essays on the Economics of Education*. Kalamazoo, MI: W. E. Upjohn Institute for Employment Research, pp. 75–109.

Miles, M. (1981) Mapping the common properties of schools. In R. Lehmig and M. Kane (eds) *Improving Schools*. Beverly Hills, CA: Sage.

Miller, E. (1995). Shared decision-making by itself doesn't make for better decisions. *Harvard Educational Letter*, vol. XI, no. 6, pp. 1–4.

Minicucci, C. and Olsen, L. (1992) *Programs for Secondary Limited English Proficient Students: A California Study*. Occasional Papers in Bilingual Education, No. 5. Spring, Washington, DC: National Clearinghouse for Bilingual Education.

Natriello, G., McDill, E. and Pallas, A. M. (1990) *Schooling Disadvantaged Children: Racing against Catastrophe*. New York: Teachers College Press.

Newmann, F. M., King, M. B. and Rigdon, M. (1997) Accountability and school performance: implications from restructuring schools. *Harvard Educational Review*, vol. 67, no. 1, pp. 41–74.

New York Times (1997) Teaching Johnny to read. January 25, Editorial, Section A, p. 22.

Oakes, J. (1986) Tracking in secondary schools: a contextual perspective. *Educationalist Psychologist*, vol. 22, no. 19, pp. 129–154.

Oakes, J. (1990) *Multiplying Inequalities: The Effects of Race, Social Class, and Tracking on Opportunities to Learn Mathematics and Science*. Santa Monica, CA: Rand.

Passow, A. H. and Elliott, D. L. (1968) The nature and needs of the educationally disadvantaged. In A. H. Passow (ed.) *Developing Programs for the Educationally Disadvantaged*. New York: Teachers College Press, Columbia University, pp. 1–20.

Peterson, P. L., McCarthy, S. J. and Elmore, R. F. (1996) Learning from school restructuring. *American Educational Research Journal*, Spring, vol. 33, no. 1, pp. 119–153.

Raywid, M. A. (1990) Rethinking school governance. In R. Elmore and Associates (eds) *Restructuring Schools: The Next Generation of Educational Reform*. San Francisco: Jossey-Bass, pp. 152–205.

Reynolds, D. (1992) School effectiveness and school improvement: an updated review of the British literature. In D. Reynolds and P. Cuttance (eds) *School Effectiveness: Research, Policy and Practice*. London: Cassell, pp. 1–24.

Reynolds, D. and Cuttance, P. (eds) *School Effectiveness: Research, Policy and Practice*. London: Cassell.

Rosenholtz, S. J. (1989) *Teachers' Workplace: The Social Organization of Schools*. New York: Longman.

Sarason, S. B. (1998) *Charter Schools: Another Flawed Educational Reform?* New York: Teachers College Press, Columbia University.

Sergiovanni, T. (1994) *Building Community in Schools*. San Francisco: Jossey-Bass.

Sharp, R. and Green, A. (1975) *Education and Social Control: A Study in Progressive Primary Education*. London: Routledge and Kegan Paul.

Shepard, L. and Smith, M. L. (1988) Funking kindergarten: escalating curriculum leaves many behind. *American Educator*, Summer, pp. 34–38.

Smrekar, C. (1996) *The Impact of School Choice and Community: In the Interest of Families and Schools*. Albany: State University of New York.

Smrekar, C. and Goldring, E. (1999) *School Choice in Urban America: Magnet Schools and the Pursuit of Equity*. New York: Teachers College Press, Columbia University.

Smylie, M. A. (1992) Teacher participation in school decision-making: assessing willingness to participate. *Educational Evaluation and Policy Analysis*, vol. 14, no. 1. pp. 53–67.

Stevens, F. I. (1993) *Opportunity to Learn: Issues of Equity for Poor and Minority Students*. Washington, DC: National Center for Educational Statistics.

Tye, B. B. (2000) *Hard Truths: Uncovering the Deep Structure of Schooling*. New York: Teachers College Press.

Waslander, S. and Thrupp, M. (1995) Choice, competition and segregation: an empirical analysis of a New Zealand secondary school market, 1990–1993. *Journal of Education Policy*, vol. 10, no. 1, pp. 1–26.

Wise, A. E. (1989) Professional teaching: a new paradigm for the management of education. In T. J. Sergiovanni and J. H. Moore (eds) *Schools for Tomorrow*. Boston: Allyn and Bacon, pp. 301–310.

Wohlstetter, P. and Mohrman, S. A. (1996) *Assessment of School-based Management: Studies of Education Reform*. Washington, DC: US Department of Education, Office of Educational Research and Improvement.

5

The Innovation Process

Amidst this constant clamor for change, recognition is emerging that successfully altering the functioning and outcomes of even one school, much less schools nationwide, is a very complex, long and often arduous process. During the first reform wave, legislators and upper level administrators somewhat arrogantly presupposed that change is something that authorities could legislate or invent, and once local site staff were exposed to the inherent wisdom of the change they would see the error of their ways and leap at the opportunity to behave as desired. The effective schools literature may also have inadvertently oversimplified outsiders' perception of the change process by citing a list of seemingly replicable factors without revealing how an effective school became so, how long it took, and if it stayed effective (Fullan, 1985). Increasingly, however, individuals in the field of innovation are becoming aware that schools are highly complex and dynamic organizations, and innovation is not a linear, rational process that can be offered like a gift, prescribed like a medication, enacted like a law, or guided with cookbooks and manuals. Still, among most legislators, upper level education administrators, the media and the public, there is no clear, coherent sense of how change proceeds at the local site level (Fullan, 1991: 4) Lacking this knowledge, would-be school reformers fall prey to faddism, superficiality, blaming the victims, misunderstandings concerning resistance, seeking premature results, and an outright failure to sustain support for reasonable change efforts

Those concerned about, involved in or affected by school change need a coherent picture of the innovation process to contextualize media decrials, "authoritative" reports, and personal efforts. This is the aim of this chapter. Toward this end, we first unpack the reform process from the perspective of its stages. Each is discussed in the context of factors that can complicate, compromise, and even derail change efforts along the way, as well as those associated with "successful" reform efforts. This section is presented not as an exhaustive review of the literature, but as an overview of noteworthy landmarks and is based heavily on extensive research conducted by Berman and McLaughlin for the Rand Corporation during the late 1970s and early 1980s. More recent literature has not significantly modified their basic findings. Progress primarily has been in the form of a reconceptualization of schools as organizations and its effect on the change process. In Part II, we discuss how organizational concepts introduced in Chapter 3 have altered the guidebook for change. As you read this chapter, consider it in the context of the following framing questions:

1. How can the way in which an innovation is introduced affect its reception and implementation by staff?
2. How long do you think it takes school staff adopting an innovation to become familiar enough with its procedures so as to feel comfortable with its implementation? What factors influence this?
3. What do you feel are the major obstacles to implementing school improvement projects and why?
4. What are the primary factors influencing whether an innovation becomes institutionalized in a school and why?

The Three Stages of the Innovation Process

Innovation is not an overnight process, particularly the innovation of large traditional organizations like schools. Estimates vary, with most researchers advising observers and implementers that even moderately complex changes take from three to five years, while major restructuring efforts can take up to ten years before reliable and stable conclusions may be drawn (Fullan, 1991: 49). In that time, school staff engage in a plethora of activities, typically conceived as a series of three overlapping stages: initiation, implementation, and institutionalization or abandonment. How each stage is handled is crucial and can significantly affect the outcomes of both the succeeding stages and the innovation as a whole. The key factors associated with each stage are discussed in turn below.

Initiation

This first stage involves activities leading up to and including the decision to proceed with an implementation (Fullan, 1991: 50). Among the factors that significantly affect its outcome and the reform effort as a whole are what and how innovations are brought to or adopted by a school, why the innovation process is being initiated, and who participates in the decision to adopt. In the first regard, innovations may take as many different paths to the schoolhouse door as their sources of origin. Thus, innovations may result from imported technology and values; perceived discrepancies between educational values and outcomes affecting those in whom one is interested (Levin, 1976); the presence of good ideas; local needs (Berman and McLaughlin, 1976); research; populations shifts; and party politics. Countless and varied, what is obvious is that, as indicated in Chapter 2, there exists a range of forces, people, and parties interested in the schooling process that extend far beyond local schools, who at any time, may seek to "improve" the operation of the system. According to Fullan (1982: 13), a close look at how decisions about change are made and what decisions are made will inspire little confidence that the majority of recommended changes are worthwhile or that the most needed changes are being proposed.

This observation is clearly reflected in one of two local, district-level initiation patterns found by Berman and McLaughlin's Rand study, labeled *opportunism*. Here, usually district-based personnel seek reform primarily as a means to bring much needed funds to their schools or to appear up-to-date and progressive in the eyes of the community.

> Local school officials may view the adoption of a change agent project primarily as an opportunity to garner extra, short-term resources. In this instance the availability of federal funds rather than the possibility of change in educational practices motivated project adoption. Or, school managers may see change agent projects as a "low cost" way to cope with bureaucratic or political pressure. Innovation qua innovation often serves the purely bureaucratic objective of making the district appear up-to-date and progressive in the eyes of the community. Or a change agent project may function to mollify political pressures from groups in the

community to "do something" about their school. (Berman and McLaughlin, 1978: 14)

From the above, it should be apparent that the primary sources of change are external to the school system (Huberman and Miles, 1984; Daft and Becker, 1978). Coming as they do not only from the outside, but usually from the top, as well, e.g., in response to constituent-motivated state legislation, they are colloquially termed "top-down" mandates. Conversely, when the initiation source is from the local school, it is termed "bottom-up" reform. Each is discussed below.

Top-down mandates

Reform by fiat or prescription is the essence of top-down mandates, and it is probably the most common means through which change is initiated in the schools. One reason for its popularity is its effectiveness in giving the illusion of responsiveness to calls for systemic change. Thus, state or federal legislators, city chancellors or district superintendents can appear to respond to their constituents' concerns by legislating change and issuing dicta. Tye (2000: 46) calls this the "magic feather phenomenon," i.e., the further a person is from the classroom, the more likely he or she is to act as if a "magic feather" may be waved and change will happen. But as schools are loosely coupled to the system and improvement is a process, not an event, this is no more than symbolic politics. Change will not proceed on autopilot once a policy has been enunciated and passed (Hopkins et al., 1994: 17).

Increasingly knowledgeable of the limitations of top-down mandates, many upper-level administrators and gurus of the major comprehensive reform models now require that the programs be invited into participating schools and that school staffs demonstrate their support through a "buy-in process," i.e., a vote to adopt from no less that 75–80 percent of the school's personnel. While this practice has the potential to unite staff around the change effort, it is no guarantee of true ownership. This strategy, powerful in its intent and its significance as an essential first step toward unifying schools around an innovation, can be misappropriated. For politicians and upper-level administrators can pressure schools to adopt improvement models sometimes by "facilitating" their introduction through the provision of money and other services. Despite the incentives, the mere act of mandating the adoption of a change program negates the goal of the buy-in. While there may be some choice in what model to select, schools, particularly underperforming schools, often cannot choose not to adopt any model. When innovations are forced upon schools in this way, their staff may not only feel little inherent need to change, they may also feel resentful and victimized as a result. Where these feelings persist, they can undermine the change effort, for minimally they can result in inadequate motivation to engage in the difficult process ahead or worse, they can elicit outright resistance to the very types of personal change required. See Box 5.1.

Bottom-up reform efforts

Much more desirable is change that results from a true sense of need on the part of the local school. When innovations are invited into a school by staff as a result of some self-identified problem-solving effort, they have usually committed themselves, in advance, to engage in a collaborative, consensual effort to bring about the problem's resolve. *Problem solving* was the other initiation pattern found at the school/district level by Berman and McLaughlin's Rand study (1977–78).

The inherent strengths of this initiation strategy are several. First, schools begin the change effort with several of the components identified by the effective schools research as requisite components, e.g., a unity of purpose, a strong commitment to address school needs and collaboration among staff. These qualities are particularly difficult if not impossible to mandate from the top down. And second, when combined with funded research, the change effort carries with it resources to address real problems or needs within these schools or districts to which they would not ordinarily have access.

However, even bottom-up initiation has its pitfalls. One clear case is the grant request process can also hinder change efforts. Unfortunately, it is not unusual for RFPs (request for proposals) to reach the local educational communities only weeks before the deadline for the submission of proposals. Schools and districts then must scramble hurriedly to learn the specific foci of the RFP, its submission procedures, and construct their proposals in accordance with the guidelines. In their haste, schools may promise to engage in activities based on an inadequate or superficial understanding of the innovation or may make small technical errors that may

Box 5.1

One suburban school district received a federal grant to conduct a comparison study of change models. Their proposal promised to compare the effects of five different reform models using schools in their district. Each of the elementary schools in the district would be assigned a different reform model, save one, which would serve as a control. As the schools were comparable demographically, it constituted a good research design. However, the schools knew nothing of the grant prior to its award and their involvement. As one of the models slated for comparison was one for which the authors had been identified as the local agents, we were asked to introduce it to personnel at the targeted school and to train its staff in the process. Initially greeted with polite hostility, our early sessions were begrudgingly attended and accompanied by surly and argumentative interactions. At one such session, staff defiantly informed us that not only was their participation worthless, the model's principles were unrealistic, for any decisions they made to change the school would never be honored by the district, offering as evidence, their being forced to adopt the program! We responded by informing both the school and the District's developer that a true buy-in was required by 75–80 percent of the school's staff. We offered to help school personnel make an informed decision by further educating them in the process, however, we insisted that the ultimate decision rested with the staff – even if they voted to reject the model and the District had to return the grant money. To everyone's surprise, District personnel agreed! When the school staff was informed of the decision there was a complete change in their attitudes. The teachers became friendly, interested in participating, willing to listen, and inquisitive about how the model functioned in an actual New York City school. Thus, once truly empowered in ways that they could understand and that were meaningful to them, they were ready to begin the task of school reform.

scuttle an otherwise sound proposal. Local level staff are suscep-
tible to such risks as they are often removed from the university
setting are not likely to come into contact with new scholarship
on education (Fullan, 1991: 53). They may, thus, naïvely promise
to implement initiatives insufficiently informed or unaware of the
underlying assumptions and the requisite work needed to introduce these reforms wisely and to the school's best advantage.

For example, one school with which the authors worked
received a grant to integrate arts into the curriculum employing
Gardner's concept of Multiple Intelligences. The faculty was soon
engaged in their own arts training; arts sessions for their students;
planning workshops with the artists; concerts and recitals. When
informed that the grant promised concrete evidence of progress,
not testimonials, but rather objective findings based on previously
published or school constructed measurement tools, they could
neither find an instrument to meet their needs nor possessed the
in-house expertise, much less the necessary time and energy, to
create one. Ergo, when schools or district personnel lack adequate
time and expertise to research fully the proposed innovation as
well as its implications, the change effort may be doomed by
weaknesses in its initiation.

Three things are important to note with both top-down and
bottom-up reform initiations. First, the initiation of change never
occurs without an advocate – one of the most powerful being
chief district administrators. With their staff and, sometimes, in
combination with school board support or mandates, they can
provide access, internal authority, and resources to facilitate
project implementation. They thus have the potential to be an
important source of district-wide changes that favor groups that
might otherwise be neglected, as well as block changes they do
not like (Fullan, 1991: 54).

Second, top-down mandates, fortunately, can become bottom-
up initiatives as Box 5.1 shows. The intent of top-down innovation is to spur schools very needy of improvement that do not
spontaneously recognize their need or where the recognition
exists but faculty are too splintered and fatalistic in their attitudes
and practices to garner the motivation and unity of purpose
needed to spark the effort. While such transformations are hard,
they can occur, but require work and a sincere effort on the part
of the project's initiators to give true ownership of the project to
the schools.

And, third, bottom-up reform is not without its pitfalls. When schools (and districts) use funded innovation to solve problems identified internally by school staff, inadequate or naïve understanding of the innovation may hinder or thwart its optimal introduction into the schools. The fact that university authorities and "experts" on education develop change models and projects does not mean that they cannot be dead wrong. They can be based on overly abstract theories not related or relatable to practice; come from researchers who have limited or no contact with nor understanding of the school; or come from reformists who are ignorant of the lessons and experiences of earlier reformers. Above all, these change initiators may fail to consider explicitly the relationship between the nature of the proposed innovations and the purposes of schools (Fullan, 1982: 18).

It is impossible to determine the proportion of bureaucratic, problem-solving, and opportunistic initiatives, however, research indicates that schools are more likely to implement superficial changes in content, objectives, and structure than second-order change (Fullan, 1991). The three factors that best predict the likelihood of reform adoption provide some clues. They are:

1. Bureaucratic safety, as when innovation adds resources without requiring behavioral change.
2. Response to external pressure (in which "adoption" may ease the pressure).
3. Approval of peer elites (in the absence of clearly defined output criteria, whatever is popular among leading professional peers is sometimes the determining criterion).

This list suggests that external change agents are prone to advocate for and have schools adopt complex, vague, inefficient, and costly innovations (especially if someone else is paying), as long as they do not have to implement them. Berman and McLaughlin *et al.* (1979) concluded that quite content with the "illusion of change," opportunistic bureaucrats often ease up on the pressure they exert for change with a school's act of adoption alone. Whatever a reform's initiation sources are, it is a good rule of thumb to determine who benefits from the change, and how sound, feasible and relevant are the ideas and the approach.

Implementation and consolidation

In the second stage of the school improvement process innovations chosen for a local site or school system confront the realities of their institutional settings, and models must be translated into practice (Berman and McLaughlin, 1976). This stage may be unpacked in a number of ways. For this discussion, we characterize it as involving two phases: start-up and consolidation. In the first phase, adopting schools must assemble the physical and human resources necessary to get the project "up and running." In the later consolidation phase, the new procedures are practiced, practiced, practiced to make the program work as it is intended or as best fits the school. To achieve these ends the various pieces must be coalesced into a working interrelated whole.

Start-up: putting the pieces in place

If the goal of implementation is for staff at adopting sites to achieve both a personal mastery of the innovation and a stable use of its practices, in launching any change project, money, time, materials, expertise and effort must all be applied in concert.

Money, time and legitimacy As with most things in this world, money is a necessary evil. It is an essential element in most innovation projects, as it is needed in adequate amounts to purchase participants' time and other requisite resources. When provided in the form of grants, it is, characteristically, earmarked for particular project use, and even for specific purposes within projects, e.g., to purchase equipment, to hire training and support staff, and to pay teachers and parents for their attendance at training workshops and planning sessions.

Time is probably the most valuable commodity in this equation. Whether compensated or not, available time for participants to plan for, to learn, to consolidate, and to refine their use of the innovation is crucial and is usually inadequate (Adelman and Walking-Eagle, 1997). Available time during the school day is rare, particularly if teachers must work together as a group or in collaboration with parents. Additionally, union contracts may prohibit or severely limit the amount of in-school time that faculty can be required to meet. They may also prohibit or constrain meetings before and after school, and on weekends without due compensation. Such limitations can severely hobble time intensive innovation start-ups. SBM/SDMTs, for example, often require extensive outlays of teacher time for initial training, regular meetings, research on school problems, the development of strategies for improved organizational functioning, and contemplative time to reflect on school practices and products. The time for these activities is always in addition to that required of the regular workday. "School based management and shared decision-making, for example, are apparently supposed to happen in the spare time of teachers and without the investment of time either to train them for these new roles or to deliberate over decisions" (Maeroff, 1993: 519).

In-school time may be created at the city and district levels by scheduling "professional" days and half days into their schools' calendar. Students are not in attendance at these times, so teachers are freed from their instructional responsibilities to participate in project training, planning sessions or other developmental activities. Principals may similarly create time by orchestrating mass preparations, small group-specific coverages, or scheduling the topic as agenda items at prescribed staff meetings. However, strategies that require the juggling of students, characteristically, counter-balance their instructional needs with the needs of the innovation project. This is fine, if in the long run the project benefits the students; however, if the innovation is short-lived and opportunistic, or comes after wave upon wave of earlier reform efforts, students may not be served.

Notwithstanding, project facilitation by school administrators sets a tone of regard for the change efforts. It signals administrative legitimatization, indicating to adopting schools and to their teachers a desire for serious endeavor at the site level, as well as a sincere commitment on their and their agencies' parts to project support. Support by school principals can be a psychological boost and was found to be a significant factor contributing to projects faring well (Berman and McLaughlin *et al.*, 1979). Support at the district level was found to be of two major types, i.e., front or back loading. With the former, moderate to high amounts of aid or support "presence" is provided at the onset of the program, but characteristically dwindles thereafter. With back-loaded aid, more moderate levels of support are provided in the beginning, but this aid is usually sustained and may even be increased as the implementation continues. Back loading tends to be superior to front loading and event-linked assistance (e.g., for conferences) and, of course, is vastly superior to low levels of assistance and indifference (Huberman and Miles, 1984).

There is an optimum balance that administrators must find in providing support and encouraging local school personnel room to own and to work through the innovation. Where site personnel feel "strong armed" by the power assertive tactics of administrators rather than helped and assisted, the pressure can backfire and can precipitate school and teacher resistance to program efforts. Conversely, implementation may also be imperiled by administrative assistance that is nonexistent. Where this happens, schools and their staff are essentially left to do the innovation on their own. This is difficult, for even the most zealous staff seldom have the wherewithal and the authority to self-manage the acquisition and distribution of supplies, the scheduling and coordination of meetings, the trouble-shooting capability, or the time and energy for the just plain hand holding that are needed. Huberman and Miles (1984: 183) concluded that for organizational change to work, systemic support is needed from at least two of the three local school levels, i.e., the principal, the district and the central office. Without it, projects of any significant size and complexity seldom go beyond this phase successfully. Moderate, top-down pressure works best, particularly when it comes in the form of advocacy, manifest as systemic assistance.

Technical expertise and its dissemination   In the start-up phase, participants must learn the rules of the game. Technical expertise may come from several sources. Most innovation models, regardless of type, use trainers to instruct school staff in the specifics of program implementation.

Project trainers should not, however, be confused with reform coaches, who have a more extensive function. According to Donahoe (1993), the function of the external coach is to prepare and organize the school for change; to identify the areas in which staff members are weak and to provide the training that they need; to help the principal adapt to a new management style; to assist in the formulation of the vision, mission, goals, objectives, and timetables; to identify impediments that are peculiar to the school and help the staff recognize and overcome them; to keep the focus of activity on improved student achievement; to recognize when schools are attempting too little or too much and then to help them establish the right pace of change; to enable schools to circumvent district and state bureaucracies and provide them cover against interference from the district; and to create networks within which teachers and principals can interact with their peers from other schools and districts. Coach/facilitators, thus, work directly with teachers, steering committees and SBM teams, as well as school and district-level administrators to help get the project on its feet. In problem solving, coach/facilitators may also need to interface with key program, district or city level personnel as the implementation's advocate (see Box 5.2). In addition, ancillary expertise may also be needed to transmit secondary knowledge, e.g., team building or conducting successful meetings for schools establishing SBMTs.

Traditionally, training workshops have been the method of choice for disseminating project knowledge. In sessions lasting a few hours or held over the course of several days, trainers dispense project information; participants are asked to engage in several illustrative activities; and in the end, all are encouraged to transfer or apply the behaviors and attitudes discussed in these sessions to their school or classroom activities. Whether held on- or off-site, prior to or during implementation, this "spray and pray" method, as it has derisively been dubbed, has increasingly come to be regarded as inadequate. Summarizing the reasons for the failure of in-service education Fullan (1991: 316) states that:

- People other than those for whom the in-service is provided frequently select topics.
- Follow-up support for ideas and practices introduced during in-service programs occurs in only a very small minority of cases.
- Follow-up evaluation occurs infrequently.
- In-service programs rarely address the individual needs and concerns of participants.
- The majority of programs involve teachers from many different schools and/or school districts, but there is no recognition of the differential impact of positive and negative factors within the system to which they must return.
- There is a profound lack of any conceptual basis in the planning and implementation of in-service programs that would ensure their effectiveness.

The negative impacts on the innovation of these shortcomings are several. Most immediately, workshop recipients typically leave these sessions with a faulty and fractured understanding of the innovation, making clarity (about goals and means) a perennial problem in the change process (Berman and McLaughlin, 1978: 27; Fullan, 1982: 66). This may be manifest in a sense of false clarity, characterized by oversimplified versions of complex concepts and project requirements (Fullan, 1991: 70).

Box 5.2

Internal versus External Coaches

Programs and gurus differ as to whether coach/facilitators should be internal or external school personnel. Some projects recommend the use of on-site personnel as a means to "build capacity" in the school, i.e., to create an ever expanding cadre of school staff who can carry on the project once initial funding has been withdrawn. Showers (1985) agrees, adding that the three fundamental purposes of coaching are to build communities of teachers engaged in the ongoing study of teaching, to facilitate the collegial study of new knowledge and skills through the development of a shared language of common understandings, and to provide a support structure with which teachers can develop new teaching skills and strategies. To increase the chances that teachers will transfer the new knowledge he supports the use of in-house coaches. Others, however, believe that coaches should initially be external, e.g., local university personnel, as a means to bring greater objectivity and authority to the implementation and decision-making processes. According to Donahoe (1993: 300), schools need an external agent to help them through the traumas of change; and like a "rebar in concrete, keeps the process from cracking and crumbling." As dynamic organizations, when disputes arise among teachers and staff concerning the implementation, "someone is needed who stands outside and looks at the school's culture and effectiveness with a cold eye and a warm heart, who would not be tempted to let difficult circumstances limit what the school believes it can achieve and cannot be co-opted by either the district or the school" (ibid.: 303). Moreover, when appeals need to be made to the principal or to district personnel, outside personnel may carry more weight and receive greater consideration than teachers.

Further complicating this issue is the question of allegiances and credibility. Is the coach user-centered or innovation-centered? The answer can heavily affect the coach's influence to perform one, extremely significant, set of functions: that of cheer leader, hand holder and general morale booster to often overwhelmed school personnel. Few things function smoothly in the schools, and innovation is characteristically fraught with worry, concern, setbacks, frustrations, and moments when all want to abandon the effort. It is at these points that the coach must be able to encourage the faculty and staff to continue with the project with the hope that things will get better.

What do you think and why?

As a consequence, their skill-specific training may have only a transient effect because the use of new materials and methods is often mechanical without an in-depth understanding of the underlying ideas (McLaughlin and Marsh, 1978: 76, 78; Adelman and Walking-Eagle, 1997: 95). Teachers may, thus, change "on the surface" by endorsing certain goals, using specific materials, and even imitating the behavior without any real sense of the principles and rationale underlying the change. They may even be able to value and articulate the goals and beliefs of a change without understanding their implications for practice (Fullan, 1991: 40). Such an understanding truly cannot be achieved overnight, for it requires resocialization – learning by doing. It is achieved gradually from using the innovation and making sense of what happens as a result, what Fullan (1982: 67) terms "coming to see the meaning of change." Unfortunately, most in-service training is not designed to provide this kind of ongoing, interactive, cumulative learning necessary to develop new conceptions, skills and behavior.

Materials   The presence of materials and equipment may be a given, but when they are not there on time, and of adequate quality or quantity, implementation may suffer gravely. When staff have been trained and are ready to put the innovation into use, all necessary materials, e.g., texts, tests, guide books and supplementary materials, must be on hand to ensure that the project's launch goes off as smoothly as possible. So materials-centered are some programs, particularly packaged instructional models, that their success becomes heavily dependent on their quality and availability. Rushed and hasty start-ups in which materials are not on hand, are not well designed, or cannot be used as expected may doom such projects to failure. According to Huberman and Miles (1984), a lack of technical readiness seemed to hurt project innovations in their study more than the presence of attitudinal or cognitive readiness helped, at least in the initial phase.

Energy, effort and resistance   No less critical in implementation start-up is the amount of energy and effort project adopters apply to the effort. Suffice it to say that some critical mass is necessary, both in terms of person power and in their willingness to participate. It is rare to get 100 percent agreement on and active participation in most naturally occurring work environments, and school reform projects are no exception. Even when participation is mandated, behind closed doors teachers may resist or merely go through the motions. Thus, willingness is an important factory. Does the faculty perceive a need for the reform? Do they have the knowledge and skills to implement the change once provided with the training? And do they have the time and the inclination to devote to the effort? Without a critical mass of ready personnel, which will vary from situation to situation, model to model, and from school to school, school implementations will be neither valid nor reliable tests of any innovation adequate to draw conclusions about its true usefulness or worth.

Teachers may manifest their willingness to participate in many forms, which in part have been found to be related to their life stages. In one classification system, Elmore (1966) describes the formation of cliques and factions organized into those who oppose change (often older, veteran teachers who believe they have mastered the system) versus change advocates (usually younger teachers just out of teacher preparation schools, with more up-to-date strategies and theories of instruction). Another way of viewing them is provided by Hampel (1995), who divides them into the leaders, or "vanguard"; the "yes, but" people, the "sleepy" people; and the "cynics." Hampel found that the *leaders* were never more than 25 percent of the faculty, usually in their mid-30s to mid-40s, largely female, and were the idealists and activists of the school. Many regarded the innovation as a midcareer opportunity, a jolt of energy, spurring them to put in long hours organizing meetings, chairing committees, writing newsletters, and exploring ideas. The *"yes, but"* group was the largest. These teachers were cautiously supportive of reform but wanted hard evidence that the ideas would work. They wanted to travel to other sites to be reassured that it would work. *Sleepy people* were mostly male, often close to retirement. They avoided extra work whenever possible, said nothing at faculty meetings, but would reveal their distaste for the new ideas by body language and lunchroom complaints. Frequently they disparaged students as undisciplined and unmotivated, blaming everything on a sad decline in conditions from the time when they started teaching. The *cynics* were the outspoken opponents, raising uncomfortable questions at faculty meetings about the equity and effectiveness of the proposed changes. They deeply resented what they considered preferential treatment of the "vanguard." The vanguard and the cynics had much in common. They often shared an abundance of energy and intelligence. Cynics, Hampel found, had often been members of the vanguard 10 or 20 years earlier. Where these latter groups are present to some significant extent, failure to address their concerns may seriously retard the reform process.

Ironically, too enthusiastic an outpouring of personnel and energy at this phase can also be counter-productive. Elaborate needs assessment, endless committee and task force debates and the like, often consume large amounts of energy and time, and ironically can create confusion and alienation in the absence of any action. Extensive pre-action discussions can actually exhaust the energy needed for implementation, so that by the time the innovation reaches the next stage, people are "burnt out" (Fullan, 1991: 62; Huberman and Miles, 1984). According to Fullan (1991: 63), as innovation is a very long process, early participation might best be viewed as something that begins during initiation, and grows and grows.

Consolidation: achieving good fit and usage

Simultaneous with program onset, the consolidation phase often begins. There is rarely a stark demarcation line between the two phases, for seldom are reform adopters given adequate and separate lead-in time for training and planning prior to formal program implementation.

With the consolidation phase, start-up elements are coalesced as staff utilize the innovation and attempt to make it work as intended. The key concept during this phase is that of "fit," i.e., the extent to which initiators and implementers are able to make the innovation fit the unique aspects of the school. In this process, participants may shift attention from doing what is required of the project to achieving familiarity, comfort and mastery of the procedures (Berman and McLaughlin, 1976). Staff may also seek to enhance the quality of the implementation. As the tasks consistent with the innovation become easier, go more quickly, produce more predictable results, and work progressively better, teachers may begin to debug, refine, adapt, integrate and to extend core program components as a means to achieve a better "fit" between the change project and the particular characteristics of the school. According to Huberman and Miles (1984) and Fullan (1993), practicing mastery is not an event but an accomplishment, gradually and often painfully achieved. Factors affecting the degree to which school staffs are able to adapt the innovation to their school are several (see Box 5.3).

Project flexibility   Each school has its own "personality," which is shaped by its unique history, the nature of the community it serves, and such internal factors as school climate and the quality of the teacher/administrator relationship. Interfacing these uniquenesses with corresponding model features is essential to changing a school and achieving a good fit between the model and the school. According to Tye (1987), by addressing these uniquenesses, change projects may access the deep structure of the system. Innovations should neither restrict nor overwhelm a school. Each reform element as well as the whole must be tailored to a school's unique characteristics and needs. Simultaneously, it is hoped, the implementation will alter the practices, culture and outcomes of adopting schools in the process. Consolidation is, thus, a phase of mutual adaptation (Berman and McLaughlin, 1976).

Perceptions vary on the degree to which reform programs should be changed and what constitutes a good fit or successful implementation. Huberman and Miles (1984) found that teachers tend to view program flexibility as a crucial factor – the most significant dimensions of which were related to their own needs and demands. Where teachers were able to adjust the innovation to suit their perceived needs, time schedules, and existing knowledge and procedures, they were more likely to regard the innovation as a good fit. Relatively small projects with moderate flexibility were most often "scaled down" to make them more manageable. For example, teachers might simplify or shorten heavily scripted lessons, continue to use familiar materials wherever possible, and adjust the cognitive demands of the content to their perceptions of their pupils' academic ability. In essence, they

---

Box 5.3

Factors Affecting Implementation

A. Characteristics of the change
   1. Need and relevance of the change
   2. Clarity
   3. Complexity
   4. Quality and practicality of program (materials, etc.)

B. Characteristics at the school district level
   1. The history of innovative attempts
   2. The adoption process
   3. Central administrative support and involvement
   4. Staff development (in-service) and participation
   5. Time-line and information system (evaluation)
   6. Board and community characteristics

C. Characteristics at the school level
   1. The principal
   2. Teacher–teacher relations
   3. Teacher characteristics and orientation

D. Characteristics external to the local system
   1. Role of government
   2. External assistance

Source: Fullan (1982)

---

made the new innovations accommodate as much as possible their existing arrangements and routines. Users essentially did as much or as little as they desired, drawing on the discretionary latitude given them by the principal or the central office staff. More ambitious projects, those requiring large-scale user changes with less latitude for discretionary modification, were more likely to leave teachers feeling overloaded and overwhelmed, depleted of energy and unable to keep up. In such instances teachers were more likely to report a poor fit and problems in implementation.

In general, downward adaptations (e.g., reduction or modifications of idealistic project goals, amendments or simplification of treatments, downward revision of ambitious expectations for behavior change in the staff or overly optimistic effects of the projects on students) tended more often to be associated with an increase in the likelihood of changes in teacher and organizational practices. Unfortunately, they also tended to compromise the full achievement of the project's goals (Berman and McLaughlin, 1976: 353; Huberman and Miles, 1984: 88). The risk in adjusting a model by simplifying the complexity and lowering the demands on teachers and students as a means to achieve greater participation and usage is that the innovations may be watered down and trivialized (Miller, 1996). In tailoring them to interface better with an adopting school's uniqueness, they may be altered to the point of compromise and allow staff to continue with their pre-existing routines with only minor modifications. Thus, "goodness of fit" is an important factor, Huberman and Miles (1984: 182) suggest that staff perceptions cannot, nor should be taken as a "strong predictor of eventual organizational change."

Insufficient adaptation of the model on the part of site personnel presents another problem. Here projects meet with indifference and resistance from the host sites, resulting in a general unwillingness to change participants' existing practices, or implementers fail to adjust or to tailor the model to the school. Berman and McLaughlin termed this "cooptation of the project by the host" (1976: 352), producing an implementation that is hollow or superficial, and where key players often report that they are merely "going through the motions." A possible reason for failing to adjust innovations may be a rigid belief that the initiators of reform efforts know best. Both situations constitute instances of non- or invalid implementations, and Berman and McLaughlin found them most often to be the consequence of opportunistic initiations and top-down mandates. In either case, the innovation is also likely to fail.

Teacher change In teachers' efforts just to get through the daily or weekly segments of prescribed activities and attain practice mastery, hopefully, they themselves are transformed in the process. As adaptation and mastery are never complete with users tending to go on to more ambitious tasks related to an innovation, Hall *et al.* (1975) have constructed a taxonomy describing the sequential progression of innovation implementation and teachers' shifting concerns related to the process. They identify five levels:

1. Mechanical use, where practice activities are difficult and disjointed.
2. Routine use, where program execution is stabilized, with few, if any changes made or envisaged.
3. Refinement, in which users vary parts of the innovation in order to heighten its impact.
4. Integration, where users combine their own efforts with those of others in extending or refining the new practice.
5. Renewal, where users seek or make more modifications in the practice.

In their movement through these levels, Hall *et al.* assert teachers shift from self-centered concerns, i.e., worry related to their personal or professional capacity to carry out the project, to greater concern with the task, i.e., concerns about efficient management; concerns about student impact or consequences; concerns about collaboration with others; and concerns about refocusing, replacement and alteration. While our own work supports a general shift from personal to more other-oriented concerns, we agree with Huberman and Miles (1984) that several of Hall *et al.*'s levels of innovation and teacher concerns were not always sequential. Multiple levels of implementation as well as different types of concerns were found to go on side by side and regression was common. These stages probably are also influenced by teachers' lifecycle stages, as well as their general sense of efficacy (Fullan, 1991). Consistent with McLaughlin (1987), we found in our own work with schools, shifts in individual interest, motivation, and involvement based on the multiple and simultaneous goals that influence individual choices and actions.

Consolidation is, thus, not a linear process, but rather is fraught with setbacks, plateaus, reversions to prior practices, or periods of "freezing" while staff gather energy and regroup. As a result of such fluctuations, there can be considerable variation among adopting sites in the extent and nature of the adaptations made to the model as well as in staff and in individual schools, depending on how each site tailors a project and themselves adapt to meet the task at hand. With increasing time, the greater are the mutual adaptations and refinements (Berman and McLaughlin, 1976: 349).

Time for consolidation Beyond the need to hone, refine and adjust new practices to a school's students and culture, time is also needed to assess both formatively and summatively the results. How much time ought to be allotted depends on one's perspective. Even when there is a critical mass of faculty who implement an innovation, time must be provided to assess and adjust to changing conditions and circumstances to avoid back-sliding (Adelman and Walking-Eagle, 1997: 104), as well as to explore and understand the outcome data. Systemic change may be undermined at the state and local levels by attempts to reduce conceptual and practical complexities in the interest of a fast-paced implementation (Little, 1993: 149).

Characteristically, the time perspectives of decision-makers and initiators of change, particularly when they are external or removed from the implementation site, conflict with that of project implementers. The former tend to have much shorter time frames than do the latter, more often motivated by political exigencies, societal pressure, or opportunism. Politically moti-vated change requires noticeable and certifiable outcome data in time for the next election campaign, contract negotiation, or closure within the public's attention span. For political opportun-ists, the three to five years typically required by most innovations or comprehensive models to evidence solid and reliable results are prohibitive. Pushed to produce timely results for top-down mandates, school administrators may put undue pressure on a school to speed up the implementation process.

> [I]mpatience arising from the desire to bring about much-needed reform results in hasty decisions, unrealistic time-lines, and inadequate logistical support during implementation because due dates arrive more quickly than problems can be resolved. (Fullan, 1982: 69)

When schools are not given adequate time to refine, adjust and integrate innovations into the workings of their schools, prema-ture summative evaluations will likely project an inadequate or even erroneous picture of an innovation's true or possible ability to effect desired change in the school setting.

When public interest and administrative support wane or shift to newer, more trendy educational panaceas, compromising the legitimacy of a project, their disaffection has been found to lead to the further disillusionment, burn-out, cynicism and apathy on the part of those at the local sites that are asked to respond to every change that comes along.

In summary, the mere implementation of an innovation cannot be assumed to provide an accurate forecast of its actual use. One must look closely at the extent and at the nature of the mutual accommodations made. Administrators can get away with mandating an innovation and still achieve high usage, but only if reasonable attention is paid to the development of staff commitment and skill (Huberman and Miles, 1984: 206). Innovation adjustment and fit are a delicate balance arrived at through reasonable and conscientious give and take on both sides. Projects must be flexible enough to address the uniquenesses of the school, and schools must be willing to hold in abeyance, if not relinquish traditional ways of doing things to allow the innovation to work as it is intended.

Institutionalization or abandonment

In this last stage of the change process, schools either take true ownership of the innovation or it is abandoned. With the former, the procedures and supports for the innovation are "built into" the school or the district. This is more than a mere continuation of the project, and constitutes, for all intents and purposes, another adoption decision (Fullan, 1991). For example, by incorporating an innovation's costs into the school's own budget and weaving its habitual ways of doing things into the fabric of the school, the organization signals its ownership. This requires a conscious decision, for often other budget items must be compromised – particularly in poorly funded schools. Where projects are not so embraced, isolated individuals may continue with their use as long as is possible, but by and large, institutional support is withdrawn.

There are a number of factors that dispose an innovation toward one outcome or the other. Huberman and Miles (1984) list these variables in three categories (see Box 5.4): supporting conditions, passage completion, and cyclic survival. Supporting conditions include those factors that would testify to a project's worth and proven ability to achieve positive results, e.g., benefit to users, support from staff and others, and the project's satisfactory operation on a daily basis. The degree to which the innovation

Box 5.4

Factors Affecting Institutionalization

Supporting conditions:
  There is a core (versus) peripheral application
  Operating on a regular, daily basis
  Provides benefits, payoffs to users
  Competing practices eliminated
  Receives support from administrators, staff, clients, other
    external sources, e.g., dollars

Passage completion:
  Goes from soft to hard money
  Job description becomes standard
  Skills required are included in formal training program
  Organizational status is established part of regulations
  Routines established for supply and maintenance

Cyclic survival:
  Survives annual budget cycles
  Survives departure or introduction of new personnel
  Skills are taught in successive cycles
  Achieves widespread use throughout organization
  Survives equipment turnover or loss (includes materials)

Source: Huberman and Miles (1984)

has been incorporated into the organizational and economic fabric of the school is reflected in Huberman and Miles' last two categories. The second category, passage completion, reflects the literal transfer of ownership from external sponsorship to the aegis of the local site, e.g., the shift in funding from grant monies to the school's own budget. The last category, cyclic survival, is an indicator of the degree to which the innovation can weather cyclic systemic occurrences that traditionally signal the end of less hearty programs, e.g., budget cycles, the loss of key administrators or staff who are the program advocates, and whether its use is disseminated to other schools or parts of the system.

These groupings are interesting, in themselves, for what they imply. Noteworthy is that the benefits to students and teachers are only one factor, and depending on the researcher, perhaps not the most important factor. For example, Berman and McLaughlin (1978) found that only a minority of innovations that were well implemented were continued beyond the period of federal funding! While differences exist among schools and districts as to what combination of factors are associated with successful institutionalization, Huberman and Miles (1984) place greater weight on the predictive ability of the last two categories, i.e., passage completion and cyclic survival. These categories privilege the financial and organizational self-sufficiency of the innovation – rather than its payoff to teachers and students.

Our own work, as well as that of Huberman and Miles (1984) and Berman and McLaughlin (1977) supports the significance of organizational survival. Crucial in this regard is the toll taken by continued change in staff and administrative turnover. According to Fullan (1982: 77):

> Since effective change depends on interaction among users, removal of key users weakens the conditions that would incorporate or help new members. While this is obvious, very few new programs plan for the orientation of members who arrive after the program gets started. And arrive they do, chipping away, however, unintentionally at what is already a fragile process.

Perhaps equally as important is economics. Economics plays a significant role throughout the innovation process, but may be even more crucial in the final phase. As Huberman and Miles' taxonomy implies, a school and district's ability to assume financial responsibility for "special projects" once external funding is withdrawn is paramount. Regardless of how successful the program is in terms of results or how favorably disposed staff and students are toward its continuation, if necessary funds are not forthcoming to sustain it, the program will largely cease to continue. Staff turnover further complicates the picture, as the ability of the school and the district to fund continuing staff development for new teachers will affect the ongoing viability of the program. These factors alone further disadvantage schools and districts in their ability to improve. Wealthy districts are far more likely to have the wherewithal to institutionalize new and needed programs than are poorly financed inner-city schools, which are traditionally severely handicapped in their ability to absorb the costs of materials, ongoing training, and personnel into their regular budgets (Yin *et al.*, 1977: 16). In doing so, they often must concomitantly remove or downsize other programs, presenting obstacles to institutionalization that innovations in wealthier districts may not face. In addition, the greater need for programs and resources in poorer districts increases the likelihood for opportunistically initiated innovations and their subsequent abandonment based on their inability to sustain them. Tye (2000) queries what would happen if poorly funded districts stopped playing this game, i.e., began refusing to accept soft money and short-term external grants in the absence of long-term commitments to successful programs.

Finally, to survive the financial crunches and personnel changes that characterize public schooling, projects often must have assistance in the form of a critical mass of strategically located administrators who are committed to the change. Change efforts can seldom overcome situations where administrators show by their behavior that they are essentially indifferent to the fate of an innovation, i.e., doing little either to assist the users to develop mastery and commitment or to stabilize use. Similarly, the departure of district-level advocates renders institutionalization unlikely.

Organizational support for institutionalization should start at the site level with clear evidence of the innovation's incorporation into the fabric of the school. By demonstrating "skill-committed use," i.e., user mastery and project stability, the local site signals to upper level administrators their commitment to continuation (Huberman and Miles, 1984). In combination with evidence of student impact, it can boost the likelihood of subsequent institutionalization, but it is no guarantee.

Administrative advocacy may be more critical at the district or central levels, for although local schools are increasingly being given greater control over their budgets, decisions and support at the district level still carry a great deal of weight. Particularly if the innovation is initiated opportunistically or via uncommitted top-down mandates, district-level advocacy may be necessary to counter possible resentment and resistance on the part of school administrators and staff. This is most likely when directives are followed by substantial assistance. However, when administrative support accompanies innovations into schools where there is little serious resistance and a reasonable degree of teacher-administrator harmony, there can be major benefits. According to Fullan (1993: 38):

> Put differently, the central and local units need each other. What is required is a different two-way relationship of pressure, support and continuous negotiation. It amounts to simultaneous top-down bottom-up influence. Individuals and groups who cannot manage this paradox become shipsawed by the cross-cutting focus of change.

Again, pressure should not be taken to mean administrator tyranny over project operations but rather firmly supported and pursued objectives in the context of personnel stability on the part of both users and administrators (Miles *et al.*, 1978: 40).

Institutionalization is not an end in itself (Fullan, 1991: 90). The improvement of practice must be a continuous process of renewal, and singular innovations are just a means toward this end. Similarly, schools that engage in major restructuring efforts should have as their ultimate goal expanding their schools' long-term capacity for continuous improvement.

New Conceptions in School Innovation

New conceptions of organizations have led to new ideas and thinking about the change process. Consistent with views of the schools as more open, irrational and complex institutions, linear, "lock-step" thinking about the implementation process has been challenged by more fluid and spontaneous approaches. While not altering the broad stages outlined above, most of the current thinking in the field asserts that the path of change cannot be mapped or planned in advance (as with the transformation analysis). Both these perspectives on the change process are currently being advocated, or offered for adoption by schools. Those that still conceptualize the change process as moving in a linear, lock-step sequence, present change agents with a planned series of strategic activities (e.g., visioning, conducting a needs assessment) in which schools are to engage in the process of transformation. The School Development Project of James Comer and the Accelerated Schools Program of Henry Levin are popular and well regarded examples of this thinking.

Conversely, those who conceptualize organizational change as a non-linear, unpredictable, and chaotic process, assert that there can be no road maps, no planned series of steps. For advocates of this school of thought, change is uncontrollably complex, and in many instances "unknowable" (Stacey, 1992). A frequent illustrative exercise asks those contemplating innovation to list all the forces and stakeholders that could figure into the solution of a problem, those that could complicate the situation, or those that would need to be influenced to make for productive change. Then realize that every predicted variable, as well as a plethora of unanticipated variables can have myriad and unknowable ramifications (Fullan, 1993: 19). This dynamic complexity, they assert, is the real territory of change, i.e., where "cause and effect" are not close in time and space, and obvious interventions do not produce expected outcomes because other unplanned factors dynamically interfere (Senge, 1990: 365, quoted in Fullan, 1993: 20). Complexity and unpredictability are not merely things that get in the way. They are normal to the schools in their day-to-day operation.

Instead of road maps and linear step-wise progressions of activities, they posit guiding principles, or lessons, that change agents should use in the innovation process. Fullan (1993, 1999), a prominent advocate of this view, asserts that rationally constructed reform strategies can never work in the face of rapidly changing postmodern environments. Quoting Stacey (1996), he asserts:

> Most textbooks focus heavily on techniques and procedures for long-term planning, on the need for visions and missions, on the importance and the means of securing strongly shared cultures, on the equation of success with consensus, consistency, uniformity and order. [However, in complex environments] the real management task is that of coping with and even using unpredictability, clashing counter-culture, dissensus, contention, conflict, and inconsistency. In short, the task that justifies the existence of all managers has to do with instability, irregularity, difference and disorder. (pp. xix–xx)

In essence, he believes that what is at the heart of successful organizations is "in-house" knowledge, i.e., skills and beliefs which are below the level of awareness and in the heads and experiences of employees. It is this expertise and wisdom that must be converted into explicit knowledge on an ongoing basis.

This is the substance of true collaboration and why formal planning fails.

For Fullan, the creative process required to recreate a comparable essence is inevitably messy, involving differences, conflict, fantasy, and emotion. It stirs up anger, envy, depression, and many other feelings. To remove the mess in the name of some common vision or shared culture is to remove the raw material of the creative activity. Creative abrasion, in fact, is sought in the form of collaborative diversity. Change agents are urged to "live on the edge of chaos," amid anarchy and an open-endedness in structure. Rather than use lots of rules, rigid structures and formal channels of communication, a system of people-based learning, framed by a few key priorities and structures should be set up. Toward these ends, Fullan offers two sets of lessons for change in complex environments (the first is shown in Box 5.5).

We believe that, finally, that there is no one panacean innovation model, policy, or practice, nor does there exist a change process that can be copied step by step for all schools. According to Fullan (1999), there never will be a definitive theory of change. It is theoretically and empirically impossible to generate a theory that applies to all situations. Definitive theories of change are unknowable because they do not and cannot exist. Theories of change can guide thinking and action, but the reality of complexity tells us that each situation will have degrees of uniqueness in its history and make-up, which will cause unpredictable differences to emerge. In each setting the innovation is transformed and adapted to the conditions of the implementing unit. Some models will have greater effects on some schools than on others. "Muddling through," then, can be seen not only as an adaptive response to demands for change but also as the more beneficial response in the long run. The history of school innovation leads researchers to believe that incremental, creeping, locally defined change is often the best. Taken together, these lessons describe a model of implementation that moves from early notions of implementation as transmission or as a problem of incentives or authority to conceptions of implementation as bargaining and transformation (Ingram, 1977; Majone and Wildavsky, 1977; McLaughlin, 1987).

Box 5.5

Fullan's Eight Basic Lessons for a New Paradigm of Change

Lesson 1: You can't mandate what matters: The more complex the change the less you can force it.

Lesson 2: Change is a journey not a blueprint: Change is non-linear, loaded with uncertainty and excitement and sometimes perverse. Under conditions of uncertainty, learning, anxiety, difficulties and fear of the unknown are intrinsic to all change processes, especially in the early stages.

Lesson 3: Problems are our friends: Problems are inevitable and you can't learn without them. Only by tracking problems can we understand what has to be done next in order to get what we want. Problems need to be taken seriously, not attributed to resistance, ignorance or wrong-headedness.

Lesson 4: Vision and strategic planning come later: Premature vision and planning are blind. A good deal of reflective experience is needed before one can form a plausible vision. Vision emerges from, more than it precedes, action.

Lesson 5: Individualism and collectivism must have equal power: There are no one-sided solutions to isolation and groupthink. Collectivism pushed to extremes becomes groupthink. Under conditions of dynamic complexity different points of view often anticipate new problems earlier than do like-minded close-knit groups.

Lesson 6: Neither centralization nor decentralization works: Both top-down and bottom-up strategies are necessary. Decentralized groups get preoccupied with governance and frequently flounder when left on their own. Mandates can put needed

---

pressure on local reform and can provide opportunities for legitimizing the efforts of local agents.

Lesson 7: Connection with the wider environment is critical
for success: The best organizations learn externally as well as internally. Individual moral purpose must be linked to a larger social good.
Teachers must look for opportunities to join
forces with others, and must realize that they are
a part of a larger movement to develop a learning
society through their work with students.

Lesson 8: Every person is a change agent: Change is too
important to leave to the experts, personal mind
set and mastery are the ultimate protection.

Source: Fullan (1999).

References

Adelman, N. E. and Walking-Eagle, K. P. (1997) Teachers, time and
school reform. In A. Hargreaves (ed.) *Rethinking Educational Change
with Heart and Mind*. Alexandria, VA: ASCD, pp. 93–110.

Berman, P. and McLaughlin, M. W. (1976) *Federal Programs Supporting
Educational Change*. Santa Monica, CA: The Rand Corporation.

Berman, P. and McLaughlin, M. W. (1977) *Federal Programs Supporting
Educational Change. Vol. VII: Factors Affecting Implementation and
Continuation*. Santa Monica, CA: The Rand Corporation.

Berman, P. and McLaughlin, M. W. (1978) *Federal Programs Supporting
Educational Change. Vol. VIII: Implementing and Sustaining Innovation*. Santa Monica, CA: The Rand Corporation.

Berman, P. and McLaughlin, M. W. with Pincus, J., Weiler, D. and
Williams, R. (1979) *An Exploratory Study of School District Adaptation*. Santa Monica, CA: The Rand Corporation.

Daft, R. and Becker, S. (1978) *The Innovative Organization: Innovation
Adoption in School Organizations*. New York: Elsevier North Holland.

Donahoe, T. (1993) Finding the way: structure, time and culture in
school improvement. *Phi Delta Kappan*, vol. 75, December,
pp. 298–305.

Elmore, R. (1996) Getting to scale with good educational practice.
Harvard Educational Review, vol. 66, no. 1, pp. 1–26.

Fullan, M. (1982) *The Meaning of Educational Change*. New York: Teachers College Press.

Fullan, M. (1985) Change process and strategies at the local level. *The Elementary School Journal*, vol. 84, no. 3, pp. 391–420.

Fullan, M. with Stiegelbauer, S. (1991) *The New Meaning of Educational Change*. 2nd edn. New York: Teachers College Press, Columbia University.

Fullan, M. (1993) *Change Forces: Probing the Depth of Educational Reform*. London: Falmer Press.

Fullan, M. (1999) *Change Forces: The Sequel*. London: Falmer Press.

Fullan, M. and Miles, M. (1992) Getting reform right: what works and what doesn't. *Phi Delta Kappan*, vol. 73, no. 10, pp. 744–752.

Hall, G., Loucks, S.F., Rutherford, W. and Newlove, B. (1975) Levels of use of the innovation: a frame for analyzing innovation adoption. *Journal of Teacher Education*, vol. 26, no. 1, pp. 52–56.

Hampel, R. (1995) The micropolitics of RE: learning. *Journal of School Leadership*, vol. 5, no. 6, pp. 597–616.

Heifetz, R. (1994) *Leadership Without Easy Answers*. Cambridge, MA: Hansard University Press.

Hopkins, D., Ainscow, M. and West, M. (1994) *School Improvement in an Era of Change*. London: Cassell.

Huberman, A. M. and Miles, N. B. (1984) *Innovation up Close*. New York: Plenum Press.

Ingram, H. (1977) Policy implementation through bargaining: the case of federal grants-in-aid. *Public Policy*, Fall, vol. 25, no. 4, pp. 499–526.

Levin, H. (1976) Educational reform: its meaning. In M. Carnoy and H. Levin (eds) *The Limits of Educational Reform*. New York: McKay.

Little, J. W. (1993) Teacher development in a climate of educational reform. *Educational Evaluation and Policy Analysis*, vol. 15, no. 2, pp. 129–151.

Majone, G. and Wildavsky, A. (1977) Implementation as evolution. *Policy Studies Review Annual*, vol. 2, pp. 103–117.

McLaughlin, M. W. (1987) Learning from experience: lessons from policy implementation. *Educational Evaluation and Policy Analysis*, Summer, vol. 9, no. 2, pp. 171–178.

McLaughlin, M. W. and Marsh, D. (1978) Staff development and school change. *Teachers College Record*, vol. 80, no. 1, pp. 69–94.

Maeroff, G. I. (1993) Building teams to rebuild schools. *Phi Delta Kappan*, vol. 74, no. 7, pp. 512–519.

Miles, M., Fullan, M. and Taylor, G. (1978) *Organizational Development in Schools: The State of the Art. Vol. III, OD Consultants/OD Programs in School Districts*. New York: Center for Policy Research.

Miller, E. (1996) Idealists and cynics: the micropolitics of systemic school reform. *Harvard Educational Letter*, vol. XII, no. 4, pp. 1–3.

Senge, P. (1990) *The Fifth Discipline*. New York: Doubleday.

Stacey, R. (1992) *Managing the Unknowable: Strategic Boundaries between Order and Chaos in Organizations.* San Francisco: Jossey-Bass.

Stacey, R. (1996) *Complexity and Creativity in Organizations.* San Francisco: Berret-Koehler.

Tye, B. B. (1987) The deep structure of schooling. *Phi Delta Kappan,* December, pp. 281–284.

Tye, B. B. (2000) *Hard Truths: Uncovering the Deep Structure of Schooling.* New York: Teachers College Press, Columbia University.

Yin, R., Herald, K. and Vogel, M. (1977) *Tinkering with the System,* Lexington, MA: D. C. Heath.

Part III

Case Study

Reforming our nation's public schools is no simple process. Any effort to improve or change the schools is rendered infinitely more complicated by those very aspects of school culture that the current wave seeks to alter, e.g., teacher isolationism; low expectations for a significant part of the student population; the plethora of often contradictory proposals currently afloat; as well as politicians' and reformists' lack of understanding of the pace of the school change process. Further complicating this process is that schools are learning institutions; and have acquired the ability to perpetuate the status quo in the midst of these efforts. The nation's history of near omnipresent change forces has created many robust and effective defense mechanisms that enable them to continue to fulfill their basic functions despite the clamor. The very robustness of these safeguards attests to their effectiveness.

Understanding the operation of these safeguards in context is the focus of Part III. In the next three chapters, institutional obstacles common to the school improvement process are explored. Specifically, we address the mechanisms, practices, contractual regulations and attitudinal sets, which facilitate the school's continuation in the midst of change, and which also pose obstacles to any school improvement or change effort. Moreover, rather than provide a dry list of variables and abstract descriptions, in this section, we seek to give the reader a sense of their dynamic functioning in the context of an actual three-year improvement effort at one urban middle school.

This Part intentionally focuses on some of the major obstacles and common problems faced by many under-performing schools in their efforts to implement several of the changes recommended in the current second wave of reforms. The reform effort described is a failed effort. We use it for what it can reveal about the power of schools to maintain the status quo. Rarely do articles expound upon the lessons learned from what didn't work, what programs failed, and what students or teachers were not successful. We believe that these typically unpublished accounts may be far more telling and valuable, for it is through our failures sometimes more than our successes that we can best understand and analyze the challenges faced.

This Part and the case study are divided into three chapters, corresponding to the traditional phases of the innovation process, i.e., initiation, implementation, and consolidation/abandonment. Each chapter is divided into two sections. In the first section, we describe the events which occurred in that phase of the school's improvement efforts, revealed through monthly field notes. In the second part of the chapter, we discuss common obstacles encountered during that phase. While many of these obstacles are well illustrated by the case study, a few are not, but still may be discussed relative to the common position of occurrence. This also well illustrates that while many problems are common to many implementations, few schools or implementations evidence all problems. And there are lessons that can be drawn from even our failures.

6

Innovation Start-up:
Early Problems and Pitfalls

For three years (from 1994 to 1997) the first author worked intimately with the faculty and administration of Professions Institute, a middle school serving grades seven and eight, in the capacity of external school reform coach. (The names of the school and all participants have been changed to protect the identity and reputation of many well intentioned individuals, who were very concerned about the achievement of their school, and most of the time, had the interests of the students at heart.) Located in the East Harlem section of New York City, the school serves a community that is overwhelmingly Latino- and African American, poor and lower working class. The Director of the school is an African-American female. During the coach's first year, the school had 15 teachers, only one of which, i.e., the special education teacher, was an African American. All the remaining teachers were of European-American descent. Many were seasoned veterans with over 15 years of experience at the school and they ranged in age from their late thirties to their mid-fifties.

Professions is one of the early "schools of choice" created in the District along with Central Park East in the 1970s. The school's original unifying theme was "professions," but by this time, students received neither special instruction nor exposure consistent with this concept. Despite this fact, staff at the school maintained some small discretionary power on student admissions. At the time the comprehensive school improvement coach was "invited" into Professions, the New York State Department of Education had recently categorized it as a School Under Registration and Review (SURR), a title given to schools where the academic scores of its students on standardized tests had been in decline for at least three years. The "invitation" was the result of a top-down mandate from the State Department of Education, which "urged" all SURR schools to select improvement models to assist them with their improvement efforts. To facilitate the selection process, New York State held a large fair where selected staff from various SURR schools heard presentations given by representatives from a wide range of improvements programs describing their models. Based on this information, and whatever additional research schools chose to conduct, schools were to select an improvement model or models. New York State also provided additional funds for the first three years to support start-up and early implementation costs. The Director of Professions and a senior faculty member selected the comprehensive model for which the first author would be their coach. Their choice was approved, via an informal consensus, by the staff of Professions Institute, but as will be seen, this in no way indicated the staff's whole-hearted embrasure of the reform model or its process. Before beginning this case study, please consider the following questions:

1. From the description above, in advance, what factors do you think make this school a positive innovation site? What factors do you think would hinder the process?
2. What type of school culture do you anticipate encountering at Professions and why?
3. If you were a new external coach embarking on just such a process, what would be your first step and why?

September 1994

My personal orientation to Professions Institute came in May through a phone conversation with Jeanna, the Language Arts teacher who along with the Director had initially selected Model X as the school's "model of excellence." She informed me that, as she perceived it, the atmosphere or school climate was problematic. Everyone existed in their own world and seldom spoke to each other or came together to do any joint problem solving or planning. There were factions among the teachers that were largely ideological in nature, and everyone seemed to have trouble communicating with the Director.

Soon thereafter, I was informed by one of the District administrators that the intelligence and veteran nature of the faculty would make this a challenging experience. In early June, just prior to my training as a coach for Model X, I visited Professions to acquaint myself with the school's personnel and its issues. This visit rapidly informed me of the truth of this warning. The Director was young, both in (relative) age and experience as an administrator – this being only her second year as the school's Director. When I queried the assembled teachers and later the Director about the school and how they accounted for it being on the SURR list, I witnessed a classic case of "blaming." The teachers blamed the students, who they said "were not the best," while the Director blamed the teachers, whom she felt had low expectations for the students.

My first impression of the school was that it had the potential to be a great school. The teachers were extremely knowledgeable and challenging. Many had seen a number of school reforms come and go, and they doubted that this reform could or would make any difference. The Director was sincere and truly believed in the potential of the students. And the student body, as a group, was energetic, good-natured children, and as yet, had not bought into the negative psychology of caste-like minorities (Ogbu, 1992). There was potential all around.

My first month with Professions Institute was like a roller coaster. Things got off to a great start, but went rapidly downhill shortly thereafter. Apparently, bad feelings between the teachers and the administrator, only thinly masked, found an escape valve through me.

On September 9th, I conducted an all-day training on Model X. There were approximately 20–25 individuals present, including the Director, Professions' teachers and para-professionals. In the afternoon several "guests" arrived, including the building Principal; the school's monitor from the State Education Department (SED); a District coordinator; and Mae Gamble. The morning and afternoon sessions were long and covered a lot of work. After the first afternoon session, there was not much time left for a presentation of the instructional component. When the teachers informed me that their dismissal time was 2:30, and not 3:00 p. m. as I assumed, I gave an abbreviated version. After the session, the SED rep commented that she was pleasantly surprised at how well things went, for these teachers were "a tough bunch," who had very definite ideas about the schooling process.

On September 14th, I met with the school's Director and seven teachers to briefly discuss follow-up and the agenda for my next meeting with the general faculty. They felt that to formally "launch" Model X at Professions Institute I should talk about scheduling the school-wide assessment process in which the whole school community studies their school to determine its present condition and challenge areas. The general faculty meeting on September 16th went well. Teachers raised questions about the scheduling of the launching, indicating that if it was held after school it would be difficult for teachers with other commitments to attend. I reminded them that unless parents and other members of the school community were present, it could not be considered a real launching. The teachers left saying that they would think about it further.

On Friday, September 22nd, I got a telephone call from Jeanna, who informed me that a dispute had arisen between the teachers and the Director over money. She asked me to come to the school to help resolve the matter. I replied that if it was all right with the school Director, I would certainly be willing to mediate. Shortly thereafter the Director called, quite upset. She stated that Jeanna had no right to call me; this act overstepped her role as a head teacher and no one other than she could invite me to the school! Over the weekend, I got several calls from Jeanna, who stated that the teachers were very angry at the Director's response. They were threatening not to continue with the launching and to discontinue use of Model X at the school. I called Mae, who urged me to have the Director meet with the teachers to discuss their concerns. She and I would function as arbitrators and meeting facilitators. Although I was not entirely comfortable with this idea, I agreed. Mae said it was wise to air these negative emotions to prevent them from hindering the school reform process. The meeting was scheduled for 2:30 on September 27th. As I had first to attend a meeting at the college, I asked Mae to begin the session; I would get there as soon as possible.

When I arrived at Professions at approximately 3:15, Mae had already begun the session. In addition to the Director and Mae, six teachers were in attendance. It became readily apparent that the teachers were using this session as an opportunity to voice long-held complaints against the Director, who sat quietly and made no attempt to reply. When Mae asked her to respond, she, making an obvious effort to control her anger, stated that she had a different perspective and didn't feel that the teachers' views were accurate. The session lasted until about 4:30, when Mae stated that dialogue was now open and would continue. I did not participate in this session, as I felt uncomfortable with both the format and the content of this interaction.

I called the Director the next night. She was very icy toward me. When I got her to talk, she stated that she had to administrate over these individuals and it was not permissible for them to talk to her in such a fashion. She felt demeaned and belittled by the experience and would never allow such a débâcle to occur again. She finally asked how I could have allowed such a thing to happen to her? I reminded her that I had not participated in the session, and said that I, too, was quite distressed with the turn of events. Referring to the faculty meeting scheduled for the next day, the Director said she would not go or would attend but would not speak, and if the teachers started accusing her of things again, that she would walk out. I promised that I would conduct the meeting and would not allow a recurrence of the previous events.

On Thursday, September 29th a general faculty-wide meeting was held. Almost all of the school's teachers attended. Apparently, teachers who had not attended the earlier meeting had learned of it and had come, eager to continue along the lines set at that meeting. Mae, I, and the SED rep had conferred prior to this session and agreed that I, as the chair of the meeting, would neither encourage nor support the teachers' "venting" at the Director. We all agreed that the reform process, i.e., structured inquiry and problem solving would address these issues in time. As the meeting began, the teachers started by enumerating their problems with the Director. To refocus their attention, I stated that based on the previous meeting, there appeared to be misconceptions concerning roles and responsibilities within the school system. I suggested that we make a list of significant school-related topics, e.g., curriculum, discipline, budgetary and discretionary spending, and indicate who had responsibility for or ownership of each. From their list it was clear that they were very much in error on many items. They had little understanding of the budget process and believed, incorrectly, that the Director had money to use at her discretion. I asked Jeanna to copy the lists and concluded the meeting by suggesting that the SED rep and I would research each activity to determine who actually held responsibility.

October 1994

October was a month spent almost exclusively addressing issues related to communication between the Director and the faculty.

The month's first general faculty meeting was held on October 6th. The Director did not attend. Mae and I met just before the meeting to discuss strategy. We decided to start, initially, with the issue of organizational responsibility but to move quickly to a discussion of the model as a means to address teachers' areas of concern. I conducted the meeting and went through the planned sequence of topics. As the teachers were still somewhat disgruntled, toward the close of the meeting, Mae encouraged them to voice their feelings. The teachers reiterated several areas of contention and cited examples of poor communication with the Director. We assured the teachers that we would do what we could. After the meeting, Mae, the SED rep, and I met to discuss the situation. We decided that the rep and I would meet with the Director to discuss communication.

On October 7th, I went to Professions to introduce Model X to the students in a student assembly. Prior to the assembly, I invited the Director to meet with Anna (the SED rep) and me. She very tentatively agreed. The assembly went very well; the Director had a very definite rapport with the children in her school. Later that evening, Jeanna called me to say that she had met briefly with some other teachers after the assembly, following a problematic interaction between the Director and a faculty member. I reassured Jeanna that I had a meeting scheduled with the Director, at which I would discuss the quality of communication between her and the faculty.

On October 12th, I attended a Parents Association meeting to introduce them to the improvement model. Prior to the meeting, I spoke with the Director and asked if the teachers had met, as scheduled, to plan the school assessment and the launching. She said they had and asked if I would meet with them to provide them with more specific information on the assessment process. The session with the parents went well. There was a very good turnout; and the parents asked a lot of good questions and made interesting comments.

Early on the morning of October 13th, Mae and I met with the head of Alternative Schools/ Special Program for the District to discuss events at Professions. He was very understanding, stating there was the potential for anarchy at the school. He correctly assessed that the Director truly wanted to do what was right but did not always know how – based primarily on her "newness" and inexperience.

Immediately after this meeting I went to Professions as requested by the teachers. This meeting went pretty well. We talked about the launching and what was involved. We set and reset dates. We tentatively scheduled the launching on the same day as parent-teacher conferences. One teacher raised a pet peeve of several teachers, i.e., money and spending. Again, the teachers felt the Director had a hidden cache of money and that mismanagement of some specific monies had previously taken place. I responded that the issue would be addressed soon.

After the faculty meeting, the Director, Jeanna, and I met to discuss some general concerns, and Jeanna said that she thought things were moving. We all felt that it was time to finally resolve the issue of money and budgetary spending. We agreed that both these issues could be readily laid to rest by having the building Principal attend the next general faculty meeting to clarify the operation of the school's budget. It also was felt that it was time to turn to issues of the curriculum and the instructional component, if possible. We briefly discussed the Language Arts curriculum, and they invited me to come in to review the various texts that were under consideration.

On October 18th the SED rep and I met with the Director at a local diner to discuss communication within the school. Initially, conversation proceeded slowly. Anna and I were careful not to offend the Director, who was still "raw" from the previous month's events when the teachers, as a group, had so severely and publicly criticized her. We talked about trust or rather the lack of it among the school's participants. By the end of the meeting, the Director acknowledged that more "professional" communication was necessary on both sides. I think we made some progress!

On October 21st, the topic for the general faculty meeting was the instructional component, and I chose to reintroduce it by showing the video, "Good Morning, Ms. Toliver," (a video of an excellent mathematics teacher who uses real-life experiences to make mathematics come alive). After the viewing, several teachers commented that Ms. Toliver really wasn't doing anything very different from several teachers at Professions. Moreover, they continued, the children in the video were gifted, and that students at Professions were not of that caliber. I responded that Ms. Toliver was a mathematics teacher at a public J. H. S. just a few blocks away. The two schools had exactly the same populations, demographically. The teachers replied that yes, the school was in the neighborhood, but they were sure a class of "gifted" students had been used for the filming. I didn't argue, and instead gave them a handout on the instructional component and asked that they consider the questions for our next meeting.

November 1994

In November the school made progress in problem solving and planning. The month began with the school-wide assessment scheduled for the late afternoon of November 2nd, at which parents, students and teachers were to attend. There was a good turn out of parents and students (almost 40), but not of faculty. Although several teachers stayed long enough to put up decorations, only two attended the actual event. Nonetheless, it went well and the parents were very enthusiastic about the nature of their involvement that evening. They asked to have the results typed up and mailed to them.

Due to the poor teacher turnout, I planned for them to do their own taking stock at our regularly scheduled weekly meeting (on November 4th). Seven (approximately half) of the faculty attended this session. They indicated, however, that they were very busy trying to complete report cards and requested that I postpone this activity until November 8th, when all the school's faculty and staff would be present for the faculty In-Service Day. I agreed.

November 8th was a full day for staff development. Much of the morning was filled with the teachers' identifying areas of concern in the school and beginning to identify what they needed to know to understand better these problem areas. I also conducted a workshop on questionnaire writing in preparation for the next phase in which teachers would develop surveys to assess the conditions in the school. In the afternoon, a guest speaker came to give a session on conducting productive meetings. I was not able to remain for all of this session (having to return to the college). Once I left, things deteriorated. I was informed later that teachers, disgruntled over long-standing issues, took the opportunity to complain, stating, for example, that they felt like they were being punished for being a SURR school by having to donate their time to implement Model X. The Reading Specialist stated that rather than do the work involved she would prefer to see the school close down. She stated, union rules obligated the system to find them other placements. This truly distressed other teachers who were interested in moving the process forward.

As a result of this open dissent, Mae, the school Director, and I met on November 9th with the building Principal, the SED rep, and the District Office's Director of Funding. At the start of the meeting, the teacher representative, Jeanna, spoke briefly, stating that she felt things really *were* getting better – despite the negative comments at the last meeting. She said, "At least people are talking about real things and don't seem so hopeless." By the close of the meeting, we decided on two things: (1) to have district personnel and the Principal meet with the faculty to answer their questions about funding, bank accounts, and other "bones of contention," and (2) to attempt to address school climate issues by immediately forming a School Climate Committee to begin inquiry on these problems (in advance of the time schedule set by Model X for the formulation of a leadership team and associated subcommittees). To facilitate the first meeting, I gave up my regularly scheduled Friday session with faculty.

On November 14th, the Director, the SED rep, and I met to problem solve further. We decided to expand upon the idea proposed at the November 9th meeting. It was becoming obvious that a committee was needed to function as a transition team relative to the SURR plan, so we decided that I would propose the creation of a temporary School Planning Committee. This committee would have two primary functions: (1) to oversee the implementation of and transition from the SURR plan to Model X; and (2) to serve as the Taking Stock/School Climate committee. I knew we were not strictly following Model X, but some issues had to be resolved immediately, months before the Model scheduled a leadership team to be constituted.

On November 28th, Mae, the Director and I met in my office to discuss how to deal specifically with disgruntled teachers. We decided that we would meet with the District's Head of Special Programs to discuss this matter. We were really stumped by this problem. We knew it was having a negative effect on the school but could not figure out how to get it resolved.

December 1994

In December, the Director, the SED representative, Mae and I, all worked furiously to put together a temporary school planning/ management team to deal with some of the teachers' concerns while, simultaneously, advancing Model X's implementation. The month began with a meeting at the district office where the Director, Mae Gamble, and I discussed the situation at Professions with the Head of Special Programs. He again restated that he was aware of the problems at Professions, and encouraged our continued efforts. He also supported our intention to bring more parents into the school's governance body as a means to introduce another perspective to these discussions.

The first regularly scheduled faculty meeting in December began with my attempting to put past events in perspective with a "Where are we now?" In this context I introduced the temporary Planning Committee, as planned. The committee's creation made absolute sense to the faculty present, as school climate had quickly emerged as a challenge area from the school-wide assessment process. After some discussion, it was decided – contingent upon approval by faculty not in attendance – that the regularly scheduled faculty meetings would serve as the temporary School Planning Committee/Leadership Team. Moreover, four faculty had volunteered and been given released time to facilitate the implementation of Model X; this body should function as a subcommittee, executing the tasks and directives of the larger body.

Later in the day, I participated in a parent workshop at the school entitled "Working Together to Improve School Performance." Parents whose children had previously been identified as having "trouble" were invited. The turnout was small, approximately five parents and their children. I gave a brief presentation on contracting. Despite the size, the parents were talkative and apparently knew a lot about how to help their children, in theory. They particularly liked developing contracts with their children, outlining what each would do to improve their child's performance.

The next regular faculty meeting began with a discussion of the temporary School Planning Committee/Leadership Team. Although I had sent the minutes of the previous meeting to the school earlier in the week, they had not been distributed to faculty. With the minutes now in hand, the faculty asked for another week to discuss the proposal with non-attendees. The first draft of questions for the intensive school-wide assessment was distributed. Faculty was asked to read them and to add questions or raise discussion questions for our next meeting. In line with the topic, "Where do we go from here?" I suggested to faculty that, perhaps, some of the school's problems would take care of themselves if we could shift our focus to instruction and curriculum. It was suggested, and I concurred, that we start by my meeting faculty on a subject area basis. I could work on instructional with teachers in the areas of Mathematics and Language Arts at their regularly scheduled subject area meetings.

On December 12th, I spent the day at Professions sitting in on separate meetings with Mathematics and Language Arts faculty. I chose not to impose myself in these meetings, but rather observed the regular content of these sessions. For both subject area meetings, the time was spent talking about upcoming testing sessions.

The last regular faculty meeting for December was on the 16th, at which time the plan for the temporary School Planning Committee was ratified. Based on my previous attendance at subject specific meetings, I proposed to continue attending these meetings for the month of January and to work with this faculty on extending and developing the themes of the instructional component in these curricula.

January 1995

Much of January was spent at Professions attending subject specific meetings with the Mathematics and Language Arts departments and working with District personnel in planning a conference. The conference was originally planned for district faculty of the four SURR schools utilizing Model X, but subsequently was changed to include faculty from all alternative schools in the District.

From my subject specific meetings, held on January 4th, 11th, and 18th, two concerns and possible solutions emerged: (1) Faculty were concerned that students often forgot the content of their classes upon walking out the door of each class session. In response, they proposed an in-service day where each subject area could present one or two key concepts that other subject area faculty would support, as appropriate, in their courses. The proposed in-service session would conclude with interdepartmental workshops on how topics in one department could logically and non-intrusively be supported in another department's classes. (2) Mathematics faculty were interested in using manipulatives but felt that they were too time-consuming and potentially disruptive for the short 45 min. periods. They requested help in their effective use within this time frame.

At the last regular faculty meeting to be held in January the functions of the two-tier, temporary School Planning Committee/Leadership Team were delineated; events related to my subject specific meetings were reported; and the proposals for the January In-Service day were presented to the larger body for approval. I was asked to query the District as to the use of the January grading day (afternoon) for this purpose.

These issues worked out as follows: (a) In-Service Day: After several planning sessions, the District informed me that the half day that the teachers wanted to use for in-service had to be used for grading papers. We could use it for training of some faculty, provided the tests still got marked. After talking with the Principal and faculty, it was decided that the two could not be done simultaneously. The idea was shelved for the time being. I like it very much and will try and revive it at the first opportunity. (b) Math Manipulatives: Bill M., the District's current Deputy Superintendent (a mathematics educator) will be brought in to work with the Mathematics faculty. He will plan a series of meetings with them to facilitate their use of manipulatives. (His techniques and the use of manipulatives are very consistent with the concepts contained in Model X's instructional component. I hope to use this as a springboard to extend the methodology of the instructional component to other subject areas.)

Several things trouble me. One is that Professions is not strictly following the process as road mapped by Model X. They are extremely reluctant to conduct the initial school-wide inquiry needed to identify and explore where problems exist. The staff seem, however, to need results sooner rather than later. They are rather doubtful and cynical, having seen a number of innovations come and go. They must begin to see progress soon or I fear they will return to their former negative mode – they are not too far from it now. They must begin to trust each other and me. Two, there are still some individuals who do not attend the Friday sessions. The Reading Specialist is one, although the Language

Arts meetings are held in her room. The male Special Education teacher is another. For work on Model X, I only see them on mandated Professional Development days. At these sessions, they are cynical and reluctant to participate. When they do, they merely go through the motions. And three, teacher reluctance to address instructional issues is disconcerting. It seems, however, that working on the curriculum in this isolated fashion might be a start in this regard and begin to win over their trust as well.

February 1995

February involved a series of well-intentioned efforts that were, at times, thwarted by cancellations and the winter break for the public schools.

The month started well at Professions. On February 1st, Bill M., from the District Office, came for his first meeting with the Mathematics faculty. At that session, issues of concern were laid out and a tentative calendar of future sessions was constructed. Included was one session to introduce him and to observe a school faculty member teach the class that Bill will use for his demonstration lesson, another session to assess the manipulatives available in the school's mathematics lab, a pre-planning session to discuss the topic he would teach, the actual demonstration lesson, and several follow-up discussions.

On February 3rd, the first regular faculty meeting of the month was held. The building Principal attended and presented the results of the Board of Education's SURR team review of the mini-schools in the building. Jeanna, who now was the head of the subcommittee of four, gave a progress report on the implementation of the school's SURR plan and how Model X had helped in their meeting several of the plan's goals. I asked one of the Mathematics faculty to report on their meetings with Bill. Following this report, I suggested the creation of a Curriculum and Instruction Committee. Committee members would sit in on meetings with Bill M. and the Mathematics faculty, so as to support and extend this work with faculty in the other subject areas. To my disappointment, one of the two key faculty members that I wanted on the committee indicated that she could not participate, due to the illness of a parent (the other faculty member was not in attendance). (I'm going to sit on this suggestion for a moment and revive it later – after I do more department-specific work.) We then turned to the issue of developing school surveys from the taking stock questions. No one had seriously reviewed the questions and, therefore, all were unprepared. I then asked the subcommittee of four to assume the task of drafting these surveys. The head of that committee agreed. The session concluded with my offering them the opportunity to have a retreat where they can focus on curriculum and teaching issues away from the school setting. They were enthusiastic about the idea. I asked if they preferred to have it by themselves or with other schools utilizing Model X in the District. They preferred the latter.

Several of the remaining meetings that were scheduled at the school were canceled, due to faculty having to cover the classes of others that were out ill. (When a school is as small as Professions, the absence of one or two people can be very disruptive.) One last regular faculty meeting was held on February 17th. Very few members of the faculty attended, due to coverages, and it was decided to hold off on any business until after the winter break. I spent my time observing in classrooms, meeting with the Director and facilitating the work of the subcommittee that was creating surveys.

March 1995

In March, District personnel, Mae, I, and the other coaches worked together to plan a retreat for District schools utilizing Model X. These schools also had a visit from the Director of Training for Model X's National Office. In addition, several District schools have decided to submit a proposal for a federally funded grant for the public schools, i.e., Goals 2000.

Model X's Director of Training, Madelia, was in New York from February 27th through March 3rd. On February 28th, all the coaches and directors of schools in that district that were implementing Model X met with Madelia to inform her of the status of the Harlem implementation. Afterward, Mae and I accompanied her on a tour of Professions Institute. On Friday, March 3rd, Madelia attended a faculty meeting at Professions, which I chaired. A representative from the District Office and five teachers were in attendance; Mae joined us later. After the meeting, the Professions Director, Jeanna, Mae and I met to hear the Training Director's reactions. Madelia voiced some displeasure with the meeting, stating that the faculty was not involved enough. She said it felt like I was pulling teeth. (It feels that way to me too, at times!) She wondered aloud if the school really wanted Model X and if it should be continued there next year. This idea greatly distressed the Director and Jeanna, who quickly informed Madelia that the school had greatly changed from the beginning of the year. They added that at least now the faculty was talking to each other about school matters. Madelia still was not happy, but offered that of all Model X schools she had visited in New York City, the environment and the students at Professions were the most upbeat. This was a positive note that pleased the Director.

My work with the school on the Goals 2000 grant proposal took up most of the remainder of the month. This grant offered public schools in New York City immediate funds for school reform efforts and professional development. This would be a valuable asset for the school, as it would provide money for the teachers to meet. It would also provide time for staff to work on identifying and solving school problems. Most schools were advised to seek professional development funds, as the largest single number of grants would be awarded in this category. Schools had very little time to prepare their proposals before the deadline date – we did not find out about the grant until the very end of February and the deadline for submission of proposals was 4:00 p.m., March 23rd.

I informed school staff of the proposal at the March 3rd faculty meeting; they, in turn, indicated that they were interested in applying. I gave copies of the RFP to the faculty and asked them to think about it. Proposal planning began on March 14th and continued on the 15th. These discussions went okay. One teacher volunteered to write a draft of the proposal and bring it to our next meeting. Although, the draft was well intentioned, it was woefully inadequate. I provided feedback to the proposal writing committee on how to improve the draft, which met again on the 17th. Midday Sunday, March 19th, I called Jeanna to determine the status of the proposal and was informed that very little progress had been made from the time of our previous discussion. I then realized that the deadline for the proposal's submission was the upcoming Thursday, and we were very far away from any state of readiness. I also realized that if I didn't write at least a draft, there would be no hope of submitting anything. Around 3 p.m. I began writing the proposal using ideas that had come from the teachers. I worked 12 hours – straight – and completed a working draft by 3 a.m.! I edited this draft on Monday morning and took it to Professions Institute for the committee's review around noon. The committee's comments were incorporated into the draft on Monday evening. Tuesday, I took the proposal in to obtain the necessary signatures. The committee and I reviewed the document again, and I made final edits that evening and the next morning, Wednesday. That afternoon, a Professions faculty member came to the College to get the document from me, obtained the signatures that were still outstanding and took the proposal to the District Office.

At our next general faculty meeting, March 24th, we discussed the upcoming meeting with SED staff and I continued to push work on the school assessment surveys. (Jeanna was making little progress with this.) Faculty voiced, with dismay and powerlessness, a chain of events that might lead to some of them being "bumped" from Professions Institute. A mini school in the building was being closed. Senior faculty from that school, had requested and been granted positions held by faculty at Professions who had less seniority in the building. The Director at Professions had just been informed that the school would be losing approximately one third of their faculty (5–6 teachers), and as yet, no one had been informed as to who would be going. This, of course, was very unsettling – and some of the staff became more agitated.

April 1995

April was a relatively quiet month. The main activity was the retreat for Model X schools in the District, held on the 7th and 8th. On the first day, the coaches were asked to present their schools to the assembly. Each gave a brief summary of where their schools were in the school improvement process. Afterward, I went over to the faculty from Professions, who were seated together as a group. Two teachers quickly commented that I was the only coach who did not say that she "loved" her school/ teachers. They seemed to be a little hurt. In response, I asked if they were pleased at how things were going. Later that evening, I played handball with two teachers.

The next day, there was some time for the coaches to work with their schools. We chose to work out a way to advance the construction of the surveys. Teachers would be asked if they wanted to work on questionnaire development. Those who did not would be asked to take the children on a half-day trip, leaving those who did with an afternoon to do some intensive work. This was a good idea. I think that all in all, the retreat went well. Teachers felt bonded to each other and to the other schools in the District.

After the retreat, I withdrew from active participation with Professions for much of the remainder of the month. I was a little disappointed that I had to do so much of the grant writing by myself, although I later found out that almost all the coaches took major responsibility for writing the grants for their schools. Still, I felt there should have been more input from the teachers and/or that they should have assumed greater responsibility. I began to feel I was doing too much for them. In addition, and contrary to the agreement made at the retreat, one of the teachers said that she didn't remember that we had agreed to organize a half-day to get the surveys written. Jeanna was disgusted and so was I. Jeanna said she would start writing the questionnaire herself, if she could learn more about the format.

I did not visit the school again until the end of the month when I held a general faculty meeting. At that meeting, I informed them that we had been awarded one of the Goals 2000 grants. (My school was the only one of the New York City Model X schools that was awarded a grant!) I gave the teachers copies of the grant and explained to them the funded activities. The teachers liked the idea of the intervisitations. I suggested that they should look to identify master teachers with whom they could visit. We also talked about the school assessment questionnaires.

After the meeting, I worked with Jeanna on the format for the questionnaire. We then brainstormed questions and began putting them into a computer file.

May 1995

This month, work focused on the taking stock questionnaire, implementing the Goals 2000 grant, and the Comprehensive Education Plan.[1]

On May 3rd, I worked with the teachers on the questionnaires. On May 5th, there was a general faculty meeting, at which we talked about getting a half-day to put together the questionnaire. At this point, the half-day for staff development did not appear to be forthcoming from the District. We also spoke about the Goals 2000 grant. I asked the teachers if they had found master teachers to visit; none had even looked, even though the grant would provide a substitute teacher if they chose to visit another school! I told them that I would also work on this. We set some tentative dates for the week of workshops that the grant would fund.

For much of the remainder of the month, I worked with the Director and a group of three teachers on the Comprehensive Education Plan. Typically, I would arrive around 1:30 and remain until 4:00 or 5:00 p.m. We worked primarily on how to provide the requested information and how Model X would fit into the plan.

I also continued to work with Jeanna on the school assessment questionnaires. Periodically, I would look at the questions that she and another teacher had developed, add questions and/or edit the documents. Toward the end of the month I became tired with the slow rate at which this process was moving and decided to complete the questionnaires myself. This decision was driven by the knowledge that if the questionnaires were going to be distributed and tallied by the various school constituencies before the end of the school year, drafts had to be completed and edited by the end of May. At the rate the teachers were moving, the first drafts would not be done in time. Consequently, I spent much of the May 27th weekend constructing the first drafts for each of the three stakeholder groups, i.e., teachers and staff; parents; and students. When the District office finally granted us a half-day for May 30th, I chose to have a large group of faculty review and edit the questionnaires. Teachers seemed content with most of the questions that related to school climate and did some good work on editing the questionnaires. There were some instances where changes were made in items where the implications for teachers might be negative. For example, they changed one question that asked: "Teachers maintain discipline by use of ridicule and repression" to "I feel comfortable with the way teachers discipline the class." From the statement "Conflicts are usually resolved without arguments and violence," the teachers elected to remove the expression "without arguments and violence." I subsequently returned the phrase based on interviews with students who stated that they would answer the question in the affirmative with the statement removed, but in the negative with the phrase added. The teachers also wanted to totally eliminate all questions related to governance on the student questionnaire. They didn't want to "give students any ideas" about their having a right to govern the school. This section was later returned after teachers were made to see that it was important to have this kind of student input. My rationale was that it was needed to parallel the sections in the other two questionnaires.

Simultaneous with this activity, three other teachers and the school Director worked in another room on the Comprehensive Plan with the SED rep. This plan worked well. My group got through with edits on both the parents' and the teachers/staff questionnaires. They promised to meet by themselves on Friday, June 2nd, to complete edits on the students' questionnaire. After the half-day meeting with faculty, I joined the group working on the Comprehensive Plan.

June 1995

In June, efforts were made to wrap things up and put things in place for the start of the next academic year. In the beginning of the month, I worked to get the surveys completed in time to have them distributed to the graduating eighth graders. Their ceremony was on June 13th and they didn't have to return to Professions. I spent much of Tuesday, June 6th, at the school working on the surveys with teachers and students. I edited survey drafts on Wednesday and Thursday, and took them on Thursday late afternoon to the District Office to be run off. The school Director then was to have someone pick them up and distribute them to each of the target populations.

The following week was commencement and I was asked to speak. I agreed. Things went well at the ceremonies and I enjoyed the event.

Later in the week, I called Jeanna to ask about holding a general faculty meeting as a way to prepare for the Goals 2000 workshops to be held at the end of the month. At that time, she told me about new problems between the staff and the Director that seem to have flared up in the last few weeks. She also indicated that only the eighth grade had been given the surveys. Moreover, as the Director kept them locked in her closet and had been out for the last two days, there was no way to get them to give to the seventh graders, parents, teachers and staff. I promised Jeanna that these issues would be addressed at the workshops, probably through the establishment of a cadre on school climate. I gave her some information on a possible intervisitation site and agreed to meet with faculty the following week for a general meeting to discuss everything.

June 21st was my last general faculty meeting. The meeting focused primarily on the upcoming workshops, who could attend, and the stipend rates for attendees. There was a great deal of confusion about both these matters. What is more, before faculty knew that they would be paid, few of the faculty volunteered to attend. Once this information was disseminated, everyone wanted to attend – but there was inadequate money to do this, precipitating calls to the District Office. I promised the staff and faculty that everything would be worked out. In turn, they promised that the surveys would be gotten to the seventh graders and that they would all complete their surveys. Unfortunately, there was no mechanism in place to get surveys to and from the parents in a timely fashion. To my dismay, faculty still had not come up with master teachers for their intervisitations! Although they said they wanted to make the visits, in over a month, none had done the work to identify model teachers to visit. Consequently, I announced that this component of the grant would be dropped.

I spent June 26th and 28th at Professions Institute working with students on tallying respondents' answers to the questionnaires. As the work was boring and tedious, students often procrastinated and many did not return after lunch. In the end, Jeanna and I did the tallying. By the 28th, it was concluded that two faculty who decided late that they wanted to attend the workshops could not. This caused some hurt feelings, as the Director insisted that two new faculty from the soon-to-be-closed mini school who would be joining the staff in the fall must attend.

The Goals 2000 Workshops were held on June 29th and 30th, at Professions Institute and on July 1st and July 3rd at the College. In attendance were ten teachers, three para-professionals, one family assistant, and one parent, in addition to the Director and myself. An outside consultant led the morning sessions on the first two days. He was excellent at team building and helping them to work together. The first afternoon we worked on forging a school vision. Initially the staff were reluctant, stating that only a year or two earlier they had created a mission statement.

Although no one could remember what it stated, they insisted that it was "good enough." After some gentle persuasion, they agreed to draft a new school vision. The product, I think, was underdeveloped. It stated

> At Professions Institute, we aspire to develop the full potential of each child. We will accomplish this through strong academics, small classes, the arts and vocational instruction. The entire school community including students, staff, parents, and others will be involved in our continuing process.

The second afternoon proved problematic. After a successful morning of activities, in the afternoon we tackled a comparison of the vision statement developed the previous day with where we were now. The group was to identify "roadblocks" and devise ways to remove them. This activity, contrary to my intentions, functioned as a disinhibitor, encouraging faculty and staff to vent about the Director. They criticized her for not attending the workshops for the first two days. (This was ironic, as the Director had spent this time at the D. O. trying to ensure that the workshop attendees would be paid in a timely fashion.) This day did not end well.

The final two days were spent working on the surveys. The Director joined us in these activities. Participants were divided into four groups, consistent with the topics covered in the surveys: School Climate, Governance, Curriculum and Teaching, Parents and Community. Each group had to analyze the tallied results related to their topic for each of the target populations. The groups also had to prepare materials and present their findings to the others. Everyone worked diligently for a day and a half analyzing the master tallies and preparing their materials. Presentations were given immediately after lunch on the last day. From these presentations, the participants identified two priority areas for work next year: discipline and communications. I was surprised that the faculty insisted on immediately selecting which of these two subcommittees they would join and briefly meeting to discuss next year's meeting schedule for these groups. Subcommittee membership conformed to existing cliques within the school: the traditionalists, led by Mrs. Di, and those that were more liberal-minded, led by Jeanna. These last two days had involved a lot of intense work. However, by the end of the last session, people began to thank me for the workshops, stating that for the first time they felt a sense of efficacy and that some things might be changing for the better. Hallelujah!

Discussion

The introduction of an innovation to a school is almost always awkward, particularly when an outside coach is involved. A getting acquainted period is necessary. At the same time that the school's stakeholders must become acquainted with the design specifics of the innovation, its work requirements, and progressively commit themselves to its implementation, the coach and the school's staff must also get to know and to trust each other. Gradually, it begins to be revealed to the school what they have gotten themselves into. In many ways, it is a time of laying one's cards on the table – before the game has even begun. This case study begins at a point that is interesting, but not uncommon. Technically, it starts at the implementation stage, for Professions' staff was mandated to and had chosen a reform model to bring to the school. In other ways, however, the school was still at the initiation point, as they had obviously not "bought into" the reform effort.

In what follows, we analyze some of the ramifications of this adoption process as well as some common culturally based features characteristic of many troubled schools. In advance, we state that a comprehensive reform model based on a strategic planning approach was used to structure and guide this reform effort. Our discussion, therefore, focuses to a large degree on the traditional roadmap concept for school change. In drawing heavily upon this troubled implementation, we hope that the reader will see how common systemic procedures; traditional school culture and individual site characteristics can adapt to and effectively repel change forces.

Technical impediments to the initiation of school innovation

Schools have a way of absorbing wave after wave of innovation. As innovation is a virtual constant for most schools and school systems, strategies have been developed that enable schools to adopt innovation after innovation and continue to function. But it is not without its costs. In this subsection we explore the specific ramifications of these mechanisms. Specifically, we explore the effects of top-down mandates, the practice of constantly adding on innovations to extant programs, and the effects of clashing program philosophies.

Top-down mandates

Change in schools or a school system is seldom self-initiated. Top-down mandates are the most common means through which change reaches our public schools. As a strategy, change by legislation or fiat rests on several assumptions that can pose problems for the innovation effort. According to Barth (1990: 38):

- Schools do not have the capacity or the will to improve themselves; improvement must therefore come from sources outside the school.
- Teachers and heads in other schools can be trained to display the desirable traits of their counterparts in high achieving schools. Their pupils then also will excel.
- School improvement, then, is an attempt to identify what school people should know and be able to do and to devise ways to get them to know and do it.

Only thinly veiled, these negative assumptions about poorly performing schools are easily perceived by educators who are the targets of these efforts. Understandably regarded as aspersions on these educators' ability and will to improve their schools, both these assumptions and the resultant mandate put into motion a negative affect that can pose a serious obstacle to the improvement process.

Told, in many cases by non-educators, not only to change what they do, but how to do it, staff at such sites may rile against such mandates. When this occurs, school staff may reject initial ownership of the innovation. Where this happens, the stage is set for a problematic implementation, as it is difficult to teach individuals what they don't want to know, much less to make them perform these tasks with any true commitment.

Such was the case at Professions Institute. "Urged" to adopt a "model of excellence" by the State Education Department, staff at Professions and many of the other SURR schools in the City felt victimized by the strategy. Although given the freedom to select from a range of established models, and facilitated in the initiation phase by the provision of start-up funds, many of the staff at Professions riled against the assumptions upon which the mandate was based. Many felt the school's categorization was unjust, as it was not they nor their teaching that was the problem, but the quality of the students. In turn, they felt no inherent need to change themselves for there was nothing that they could do to alter the school's student achievement patterns. For her own reasons, the Director was cautious in embracing the project, not happy to have a SURR school as her first administrative responsibility. Thus for both the Director and staff, the status now attributed to the school made this a culture of failure.

Change by legislation and fiat feels very much like what it is: an issue of control, which creates a major obstacle to ownership by school staff. It tends to disregard the need for faculty ownership, presupposing that external pressure can provide the motivation for change to occur (Hopkins *et al.*, 1994: 3, 28). The inherent weakness of this approach is that as schools are loosely coupled organizations, there can be no guarantees of compliance. Having a certain amount of autonomy despite being connected and responsive to the larger system, schools and teachers can in their hearts reject the innovation and engage in passive noncompliance. In a reanalysis of the Rand data, McLaughlin (1990: 12) concluded that it is exceedingly difficult to change practice across levels of government. Particularly in regard to the current wave of reform, focused as they are on changing the culture of the school, these changes require internal motivation on the part of teachers and a personal commitment to the change effort, variables that cannot be mandated from above (Fullan, 1992). Therefore, despite having gone through an "urged" buy-in process, the project began with few, if any, faculty assuming ownership. This was very apparent in the actions of the Reading Specialist and the male Special Education teacher, who never attended any of the Friday sessions. In fact, they were only seen at professional development sessions when their attendance was mandated. Behind their closed doors, the project was ignored. They resented the project and its implications, so poignantly expressed by the Reading Specialist at one of these sessions. In the coach's words, the entire first year was spent getting staff to "buy into" the reform project and to assume some ownership of the implementation. This was not achieved to any degree until the Goals 2000 workshops in June.

Add-on, add-on, ad infinitum

A very common consequence of the symbolic politics of school improvement is that schools become inundated by the plethora of mandated innovations. Desperate over the seemingly intractable nature of students' poor performance, some state legislators, chancellors and district superintendents have resorted to a shotgun strategy for reform, i.e., blanketing local sites with an odd assortment of promised "solutions," improvement programs and other initiatives in the hopes that one or some unknown combination will magically result in increased student performance. Schools may, thus, be ordered to respond to some initiatives, and themselves invite in other innovations through grants. Each new program is added to those already existing. Many schools have, therefore, become the site of a bewildering array of programs, materials and personnel. Adopted piecemeal, each effort is often independent from the others, with little if any thought given to their compatibility with each other or their total coherence with the local school. According to Fullan and Miles (1992), schools and districts are overloaded with problems and, ironically with solutions that don't work. The problem is not really lack of innovation, but the enormous overload of fragmented, unco-ordinated, and ephemeral attempts at change.

The increasing sum total of unco-ordinated programmatic demands can overload a school community. As each new program is added, it competes with the school's existing improvement efforts for the available time and personal commitment of administrators, staff, parents and students. Which of the various programs will ultimately be given implementation priority in the minds of local school staff often has less to do with what benefits students than with the program's advocates. In such an atmosphere, teachers can rapidly become "meetinged out," parents feverishly sought to serve on committees or to be served by affiliated social service agencies, and students literally pulled from their classrooms variously to receive an array of unco-ordinated program services. Both these strategies, i.e., add-on, add-on, and "going through the motions," have become common tactics used by public school systems in response to the demands placed on local schools. It creates the illusion of compliance with little of the substance. Unable to adequately focus on and implement any one program well, most, if not all, are given short shrift, increasing the likelihood of their failure.

When a school becomes overwhelmed with the sheer volume of in-house help programs and the complexity of their everyday implementation requirements, schools need to be rescued from their rescuers. Characteristically unable to voice these problems with the bureaucracy that imposes both these demands and consequences for noncompliance, local staff may displace their resentment onto the innovation programs themselves. In adding programs helter skelter, *ad infinitum*, public school systems create the conditions for staff resistance and distracted implementation, laying the foundation for project failure and the welcome return of the status quo.

While poorly performing schools may be needy of not only these but additional services and programs, the unsystematic introduction of programs is a decided liability. Characteristically, it results in wasted resources, the duplication of services, the loss of valuable instructional time, and inadequate time and studied effort devoted to any one of these projects. It also makes it impossible to determine the relative contribution of any one program on student achievement.

Clashing philosophy

Where schools house an array of independent, unco-ordinated innovations it is inevitable that programs will be introduced that clash in their educational philosophies, assumptions, and goals. As programs differ in their underlying assumptions and belief systems, they will also differ in their methodological approaches to instruction and in their conceptions of control and school governance. Juxtaposing them without knowledge or forethought may produce projects that work toward contradictory ends. For example, it is not uncommon to find comprehensive models that seek to extend teachers' use of constructivist models coupled with highly prescriptive, "teacher-proofed" instructional programs that remove all discretion in planning classroom instruction. Similarly, SBMTs and other programs that seek to increase teacher responsibility for school governance coexist with mandates aimed at increasing state and federal control of public schools.

The consequences of this cohabitation are difficult to calculate. As the paradoxes increase and the scale of complexity in post-modern society accelerates, educators are challenged in their ability to synthesize polar opposites and to build upon this framework. Failure to do so risks undermining a school's unity of purpose, where it exists, and may leave teachers confused, frustrated and resentful of the necessity of satisfying seemingly contradictory objectives. According to Hargreaves (1997), the result is an increase in the chaos and complexity of the schools.

Cultural impediments to school reform

In an innovation's first year, mutual adaptation is necessary if it is to succeed. With most comprehensive models, it is anticipated that teachers will adapt model components to the perceived needs and reality constraints of their student and parent populations. Accommodations should be expected to fit the time constraints and workloads of the teachers. However, save for either compressing or extending a model's event timetable, few comprehensive models allow for other aspects of a school's culture that may significantly interfere with or necessitate major modifications to the event roadmap. Always an issue, is how much adaptation is appropriate before a program is compromised and schools, in effect, are doing what they always have done.

Premature visioning and unity of purpose

The first element in the transformational approach to school reform is school-wide development of a mission statement or vision. The aim of this activity is threefold: (1) to develop a goal and set a direction for the school; (2) to establish a basis for comparing where the school is now with where it wants to be in order to identify discrepancies and areas of challenge; and (3) to create a unity of purpose among the school community. This is all very logical and makes absolute sense except where particular school cultures pose obstacles to any productive activity along these lines.

To accomplish this task, there are contextual preconditions, although they are not determinative. Louis and Miles (1990: 220–221) list three: (1) the presence of a principal who is willing to "think vision" and share with others vision development and ownership; (2) a reasonable level of staff cohesiveness; and (3) some school-based control over staffing. This list recalls the characteristics of effective schools and small independent schools during their theme-based establishment. For such schools, visioning at the onset can create the unifying principle(s) that will guide the innovation process.

However, for truly troubled schools where these conditions are not present, these tasks may be counter-indicated at the start-up phase. At Professions Institute none of the conditions were present. The Director may have had a vision, for there were things that she wanted and sought to do that were consistent and constituted some form of whole. But she failed to communicate her vision, in whole or in part, to the staff. Staff also lacked cohesiveness, and had difficulty engaging in this task and other co-operative activities in any meaningful way. And as you will see in the next two chapters, the school's inability to control staff turnover repeatedly undermined morale and maintained the balkanized atmosphere of the school.

An additional factor not mentioned by Louis and Miles, but which we found to be quite influential is staff expectation regarding students' ability to learn. Staff at the school perceived their problems not to lie with the school but with the students, whom they felt did not have the ability to do better. As there was nothing wrong with the school that they could fix, it was perceived as a waste of time for them to set lofty visions for the school and its students. Why set as a mission for oneself or one's organization something that cannot be attained? Their previous mission statement was hollow and lay abandoned. Why attempt to "facilitate" another such effort under the same conditions? When urged to engage in the activity again, in keeping with the model's roadmap, staff rightly asserted that they had a vision statement that was good enough. The fact that no one could restate it, that it did not serve the purpose of unifying the school around a singular set of goals, and that no one was interested in reformulating it should have clearly signaled that a repetition of the exercise could only produce another hollow statement. When forced to "go through the motions," the school's balkanized culture, staff's low expectations for students, and their general lack of enthusiasm for the reform process led to the production of a trite, meaningless statement no better suited to serve as a unifying force or guiding vision than the previous one.

In retrospect, it would have been more worthwhile to position this task where it constituted a logical next step in the gradual development of a truly collaborative school culture. Both visioning and the establishment of a unity of purpose are highly sophisticated, dynamic processes that are neither well understood nor easy to attain or sustain (Fullan, 1991: 31). As such, mapping or grafting them onto school cultures unready to embrace these tasks productively can only produce the formulation of hollow trite visions, that are posted only to be forgotten and ignored, and contrived collegial settings where true consensus and the spirit of collaboration are typically absent.

Start-up time and problem solving

A school's vision is a long-term goal and must be distinguished from its short-term goals. These are incremental, measurable improvements that can be achieved relatively quickly, and are the basic products of a school's problem-solving mechanism. Despite research which indicates that teams working toward the achievement of clear, inviting and doable short-term goals can drive and promote effective teamwork (Bullard and Taylor, 1993: 123), several of the major comprehensive models delay faculties' engagement in short-term goal setting and problem solving only after a long series of preliminary start-up activities. These activities, which, characteristically, include the constitution of the SBMT, its various subcommittees, and training in action research, or the inquiry process, can easily encompass the entire first year of the innovation process. Although valuable activities, we have found that where the school culture clearly signals that staff cohesiveness and a willingness to co-operate may be difficult to sustain, lengthy start-ups may be counter-productive and quickly exhaust any fragile momentum that may have been aroused.

At Professions Institute, the school's high degree of balkanization suggested the staff's need to engage in some meaningful activity that if successful might rally their spirits and bring them together as a group. Although there was little trust and morale was low, faculty were upset enough over particular issues that they might be enlisted to resolve them. In fact, the teachers literally held the change process hostage, threatening not to go forward with the effort until their concerns were addressed. Wanting to adhere to the model's roadmap, the coach found herself literally having to suppress faculty eagerness to address these problems, asking them to wait until the appropriate subcommittees were formed. Faculty was neither appeased nor pleased. Sensing the potential of further alienating faculty from the process and their need for an early "win" to unify and inspire them, the coach deviated from the prescribed roadmap by supporting the creation of a school climate subcommittee to address their concerns in this area. This strategy led initially to staff's early co-operation with the effort, but ultimately became derailed by the faculty's inability to clearly identify a single school climate problem upon which to focus. However, had they been denied the opportunity to engage in this exercise, the credibility of the innovation effort may have suffered – precluding further willingness to participate on their part.

While schools do need to take stock of where they are, we again agree with Fullan (1991: 62) that faculty may expend excessive amounts of time and energy conducting elaborate needs assessments and engaging in endless committee and task force debates which can create confusion and alienation in the absence of any action. Lengthy start-ups may also exhaust crucial momentum needed for implementation, so that by the time people reach the action stage they are "burnt out." Schmoker (1996: 59) states that palpable gains are the key to leveraging change in systems undergoing change because they can unravel the "tangle of debilitating patterns that are reinforced by formal and informal institutional mechanisms." It can mean the difference between a rapid sequence of successes that sustain momentum and a mere plodding along with no palpable excitement. Schmoker believes that it is crucial for institutions carefully to establish concrete and achievable short-term subgoals. "Otherwise people are unrealistically expected to maintain a high affect as they slog toward goals they can only attain months or even years later." Similarly, Louis and Miles (1990) found that an *evolutionary approach* to planning, with plenty of early action (small-scale wins) to create energy and support learning "works best."

Addressing negative affect

Once teachers have mastered their school culture, i.e., adapting to and internalizing traditional ways of being, feeling and handling the environment, change to that culture is not an easy task; and conflict, anxiety and hostility are very natural and very human by-products. All change processes, especially at the early stages, are periods of general uncertainty, in which anxiety, difficulties, and fear of the unknown may be common responses to transition (Fullan, 1993). When rules, meanings, and standards for action are altered, individuals are often thrown off balance, no longer understanding and frequently becoming unsure of what is going on. In such situations, individuals can lose their framework of reality, their confidence in their ability to know what to do. As it is a human quality to seek stability, consistency and meaning, resistance to change is a ubiquitous phenomenon, particularly when individuals are unsure of, take issue with or feel victimized by the goals and reasons for the upheaval.

One very human response to such situations is to defend both oneself and one's culture from the onslaught and to seek the return of the status quo. For reform participants, innovation may signal not a time of opportunity, but rather one of upheaval, disorientation, anxiety and work. Particularly when imposed from the outside, as is common for school reform, change efforts are likely to engender feelings of confusion, dismay, hostility and resistance in school staff. So much so in fact, that affective problems during school improvement efforts tend to be pervasive, multiple and often nearly intractable (Louis and Miles, 1990: 295).

Despite the understandable and often inevitable negative affect that school reform frequently engenders, these aspects of the school change process have frequently been neglected and ignored by repeated waves of change agent. Most improvement models focus, instead, on the cognitive aspects of improvement (Noddings, 1992), i.e., the knowledge, skills, decision-making aspects of educational change that are rational, calculative, masculine and managerial in nature (Hargreaves, 1995). When affect is discussed, the emphasis has typically been on the positive and facilitative aspects, e.g., trust, collaboration, communication, and risk taking, all the while scrupulously eschewing the negative and emotionally volatile aspects of the change process.

An unintended by-product of this crucial (lie of) omission is that change agents may not be prepared for the negative affect that often accompanies school reform efforts – as was the case at Professions Institute. Although the coach both received training from and gave instruction in the basic principles of two of the major comprehensive models, she was nonetheless totally unprepared for the intensity of negative emotions encountered at Professions. Forthrightly informed by the faculty that the project could not go forward unless animosities between the faculty and the Director were addressed, she, literally, was on uncharted ground. When on the advice of the second author she attempted to address some of their concerns, she unleashed even more intense emotions among participants. Fearing an irretrievable deterioration of the situation, the coach retreated from the chaos that appeared to be descending upon the project. In attempting to resolve these issues, she appealed to the process: the road map, team-building workshops, and group priority setting, as "safe" vehicles for the resolution of these conflicts. As future chapters in the case study reveal, these processes were inadequate to resolve these conflicts and resentments. The coach quickly learned that:

> If educational reformers and change agents ignore the emotional dimensions of educational change, emotions and feelings will only re-enter the change process by the back door. Festering resentment will undermine and over-turn rationally-made decisions; committee work will be poisoned by members with unresolved grudges and griev-ances; passive-aggressive leadership that masquerades as rationality and reasonableness, will engender frustration among followers who are exposed to it; and pedagogical changes will fail because they have not engaged with the passions of the classroom.

As this first year of reform efforts at Professions Institute revealed, obstacles to school improvement may come from myriad sources. This effort was initially disadvantaged by the nature of its intro-duction, resulting as it did from "top-down" urging by the State Department of Education. Despite SED's facilitation, in the form of funding and the provision of a monitor who periodically visited the school and worked in collaboration with the reform coach and the Director to problem-solve, the initiative was not embraced by the majority of the faculty until late June. Owner-ship was a main issue. Faculty was reluctant not only to embrace a time-consuming effort that they perceived as a punishment for events that were beyond their control, they assumed neither ownership nor contribution for the students' poor performance. So adamant was this belief, that many were hostile to discussions of ways in which their instruction might be changed to improve student performance. The school's balkanization also seriously interfered with the model's implementation, indicting that faculty or a school culture may need to evidence a level of readiness before implementation efforts can begin in earnest. While not ready for some activities, they desperately needed others. For example, they wanted to try small collaborative problem-solving efforts, which may have rallied them, but were delayed by the coach's attempt to adhere to the Model's road map. As a result, much of this year was spent merely going through the motions.

Study Questions

1. What are some of the positive qualities of Professions Institute that could be used to work in its favor? How might these factors be used to help the course of school improvement?
2. The school culture at Professions has been described as balkanized. Explain why.
3. From the limited descriptions of faculty provided, can you identify the faculty types described in Chapters 3 and 5? Which faculty members would be placed in the various categories?
4. How would you, thus far, describe the leadership style exhibited by Profession's Director? What leadership type do you think would optimally advance the implementation process here?
5. What reasons does faculty at Professions Institute give for initially rejecting empowerment and the school improvement project? How would you address these problems?
6. Why is Professions steering committee a SDMT and not a SBM/SDMT?
7. Describe the order in which Profession's SDMT addresses issues. Explain how it is or is not in line with the research.
8. Why do you think there is so much dissension between the faculty and the Director? What do you think the Director can and should do to establish a better working relationship with her faculty?
9. List the major obstacles at Professions Institute that must be overcome for reform to succeed.
10. What would you do in that situation to help facilitate better communication among the stakeholders here?

Note

1. The Comprehensive Education Plan is a SED-mandated school activities plan that all SURR schools must complete on a yearly basis. These plans outline what activities the SURR school will conduct to improve the academic performance of its students, including staff development and curriculum.

References

Barth, R. (1990) *Improving School from Within*. San Francisco: Jossey-Bass.

Bullard, P. and Tayler, B. O. (1993) *Making School Reform Happen*. New York: Allyn and Bacon.

Fullan, M. (1992) *Successful School Improvement*. Buckingham: Open University Press.

Fullan, M. with Stiegelbauer, S. (1991) *The New Meaning of Educational Change*. 2nd edn. New York: Teachers College Press, Columbia University.

Fullan, M. (1993) *Change Forces: Probing the Depth of Educational Reform*. London: Falmer Press.

Fullan, M. and Miles, M. (1992) Getting reform right: what works and what doesn't. *Phi Delta Kappan*, vol. 73, no. 10, pp. 745–752.

Hargreaves, A. (1995) Renewal in the age of paradose. *Educational Leadership*, vol. 52, no. 7, pp. 14–19.

Hargreaves, A. (1997) Rethinking educational change: going deeper and wider in the quest for success. In A. Hargreaves (ed.) *Rethinking Educational Change with Heart and Mind*. 1997 Yearbook of the Association for Supervision and Curriculum Development, Alexandria, VA: ASCD.

Hopkins, D., Ainscow, M. and West, M. (1994) *School Improvement in an Era of Change*. London: Cassell.

Louis, K. S. and Miles, M. B. (1990) *Improving the Urban High School: What Works and Why*. New York: Teachers College Press.

McLaughlin, M.W. (1990) The RAND change agent study revisited: macro perspectives and micro realities. *Educational Researcher*, vol. 19, no. 9, pp. 11–16.

Noddings, N. (1992) *The Challenge to "Care" in Schools: An Alternate Approach to Education*. New York: Teachers College Press.

Ogbu, J. (1992) Understanding cultural diversity and learning. *Educational Researcher*, vol. 21, no. 8, pp. 5–14.

Schmoker, M. (1996) *Results: The Key to Continuous Improvement*. Alexandria, VA: ASCD.

7

Development

The second implementation year, ideally, is a year for consolidation. Faculty practice and use the structures, the processes, and the skills acquired during the start-up phase, both to tailor the innovation to the school and, in turn, hopefully to have it changed by the model's functioning. At Professions, a number of detours had been taken from the road map the previous year, and as a consequence, some of the components were not in place. Most notably absent was the instructional component; as last year, faculty had fiercely rejected the idea that their instruction could possibly be a contributing factor to the students' poor test scores. What was in place was a modified faculty SDMT and subcommittees that had been formed at the June Goals 2000 workshops. The plan this year was to use these structures and the good feelings from the June workshops to put the other pieces in place. As a consequence, the second year was both a start-up and a consolidation.

In this chapter, we explore how innovation implementation can progress at the same time that schools stagnate. Before beginning the chapter, the reader is asked to consider the following framing questions:

1. Recalling the events from Year 1, what are the school's strengths and challenges in regard to the implementation for Year 2?
2. What would be the first thing that you would do to get this year going well? And why?
3. What, if anything, would you scrupulously seek to avoid? And why?

September 1995

Year 2 at Professions Institute began with a good deal of upheaval and time spent reviewing the previous year's progress for new faculty and staff. This was necessitated by a number of staff changes resulting from the closing of another mini school in the building. This event led to five teachers at Professions Institute being "bumped," or displaced by faculty from this school. Professions received three special education teachers, one mathematics teacher, one social studies teacher, and several para-professionals. As a result, both of its special education teachers, a mathematics/social studies teacher, and a language arts teacher, were forced to leave. One of the social studies teachers scheduled to be bumped began grievance procedures and was subsequently rehired as a language arts teacher. At the start of the year, staff uncertainty remained, as an art teacher in the school upstairs indicated she wanted the position of the art teacher at Professions.

On September 6th, there was an all-day workshop intended to acquaint new faculty with Model X; to inform everyone of the progress that had been made during the Goals 2000 summer workshops; and to obtain consensus on these issues. While these goals were achieved, the teachers were very distracted, wanting instead to begin setting up their rooms. Several review and briefing sessions were held over the next week. On September 11th, veteran and new mathematics faculty met to review the department's work last year with Bill M. On September 14th, Language Arts faculty met to review and discuss the most recent changes to New York State's reading test, i.e., the Degrees of Reading Proficiency (DRP). The test will now require more "higher order" thinking. I also asked them how I could assist them this academic year.

This year I am to be assisted at Professions Institute by a Professional Development Associate (PDA), a teacher on sabbatical leave from another school who has elected to spend this time working with the project for credit. I met with her on September 12th, where all such teachers joining the project came for an orientation to Model X. Her name is Karen W.

As the faculty had already set their priorities and established their subcommittees at the summer workshop, according to Model X's road map, we are now ready to begin the problem solving process. In preparation, I introduced and explained the

Inquiry Process at a general faculty meeting on September 15th. The subcommittee on discipline had already met. Mrs. Di, the head of that subcommittee, stated that they had decided to add a bathroom period after lunch. I responded that the decision "jumped the gun," as it had not been made through the inquiry process. They asked if they could, nonetheless, implement this strategy and engage in the inquiry process next time – "because all the faculty were unanimously in favor of this change." I agreed, reluctantly, sensing that they needed to feel some sense of efficacy. Subcommittee meetings were now added to regularly scheduled general faculty and departmental meetings.

The Language Arts faculty met on the 21st and continued their discussion of the new format of the DRP. The Reading Specialist, who had represented the school at these district meetings, felt that we could more effectively prepare students for the new requirements through greater interdisciplinary practices (e.g., word problems in mathematics).

The first general faculty meeting was the 18th, about half of the faculty voluntarily attended (!). I introduced Karen W. to the school's staff, and subcommittee representatives gave status reports. Mrs. Di, speaking for the discipline cadre, said they were moving along and had targeted conduct in the halls as their first issue. They were attempting to identify causal factors. Jeanna, speaking for the communications/climate subcommittee said they were having trouble. The school's secretary, who had been made the head of the committee, had resigned, upset at the events of the first meeting. The remaining subcommittee members had not met since then. I got dates for subsequent committee sessions in order to attend.

Following the general faculty meeting, the Director, the school's SED representative, my PDA and I met. The SED rep indicated that the State was very serious about SURR schools implementing the changes outlined in their Comprehensive Plans. The Director suggested that she and I reiterate to teachers the instructional objectives stated in the Plan in next week's subject area meetings; and the SED rep would subsequently meet with the general faculty to inform them of SED's position.

On the 28th, I first met with the communications/climate subcommittee. The secretary did not attend. The Director came in with an agenda that she proceeded to present. Jeanna objected that the function of the subcommittee was not to implement action plans that had been unilaterally decided, but to engage in inquiry. She asked me for procedural clarification and support; I seconded the substance of her remarks. This left the cadre without a clear plan of action. I suggested that they review the survey results for issues for the next meeting. They agreed, but seemed displeased over the Director's attempt to appropriate the meeting. I then went to attend the regularly scheduled meeting of the L. A. faculty, where the Director and I began discussion of the school's Comprehensive Plan. The Director stressed the significance of the Plan's implementation offering in way of support, the Chancellor's review team report. This meeting was somewhat overshadowed by the events of the previous meeting.

My apprehension about that meeting was confirmed later that evening when Jeanna called me at home. She said the other cadre members were very upset, and indicated that another subcommittee member intended to resign. I tried to explain to her that the Director was used to a top-down leadership style. Until she began to trust that the teachers would be responsible and put children's learning as their first priority, we could expect her to attempt to direct the group. I offered to reiterate to the Director the goals of Model X in regards to teacher empowerment and decision-making.

The last general faculty meeting for the month was held on the 29th. Subcommittee representatives gave status reports. The discipline subcommittee offered a number of possible reasons and remedies for the chaotic condition of the halls. I reminded them that the process required fact-finding, not jumping to solutions. The committee accordingly decided to make up a questionnaire asking students for their input on the issue.

October 1995

October was primarily spent trying to get the subcommittees to use the inquiry process and attempting to incorporate the instructional component unobtrusively into the subject area meetings. Work in the discipline subcommittee progressed, but the communications/climate subcommittee was falling apart – largely due to teachers' reactions to the Director. Early in October, I got the Director to agree no longer to attend meetings of this subcommittee. I thought this might give staff the opportunity and the space to become empowered. I now have to persuade disgruntled faculty to come back.

Introduction of the instructional component was moving very slowly. Teachers seem to resent the idea that there is any need to change or improve their instructional techniques. In general faculty meetings, any formal mention of the instructional component was greeted negatively. However, in subject area meetings, it was possible to talk about the concepts contained within it as individual principles and practices.

On Thursday, October 5th, Bill M. came from the D. O. to continue his meetings with the mathematics faculty. This time, he wanted to help them set up the mathematic calendar for November and December. Bill recommended that all students be given a monthly skills test in mathematics, formatted like a standardized test. The next several meetings were to be devoted to constructing the monthly mathematics tests. Bill also suggested topics for possible hands-on activities and he promised to give the demonstration lesson and to pick up the events planned last spring. Toward this end, Bill suggested that our meetings be held in the mathematics lab, where each week the head of the math lab would demonstrate an activity done with manipulatives. Later that same day, I met with the Language Arts staff. This meeting involved presentations by those who had just attended the NYS Middle Schools Conference.

At the first general faculty meeting in October, discussion of the school calendar grew controversial. The teachers wanted a graphic events calendar, rather than or in addition to the monthly, weekly and daily "News of the Day" that the Director disseminated. Teachers complained that the newsletters were too wordy and it was difficult to cull information. The Director refused to reproduce the information in a different form. She asserted, moreover, that there was a large calendar in her office for that very purpose that was not being used. After some discussion, the body decided to explore alternate formats. The subcommittees reported on their progress. The communications subcommittee still has not been able to select a topic and has fallen apart.

I met with the mathematics faculty again on October 10th. We spent the session talking about the format for the monthly mathematics skills tests for students.

On Thursday, October 12th, I spent my morning trying to pull together the communications subcommittee. There was to be a meeting of the committee at 11:30, however, Jeanna was out, and consequently, no one else on the committee "knew" there was a meeting. I spoke individually to old and potential members, trying to get the former to return and the latter to join the committee. The teacher who had resigned reluctantly agreed to return, the secretary made no promises. One of the new special education teachers, Ms. B., agreed to join the committee, as did the new math teacher, Mr. L. (whom I pulled from the discipline committee). Mr. L. is very helpful – when he decides to participate. I then went to the meeting of the language arts faculty. We reviewed the Comprehensive Plan in preparation for the SED rep's visit. From there, I went to see Mrs. Di, the head of the discipline subcommittee, to talk about tomorrow's general faculty meeting. She stated that instead of focusing on Model implementation, the teachers wanted the meeting to focus on routine school matters, e.g., report cards. I encouraged the Director to go along, and so we postponed the SED rep's visit to give them this time. Mrs. Di was asked to forward information to the Director on who would chair the session, with a copy of their agenda so the Director could duplicate it. By Thursday at 2 p.m. none of this had been done. When I saw Mrs. Di, I stressed the lateness of the hour. She in turn talked to two other teachers, and together determined that the Director should chair the meeting (!) and that they would get an agenda to her as soon as possible. They asked me to attend.

I talked to the Director that evening on the phone. She found their asking her to chair ironic. At first she said she didn't want to do it but later agreed and talked about setting "ground rules." I responded that we had made a lot of progress on team building this year and that she needed to reinforce these gains by being particularly positive. I offered to sit at the back of the room and monitor her "niceness quotient." We laughed. The meeting went very well. It was efficient, a lot got covered, and everyone went away surprisingly pleased.

Meetings with subject area faculty continued. The mathematics faculty continued to work on the monthly mathematics skills test. They seemed to have made little progress from our last meeting. I tried to get them to set some tentative milestone dates for test completion and administration. We had a good discussion on making mathematics instruction more relevant to students' future careers. Mr. L. pulled out some excellent text/workbooks and offered to let Mr. G. use them. On the 19th, I met with Language Arts faculty. We further discussed the guidelines for the new reading test, as well as instituting weekly, school-wide skills tests in the area. On Tuesday, October 24th, I went to Professions for a math faculty meeting and found it was not being held as usual in Mr. L.'s room. I found Mr. G. in the office. He said Mr. L. said he was "meetinged out" and wanted to attend mathematics meetings only once a month, as mandated by the union. The Director was not there. I saw Mr. L. in the hall (he admitted he had tried to "hide" when he saw me) and invited him to meet with Mr. G. and me. I reminded Mr. L. that the monthly skills tests could not be completed if they met only once per month. He reluctantly agreed to meet regularly but only until the skills tests were constructed. He said he felt there was no need to meet more often and that even if the school was closed, he would not lose his job because the union required his transfer to another school. (This was the second time I'd heard this comment.) The Director was upset when I told her about Mr. L.'s reluctance to meet. She said she would talk to him.

The SED rep was scheduled to discuss the Comprehensive Education Plan with the general faculty on October 20th. When she canceled the meeting the day before, the Director, Karen and I took the opportunity to plan for the month of November.

Around this time I was informed that the new Request For Proposal (RFP) for Goals 2000 had been distributed. The Director, "of course," expected me to write Professions' proposal as I had done the year before. However, Mae and the Head of Funded Programs at the D. O. had decided that all four Model X middle schools in the District should write a joint proposal. This way the project could ask for up to $120,000. As my proposal was funded the previous year, it was decided that I should write this one. We met on October 25th to brainstorm. Initially I was asked to survey the Comprehensive Education Plans for common elements, which would then become the professional development topics for our joint proposal.

On October 27th, we held our monthly meeting for all the coaches, PDAs, and participating school directors utilizing Model X. State Education Department representatives frequently attended to be updated on the status of the implementation. Prior to the arrival of the State reps, the coaches reported on the status of their schools. Last year, Professions was behind the other Model X schools in its implementation, but now it appeared to be the furthest along. The State reps informed us of their priorities. Anna, Professions' SED rep, again emphasized the need to have the schools focus on their Comprehensive Education Plans.

On October 30th, Anna presented the position of SED to the

general faculty of Professions. Before her presentation, I pushed faculty to agree on topics for the in-service day on November 8th. Previous requests had resulted in indecision and now there was no time left, as the district was pressing the Director for her agenda. It was still like pulling teeth, but the staff finally agreed on conflict resolution and how to hold productive meetings. Anna followed by talking about the State's emphasis on the Comprehensive Plan. The tone of the meeting quickly turned when Mrs. Di began to complain about the NYS Middle School's Conference held earlier in the month and how it had crippled the school by taking so many teachers away from the school to attend. The meeting ended with her screaming at Anna.

On the last day of October, I met with Mae and the D. O.'s Head of Funded Programs to work further on the Goals 2000 proposal. I had previously identified the common professional development topics from the four schools' comprehensive plans and we now discussed a series of events that would implement this wish list.

November 1995

November was spent on facilitating the subcommittees, pulling together the in-service day, working on the mathematics and language arts skills tests and writing the Goals 2000 report.

On November 3rd a general faculty meeting was held. In addition to subcommittee updates, the faculty was also informed that with their in-service day just four days away, I was having difficulty finding a consultant to conduct the workshop. For me, the next several days were a nightmare. Finding a consultant willing and ready to conduct a session the following Tuesday was complicated by the fact that all the public schools in New York City were also having their in-service training on that day, and consequently, there were no consultants available. I finally found a consultant firm in Westchester that offered the kind of training needed. The arrangements were confirmed on Monday, November 6th.

The in-service day went well. The consultant decided to devote the entire morning to conflict resolution. A very low key individual, he did okay; the staff enjoyed him and came away thinking about how they could use the information provided in their own lives as well as with Professions' students. The afternoon was to be spent in subcommittee meetings – although faculty indicated that the Director had promised them that they could do their paperwork at that time. After lunch, faculty, consequently, dispersed to their own rooms. With the Director nowhere to be found, I literally went around pulling faculty from their rooms to conduct their subcommittee meetings. However, once the two groups were rounded up, they spent the remainder of the afternoon working in their subcommittees. The discipline subcommittee developed a plan for facilitating orderly hall transitions that contained a set of consequences including "confronting" lax teachers and imposing "consequences on late students." However, these terms were not spelled out. The communications subcommittee again attempted to come up with a topic for inquiry. A number of ideas were suggested, none were seconded and it was finally decided that the chair of the subcommittee, Mr. T., would construct a one-page faculty survey to gather issues on which the subcommittee should focus. At the end of the in-service school day, I met with several faculty members to discuss the writing of their portion of the Goals 2000 report.

I also continued with my writing of the Goals 2000 report. Writing the actual first draft took three days. Edits took an additional day and a half. There were several meetings with the D. O.'s Head of Funded Programs and Mae to work out the fine points of the proposal.

I met with the Language Arts faculty on November 30th and with the mathematics faculty on November 21st and 28th. Most of the time was spent discussing the skills tests. The mathematics faculty finally completed construction of their first monthly test. It will be administered on December 8th. The language arts faculty is still working on their first test; language arts tests are to be administered weekly.

There was a general faculty meeting on the 15th. My PDA, Karen, led part of the session. She reported on the status of the two subcommittees. We had previously agreed that the discipline committee had to further refine their proposed plan in addition to spelling out what each of the proposed consequences meant. The head of the communications subcommittee, Mr. T., indicated that he had constructed his survey and would distribute it to faculty soon.

There were no subcommittee meetings after the middle of the month. The school was preparing for the parents' "Options Fair," housed in the school.

December 1995

December began with a general coaches meeting with SED and district personnel. Some schools are really not doing well, Professions seems to be making more progress than the others.

At Professions, December continued much as the previous month. That is, the subcommittees met (one decidedly more than the other), and the general faculty meetings continued to be used as steering committee meetings. However, the previous month, Anna, the SED rep, strongly suggested to the Director that the school institute a curriculum and instructions cadre that would focus their activities on implementing the Comprehensive Plan.

My first meeting at Professions was on December 5th with the mathematics faculty. I arrived early and took the opportunity to talk to several teachers. They stated that morale was down, due, they believed, to the disruptive behavior of special education students when in the hallway – students in one class, in particular, were said to yell and curse at each other and to insult the teachers in the rooms they passed. They also mentioned the District might move part of one of two nearby schools to the junior high housing Professions Institute. The faculty is worried about being "bumped" again. I listened but could do little more.

That Thursday, December 7th, I attended a meeting at Professions on the School Wide Projects program. This program allows schools to receive part of their budget money directly from the State, circumventing some of the existing district-level oversight. Each of the mini schools within the building may choose separately whether to defer the decision or accept the plan for adoption next academic year. Attending the meeting was the District Coordinator of Special Education. I asked him how he understood the problems teachers were having with these students. He indicated to me that some of the children were probably miscategorized and needed re-evaluation; documentation also needed to be gathered. He further stated that he was being pressed to "move students" rather than provide teachers with classroom assistance. Although he promised to see what he could do, he did not hold out much promise. Following this meeting, I met with Professions' Language Arts faculty. The meeting focused on the preparation of the weekly tests.

The week ended with a general faculty meeting. It was fairly well attended. We had subcommittee updates, and talked about combining the Mathematics and Language Arts faculty once per month to constitute a Curriculum and Instruction cadre. Faculty said they were "meetinged out." We'll see. Things seem to be moving along – for how long I don't know.

The first meeting of the Curriculum and Instruction cadre was held on December 13th. I could not attend and Karen sat in for me. At the meeting, the SED rep, Anna supported my previous suggestion that this subcommittee meet once per month and that the subject specific meetings be continued. Teachers wanted to know if these meetings would be voluntary and again stated that they were "meetinged out." Anna reminded the faculty that if the students' scores did not improve, there was a major possibility of the school becoming a "corrective action" school. Schools with this designation must be reorganized, and administrators as well as teachers may be removed. Karen said this did not sit well with them.

My last meeting at Professions for December was a general faculty meeting held on December 15th. (The month was ending early due to the winter holiday.) The discipline subcommittee presented a list of suggested activities. Mr. T. gave an update on the communications subcommittee, stating that his faculty survey found that: (1) work needed to be done on the "News of the Day" (put out by the Director). It was too wordy and faculty found it difficult to glean important information; (2) there were too many teachers out of the building attending meetings on any given day; (3) too much time was wasted in meetings; (4) bathroom time rules (instituted by the discipline subcommittee) were not being adhered to; and (5) teachers were inconsistent in standing in the halls to monitor students' changing periods. I suggested that the communications subcommittee meet to decide which of these issues to address first and to come to the next meeting with the decision. Toward the end of the meeting, faculty indicated they were displeased with how senior activities were being handled. They asserted that the Director was delegating to others (parents), activities that they formerly had control over. They asked me to talk to her about this.

After the Christmas holiday, I don't intend to return to Professions for the month of January. I have time off at the College and think I will use the month to write. Moreover, I want to see how the school gets along without me for a while. It is clear to me that I am doing too many activities that should be done by the staff. I am going to use this opportunity to give them some room to work on their own.

February 1996

After my hiatus for the month of January, February got off to a surprisingly good start. We continued with the weekly subject area meetings and began planning for the standardized tests. Two things troubled me, however. The faculty was functioning, but not necessarily in accordance with Model X guidelines. That is, they were working to improve Professions but without following the Model. For example, they often met informally, rather than holding formal sessions to which all subcommittee members were invited. Minutes were, therefore, seldom taken and were never posted. Similarly, faculty continued to leap to possible problem solutions without going through the inquiry process. I need to steer them back to the Model without raising opposition.

The Director and I met on Saturday, February 3rd, and Tuesday, February 6th, to plan for the month. She raised the issue of changing the name of the school. She said that she would broach the subject with the faculty later this month. She also said that she would remind them of the concerns raised by the City monitors in preparation for a site visit by SED personnel. I said I would discuss these latter topics with the faculty at the first general meeting.

The first general faculty meeting for the month of February was on February 9th. It was surprisingly well attended. Faculty seemed genuinely pleased to see me back. It was a good meeting. The subcommittees reported on their activities. The discipline subcommittee, as expected, was moving rapidly. Mrs. Di said teachers were standing in the halls while students changed period, and as a result, the halls were quieter. The communication subcommittee didn't have much to report. They had not met and stated they were still floundering. As a result, I held a vote to disband the cadre. All agreed, and in fact, the committee members seemed relieved. I asked if there was some other topic that might interest them that was related to the data revealed by our earlier investigation. The faculty offered suggestions. It seemed that most wanted some kind of activities committee, i.e., a group of staff that would work on fun activities or competitions involving students. The activities committee was thus formed. We also talked about the upcoming SED visit and noted challenge areas from the City monitors' report, e.g., bulletin boards, display of children's work, activity-based instruction. The teachers had already begun working on the halls. There had been a real improvement from December and I commended the teachers on their efforts. I also raised the issue of the next staff development day, scheduled for March 8th. One of the science teachers offered to lead a workshop on new computer software!

Early the next week Jeanna called me about the activities committee. She said she was floundering a bit and few faculty members seemed interested in joining. She also said that at the general faculty meeting the Special Education faculty felt left out. I suggested that the activities committee would be a good forum to get the Special Education faculty involved. Activities should be devised in which special education students could also participate. Competitions should be chosen in which special education students had a good chance of doing well.

I returned to Professions a week later (i.e., February 16th) for the next general faculty meeting. We talked about the curriculum and instruction committee. The Director indicated that it was for the purpose of improving instruction and generally preparing students for the standardized tests. However, it should not be restricted to the areas of math and language arts. We also briefly discussed the new activities subcommittee. Jeanna said she would be in touch with faculty about joining and announced a meeting for February 29th at 11:30.

On February 27th I met with the Mathematics faculty. They were all busily preparing for the standardized tests in mathematics that would begin early in March. At this meeting, Mr. S. (faculty from another school in the District who was stationed at the D. O. awaiting action on a grievance and was contributing services to its schools) indicated that analysis of students' monthly math tests indicated that there were students with little or no knowledge of basic mathematics facts. I asked if there was anything that could be done with them before the standardized tests were begun, e.g., pulling them out for drill in their mathematics facts. All teachers said it was too late. I countered that the tests were still two weeks away and every effort had to be made to see to it that students did the best possible. Mr. S. volunteered to take groups of children out for drill and practice for part of the time that he was at Professions.

On February 29th, I inadvertently came in on the school's

Curriculum Planning meetings. Almost the entire faculty was there. They were discussing what to do with the school's former "elective period," the last class hour on Wednesday. Evidently the previous arrangement was not working. Faculty wanted to do enrichment for bright children. I suggested that additional work be done with poorly performing students. I was outvoted and faculty elected to hold the majority of students in the gym that period and allow good students to do enrichment, e.g., good seventh graders would be allowed to sit in on eighth grade classes. Later that day, I attended the Language Arts faculty meeting. The meeting began fretfully. The weekly skills tests they agreed to give students were missing and the Director had xeroxed other tests that the teachers felt were much too advanced for students. This issue was resolved and I then proceeded to ask faculty if they had analyzed the results of the weekly tests. All said no. Only one teacher had her data with her. She tabulated the results as we sat there and found that almost two-thirds of her students received failing scores on a test which focused on discerning the main idea from texts! I asked her what she planned do about it, to which she replied "Nothing." She then said that she was going on to the next topic: "Inference." I asked her how could she teach inference if students had no concept of the main idea. She shrugged and asked me for suggestions. I offered her some ideas from my knowledge of metacognition, e.g., having students write short paragraphs with one thought and exchanging these paragraphs with other students to see if they could guess what that thought was or give the essay a title. She said she would try it.

March 1996

It is March and I am still trying to get faculty at Professions to function more in keeping with the processes of Model X. They are not using the inquiry process in their problem solving and are very reluctant to focus their attention on instruction.

Meetings at Professions began with the weekly meeting of Mathematics faculty, on March 5th. We discussed student preparation for the standardized tests.

On Thursday, March 7th, I met with Karen, my PDA, at the College to discuss my concerns about how to get Professions back on the Model X "track." Right now the general faculty meetings are functioning as the School Leadership Team and we have no

School As A Whole (SAW) meetings. We decided that the creation of the SAW should be shelved until next year, as this committee is heavily dependent upon parent involvement – a place where Professions is very weak. We also discussed refocusing the activities committee; making it again into a school climate cadre, more in accordance with Model X's subcommittees. Karen will help facilitate the work of this cadre; and I will continue to infuse the principles of the instructional component into the agenda of the subject specific meetings.

On Friday, March 8th, all New York City public schools had an in-service half-day. The Director had arranged to have a presenter from the UFT present on ways to make instructional content more meaningful to adolescents. This caused some confusion, as faculty thought that Mr. D. was going to present a workshop on computer software, after which staff would have the opportunity to reconsider the plan for the elective period – which had fallen through. A compromise was reached wherein the UFT trainer would present for half the afternoon, followed by Mr. D. Some teachers were a bit disgruntled by this, as in their minds, the Director had unilaterally set the agenda for the afternoon. The union trainer was good, but not great. The Professions audience was polite, but it was obvious that they got little out of it. Mr. D.'s presentation went better. The faculty seemed really interested in the new software he highlighted. Afterwards, I talked to several teachers about the confusion, for I had known about the UFT presenter for months in advance. They told me that the Director had not informed them of her coming. Teachers had been given a previous opportunity to meet on the issue (and had not done so), and they just assumed that it could be done today.

The following week, the Mathematics faculty was engaged in testing. I met with the Language Arts faculty on Thursday, March 14th. We discussed the best practice tests to use for the upcoming standardized tests. I advised teachers on possible metacognitive strategies to use with Star Lab students who were having difficulty with reading comprehension, and suggested ways to get them to "click" on and attend to the day's lesson. I am going to make a real effort to get someone here to work with faculty on the use of more "powerful" reading strategies. After this meeting I had a fortuitous meeting with two, rather vocal, faculty members. One, in particular, Mrs. Di, complained about the Director increasingly making unilateral decisions that either infringed upon projects that were the purview of others or went against decisions previously made by a group. As an example, Mrs. Di stated that each year she takes the initiative to put together a science fair displaying projects done by students in her classes. The fair is held in the library. This year, without consulting with her, the Director had someone from another school in the building do the lettering for the sign and asked students in special education to be the greeters and "man" the tables outside. While I thought the latter was a good idea, Mrs. Di was livid and informed the Director that these students' involvement would take place "over her dead body." The Director later conceded. The two were also butting heads over the plan for the elective period. When the teachers could not meet during last week's in-service day, no alternate date was set to meet and the Director subsequently instructed the teacher who typically does program scheduling to make up a schedule for the period without their input. Mrs. Di stated that staff was so disgruntled at this point that they believed few would attend the general faculty meeting the next day. Later that evening I spoke with the Director. She was equally livid at the teachers for "dragging their feet" on the issue of the elective period. Their delay, she asserted, was resulting in a safety prob-lem, as children were not being adequately supervised during this time – the gym teacher could and would not assume responsi-bility for all the children excluded from the enrichment activities. I decided to cancel the general faculty meeting to prevent it from becoming a shouting match.

The next week I met with the Mathematics faculty as usual. We discussed the students' results on the first of the two stand-ardized tests, the PAM, and preparation for the next one, the California Achievement Test in Mathematics. Professions stu-dents did poorly on the PAM – as anticipated – for it focused on solving word problems. Math faculty also mentioned that while the scoring had become more realistic, i.e., awarding partial credit for written calculations, it penalized students who could do work successfully in their heads. I again suggested that rather than cram preparation for the test, one weekly period should be devoted to instructing students in test taking skills and rotate the specific subject content. This could be done during the time now blocked out for the elective period. We briefly discussed the writing of next year's Comprehensive Education Plan, which needs to be done now. Some activities were proposed to improve students' mathematics performance including students' maintenance of journals and mathematics vocabulary lists; greater use of manipulatives and calculators; and designing mathematics games.

March 20th was spent in the field. It began with a meeting at Professions with the SED representative, my PDA, and the Director. We primarily focused on my concerns relative to Model X's process and the plans Karen and I had made to realign the process and to shift the school's focus to instruction. Anna agreed with the shift and suggested in-class observations of faculty to support the instructional component. The Director and I both felt teachers would not be receptive to this idea and reminded them of the math faculty's previous enthusiasm re. Bill M.'s planned demonstration lesson set for last year that never occurred. Anna suggested the use of inter-class visits; the Director said this had already been done. Anna then suggested that the Language Arts faculty be asked to write a curriculum outlining the topics and skills that should be covered and setting a time table for their presentation. She also suggested that instruction in test taking skills be integrated into content area teaching rather than done as a separate period. I indicated my doubt that teachers would do this and suggested that someone "model" such a lesson for the teachers. We then planned the agenda for the general faculty meeting scheduled for Friday. Following this meeting, Mr. L. invited us into his mathematics class to observe a student give a lesson while he coached.

The next day, March 21st, I met with the Language Arts faculty. We discussed topics and skills that remained to be covered this year. This partial curriculum could also be used as the start of Language Arts plan for the Comprehensive Plan.

Friday, March 22nd, the general faculty meeting was held. The discipline subcommittee's report took most of the time. Mrs. Di complained about teachers not enforcing the rules agreed upon. Some teachers mentioned that they were shaving points off students' grades for violations of rules and procedures. The SED rep stated that she thought this practice violated State regulations and offered to check the written policy on this matter. She said with certainty that such a matter could not be decided without a formal vote, and that parents needed to be present. A spokesperson for the Language Arts teachers informed faculty of their plan to post the topics they would be covering in their classes in the hall for all to see and elaborate upon. Anna said she would return next week to outline to faculty the State's new requirements for next year's Comprehensive Educational Plan.

The first meeting of the school climate subcommittee was held on March 28th – Karen attended. They talked about challenge areas and offered possible suggestions for first time events, e.g., a school banner competition and original poetry/raps by students. They also brainstormed obstacles to accomplishing these activities, e.g., resources. Later that day, I met with Language Arts faculty. We continued to plan the curriculum for the remainder of the academic year and for next year. We also discussed how to approach the teaching of expository text to seventh and eighth graders.

The last activity of the month was a general faculty meeting on March 29th. Anna presented the new requirements for writing the Comprehensive Plan. She stressed which pages were different from the plan they wrote last year. We also discussed the posting of all curricular topics for the remainder of the year. Faculty suggested that these listing be posted in the lounge. All agreed that someone from each subject area would do this. I then went on to mention my concerns regarding our noncompliance with Model X's practices. I mentioned the need to create a SAW, which led to a reaffirmation of the need for greater parental involvement. Anna ended by saying we needed two parents present for the next meeting, when the discipline subcommittee would present their plan for ratification by community consensus.

Our Goals 2000 grant proposal was not chosen for funding. Mae and I requested an explanation of why we had lost. We found that although two of the three judges gave the proposal their highest rating, the third judge gave us very poor ratings on all categories due to one technical flaw, i.e., the absence of a signed list of committee members who made up the plan from each of the participating schools. This judge had repeatedly deducted for this omission in each of several categories. We missed the cut-off by one point! How ridiculous and frustrating!

April 1996

After the College's spring break I returned to my work at Professions on April 18th. The morning began with a meeting with the District Superintendent, several District office heads, and Mae. The meeting was to discuss how Model X schools might obtain more in-service days and/or conference time. Mae also presented our plan to offer two summer workshops, i.e., a three-day Introduction to Model X for teachers and a one-day Leadership Workshop for principals and directors of schools using SBM/SDM. They seemed receptive to both and said they would put together a list of attendees. Mae and I are trying to strengthen our working relationship with the District. In the afternoon, I went to Professions to attend the weekly meeting of Language Arts faculty. They were still discussing the curriculum for the remainder of the academic year and the language arts portion of the Comprehensive Education Plan.

The following day, the general faculty meeting was held, at which the discipline subcommittee was to present its plan. Although Anna had specifically urged the Director to get parents to attend this meeting – and the Director had called several parents and gotten two promises of attendance – none appeared. Several students were also invited – none showed. The meeting began with a report from the school climate subcommittee. As I had previously urged Karen to have its members engage in the inquiry process, they reported that they were developing a survey to poll students' activity preferences, and offered some choices that would be included in the survey. The discipline subcommittee then presented their plan. Discussion was most intense concerning the issues of bathroom passes and escorts. Some faculty objected to the practice of allowing only one child at a time out of the room and of insisting that special education students be escorted to the bathroom. The most vociferous committee members strongly pushed for rather punitive consequences to infractions. In the end, all points of the plan were passed by consensus. The Director, Anna and I met afterward. Anna was disturbed and strongly urged us to have students at all meetings, consistent with Model X policy. The Director said she had been trying to get students to attend, but they often did not want to give up their lunch periods. I suggested that the School Climate Committee, composed of more moderate regular education and special education faculty might be used as a counter force. I offered to attend their next meeting to suggest positive options for upcoming activities.

On April 23th and 25th, I, respectively, attended the Mathematics and Language Arts faculty meetings. Unable to get faculty to volunteer to work on the Comprehensive Plan after school – as no money was available to pay them for this extra time, the Director wanted faculty to use the mandated monthly subject-area meetings to work on the Comprehensive Education Plan. As the Director did not attend either of these meetings, I broached the idea to faculty. They resisted the idea and to a man vowed not to work on the Plan during these sessions.

On Friday, April 26th, I, rather than Mae, chaired the monthly coaches meeting with the State reps. We reviewed the progress at each school. However, I took this opportunity to ask State and City representatives about funding for next year, as well as the decision-making criteria for the designation of "Corrective Action." We were told that next year was the last year that New York State intended to fund existing SURR schools. New SURR schools would have only one year of funding. SURR schools coming off the list for next year would not be funded – this included two, and perhaps all three of our schools. Two of our three SURR schools in Manhattan had come off the list, only Professions was left. Everything depended on students' scores on the Degrees of Reading Proficiency (DRP) test. If students' scores went up this year, Professions would come off the list; if not, it would become a Corrective Action School. SED was also changing its criteria for SURR designation. In the future, standardized test scores of special education students would be taken into consideration – currently they were not, although the scores of students assigned to resource rooms and labs were included. This was the first any of us had heard about this. We were also informed that in large part due to limited future funding, all brand new SURR schools had opted to adopt Reading Recovery, a curricular approach, rather than any of the other, more long-term, comprehensive reform models. We were also informed that schools that had chosen to obtain their funds directly from the State through the School Wide Projects (see December report) could vote to use part of these funds to continue work with Model X. I rushed to inform the Director, who had not attended the meeting. This was dismaying, as initially the State had given us a three-year commitment. From where would the funding come for next year? We were just getting these schools to work in a participatory manner and funding was being removed! If they had no coach, use of the Model would not be continued – that was obvious.

May 1996

This has been a month with several ups and downs. Much of this month I had the feeling that many of the gains that had been accomplished during the first year and a half at Professions were being lost, largely due to continued lack of communication between faculty and the Director. The school climate began to deteriorate shortly after my return to the school in February, but the pace accelerated significantly this month. Interestingly, and contrary to last year, the site visit by Model X's Director of Training was a boost.

The month began with a general faculty meeting on May 1st to inform them of the significance of the upcoming DRP. The Director tried to cast this in a positive light, i.e., she focused on urging faculty to teach reading and language arts skills at every opportunity. At the meeting, faculty seemed to respond well.

The discussion of language arts strategies continued in the weekly Language Arts faculty meeting. I was able to get a reading specialist from the College to meet with Professions faculty once a week for three weeks to work with them on constructivist strategies for use in their classrooms. During this first session, Adam had to convince the faculty of his relevance, i.e., his previous experience with a similar population (i.e., poor and working-class minority adolescents). He also had to convince them that he had no intentions of telling them to abandon their tried and true instructional approaches. Instead he advocated a middle of the road position: keep what works and expand their existing repertoire with some progressive strategies. He passed these tests well. The session ended with him giving them handouts on ways to extend students' thinking, how to make discussions more meaningful, and an article on the dialogue between constructivist and traditional approaches.

On May 7th, the Mathematics faculty used their weekly session to discuss the new automated system for recording and tracking student performance. Two of the three mathematics teachers and the Director are to go to the District for training. Following this meeting, the Director and I met to discuss events at Professions. I told her that I felt we were losing ground relative to school climate. She countered that the faculty seemed to rally on the issue of the DRPs, and that things would improve.

May 9th began with my meeting with Mae to begin planning

the summer training workshops. Afterwards, I accompanied the College reading specialist to Professions for his second meeting with the Language Arts faculty. The day's session focused on reading instruction through task-based learning and teaching. The faculty, with one exception, was particularly enthusiastic about these pre-reading activities.

On May 10th, the Director, Karen and I met for an extended day to begin to write the Comprehensive Education Plan. We got a lot of work done, but left out major areas that had to be completed by the subject area faculty. We tentatively set a timetable of afternoon dates for the completion of the write-up with faculty.

My first meeting with the school climate subcommittee came on May 14th. I suggested that they needed to research why the school's climate was a problem. One teacher suggested that the committee choose a theme on a monthly basis that would become a central concept around which to rally the school, e.g., responsibility. Another teacher suggested that we bring student government to the school. These ideas would be posed at the next general faculty meeting. When I reminded them that they were not following Model X's process and were jumping to solutions without having first clearly defined a problem, they stressed that something needed to be done now. Dismayed, I then went to meet with the Mathematics faculty for their weekly meeting. I remained at Professions after this meeting to help faculty write the Comprehensive Education Plan. However, none were willing to stay and participate, and at 3:30 I left.

On May 15th, the project was informed that, at best, SED would provide funds for only one more year at Professions and not at all for the other Model X SURR schools. Mae and I decided to write the Deputy Commissioner a letter, emphasizing the importance of continuing our funding for all current Model X schools, for at least the 1996–97 academic year.

On Thursday afternoon, May 16th, the College reading specialist had his last workshop with Professions' Language Arts faculty. I think, in all, they were very impressed with him. They said they had learned a lot and were pleased that I was able to follow up on their request for assistance. I also think the experience was crucial in focusing their attention on the importance of instruction and their ability to improve upon their existing strategies.

We had the next general faculty meeting on May 17th. Subcommittees reported on their activities. All subcommittee representatives had something to say – even groups that previously had been relatively nonparticipatory. For example, Jeanna, speaking for the Language Arts Cadre, talked about the workshops held by the College reading specialist; a special education teacher, speaking for the school climate subcommittee, spoke about reinstituting student government, the monthly project themes and the upcoming student questionnaire. There was only time left to mention the upcoming visit to the school next Friday of Model X's Director of Training.

This week, the Training Director for Model X's National Center visited us, their New York City team. I met with the Director when she first arrived on Monday May 20th and briefly reviewed with her recent happenings of the New York implementation. On Tuesday, Mae and I took her to lunch, for more information sharing. Later that day she accompanied us to a meeting of an independent research group in which we participate. The City's Chancellor of Education spoke. In the evening, the Director had dinner with all the coaches from the New York City team.

Karen and I had been meeting with the school climate subcommittee. Based on meeting attendance and her visits to the school, she informed me "morale among faculty was definitely very low." In her opinion, the faculty comprising this group was the most amenable of the school's teachers. If they felt this way, then things must be truly bad. On May 20th and 30th we met with subcommittee members to plan further and to write a student climate survey.

Later that same day, Karen met with the Director and several other teachers to finish writing the Comprehensive Education Plan. Only a little work remained to be done on the Plan at the end of this meeting. On May 23rd and 30th, I met with the Mathematics and Language Arts faculty, respectively, to help complete their sections of the Comprehensive Plan and to plan for next year's language arts activities.

Model X's Director of Training visited Professions on May 24th. She first toured the school and then attended a general faculty meeting. This turned out to be a good session. We began with subcommittee reports. At one point, Mrs. Di complained that teachers who previously had agreed to go along with the discipline subcommittee's new policies were not following through. I asked the Training Director for her advice and the faculty got into a real dialogue with her. She said the problem was due to a circumventing of the inquiry process, which resulted in a false consensus on the issue. She suggested that they return to these same issues but use true inquiry. The meeting ended well. Afterward, Model X's Training Director, the Profession's Director, Anna, Karen and I met to get her impression of Professions. To all our surprise, the Training Director was rather enthusiastic. She stated that she'd seen major progress in the school from last year. Faculty were involved in discussions of school business – whereas last year they were lethargic; the halls now looked brighter and displayed student art work; and while she realized certain procedures had been circumvented, she felt that a realignment could be effected. She suggested that for the remainder of the academic year faculty should: (1) make a conscious effort to align their school improvement activities more with Model X's guidelines – perhaps through another "buy-in;" (2) revisit the process (particularly in regards to the inquiry process); (3) forge a new vision statement in preparation for next year; and (4) plan ways to increase parental involvement. She stated that next year she wanted to see greater student participation and general faculty meeting led by teachers.

June, 1996

June is always a month of endings and beginnings. This June began with a coaches' retreat at Stanford University. On Wednesday of the same week, Karen was to present the student questionnaire generated by the school climate subcommittee to the general faculty. However, no one attended the meeting except faculty of the school climate committee and the Director. It was, therefore, decided to distribute the questionnaire to students, without faculty consensus, in order to catch eighth graders before their graduation.

I returned to Professions the following week and first attended a Mathematics faculty meeting on June 11th. We discussed students' scores on the California Achievement Test in Mathematics. Scores of eighth graders went down by 4 percentage points. The mathematics faculty stated that the statistics were confusing, as these students were not the same as the previous year, and in fact, these eighth graders had started from further behind than last year's eighth graders.

I feel the morale at Professions plummeting. I'm sure, in part, this is due to the possibility of the school being given "Corrective Action" status on the basis of their poor test scores. All standardized test scores are in, except for the one critical one, i.e., the DRP. Students' scores fell on both the CTB and the California Achievement Test in Mathematics. Teachers complained that recently the Director had taken to absenting herself from the school more than usual. She may be trying to dissociate herself from the projected results. Regardless, the faculty feel abandoned and without leadership in the midst of an impending crisis.

On Thursday, June 13th, I met Karen at a restaurant for a review of the year's work. We talked a lot about school climate and the need for me to talk to the Director regarding her leadership style. As I later had to meet with Language Arts faculty, I asked her to accompany me. Not to my surprise, she declined, saying that the morale of the school now depressed her. When I arrived at Professions, the Director was holding another meeting, updating faculty on a visit made by some Professions faculty to another junior high school, which was presented as a model school. The Director wants to copy their example of mainstreaming special education students (especially Profession's MIS II class) not only throughout the regular education classes, but throughout the building's three mini schools. The faculty supported this idea, and the Director will present this idea to the building Principal.

Previously, the Director had requested that I write a grant proposal to obtain outside funding for Professions. We met on June 14th to discuss the proposal. On the following days, I worked on the proposal.

On June 21st, we attended the D. O.'s final principals' meeting. Each school principal talked about the progress they had made for the academic year. Profession's Director took this opportunity to announce that the school's DRP scores went up (!) and so her school will be coming off the SURR list for next year. We then formed principal–coach pairs to discuss the accomplishments and challenges experienced this year and to plan initial activities for the 1996–97 year.

I wanted to hold one last general faculty meeting to outline the tasks suggested by Model X's Training Director. I called the Director and set the meeting for June 25th. I arrived, but few teachers were in attendance – even the Director was nowhere to be found! I used the time to talk informally with the faculty present. Mr. L., the school's best math teacher, informed me that he has requested a transfer to the new JHS that will be coming into the building next year. Low school morale forced his move – he'd only been at Professions one year! He stated that he was tired of the chaos, teachers who can't control their classes and teachers who too vociferously force their views on others. He commented that the Director did try, but often the problem is bigger than her ability to cope. A second math teacher is retiring. This leaves only one of the school's three mathematics teachers in place for next year – the one judged by most to be the least competent! The computer teacher has also requested a transfer to the newly arriving school. The school will also lose the most problematic of its special education classes. Teachers thanked me for my efforts; they said that things looked for a while like they would change, but there was too much "negative history" to overcome. To my amazement, one teacher said that he's almost sorry the school did not go into corrective action, then a new administrator would have been appointed and at least 35 percent of the existing faculty would be changed.

Discussion

This second year of the implementation, Professions' staff made some notable progress, but in other ways moved very little. The SDMT continued to function, at times it even seemed to gather momentum. Subcommittees made efforts to identify key problem areas within the school related to their designated priorities and to problem solve in these areas. There were attempts to focus on instruction, largely structured around preparing students for upcoming standardized tests. And the school, for a long moment, made some progress toward working together as a whole. But by the end of the year, despite their students' rising scores on the one standardized test that determined their fate, a pall had fallen over the school's improvement efforts. Old and new obstacles and conflict reared their heads to leave the school at the end of the year in a state of despondency. Let us try and unpack some of these obstacles. Again, we will consider them from the perspective of technical and cultural opposition.

Technical obstacles to reform implementation

Among the various institutionally-based obstacles that may characteristically interfere with the implementation phase are contractual restrictions. Like most hierarchical public institutions,
school systems are literally blanketed with layer upon layer of
regulations and policies that govern the activities of its stakeholders in their institutional interactions. Meant to ensure the system's
productive and smooth operation, as well as the fair and impartial
treatment of all parties, these rules and regulations structure
matters from the most vital to the most trivial aspects of the
schooling process. Particularly in states that have strong labor
unions, these rules and practices constitute one of the system's
adaptive responses to change demands, i.e., ensuring that, in
many respects, the school's basic operations proceed as usual, by
confining changes to those that can function within these bounds.
For changes that are ill conceived, they are appropriate defenses,
but they can also lead to "fatal half-measures," i.e., actions that
bend, rather than break, the traditional model, making it easier
to go back than to go forward (Donahoe; 1993: 298). So omnipresent are these myriad rules and regulations that they become
a serious factor and a major contextual component with which
all change efforts must contend where they exist.

How well change agents can navigate their innovations through
the schools' regulatory maze as well as through spontaneously
occurring events is critical, affecting not only the quality of the
implementation, but the project's ultimate success. Below we
consider the effect of contractual restrictions on teachers' time
and activities; job protection; and high staff mobility rates.

Time and activity constraints

In garnering the time needed for implementation consolidation,
reform projects can encounter obstacles in the plethora of rules
regulating teachers' time and activities. In many cities and states
across the nation, the amount of time and the conditions under
which teachers can be required by school officials to meet on
school-related matters during the school day are limited by
contract rules, usually to no more than one 45-minute period
each month. Other time spent in meetings must be voluntary if
conducted during the school day, and compensated if conducted
during off-school hours. In fact, in interviews with union leaders

in 30 California districts, Little *et al.* (1987) found that most local leaders constrained administrators' access to teachers' time (for the purpose of school- or district-initiated staff development) as a central focus. Such efforts and restrictions on teacher time can impose nearly insurmountable obstacles for inadequately funded change programs.

When time is provided from local and district level personnel, it too often is makeshift and impossible to sustain over an extended period. Staff, correctly perceiving that these practices cannot be maintained in their current form, may logically and justifiably regard both jerry-rigged schedules and the change efforts, themselves, as temporary, and undeserving of any true investment of personal time and effort. Such time constraints and weak institutional responses make it easier to do little or nothing and simply wait for funding or advocacy to be withdrawn to return to the status quo (Fullan, 1993: 3). In so doing, the schools' time policies not only prevent significant change in and to the schools, but retard serious disturbance of the schools' deep structure.

At Professions, time for teachers to attend all the variously required and requested meetings was clearly a rare commodity. The project's vital SDMT meetings were voluntary, as were subcommittee meetings. Subject specific meetings were voluntary beyond one per month. Goodwill toward the project was, therefore, essential as much depended on faculty willingness to attend all the meetings required. Some faculty never attended any of the voluntary meetings and for other faculty, commitment varied. During one of the school's professional development days, the coach had literally to pull teachers from their rooms to engage in subcommittee business. Moreover, the inability to bring in needed external funds to sponsor June workshops this year meant the year ended on a decidedly low note. Faculty and staff needed an extended, unifying work experience – similar to the one provided by the Goals 2000 grant the previous summer – to bring them together and build upon, modify and extend problem solving efforts advanced during the year.

Job protection

Most individuals think of schools as places where children are prepared for the future generation; more so perhaps, schools are major job providers for adults. In fulfilling their mission, thousands upon thousands of adults are employed; and large and powerful organizations have arisen that have as their mission to obtain the best possible work circumstance for their adult constituents. Their concerns, therefore, focus on protecting jobs, budgets, programs, facilities, turf, and enrollments (Smrekar and Mawhinney, 1999). Job protection is a primary concern. Irrespective of student achievement outcomes, elaborate contracts are drawn detailing staff rights, privileges, tenure conditions and due process. To safeguard against favoritism, patronage, and discrimination in hiring, an elaborate process has evolved. Hartocollis (1997: B4) writes:

> The hiring of able and committed teachers is the most important ingredient in the success of any classroom and any school. Yet . . . a dizzying web of state laws, city regulations and the teachers' contract . . . exist to make that process a convoluted, Byzantine, bureaucratic nightmare.
>
> Teachers looking for jobs in N. Y. City are assigned to schools at random by the Central Board's personnel office in Brooklyn. They are not required to visit their school before the school year starts or to be interviewed by the principal who will be their boss, their fellow teachers or the parents whose children they will be educating.

Once hired and allowed to remain to the end of their probationary period, usually lasting one year and a day, a number of mechanisms have been written into the contracts of school personnel to ensure their continued employment. Horror stories abound of administrator efforts to remove poorly performing teachers. Lengthy "paper trails," grievance hearings, mandated retraining efforts and appeal channels must first be exhausted before any definitive action may be taken. Similar difficulty may be met in regard to the removal of principals – as in some states and cities, like New York until recently, principals may be granted tenure – for life – to their school buildings.

The staffing problems these regulations create for school improvement were clearly illustrated at Professions. Professions had a hard core of veteran teachers, some quite good and a very few quite bad. In the classes of these poor teachers, students lost academic ground each year, making the raising of their scores in those subject areas difficult. For example, as alluded to in the June report, with the transfer request of the new mathematics teacher, who was the school's best, this left one very poor performing math teacher whose classroom management skills led to students' consistent under-performance. A long-time veteran, the sheer effort to remove him would have been costly with no guarantees. The mathematics teacher who visited the school that year and provided test prep assistance was a clear example. Bad performance had precipitated his removal from his previous school, but the grievance process kept him at the District Office until all channels of recourse had been exhausted. These rules, initially intended to avoid the capricious or punitive removal of school personnel based on whim, discrimination, politics, and unfounded disfavor, on the one hand, ensure impartiality and due process, but on the other, allow teachers and principals who are unable to improve the academic performance of students to remain year after year. Assurances of job tenure, irrespective of student performance, can, thus, have the unintended effect of allowing overburdened and uncommitted faculty to decline to participate in school improvement efforts with no concern for consequences. And as research indicates, these conditions disproportionately befall urban schools; particularly those populated by poor and minority students (Darling-Hammond, 1994).

Closely associated with the above is the system's emphasis on seniority. Senior staff may "bump," or displace newer staff within a building, with no regard to matters of community, excellence, or work performance. This posed major problems at Professions, as several of its faculty were displaced by more senior building staff from other schools. Occurring at the start of the academic year, it produced such negative affect that it overwhelmed and displaced all the good feelings that had been engendered by the earlier Goals 2000 workshops and caused the school year to begin with the entire community feeling hopeless and powerless.

While we are sure that those who abuse the safeguards of job protection are few in number, if even 1 percent may be so categorized, this equates nationwide to hundred of thousands of students each year who risk not only the loss of valuable instructional time but damage to their psyches and professional futures, as well. Despite repeated efforts to simplify personnel processes and the unions' assertions that the "layers of bureaucratic impediments must be peeled away so that flexibility, creativity, entrepreneurship, trust and risk-taking become the new reality of our schools" (United Federation of Teachers, 1995: 1), regulations continue to be major obstacles to many reform efforts.

High student mobility and staff turnover rates

Few innovations can weather excessive turnover in its primary personnel and student populations – problems that characteristically plague schools with high populations of poor and under-achieving students. In many inner city schools, only a small percentage of students enter at the school's lowest grade and remain until graduation, as the families of these children tend to move often. These schools also face high staff turnover. Typically lacking those factors most commonly associated with attracting and retaining quality teachers, these schools become staffed by a disproportionately high percentage of newly certified and uncer-tified teachers, many of whom may be poorly prepared academi-cally or come from lesser quality teacher preparation programs (Report of the National Commission on Teaching and America's Future, 1996). Unable to start their careers in more attractive schools, many such teachers acquire their early teaching experi-ence in poorly performing schools, before moving out and on, spurred by marriage, burn-out, economics, a more congenial work environment and the desire for greater proximity to home.

The problems high student mobility create for school improve-ment efforts are several. High student mobility often precludes the cumulative effects of particular innovations on children over time. When children depart, their learning in general and the effect of the project in particular are very likely to be disrupted, the latter not likely to be continued in another school. High student mobility may also invalidate assessments of an innova-tion's effectiveness. Even when evaluations of program effective-ness are conducted after the second or third year of implementation, if a significant number of students are new arrivals to the program, their performance is not a fair reflection of program outcomes at that point in time.

Professions found itself in a curious position in this regard. Students were only in the school for two years. Testing was conducted on children in the eighth grade. By the time their scores on standardized test were received, they were preparing to graduate. Disaggregation of these data could still help the school, but only if it was assumed that the same patterns existed with the students that remained or if faculty chose to research the persistence of failure patterns over student cohorts. The faculty was neither inclined to make these assumptions, nor viewed it as a problem that needed to be assessed or addressed.

The effects of staff turnover on school innovation were described in Chapters 4 and 5, and are illustrated well in the reform efforts at Professions. Yearly, the school turned over 25–30 percent of its staff for various reasons. This academic year, the school's entire special education faculty was replaced, and at the end of the year, a number of Professions faculty opted to transfer out of the school. Such high teacher turnover set the program back, as each year, the in-coming staff had to be trained and integrated into ongoing project efforts. This can be awkward. For example, the new Special Education staff were reluctant to join existing subcommittees, although these committees were fairly new in their creation. One teacher commented that each year it was like starting from scratch.

Cultural impediments to reform implementation

Strong conservative school cultures can exert counter-productive forces at the local site level that may seriously undermine reform implementation. Old traditional practices and deep-rooted assumptions die hard, particularly where they are supported by the larger society.

Obstacles to leveling the school's hierarchical structure

As previously indicated in Chapter 4, efforts to reform the school's hierarchical structure through the institution of SBM/SDMTs are grounded in a number of assumptions that may not be borne out. Particularly in poorly performing schools housed in poor, disenfranchised neighborhoods, staff and parents may be reluctant, unprepared and just too overburdened to assume these roles and functions. In particular, parents and teachers in these schools have for so long been peripheral to the formal policy-making process of public schools that many have acquired a learned helplessness concerning their ability to engage in these activities, needing extensive support and hand holding.

Troubled school cultures can exacerbate faculty and parent apprehensions of possible negative reactions concerning decisions made by school teams. Participants weigh the degree to which they feel their decisions will be honored, the worth of standing out and calling unusual attention to themselves, and the perceived emotional costs. Johnson (1990: 189) in extensive interviews with teachers found that their decision not to participate, while often assumed to illustrate a lack of interest, more often was related to disbelief in their ability to have a real influence. We have found this to be a major problem in many troubled schools, where dictatorial and authoritarian administrators, well intentioned as their goals might be, bully, circumvent and/or ignore the products of these teams. Being deprived of any genuine chance to influence policy and not wanting to create bad feelings, staff choose to withdraw and became increasingly cynical. Equally as devastating is a lack of emotional support for or a rejection of team decisions by the other faculty. Site-based management, by its very nature, requires risk-taking, confidence and trust – factors that are uncharacteristic of teachers as a group or the culture of most public schools (Tye, 2000: 130–133). In developing plans for the school as a whole, team members must not only accept responsibility for their successes, but also for the possible failure of their efforts. While anxiety and fear of the unknown are intrinsic to any change process, especially in the early stages (Fullan, 1993: 25), team members must feel either confident in the wisdom of their plans or trust that the other stakeholders will regard their actions as sincere experiments intended to improve the school (Rosenholtz, 1989).

At Professions, all these negative factors were operative. Efforts, admittedly weak, to recruit parents for SDMT participation were a decided failure. Whether information was given to them on the need for their input on issues related to consequences to their children for rule infraction is an unanswered question, but it is doubtful that they would feel that they had the wherewithal to alter the will of teachers in this regard.

Teachers were also initially disinclined to participate for a myriad of reasons, not the least of which was disbelief that the Director would honor the process. These doubts were borne out when the Director attempted to misappropriate the group as a vehicle for her own purposes, leading to its initial disarray and dissolution. Later efforts to revive and bolster this group were also thwarted by group members' fear that their decisions would not be valued and honored by other faculty members. This team's membership, comprised of less self-assured and dominant teachers, exacerbated the normal fear associated with any change process, preventing them from perceiving the situation as anything else but threatening.

In extremely balkanized schools, trust and risk taking, commodities essential for decision making, are often absent, virtually guaranteeing that products coming from such groups will not be well received by members of the other committees. At Professions these teachers' fear of being ridiculed, losing face and of their ideas being rejected was so great that subcommittee members were totally debilitated, unable even to select a topic upon which to work and reluctant to voice their ideas in a large group meeting. Wanting to avoid further disapproval or confrontation, they were paralyzed by their attempts to anticipate the other teachers' objections.

Such apprehension was common in other schools in which we have worked. Fear of disapproval by other faculty members plagued SDMT functioning. We were constantly being asked: "What if our plan fails?", "What if the other teachers don't cooperate?" Overwhelmed by these efforts, some committees seldom got beyond this stage in their planning, in effect, inducing their psychological paralysis.

Creating excellence with equity

Central components of many current initiatives are efforts to undo the traditional practice of sorting students, ostensibly by ability levels, into gifted, regular and special education tracks and to have teachers adopt high expectations for currently underperforming students. Despite this pressure, indications are that the personal beliefs and desires of many educators as well as community groups do not support this reform component.

Both the school and the larger culture may exert strong forces against teachers' beliefs in both their ability to achieve and in the value of achieving these ends. The effect of teacher beliefs on the outcomes of such efforts was strongly illustrated in a major study conducted by Oakes, Wells, Yonezawa and Ray (1997) of 10 secondary schools undergoing detracking spread across the country. So tenacious were traditional views of student abilities that at several schools teachers were found who retained vestiges of a nativist (i.e., genetic deficit) view of intelligence. While these teachers were more likely to actively resist reform, change efforts were also jeopardized by well-intentioned educators whose everyday "common-sense" actions unwittingly reinforced and reconstructed the logic behind traditional grouping practices (Wells and Serna, 1996). According to Oakes *et al.*, in the process of implementing structural and technical changes, they confronted (mostly) taken-for-granted conceptions of intelligence and ability, racial differences, merit and deeply entrenched traditions of valued curriculum and appropriate practice at the school, some of which reflected deep-seated racist and classist attitudes and prejudices.

In our work with schools and at Professions in particular, we found many of the same attitudes. Assuming that many, if not most, poor and minority children simply cannot achieve current standards of academic excellence, teachers made little effort to push these students in preparation for the tests. When preliminary mathematics tests revealed that students were lacking in some of the most basic skills, teachers saw no reason to make any effort to give them these skills, stating that "it was too late" and wouldn't make any difference at this point. Similarly, when preliminary reading tests showed that most students were unable to discern the main idea of stories, the teacher felt no personal responsibility and intended to go on to the next lesson. Clearly, among these teachers there was no expectation of excellence, which made them disinclined to work toward changing the status quo in regard to students' performance So deep-rooted were these teachers' assumptions about the relative immutability of students' academic outcome patterns that in their development of a free period activity, they actively sought to sort students in an effort to triage those believed to be capable of and willing to learn from those they believed to be hopeless, corralling the majority of students in the gym where they lost valuable instructional time.

A similar nonchalance was present even among the school's more progressive teachers, who tended to adopt more of a "you poor dears" attitude. Believing that it morally wrong to penalize or to "hold these students back" because of their shortcomings, they would give them grades incommensurate with the level of work. As previously noted, such efforts to protect students' self-esteem through unwarranted grades and to condone a lack of effort, obscure the connection between work and accomplishment, and set the stage for future failure (Tomlinson, 1992).

Rosenholtz (1989: 82) similarly states:

> Missing in more learning impoverished settings is the sense of teaching as a complex undertaking that requires an ever-expanding repertoire of strategies, that takes into account differing student needs based on contextual or population differences, and that matches particular teaching strategies

with different requirement or purposes. Most conspicuously absent from teachers' consciousness is the primacy of tending to individual students learning.

Not only do many educators and members of the larger society believe that the task is undoable, many also do not value such efforts – particularly when they fundamentally alter the way schools allocate their most precious resources – jobs, time, materials, and high achieving students. When innovations challenge traditional resource allocation patterns, entrenched assumptions about "merit," and which students "deserve" the best that schools have to offer (Oakes *et al.*, 1997: 50), the societal status quo is threatened. Similarly threatened are an entire educational industry consisting of educational specialists who have heavily invested of their time, money and skill in these distinctions among students and the extant sorting practices. For those who have prospered from this arrangement, the threat of its deconstruction can be very alarming. For example, in one school in which we worked, a teacher of the gifted asked openly why she should buy into the reform package when it threatened her job as she knew it. At Professions, teachers supported the distribution of their special education students throughout the school, but, as a whole, had true disdain for them and did not want them in their regular classrooms.

Many parents similarly do not endorse detracking. The Oakes *et al.* (1997) study found resistance and opposition from parents who feared that detracking would jeopardize the benefits their children received from the status quo. "The pressure placed on most schools by savvy parents who want their children enrolled in the 'best' classes may be the most salient of all of the responses to detracking" (ibid.: 55). Because schools need political support – not only for funding and physical resouces, but also for credibility – tracking policies that provide advantage to more privileged children have been exchanged for the political credit that more advantaged and involved parents bring to a school. Parental resistance is particularly contentious among parents who feel their school is neglecting "gifted" students, or using resources "meant" for one group of students on other, "less deserving" students. These researchers found that many parents of students in high track classes exuded a strong sense of entitlement, asserting that because their children are more intelligent and talented than other students they were entitled to more – resources, teacher time, challenging curriculums, and better instructional strategies. Fear that parental opposition will lead to white and wealthy parents abandoning the schools, taking the school's political credibility with them, compels even reform-minded individuals to proceed with caution, and to abandon unpopular reforms out of frustration. Frequently schools and districts will respond to parental resistance by reigning in the reform. At Professions, concern over parent and student sentiments in these regards is manifest in the third year, when overcrowding at the school gives faculty the opportunity to identify 6–7 female students for enrollment at a newly created special school. Regarded in the community as an honor school, the faculty team with this task are very hesitant to estrange students and parents by their choice.

Obstacles to modifying instruction

Despite research that overwhelmingly shows the best way to improve student achievement is to change teachers' instructional practices, this change has been woefully slow in coming. Despite the constant introduction of packaged programs and urgings to use the latest adaptation of constructivist or behavioral approaches, teachers continue to teach much as they did prior to these innovations. Long-term change is seldom achieved as the needed supports are seldom present nor do teachers value or see any real need to alter their practices. According to House (1998), the instructional practices utilized by teachers at any point usually reflect the sum total of their practical knowledge, constructed sometimes painfully, but certainly arduously over a long period of time beginning from their earliest experiences as students. He refers to these skills as assets, the product of teachers' investment in time, effort, educational costs, and career experience in themselves and in their profession (ibid.: 83). It is natural, therefore, for teachers to be disinclined (and perhaps not easily able) to set aside extant practices based on unguaranteed claims and, what is for them, a distant and questionably relevant research literature.

This reluctance to change teaching practices was clearly evident at Professions. Teachers, in fact, reacted hostilely to any large group discussions of altering instructional practices. "There was no need." "They were using these new practices anyway." So intense was teachers' defense of their instructional sovereignty, that the coach was forced surreptitiously to infuse discussion of the model's instructional component into small group, subject-specific meetings, being careful never to mention the name of the project's instructional component. Even after bringing in instructional specialists in both mathematics and literacy to work with the teachers on new ideas and the efficient use of manipulative features, it is seriously doubtful whether more than one or two teachers attempted to follow through on the suggestions. It was obvious that for some teachers, demonstrations and discussions of how to transfer the new practices to their classrooms were inadequate to spark an intrinsic understanding among the teachers such that they felt knowledgeable and confident enough to attempt the methods on their own. Several teachers truly gave the impression that they were giving their best effort, inadequate as it was. For example, the Language Arts teacher who found that her students did not know how to extract the main idea from written text, when asked what she would do, was truly at a loss as to how to reteach the topic differently and could see no recourse but to proceed to the next lesson! To be sure, she is not the only teacher to face this challenge.

This is not to criticize teachers in these regards, for their actions are logical as well as practical in the context of school administrators' and legislators' opportunistic tendency to adopt symbolically wave after wave of innovation. According to House (1998: 83):

> Why should teachers risk assets built up over many years by switching to new teaching materials or techniques of doubtful quality? Their education and professional experience might be devalued . . . Most reforms are the simple ideas of political and educational entrepreneurs. Almost all become fads only to disappear eventually. Why bother?

Where teachers doubt their own ability readily to change current practices or see little value in doing so, based on the belief that "this [innovation] too will pass," there will be little motivation to try. Under such circumstances, it is infinitely easier to simply close their doors and to continue to do what they have always done or to shape the new to conform to the old.

In summary, Year 2 of school reform efforts at Professions Institute continued to reveal the types of organizational and cultural obstacles that can plague the innovation of poorly performing inner city schools. While high staff turnover is a common problem in poor urban schools, at Professions it was exacerbated by job protectionist contractual obligations that permitted more veteran teachers from other mini schools housed in the same building to "bump" less senior teachers. Such events can depress and overshadow laborious gains otherwise made. Also illustrated was the difficulty faced in deconstructing a school's organizational hierarchy. Many staff as well as parents were reluctant to devote scarce time to sit on SBMTs, or assume responsibility for making such decisions. Cultural factors at the school also made this task infinitely more threatening. This year also illustrated the folly of total reliance on standardized tests, as students' scores went down on all test instruments save for the one crucial test. And finally, we saw that while some faculty welcomed instructional assistance, others did not, despite their inability to use alternate instructional strategies when familiar methodologies failed. These obstacles were not insurmountable. Progress was made, as clearly seen by the Model's Director of Training. The challenge is to build upon it.

Study Questions

1. What are the major school climate issues faced this year by Professions Institute? How, if at all, do they differ from Year 1?

2. How would you characterize the Director's actions relative to the subcommittee of which she was a member? How do you think her actions affect the functioning of the subcommittee?

3. How, if at all, has the communication between the Director and the staff changed from Year 1 to Year 2?

4. What leadership style do you think is needed at this stage of the implementation and why?

5. What do you think should be done to facilitate greater receptivity on the faculty's part to the instructional component?

6. What are the operational and attitudinal problems faced by the various SDM subcommittees? How do they compare with those outlined in Chapter 4? What would you do to help make these committees more productive?

7. In what ways have faculty at Professions failed to adopt the attitudes needed to facilitate reform implementation? How might these attitudes be encouraged in faculty?

8. Identify the external resources available to Professions Institute to aid them in the improvement process. How might the staff make better use of these resources? What factors prevent them from doing so and how could these factors be removed?

9. Who is taking the majority of the responsibility for ensuring the model is in place? How might this balance be shifted to ensure more effective reform?

10. How are regulations from the state and from the union affecting the reform process? In your opinion, which set of regulations is posing the greatest difficulty to the implementation process? Explain.

References

American Federation of Teachers (1995) *Making Standards Matter.* Washington, DC: AFT.

Darling-Hammond, L. (1994) Performance-based assessment and educational equity. *Harvard Business Review*, vol. 64, no. 1, Spring, pp. 5–30.

Donahoe, T. (1993) Finding the way: structure, time and culture in school improvement. *Phi Delta Kappan*, vol. 75, December, pp. 298–305.

Fullan, M. (1993) *Change Forces: Probing the Depth of Educational Reform.* London: Falmer Press.

Hartocollis, A. (1997) Convoluted system of teacher hiring spawns backdoor alternative. *New York Times*, Wednesday, September 3, Section B, p. 4.

House, E. (1998) *Schools for Sale: Why Free Market Policies Won't Improve America's Schools and What Will.* New York: Teachers College Press, Columbia University.

Johnson, S. M. (1990) Redesigning teachers' work. In R. F. Elmore and Associates, *Restructuring Schools: The Next Generation of Educational Reform.* San Francisco: Jossey-Bass, pp. 125–151.

Little, J. W., Gerntz, W. M., Stern, D. S., Guthrie, J. W., Kirst, M. W. and Marsh, D. D. (1987) *Staff Development in California: Public and Personal Investment Program Patterns and Policy Choices.* San Francisco: Joint Publication of the Far West Laboratory for Educational Research and Development Policy Analysis for California Education.

Oakes, J., Wells, A. S., Yonezawa, S. and Ray, K. (1997) Equity lessons from detracking schools. In A. Hargreaves (ed.) *Rethinking Change with Heart and Mind.* Alexandria, VA: ASCD.

National Commission on Teaching and America's Future (1996) *What Matters Most: Teaching For America's Future*. New York: Carnegie Corporation of New York.

Rosenholtz, S. J. (1989) *Teachers' Workplace: The Social Organization of Schools*. White Plains: Longman Inc.

Smrekar, C. E. and Mawhinney, H. B. (1999). Integrated services: challenges in linking schools, families and communities. In J. Murphy and K. Seashore Louis (eds) *Handbook of Research on Educational Administration*. San Francisco: Jossey-Bass, pp. 443–459.

Tomlinson, T. (1992) *Hard Work and High Expectations: Motivating Students to Learn*. Issues in Education. Office of Educational Research and Improvements. Washington, DC: US Department of Education.

Tye, B. B. (2000) *Hard Truths: Uncovering the Deep Structure of Schooling*. New York: Teachers College Press, Columbia University.

United Federation of Teachers (1995) *Agreement between the Board of Education of the City School District of the City of New York and the United Federation of Teachers*. October 16, 1995 through November 15, 2000, p. 1.

Wells, A. S. and Serna, I. (1996) The politics of culture: understanding local political resistance to detracking in racially mixed schools. *Harvard Educational Review*, vol. 66, no. 1, pp. 93–118.

8

Decay

The third year this innovation project at Professions Institute was the last year of project funding by the State. Therefore, a decision had to be made whether the project would continue and be funded from the District's own budget. There were some factors to support its continuation. One being that students had evidenced progress on the one standardized test that was the deciding factor in determining their status as an SURR school. Had their scores not evidenced this progress, the school would have likely gone to the next punitive stage of Corrective Action. The other positive factor was strong, obvious and consistent support at the District level. Still many problems remained. The school still lacked a sense of unity, progress was made in fits and starts, morale was low, and communication among the administration and staff remained problematic.

In this last case study chapter we see how tenuous are the strings that tie the school to the innovation, and how rapidly they unravel without diligent maintenance. Before reading this chapter, please consider the following questions.

1. How do you feel the faculty at Professions regard the coach and the project at this point in time?
2. Do you think that as a whole they would support the project's continuation? Why?
3. Whose decision is it to continue this project? What are the various scenarios for its continuation or abandonment?
4. How would you recommend that this third year be begun?

September 1996

For the second year in a row, the academic year at Professions began with staff upheaval. At the end of the previous year, several teachers retired and several others requested that they be transferred to the mini school newly introduced to the building. With this turn, Professions lost the best two of its three mathematics teachers (one by retirement and the other by request); its computer science teacher; and one of its social studies/language arts teachers.

Dismayed by the low staff morale at the end of the 1995–96 academic year, I was tentative about meeting with the Director to discuss plans for the new year. When I arrived on the afternoon of September 5th, the Director was talking with her new Language Arts teacher. When they finished, I asked the Director how she felt the previous year had gone. To my amazement, the Director said she felt things had gone pretty well, "although it could always be better." I suggested that we start the new year with another taking stock.

The next week, Professions held its first mandatory general faculty meeting. At that meeting, the Director informed staff of her goals for the year, e.g., moving the school from the second to the third quartile in their standardized scores and improving attendance. The SED representative, Anna, briefly spoke about the new State Education Department requirements for SURR status, and indicated that while Professions met the old requirements for coming off the list, the new requirements might put them back on the list. I followed, by introducing my new Professional Development Associate (PDA), Vernese, and stating that this would probably be my last year at Professions, as their forthcoming non-SURR status would stop their school improvement funding from the SED. On a more positive note, I continued that there was still time to do a number of things and suggested that at the first Model X meeting, we should make plans to conduct another taking stock of where we were. Faculty seemed genuinely disappointed at this announcement, and commented that it was unfair for the SED to stop funding and that if I was truly committed to them, I would donate my time for free (!) When the meeting was over, the Director, the SED rep, my PDA and I met. Anna informed us of the State's focus areas, i.e., attendance, instruction and parent involvement. She urged us to create a parent subcommittee but without going through a lengthy process.

The second week I received an irate call from Jeanna, who informed me that the Director had made a number of unilateral decisions that had alienated many of the teachers. For one, she had told the new instructors to "stay away from" a particular veteran faculty – Jeanna included. Second, she had decided to institute school uniforms, which the teachers felt should have been a joint decision involving them as well as the students. And last, she had decided that there should be a student government this year and was starting to put this together with the help of social studies faculty – again, without first discussing this with the faculty. As a result, Jeanna doubted that anyone would attend the Steering Committee meeting on Friday, September 20th, out of disgust. This was a prophecy, as neither faculty nor staff appeared for the meeting. What a way to begin!

The following week, I attended three meetings at Professions. The first was a meeting for Social Studies faculty, at which I was surprised to see the Special Education teachers and a number of students in attendance. We reviewed a range of social studies text for possible selection. We also discussed the eligibility requirements for the new student government elections, which are to be held in November; campaign activities; and the responsibilities of each office. Thursday, Anna and I attended a meeting of the Language Arts faculty. When the Director asked the faculty to report on the progress of their respective classes, we were surprised to hear the new Language Art teacher say that all the students in one of her classes, i.e., 8–13, would fail the first marking period. She explained that the students refused to behave, even to open their books or to do any work at all. After this meeting, the Director, the SED rep, and I met. We all soon realized that this problem was created by the way in which students had been organized. Just before the end of the previous academic year, the teachers had placed all seventh grade students whom they regarded as troublemakers into one eighth grade class. Anna strongly urged a reorganization of the entire eighth grade, as the faculty had created one virtually dysfunctional class that could not be taught by anything less than a master teacher. This was triage! We also felt that in the meantime, it would be good to have my PDA, Vernese, work with the new L. A. teacher one day a week. I informed Vernese of this on Friday, September 27th, just before the general faculty meeting. I led the session, discussing the possibility of doing another school assessment. I also raised the issue of class 8–13. Teachers indicated a similar problem was being had with 7–13. I offered the reorganization plan. We agreed that I would return to discuss the matter further with faculty at a meeting the following week.

October 1996

There were several issues that took center stage in October, primary among them were problems with 8–13 and with the new Language Arts teacher.

The first general faculty meeting of the month focused on what to do with 8–13 and 7–13. Two veteran teachers (Mrs. Di and Mr. D.) came eager to address the matter. Mrs. Di began by stating that the faculty had labored long and hard to create the current class groupings and felt the groupings worked. That is, that there were two classes on each grade level that faculty felt could be taught successfully. Admittedly, 8–13 and 7–13 were problems, but only for some (i.e., their Language Arts and Mathematics teachers) but not for others. Mrs. Di further stated that to distribute the troublemakers throughout the other two classes risked making the now functional classes dysfunctional. Despite my assertions that the research literature supported more heterogeneous groupings of students, the faculty and staff soundly rejected the reorganization proposal. A meeting had already been set for the next day on how best to manage the existing two problem classes. At the end of our meeting, the Director and I met to discuss strategy. The Director said she was tired of fighting with the teachers and was willing to go along with keeping the classes as they were. I offered that it might be a good time to give teachers responsibility for developing a plan that would ensure that the two problem classes were given academic instruction, despite their misbehavior. I later attended the weekly meeting of the L. A. faculty, where a representative from the Harcourt Publishing Company presented the Open Court reading series to the faculty. At the end of the day, the Director and I met with the building Principal to discuss the outcomes of the various meetings.

The next day, October 4th, I met with the Director and a group of faculty to develop a plan for managing the two problem classes. I tried to emphasize that the faculty had to assume joint responsibility for ensuring the learning and academic growth of students in these classes. The Director then announced that she had called the District and its Director of Alternative Programs had stated that, as Professions was overcrowded, six students could be removed from the school. Moreover, a new all girls junior high school had just been created in the district, and the six removed students, if females, would be given admission to this new school. The remaining students could then be reshuffled to facilitate classroom management. The faculty seemed genuinely enthusiastic about this proposal and agreed to meet again to identify the girls to be transferred. I was less enthusiastic as it allowed faculty to delay further any real discussion of how students in these two problem classes would be meaningfully educated.

I returned to Professions on October 7th, the date that had been set to select the six students who would be transferred. When I arrived I was surprised to hear that the faculty didn't remember that this meeting had been set at the end of the previous meeting. Many were reluctant to meet. I insisted that the meeting be held. As it was now October, if students were going to be transferred, the earlier this was done the better. The resulting group of faculty was small, i.e., five teachers and one parent, and all seemed extremely reluctant to make the selection. Repeatedly in the process of discussion, one or another teacher voiced uneasiness with being asked to assume, what was to them, such a grave responsibility. They couldn't decide on what basis to make the selection of the six girls. Either they could choose girls that were good academically, thus rewarding them for their efforts or choose those who they felt were beginning to fall prey to the temptation of boys or be otherwise negatively distracted by the climate at Professions. The more they deliberated, the uneasier they became and finally concluded that the Director should make the decision. I reminded them that they were constantly complaining about the Director doing things unilaterally, and now when given an opportunity to make an important decision, they shifted the responsibility back to her. I offered a counter-proposal: choose a slate of more than six girls, some of whom meet the first criteria and others who meet the second; forward the entire slate to the Director and allow her to make the final decision. Faculty countered that there might be opposition from students and parents (one of whom was attending the meeting and wanted her daughter to be transferred). In the end, they decided not to create a list, but rather to do the selection by lottery! They wanted all parents to be notified of the possibility of transfer, and all who wanted their children to be transferred or all students who wanted to be transferred to inform the school. These students' names would then be pooled, and the six names anonymously selected from the pool. I was thoroughly disgusted!!! The faculty had totally refused to make an educationally sound and needed decision, wanting above all else to avoid any responsibility for or negative reactions to their plan's outcome. But to create a lottery was absurd considering the amount of time required to implement it!

I did not want to show my displeasure with the staff at Professions and so I stayed away for a while. Almost two weeks later, the Director called me, having correctly concluded that I was probably disgusted with the events at the school. She asked that I not give up on them. I suggested that as both Model X's creator and Training Director were in town for the year, that I raise the problems of Professions with them. A subsequent meeting was set between the three of us for October 22nd, at Hunter College. At this meeting, the Training Director suggested that the Director adopt the role of facilitator and consciously seek to praise her faculty. I would meet with and engage them in mini school assessment exercises as a way to determine their commitment to the Model. My first meeting was to be with the L. A. faculty, where I was to query them as to the purpose of their weekly faculty meetings. At the next general faculty meeting, I was to ask them to interpret the school's Vision/Mission statement and to provide evidence of its implementation.

The best laid plans of mice and men . . . I arrived at Professions on October 24th, for the L. A. meeting, but no one was there. I tracked the Director down in Jeanna's room. She said the meeting had been canceled because an unusual number of faculty was absent and the remaining faculty had been reassigned to coverages.

Around this time, my Professional Development Associate, Vernese, who was working with the new L. A. teacher, informed me that not only did the new teacher have very poor instructional and classroom management skills, but worse yet, she had little desire to change. The new teacher also resented Vernese's presence in her class and said she was being "helped too much by too many people." In fact, earlier that week, when Vernese came to help her, the new teacher had gone to get the school's union representative, who aggressively queried Vernese about her presence there.

I finally held my general faculty meeting on the 29th. I spent the period briefing them on the criteria that the SED would use in their site visit (the visit was to be the final element in the State's decision whether to remove Professions Institute from the

SURR list). One of the several criteria used to evaluate schools was the degree to which they had adhered to their selected model of excellence. The faculty all knew that, at this point, they had not been adhering to the process. The subcommittees had not met this year and many things were in general disarray. One teacher commented that even when they make decisions their plans are not implemented, asking the Director in way of example, what had happened to the names of the six girls they had selected to be transferred to the all girls school? (I was surprised, for I was not aware that a subsequent meeting on the issue had taken place!) The Director responded that the delay was at the district level. The teachers' sense of frustration and anger was palpable. Another teacher then asked what was the worst thing that could happen as a consequence of negative findings by the SED. I responded that the school would go into "Corrective Action," a process in which, to the best of my knowledge, mandated the school's reorganization. In it, the school was closed and reopened as a new school with a new name and new Principal/Director. Only 50 percent of the original school's faculty could remain, based on seniority. Those teachers who remained would lose their seniority to the school – as the school would now be considered new; while those who left would retain their seniority in the system. Mrs. Di objected saying that the union would never allow them to lose their seniority. I reiterated my position, but she refused to admit this possibility. Another teacher said that perhaps it would not be so bad for the school to go into Corrective Action. A third teacher asked me what I thought was the main problem with the school. I replied that faculty and staff lacked any unity of purpose. Mrs. Di again disagreed. The meeting closed with my asking them if they wanted to stay with Model X and to put their subcommittees back together. They said that it was too much to think about and that we should discuss it at a later meeting.

Afterward, Jeanna pulled me into her room to update me on her current problems with the Director. She said that she and the new teacher had become friends, despite the Director's admonition to the young teacher that she avoided any association with Jeanna. She said the Director was now persecuting the new teacher because of their friendship. She also asserted that the Director had put someone into the new teacher's class to spy on her. I told Jeanna that I had put the person into the class, and that it was my Professional Development Associate, Vernese.

Jeanna responded that she was still hurt by the Director's asking "everyone else except me to mentor" the new teacher. Jeanna also informed me that it was on her advice that the new teacher had gone to the union representative to complain about Vernese's presence in the room – which led to his confrontation with Vernese. If the union rep was out of line it was because he was mad at the Director for circumventing his authority on an earlier occasion. She finally noted that the Director had unilaterally decided to have students wear uniforms.

I later met with the Director and informed her of my conversation with Jeanna. Together, we later met with the school Principal, who supported our recommendation to begin to gather the paperwork in case documentation was needed. The Principal also wanted to speak with Vernese to find out what had happened.

That evening proved hectic. I first got a call from Mae, who informed me that she had just received a call from the District's union representative. Apparently, the District representative had been called by Professions' union representative and informed of the incident. The District's union representative told Mae that she had heard that there was "some kind of problem involving implementation of Model X and the new Language Arts teacher at Professions." As it was explained to her, we had assigned someone to the new teacher's class, giving the teacher no choice in the process. The new teacher did not want the assistance and felt the coach's assistant was an intrusion. Mae responded that we had only wanted to help the new teacher, who was obviously having great difficulty with the class. The representative reiterated that the teacher did not want help. Mae assured her that as we had no intentions of causing any trouble and would withdraw the PDA from the class. Mae immediately called me to ask me what had happened. When I explained to Mae the chain of events, including what I had just heard from Jeanna, Mae was flabbergasted at how fast the issue had escalated. I assured Mae that I would immediately call Vernese and ask her not to return to the new teacher's class. I did so, and in addition, informed Vernese that the building Principal wanted to talk with her regarding her confrontation with the school's union representative.

Later that evening, I got a call at home from one of the special education teachers, who had never phoned me before. She said she and several other teachers were disturbed by the events of the general faculty meeting. They were angered by my assertion that they lacked unity of purpose. According to them, I had not been present when the Director had been out for a whole week due to illness. It was then, they contended, that the school had worked fine; faculty had rallied to make decisions, as appropriate, and a lot had gotten done. The problem was the Director and I had no understanding of how much the staff despised her. She also informed me of the complaints mentioned earlier by Jeanna.

I then called Jeanna to get more information. She informed me that after the general meeting the faculty remained agitated, blaming the Director for most of the problems. So intense was their animosity toward her and their wish to rid themselves of her that some voiced serious consideration of Corrective Action as a desirable solution. She further said that the teachers were hurt by my comment, for they had always felt I had been honest and supportive. She said that the teachers did not want to lose me.

November 1996

November began with a planning session on November 4th at which Model X's Training Director and I proposed how to proceed at Professions. We decided that the following day, which was to be a Faculty In-Service Day, we would begin the process of getting the faculty to re-evaluate the status of the school relative to the change process. We made up an agenda which began with their revisiting their vision statement and a discussion of the change process. By the end of the meeting, we felt good about our plan and thought it would get the school back on track with this as a first step.

How foolish we were! The session, led by the Training Director and myself, failed to bring the faculty to consensus on any agenda items. After the warm-up activity, we attempted to revisit the school's vision statement. Worksheet questions asked "What does this statement mean to me?" "How do I own/live it?" Faculty objected to doing the task, stating that it wasn't clear what was expected of them. The Training Director turned this question around and asked them what they wanted from the school and how could Model X help them to further their own goals for the school? At this point, the meeting rapidly began to degenerate. Faculty again began to complain about how problematic it had been to get anything to work, how some faculty consistently undermined subcommittee efforts to institute change, and how they desperately wanted or needed to make something work. They felt that once they had accomplished something, they would feel more motivated to continue with the improvement project. This discussion took the whole morning. At this point we adjourned for lunch to return in the afternoon to make plans as to how we would proceed.

At the afternoon session, it was decided that faculty would focus on discipline as a school-wide project and to work on hallway transitions in particular. Three general rules were to be implemented: (1) maintaining uniform traffic flow with all west-bound traffic on one side of the hall and all eastbound traffic on the other; (2) quiet, expeditious hallway movement; and (3) respectful conduct during transitions. Staff also decided to have all the clocks in the school synchronized with the one in the main office. Model X personnel would not interfere or involve them-selves with staff at Professions for about one month while they were implementing this plan. We would check their progress in December, after they had achieved some successes on their own, and we would carry on from there.

The Director was to call a "town meeting" to inform the students of the plan. I went back to the school on November 7th to help the Director and two of the teachers plan the town meeting.

Vernese also returned once more to the new teacher's class, for she had promised her students that she would give them a lesson on a particular topic and wanted to keep her promise. The new teacher wasn't pleased but permitted Vernese to give the lesson. According to Vernese, the lesson went well, except for one female student who sat and cried during the entire session, ignored and uninterrupted by the new teacher. Afterwards, Vernese took the girl outside and asked her what was wrong. In response, the student related how much she hated the new teacher who evidenced little or no concern for them or for their feelings.

Toward the end of the month, an unfortunate incident occurred with the new teacher's class while they were in the Star Lab. As the Star Lab teacher was out, the new teacher and the lab's para-professional were in charge of the class. A disagreement broke out between the para-professional and a student, and the para was provoked to the point of throwing a chair at the student.

The whole time, the new teacher was said to have done nothing to nip the situation in the bud, or once the matter escalated, to intervene to stop it. Charges were being brought against the paraprofessional.

December 1996

Due to the holiday, December was a short month. On December 6th, I called the Director to get an update on the progress of the discipline committee's project. She informed me that while some progress had been made, a good number of faculty were not participating, which was seriously undermining morale and preventing any real success coming from this effort. I then called Jeanna to get more information. She said that the town meeting had gone well and initially the children had begun to follow the rules, i.e., walking on the right side of the hall and talking more quietly. However, things were slowly getting out of control again, because some teachers, mostly those at the end of the hall that housed the special education classes, did not come out of their rooms to supervise students who were violating the rules. Her own morale continued to be depressed by the Director's opposition toward Jeanna's friendship with the two new teachers. To make a public declaration of their friendship and of their unwillingness to have their social and professional relationships dictated by the Director, the three teachers had begun sitting together at meetings and demonstrably associating together as much as possible. Jeanna suspected that the Director was now trying to get rid of the new teacher, for which she partly blamed herself, as she had advised the new teacher to call in the school's UFT representative and to object to the presence of my PDA in her room. She was particularly hurt that her advice might have harmed the new teacher, as Jeanna stated, she now regarded herself more like a mother than a mentor to the new teacher. Jeanna said that, in many ways, the new teacher was much like herself as a beginning instructor, i.e., idealistic, wanting to try new methods and struggling to make her training work with this particular student population. Her anger about what was happening with the new teacher made her disinclined to go along with anything else that was happening in the school, in way of protest.

I returned to Professions on December 10th for the half-day of in-service workshops. I began the session by asking for a status report focusing on the implementation of the discipline plan. Faculty reported pretty much the same events as those related by Jeanna. The faculty asked how the Model would analyze the problems they were having. I responded that the staff obviously lacked unity of purpose and an initial consensus in regards to the plan. Special education teachers defended their lack of participation by stating that they could not leave their students to stand in the halls during transitions. There was some true discussion and I think this portion of the meeting went okay.

I next distributed a mini school assessment questionnaire prepared by the Model's Training Director, as a pilot. The questionnaire asked the school's staff to evaluate the status and operation of Model X at their school. (All Model X schools in New York were being requested to complete these forms.) The surveys took much longer than expected and faculty balked at the nature of many of the questions. Some teachers complained that the survey felt like a test, others said it required too much writing, while yet others simply said that they didn't understand what the questions were asking. A few teachers, but non-teaching staff in particular, left large portions of the survey blank.

As we had agreed at our last meeting the previous month, I asked staff to decide on whether they wanted to continue with Model X at Professions and, if so, to discuss the next steps. So much time had been spent with the questionnaire that little was left for this important discussion. No consensus could be arrived at in the time remaining and so it was decided to table this discussion until our next meeting. Staff indicated that things should be left as they were for now. We would pick up from this point after the holidays. *In toto*, the meeting had not gone badly and I felt like they might be coming back together. I was encouraged.

January 1997

The next two months were very difficult for me. My father is old and very ill. I had a few meetings with the Training Director and Mae to talk about Professions' implementation of the Model, but most of January was spent with my parents – particularly as the college was in recess for the winter break.

February 1997

In February my father's condition worsened and he died on the 18th. I could not think about Professions.

March 1997

In early March, I received a call from Jeanna. Having heard about my father, she offered her condolences. Routinely, I asked her how things at Professions were going, to which she replied "terribly." She said faculty morale was almost as bad as it had been before Model X was brought to the school. The building Principal was out on medical leave, and Professions' Director was temporarily functioning in her stead, necessitating her absence from the school's floor for much of the day. When she was there, the Director yelled and seemed a bit anxious, perhaps fearful of her students' performance on the upcoming standardized tests. According to Jeanna, things were rapidly falling apart. "I know your father just died," she said, "but people are feeling that you have abandoned us in our time of need." Jeanna added that the teachers felt there was no one to defend them from the Director or to act as an intermediary.

March 14th was the monthly meeting for Model X coaches; the topic was the instructional component. As many schools wanted to know more about this aspect of the program, all coaches were asked to bring faculty from their school to partici-pate. I invited the new mathematics teacher and one veteran. This session went particularly well and the two Professions teach-ers said they felt excited about the prospect of trying out some of the methods learned from the session with their classes.

A faculty in-service half-day was scheduled for March 18th. The coaches meeting on the instructional component had gone so well. The two Professions' teachers that attended were so excited that they had begun to develop an interdisciplinary lesson. Last year, I had tried to work with language arts and mathematics faculty on the topic, but there was little effort to translate the activities and ideas brought to them to their classrooms. I thought the half-day would be an excellent opportunity to revive and present the topic to the faculty. I also hoped that by refocusing their attention on classroom instruction (an activity area more within their individual control), to revitalize their program participation and to provide them with some success. Model X's Training Director and I began to plan for the half-day session, repeating some of the activities from the earlier workshop. For example, we planned to begin in the same way that we had at the monthly coaches' meeting, i.e., by asking faculty how they would treat all children as gifted and talented; reporting out; viewing a videotape; followed by a discussion. The session would end with the demonstration lesson put together by the two Professions teachers who had attended the session. They were a little anxious about the prospect of presenting before their colleagues, but were willing to do it.

In accordance with our plans, faculty began the meeting by listing how they would treat Professions' students as gifted and talented. During the reporting out, I listed the recommendations on the board. There was a noticeable difference between the list generated by the coaches and teachers at the earlier meeting and those generated by Professions' teachers. The latter list contained much more limited and less challenging activities. The differences were characteristic of their low expectations of students. When prompted to think up some more dynamic responses, one teacher stood up and objected to the activity saying it seemed artificial when other more pressing issues, related to school climate, were facing them. They objected to the Director's lengthy absences from the floor and offered, as evidence, her absence from the meeting. Although, admittedly, I had worked very hard to help them, they said that everything they tried was failing and they felt that things were nearly back to where they were before. Mrs. Di now objected to the activity, asserting that most of the instructors at the school didn't need help with instruction. Spreading her hands, she asked if anyone disagreed with this statement. No one responded, for to do so would be to admit that they were less than proficient in their skill!

As it was getting close to the end of the hour, I suggested that we allow the two teachers who had prepared a demonstration lesson to give it, as they had made a great effort to plan an interdisciplinary lesson and had already laid out the materials. I was stunned at what happened next. One teacher stood up and said, "I commend the two teachers for their effort, but I for one don't want to see it. They can present it at another time." She would rather continue the discussion. She asked if anyone else wanted to see the lesson and no one raised their hand. I could see the hurt and disappointment on the faces of the two teachers. I couldn't believe they would be so insensitive to two of their own. Although we were still talking, when the scheduled time arrived for the meeting to be over, faculty began to stand up and leave. The Training Director was livid. She couldn't believe things had become so bad in so short a period of time.

The following Friday we had a general faculty meeting to discuss what had occurred during the half-day session. Previously, I had called the Director to inform her of the events; she said she was not surprised. Just before the meeting, I visited the female teacher who was to have given the demonstration lesson. She was surprised and hurt at how she had been treated. She said she had enjoyed the morning at Hunter College and had become excited about the possibility of learning to teach better; she just wanted to share it. She didn't understand their response. She added that she had previously regarded as friends some of the very teachers that had declined to see her lesson, often eating lunch with them in their rooms and sharing preparation periods together. What had happened at the meeting made it increasingly difficult for her to continue to maintain this attitude. As a result, she was beginning to withdraw from them socially, she was more by herself.

At the start of the next general faculty meeting, I asked teachers, "Where is the school now and where would you like to go?" There was silence. I followed by asking them if they wanted to continue with the project. A lengthy discussion ensued in which staff enumerated their problems with the school. Among the list of misfortunes, they included their recent problems implementing the hall transition plan (citing as impediments a lack of effort and consensus among faculty to participate in the plan; the school's high teacher absentee rate; and the need to cover the duties of the absentees). This left them with precious little time or desire to do anything else, including the work required for the Model. Then, one faculty member offered that the staff was divided and morale was low. She continued by asking where I had been while things were falling apart during January and February. I responded that staff should have called their own meetings to discuss and resolve these challenges to their plans and asked how they intended to regain the spirit needed to move forward with the school improvement efforts. The Training Director added that Model X was not a panacea, but rather a vehicle to provide schools with an effective means of working together. I added that it was their, not our, responsibility to effect change in the school. They countered that many of the factors that interfered with their progress could not be readily addressed – nothing could be done. We responded that our intentions were good, but the staff did not have the Model's goals as a priority – there was no common purpose at Professions. The Training Director further informed them that Professions was not so different from many other schools she had seen across the country, many of which do succeed. The one basic difference, she commented, was that they embraced the process and took action, rather than talk all the time. I again raised the issue of unity of purpose. At this point Mrs. Di countered that there was unity of purpose in the school. She stated, however, that it was situation-specific. For example, when a situation arose, staff would rally to solve the problem. She said she liked Professions the way it was. Another teacher retorted that things were chaotic, divisive and getting worse. A third teacher said he felt problems at Professions were intractable and could not be changed. I asked staff why they thought their plans always fell apart. One staff member responded that unco-operative teachers were not confronted and made to conform or go along with the plan. I asked if they felt counter-productive behavior could be changed and if the Model X could help them do this or help them improve the school in general. There was silence. Consequently, I asked them to think about the school's relationship with the program again. For our next meeting on April 4th, they should be prepared to make some definite decisions.

After the meeting, I met with the Director and the school Principal to inform them of the meeting's outcomes. Upon hearing the events, the Principal bluntly remarked that she was surprised Model X had lasted this long at Professions. She felt that the teachers' attitudes were definitely hindering any progress the school might make. She added that while the teachers were capable, their first interest was not the children. If they would only change their attitudes and shift their focus to the children, then the school could make progress. The Training Director said that the district should be informed of the program's status at Professions. She wanted to stay at Professions, suggesting that if the general staff voted us out, she would be willing to work with individual faculty on the instructional component.

We made an appointment with the District Superintendent for the afternoon following the April 4th meeting.

April 1997

On April 4th, the Training Director and I arrived at Professions for the general faculty meeting. She opened the meeting by asking if faculty had a chance to meet to confer on the issue or if this was their first meeting since our last. They indicated that they had met informally and talked about the program's continuation. I asked what was the general consensus of the faculty, and what did they want to do. They replied that they wanted a vote, but that it should be a secret ballot.

Faculty began the voting process. At that point, the school's UFT representative abruptly entered the room. He said that the faculty had called him in to supervise the voting process. I replied that they had already completed writing down their votes, which just needed to be collected and tallied. He replied that no vote could take place without him; the vote had to be secret; and that all school administrators and Model X personnel had to leave the room during the process. He then, rather rudely, informed us that we had to leave the room immediately. The Director, the Training Director, Vernese and I exited to the hall. Waiting for the results, we were strangely quiet. After waiting for what seemed like an interminable length of time, the UFT representative stepped out of the classroom and asked us to come in.

As we stood in the front of the room near the door, the UFT representative informed us that the staff had voted 75 percent to 25 percent to opt out of the implementation for the remainder of the academic year. The Training Director was stunned and hurt. Initially she tried to talk to the teachers, stating that we were there to help ("empower") them and didn't understand their vote. Still holding open the door, she offered a willingness to continue to work on the instructional component with those individual teachers who so desired. At this point, a teacher objected to this idea, stating that none should be allowed to work with us, even if they wanted to do so on an individual basis. As she phrased it, "it would encourage them to feel better than those who do not seek your help; like they're more hard working." The Training Director asked how could they stop an individual from seeking our help. A second teacher supported the first, offering that as the majority wanted the program removed for the remainder of the year, everyone should go along with the vote. Seemingly, in way of consolation, a third teacher sought to reiterate that we were only being asked to leave for the remainder of the academic year, i.e., only two months, and conceivably, they might request that the Model return next year.

Distressed by all these actions, the Training Director asked the teachers why the program had been treated with such disregard. "This is a reciprocal relationship," she said, "we too have to be willing to go back into a school." At this point the meeting ended. In her office, the Director apologized for the faculty. The Training Director and I then went to the district office to inform the superintendent.

Echoing many of the same sentiments voiced by the Principal in the earlier meeting, the Superintendent said that she had expected the worst, and was surprised that the project had lasted as long as it had. She informed us that the District was having similar problems with several of its smaller schools, they seemed just not to be working – regardless of the type of assistance provided. The Superintendent encouraged the project to remain with the District and together with Mae, who had joined us, we discussed other district schools that might be more responsive to the change process.

That evening, I received calls from two Professions' teachers. Both apologized for how we had been treated by the UFT representative, saying I looked so disappointed at the outcome. They both wanted me to know that the vote had little to do with me or with the Model. Both said the faculty was so mad at the Director, they wanted to "punish" her by causing the failure of the project as she was very heavily invested in it. "We wanted to hurt her," they said. "It had nothing to do with you or Model X."

Discussion

In this third, and final, year of this reform project at Professions Institute many of the problems previously plaguing the school continued to undermine the project and the school's functioning as a whole.

Technical obstacles to implementation

Ex-school infrastructural obstacles to reform continuation

Schools in the midst of innovation clearly need a great deal of support from all levels of the system, particularly from their districts and their states. Moreover, accountability mechanisms at these levels also need to mirror and support the innovations made at the local school level, if these agencies are to signal to the schools their serious intent relative to these changes. For example, with the current reform wave, principals are told to share, if not cede, a portion of their power and decision-making responsibility to teams comprised of faculty and community members, while at the same time, they, not their SBMTs remain accountable for school and student performance. While Chicago is a noteworthy exception, in most other states and cities not only do upper-level administrators continue to function on the basis of a local site leader embodied in the principalship, but ever greater individual responsibility and consequences may be placed on principals (and superintendents) for poor school performance. Increasingly, where principals were once granted life-time tenure to their buildings, these security blankets are rapidly being withdrawn. In their stead, site-level administrators are finding short-term con-tracts, renewable contingent upon the improved academic per-formance of their schools, and a shortened grievance process sometimes from years to months. In light of the stepped-up demands and the higher cost for failure, many principals are understandably less inclined to relinquish control and share decision-making responsibility with stakeholder teams, strength-ening teachers' perception of the futility of these efforts.

This was clearly seen at Professions, as District and State-level administrators continued to interact with the school via trad-itional governance channels. While both the District Office and the State Education Department did a great deal to encourage and to problem-solve relative to the new governance structure at Professions, neither agency placed responsibility on the SDMT for work and products – save for the creation of a comprehensive education plan for the next academic year. Professions' SDMT did not have control over the school's budgets, although they could have opted to do so through a plan but did not. Efforts to get the team to address issues of student performance and instruc-tion were greeted with hostility. Despite these failures, external agencies did not clearly signal their dissatisfaction with the actions of the team.

This failure to transfer expectations and responsibility for critical governance and instructional matters to such teams clearly signaled to teachers that upper-level administrators at the city and state levels had few expectations for the continuation and permanence of these organizational structures. Faculty read these signals. Already overloaded by the presentism of their day, they regarded the work of these committees as just another temporary fad that would soon be gone. Why waste the time and effort? For example, at Professions only a very small cohort of voluntary faculty took an active role in the planning and writing of the school's comprehensive education plans for the next year. Most faculty did not even regard it as a document of any relevance to their daily functioning. And last but not least, these agencies' continued functioning with the Director along traditional lines sent a clear message to Professions faculty that she would be held responsible for the failure and discontinuation of the project.

Throwing the baby out with the bath water

Another way in which external agencies clearly signal to schools the lack of seriousness given to any innovation is not only the opportunistic adoption of faddish innovations, but their premature abandonment as well. When programs are popular, they ride on a wave of fairly uncritical support. At these times, the public, politicians, and high-level educational administrators seldom seek to explore these projects' underlying assumptions, the appropriateness of their unqualified extension to dissimilar populations, and challenges relative to scale and major upsizing requirements. Blind to these complicating factors, when once faddish programs fail to produce on promised outcomes in the characteristically unrealistic time frames allotted, they are unceremoniously and often unfairly abandoned. Conversely, in bureaucrats' search for opportunistic initiatives to ally public discontent with the system, existing programs that produce steady, but not stellar outcomes may be discarded to make way or provide funds for newer innovations. In both these instances, "the baby is thrown out with the bathwater."

In the precipitous rejection of innovations that may have produced more impressive results if introduced into an environment of earnest application and serious formative assessment, host schools often fail to explore vital questions that may significantly improve performance. Troubled schools that are engaging in innovation need to ask, for example, if differences in the subject populations affect the relative success of specific innovations within and between schools, and why this might occur. Based on this knowledge, school personnel further need to ask if these programs should be retained for particular populations and new programs sought for other students. Can these programs be adjusted to make them work more effectively? What are the costs of needed modifications, and are these steps worth taking? As Cuban (1990: 6) states:

> Reforms return because policymakers cave in to the politics of a problem rather than the problem itself. Reforms return because decision makers seldom seek reliable, correctly conducted evaluations of program effectiveness before putting a program into practice (Slavin, 1989). In short, were policymakers to pursue a rational course of analysis and decision making and, where fitting, use research and evaluation results properly, there would be no need for the same solutions to reenter the policy arena.

Most unfortunately, as the decision to retain programs is often not based on student outcomes or benefit to the school, innovations can and are discarded for less than moral reason. This occurred at Professions. First and foremost, Professions' faculty chose to focus almost exclusively on its governance component and to de-emphasize the instructional and the affective components of the innovation. This narrow selectivity of focus was earlier noted as a shortcoming of pure governance models. Minus the other two essential components, the school cannot be said to have given the model a true and valid test, and its rejection must, therefore, be regarded as premature. Moreover, events suggest that the model had the potential to improve the school, e.g., despite faculty's rejection of the formal instructional component, its infusion into subject area meetings may have contributed to student improvement on the critical standardized test. Nonetheless, factors totally unrelated to student performance motivated teachers to reject its continuation, e.g., animosities and antagonisms with the administration, work overload occasioned by the project, and a misguided use of union power. As a result, whatever potential the model had to improve the school and student performance had the effort continued was precluded. Such instances strongly support Fullan's (1999) and Sergiovanni's (1992) notion for the use of moral purpose and the greater good as guiding principles in the reform process.

When innovations are repeatedly discarded prematurely with little attention paid to their true value, the resulting waste of time, effort, resources and optimism can take a serious toll on all involved. It is no wonder that veteran teachers who have witnessed wave after wave of reforms come and go, perceive insight-fully that it is easier for the systems' administrative elite to legislate policy and to mandate the adoption of every new pedagogic fad than to commit themselves to school and student improvement. Faculty will, thus, hold their enthusiasm and effort in abeyance, prophetically predicting that "this too will pass."

Cultural obstacles to reform continuation

Obstacles to reforming teacher isolationism

Deconstructing the physical and emotional barriers that prevent teachers from coming together amongst themselves and with school administrations is integral to current efforts at altering the culture of the school. Current reform efforts urge teachers to adopt attitudes conducive to group problem solving, to join SBMTs and to engage in mutual professional development efforts through collaboration. However, as Sarason (1990) notes, there is nothing automatic about this process, and in fact, it is very difficult to bring about these ends. Superficially changing organ-ization of staff is not the same as changing their norms, habits, skills and beliefs (Fullan, 1991; 1993). As discussed in Chapter 3, the walls isolating teachers in their classrooms may be regarded as kindly, perceived as protective barriers safeguarding scarce resources, shielding teachers from the judgmental eyes of col-leagues and superiors, and providing a niche where they may safely experiment and rule over their little domains.

At Professions, new teachers were quickly socialized to the system's isolationist culture and fiercely defended their rights in this regard. Veteran faculty resented the Director's use of mentors from outside of the mini school to orient new staff members. Jeanna, in fact, complained and sought out two of the new teachers to orient them to the school's culture. The new Language Arts teacher was given a crash course on the school's individualistic, sink or swim culture, and the view that expertise in teaching is something possessed or acquired on one's own, rather than developed collaboratively. Thus, when the project's coach sought to place a sabbatical teacher in the new teacher's classroom to provide assistance and advice, the new teacher was advised to complain to the union on the grounds of harassment. When she complied, precipitating union concern, a clear message was sent to both the project's staff and local school administrators that regardless of teacher need, maintenance of the school's isolationist culture took priority and would be defended at all costs.

The school culture at Professions also discouraged teachers from seeking additional professional development where it threatened the existing pecking order by allowing some staff members to be viewed as "more willing" than others to work and improve their skills. Thus, when one veteran teacher and a new teacher returned to school enthusiastic about new collaborative instructional skills they had acquired under the aegis of the innovation and sought to share this knowledge with the staff, they violated the school's culture by standing out and daring to be different. The consequences were swift and devastating. When they sought to share their new knowledge with staff back at Professions by presenting a integrated lesson at one of the weekly staff meetings, staff voted not to witness the lesson! To prevent any possibility of a future recurrence, "so that teachers would not feel that they were better than anybody else," leaders of the conservative faction successfully moved to forbid other faculty from attending future workshops – after the school had voted to discontinue the project.

For individuals who have come to value these aspects of school culture, neither providing meeting time, nor organizing joint problem-solving sessions are any guarantee that once brought together, teachers will embrace either in spirit or in action the collegiality that is the goal of these reform efforts. Nor can it be assumed that teachers know how to work together in ways likely to produce more engaging curriculum and improved student performance (Wehlage et al., 1992: 76). Rather than creating a true collaborative spirit, on the order of the effective schools model, such "contrived collegial" situations (Hargreaves, 1997) typically produce no more than a superficial semblance of this ideal. While simulating the outward forms of collaboration, i.e., the organizational structures that typically accompany the products of true school reculturation, forced decision-making "communities" seldom achieve the spirit of true interdependence

(Grimmet and Crehan, 1992). Hargreaves (1997) characterizes such contrived situations as:

- *administratively regulated*: they do not evolve from teachers' own initiative but are an administrative imposition that requires teachers to meet and work together;
- *compulsory*: they make working together a matter of compulsion as in mandatory team teaching, peer coaching or collaborative planning;
- *implementation oriented*: they require or "persuade" teachers to work together so as to implement other people's mandates.

Some assert that such communities can do harm by gratuitously taking teachers away from valuable activities with students, and contrary to popular opinion, can reduce innovation and imaginative solutions to school problems when "groupthink" carries the day (Fullan, 1993: 33). Such "collaborative pretenses" enable teachers to give surface support simultaneous with deep-seated rejection of educational change. Worst of all, Hargreaves (1997) asserts, by making collaboration into an administrative device, contrived collegiality can paradoxically suppress teachers' desires to collaborate and improve among themselves (ibid.: 73–74). Thus, despite teachers' avowals of the value of their relationships with colleagues, true collegiality and the deconstruction of the emotional walls separating classrooms may not be goals that are highly valued at many local sites. Where such reform efforts are undertaken at schools, like Professions, with entrenched isolationist cultures, both reactive (protective) and proactive (efforts to influence others) defense mechanisms (Blase and Anderson, 1995) may be brought to bear to maintain the status quo. Thus, contrary to the goal of advancing unity, community and trust, in forcing collegiality, teachers may be thrust into a more antagonistic position with their colleagues as they try to reassert cultural norms.

Obstacles to reculturalization by workshops

Staff development workshops, long used as the primary vehicle through which implementers are trained in program specifics, have been extended to produce attitudinal change as well. Increasingly, however, their effectiveness in both teaching project specifics and in the reculturation process is being questioned.

According to Schein (1992: 22), to unlearn counter-productive beliefs and actions, and to acquire new ways of acting, espousing and believing, require us to resurrect, re-examine, and possibly to alter some of the more stable portions of our cognitive structures. Such activities necessitate "frame breaking," i.e., altering long-held and habitual patterns of action and ways of knowing that have become second nature. Breaking with the old is difficult, because the re-examination of basic assumptions temporarily destabilizes one's cognitive and interpersonal worlds, releasing large quantities of anxiety (ibid.). As indicated above, this can be a massive process, for it involves altering a network of interrelated belief systems, the practices and interpersonal relationships built upon them, in fact, the very nature and functioning of all group members within that culture.

Change of such enormity cannot be done through workshops. Research shows that as a technique, workshops have been of relatively little success in attitude change. Characteristically, the good feelings immediately engendered in team-building sessions are short-lived. Similarly, studies on the effectiveness of pre-service training in multicultural education have found that efforts to change trainees' stereotypic attitudes and behavior had little or no effect (Grant and Tate, 1995). A similar lack of significant results were obtained by Sleeter (1993) and Haberman and Post (1992), leading Sleeter to conclude that, in general, (White) students and teachers used their experiences and training in multicultural education selectively to support their initial preconceptions, and that teacher education in this area tended to reinforce rather than reconstruct how these individuals view children of color. In explanation, Schein (1992) states that rather than tolerating such anxiety levels, we tend to want to perceive the events around us as congruent with our assumptions, even if that means distorting, denying, projecting, or in other ways falsifying to ourselves what may be going on.

Attitudinal change can be achieved, but it is difficult. According to Pink (1989: 22–24), schools need additional critical supports and resources on the order of university presence at the early stages, external conferences, visits to other sites, in-service training and materials, as well as an awareness of the need for improvement and a mechanism to facilitate content implementation in their classrooms. In addition, typical barriers to the learning process (e.g., district interference, lack of sustained central office support, underfunding, high teacher turnover, work overload, and a lack of awareness of the limitations of teacher and school administrator knowledge about how to implement the project – among others) must be minimal. However, even when many of the additional supports are present and barriers are few, the fragile network can deconstruct and the traditional culture of the school can tenaciously reassert itself. Thus, consistent with Sirotnik (1990: 102), we have concluded that:

> conflict is not something that can be eliminated through sensitivity training and the other organizational development devices that flourished during the application phases of human relations theory. Differences in economic structure and power positions cannot be communicated away . . . The idea of "communication" in organizational development terms, of course, bears little resemblance to the idea of "communicative competence" in the critical-dialectical tradition. In the former, people are "trained" to relate to one another, to become conscious of their own hang-ups, and to finds ways of diminishing (if not eliminating) conflict with the existing parameters of the organization. In the latter, people continually struggle not only with interpersonal relations but with the very structures and conditions within which they work – conflicts in values and human interest are the very substance of the discourse. From the human relations perspective, then, schools would be more like centers of therapy than centers of change.

In combination, how these various features of institutional practice and culture affect commitment to school innovation and, ultimately, to student achievement will vary from school to school. Whatever the stance of the teachers in a school, the balance of young and old, supporters and detractors is crucial. As younger teachers often take their cues from veteran teachers, support from the latter group, at least to some degree, is crucial in shifting the balance in favor of a proposed implementation. If there is one cardinal rule of change in human condition, it is that you cannot make people change. You cannot force them to think differently or compel them to adopt new ways, i.e., skills, creative thinking, and committed action (McLaughlin, 1990).

This discussion in no way is intended to indict administrators or teachers as a group. In our work, we have found many new as well as veteran teachers and principals who were ardent supporters of and advocates for change. These individuals were hopeful and, most often, placed children first. What we reported were efforts in one very troubled school. The variations among schools in their culture and in their ability to embrace improvement efforts have been characterized by Hopkins, Ainscow and West (1994), adapting the work of Rosenholtz (1989), as follows:

- *Stuck schools* are often failing schools. Conditions are poor, teaching is an isolated activity, and a sense of mediocrity and powerlessness pervades. Expectations from all around are very low, and external conditions are blamed for the situation. One typically hears phrases like, "There's not much we can do with these kids," "We've tried change before, but it doesn't work." As the school is buffeted by the winds of change, it responds capriciously if at all, and in many ways these schools may be regarded as being inactive.

- *Wandering schools* have experienced and are experiencing too much innovation. These schools have all the appearance, but little of the reality, of change, and staff quickly become exhausted and fragmented. Overall, there is movement going on but it lacks a settled route or a clear destination. Sometimes this involves a lack of agreement about purpose, with groups or individuals pursuing their own aims.

- *Promenading schools* often seem to be living on their past achievements, which may well have been impressive. They do not move fast or far, and when they do, this may be for display rather than exercise. Promenading schools are often traditional schools with a stable staff that have enjoyed success in more stable times but are currently reluctant to change. One often hears from staff that they "are pretty pleased with the way thing are . . . there is no real reason to change." These are in fact very difficult schools to change.

- *The moving school* is an ideal type of "active" school which has achieved a healthy blend of change and stability, and balanced development and maintenance. Internally the school is relatively calm as it adapts successfully to an often rapidly changing environment, its culture and traditions, and the staff are often heard to say that "we try to keep abreast of developments and everything under review."

In conclusion, as this part reveals, by their very nature, most large institutions are conservative, preferring long-term stability and predictability over quixotic movement. The system of public schooling is true to this mold. Inevitable as change can be, equally as predictable are the many forces that may interfere, block or simply retard its movement when change efforts present themselves at the schoolhouse doors. At this point, traditional but derelict patterns for adopting reforms, hostile rules and regulations, and counter-productive beliefs and assumptions will surface to become almost insurmountable obstacles to school improvement. While these adaptive responses allow the schools to fulfill their mission in the midst of near constant demands for change, innovations remain on borrowed time, such that it is easier to go back than to go forward. How school personnel perceive and come to terms with the reality of change in the context of their daily lives is crucial (Fullan, 1982: 42–46; Johnson, 1990: 172, 201; Tipton, 1988: 5). Ultimately, to get the needed gains for kids, we adults must expect and endure the pain that comes with ambitious rethinking and redesign of schools. To pretend that serious restructuring can be done without honest confrontation is a cruel illusion (Sizer, 1991: 34). Innovations in schools are unlikely to be of a very radical kind unless they produce fundamental changes in the ways in which educators perceive their tasks, think about children and do their work.

Study Questions

1. How did the changes in faculty staffing affect the implementation? What additional difficulties were presented by these changes that were not present the previous year?

2. Over the three years of Model X's implementation, how, if at all, have the faculty's attitudes toward empowerment changed? Give an example of faculty behavior to support your response.

3. In your opinion, what were the critical turning points in Model X's implementation where things could have gone differently? What forces prevented or interfered with their positive outcomes? How might these forces have been changed or addressed?

4. In your opinion, what, in general, were the major factors leading to the demise of Model X at Professions Institute? Which of these factors could have been controlled and how? Which could not have been controlled or altered and why?

5. In your opinion, what other combination of improvement programs might have been more effective with Professions Institute? Explain.

6. For each of the stakeholder groups listed below, explain their influence on the reform implementation process and give supporting evidence:
   (a) State Department of Education
   (b) City Board of Education
   (c) City's teachers' union
   (d) Philanthropic foundations
   (e) Parents

7. Where in this school's improvement efforts do you see examples of conflicting goals and practices?

8. What counter-productive attitudes among administration and faculty were in evidence in this reform implementation?

9. Based on this case study, in what ways have you changed your thinking about the transformational and chaos models of school reform? Which do you think is more applicable and why?

10. In your opinion, could this reform implementation have been saved? Explain how or why not.

11. How would you change school reform to facilitate a more efficacious process?

References

Blasé, J. and Anderson, L. (1995) *The Micropolitics of Educational Leadership: From Control to Empowerment*. New York: Teachers College Press.

Cuban, L. (1990) Reforming again, again, and again. *Educational Researcher*, January, pp. 3–13.

Donahoe, T. (1993). Finding the way: structure, time and culture in school improvement. *Phi Delta Kappan*, vol. 75, December, pp. 298–305.

Fullan, M. (1982). *The Meaning of Educational Change*. New York: Teachers College Press.

Fullan, M., with Stiegelbauer, S. (1991). *The New Meaning of Educational Change*. 2nd edn. New York: Teachers College Press, Columbia University.

Fullan, M. (1993) *Change Forces: Probing the Depth of Educational Reform*. London: Falmer Press.

Fullan, M. (1999) *Change Forces: The Sequel*. London: Allen Lane.

Grant, C. A. and Tate, W. F. (1995) Multicultural education through the lens of the multicultural education research literature. In J. Banks and C. M. Banks (eds) *Handbook of Research on Multicultural Education*. New York: Macmillan Publishing, pp. 145–166.

Grimmet, P. P. and Crehan, E. P. (1992) The nature of collegiality in teacher development. In M. Fullan and A. Hargreaves (eds) *Teacher Development and Educational Change*. London: Falmer Press, pp. 56–85.

Haberman, A. and Post, J. (1992) Does direct experience change education students' perceptions of low income minority children? *The Midwestern Educational Researcher*, vol. 5, no. 2, pp. 29–31.

Hargreaves, A. (1989) Educational policy and educational change: a local perspective. In A. Hargreaves and D. Reynolds (eds) *Educational Policies: Controversies and Critiques*. Lewes: Falmer Press, pp. 213–217.

Hargreaves, A. (1997) Cultures of teaching and educational change. In M. Fullan (ed.) *The Challenge of School Change*. Arlington Hts., ILL: Skylight.

Hopkins, D. Ainscow, M. and West, M. (1994) *School Improvement in an Era of Change*. London: Cassell.

Johnson, S. M. (1990) Redesigning teachers' work. In R. F. Elmore and Associates (eds) *Restructuring Schools: The Next Generation of Educational Reform*. San Francisco: Jossey-Bass, pp. 125–151.

McLaughlin, M. (1990) The RAND change agent study revisited. *Educational Researcher*, vol. 5. pp. 11–16.

Pink, W. T. (1989) Effective staff development for urban school improvement. Paper presented at American Educational Research Association Annual Meeting.

Rosenholtz, S. J. (1989) *Teachers' Workplace: The Social Organization of Schools*. White Plains: Longman Inc.

Sarason, S. B. (1990) *The Predictable Failure of School Reform*. San Francisco: Jossey-Bass.

Schein, E. H. (1992) *Organizational Culture and Leadership*. 2nd edn. San Francisco: Jossey-Bass.

Sergiovanni, T. (1992) *Moral Leadership*. San Francisco: Jossey-Bass.

Sirotnik, K. (1990) Society, schooling teaching and preparing to teach. In J. Goodlad, R. Soder, and K. Sirotnik (eds) *The Moral Dimensions of Teaching*. San Francisco: Jossey-Bass, pp. 296–327.

Sizer, T. (1991) No pain, no gain. *Educational Leadership*, May, pp. 32–34.

Slavin, R. E. (1989) Riding the pendulum of educational change. *Phi Delta Kappan*, vol. 70, no. 10, pp. 752–758.

Sleeter, C. (1993) How White teachers construct race. In C. McCarthy and W. Crichlow (eds) *Race, Identity, and Representation in Education*. London: Routledge, pp. 157–171.

Tipton, F. (1988) Educational organizations as workplaces. In J. Ozga (ed.) *Schoolwork: Approaches to the Labor Processes of Teaching*. Milton Keynes: Open University Press.

West, P. (1994) Efficacy of U.S. aid for science, math questioned. *Education Week*, vol. 14, no. 14, p. 1.

Part IV

Reforming School Reform

In previous Parts, we attempted a number of things, i.e., to set the context for the current debate on school reform, to lay out the major proposals and realities of the reform process, and to illustrate the dynamic interaction of various components of reform through a longitudinal case study of a real school improvement effort. To some readers, this portrait may seem a little bleak, with too many competing forces, institutional obstacles, and power struggles over issues other than student learning. While these challenges are very real and great, the situation is not without hope.

In this last Part, we combine these realities with the hope of school reform in the twenty-first century, and make recommendations as to how traditional modes of school reform may be changed. We think Jane David's (1990) conceptualization of the schools as at the center of an interlocking jigsaw puzzle is very apt. Surrounding the schools are inter-linked, ever widening concentric circles consisting of the institutions, agencies and groups of individuals needed to support the schools and their reform efforts. In this Part, we start at the center and move outward to the need for public and societal support. Thus, Chapter 9 addresses changing school reform at the level of the local school. We specifically discuss transformational change in the school's cultural artifacts and beliefs from the lessons we have learned. From this perspective, we also discuss how the reform process might be adjusted. In Chapter 10 we discuss the ways in which the educators, i.e., teachers and school administrators, might be better prepared for the challenges ahead. And in Chapter 11, we discuss how systemic and governmental agencies, at the district, state and federal levels, as well as parents and society as a whole are needed to scaffold the schools during this change process. As we hope to show, it takes minimally a village, but optimally a nation to raise a child.

Reference

David, J. L. (1990) Restructuring in progress: lessons from pioneering districts. In R. F. Elmore and Associates (eds) *Restructuring Schools: The Next Generation of Educational Reform*. San Francisco: Jossey-Bass, pp. 209–250.

9

Transforming Schools

The history of public schooling in the United States might well be characterized as change in the midst of stability. While the nation and the times have advanced, the basic goals for public schooling, and many of its most fundamental structures have changed little. For example, changes in immigration and migration patterns, our conceptions of human rights, the nature of the family, and in the amount and types of necessarily transmittable information have changed significantly since the time of our founding fathers and put pressures on the institution of schooling to adapt. Notwithstanding, the public still looks to its educational system to meet long-held expectations, e.g., to remedy societal ills, to be the vehicle of upward mobility, to identify, sort, and prepare our youths for their future lives as workers and citizens, in essence, to be the hope of the nation (Ravitch, 1994: 124–127).

Struggling to fulfill its historical goals and function in a rapidly moving world, the schools have become deluged with tasks, hidden agenda and missions, and run the risk of losing their way. Thus:

1. Schools are being asked to provide the "family" network that may no longer exist in the home or in the community due to poverty, un- and under-employment, dislocation, and the necessity for two income families.
2. They are being blamed for and mandated to prepare students that previously would have dropped out and been absorbed by a factory economy to levels of academic proficiency previously unknown to the system.
3. Consistent with "one stop shopping," schools are being urged to become the hub linking a range of social services including education, health, employment and recreation.

This transformation would have them house social service referral and treatment centers, as well as off-site clinics for both students and their families.

4. Based on the knowledge that parental involvement in schools facilitates student success, schools are being mandated to involve parents in governance and decision-making capacities, in addition to their traditional school roles as fund raisers and auxiliary supports.

5. Plagued by adolescent drug use, teenage pregnancy, and a rise in other forms of general adolescent anomy, schools are being asked to add preventive education on sex, AIDS, drug abuse, child abuse, and violence to their curriculum – topics formerly handled by the family or church – and mandated to become student and family watchdogs in these regards.

6. And based on the nation's burgeoning immigrant and ethnic minority populations, schools are being implored to facilitate students' positive ethnic awareness and the maintenance of their mother tongues, at the same time mandated to advance their knowledge of English and other academic studies sufficient to reap the rewards of their adopted land.

If the schools are to respond to these and other pressures, are old conceptualizations of their mission still viable or ought they be revisited? Should there be a reprioritization of the functionalist ideals of the system's founding fathers, as some conflict, and others may no longer be viable? Who should decide and at what level should this debate take place?

In this chapter we explore both the debate and the realities of the goals of public schooling, as well as make some recommendations as to how these realities can be shaped to ensure that all children benefit and the current objectives of second-order change be advanced. Before reading this chapter, the reader is asked to answer the following framing questions:

1. If the mission or goals of public schooling are to be revised, at what level should this discussion take place and why? What factors, do you feel, are most important to consider?

2. What is or should be the role of national and state standards in terms of the mission of public schooling?

3. What key factors would most likely ensure that the nation's neediest children are fairly served?

Purpose and Goals in Public Education

Change and consensus in the schooling process

A very public debate currently rages on what should be and who should formulate the goals and objectives of public education, albeit largely confined to scholars and the elites of various interest groups. On the one hand, some maintain that party and interest group politics precludes consensus, and that agreement can never be or is far from being achieved (e.g., Cohen, 1990; House, 1998). This implies that there is still some choice in whether goals for public schools and standards for learning will be set, as well as at what level the substance of these standards will be decided. Our nation's long history of interest group and party politics encourages this perception, as well as the view that the various groups do not want the same things from schools. Consequently, scholars and many educators continue to rile at the setting of standards and the increased use of standardized tests as society's gatekeepers (e.g., Goodman, 1994).

On the other hand, there are those, like Tye (2000), who assert there is consensus. Working on this assumption, Republican President Bush initiated and Democratic President Clinton later signed into law Goals 2000 (see Box 9.1), legislation establishing a set of national education goals to move the country toward a national consensus. Shortly thereafter, state governors in collaboration with business leaders (reminiscent of the Administrative Progressives of the early 1900s) further advanced the centralization of public schooling by setting more specific educational objectives in the form of state and performance standards. At the National Education Summit of 1996, they also endorsed the use of standardized testing as a viable means to improve the schools. They thus declared:

> We believe that efforts to set clear, common state and/or community-based academic standards for students in a given school district or state are necessary to improve students' performance . . . We believe that setting clear academic standards, benchmarking these standards to the highest levels and accurately assessing student performance is a state, or in some cases a local, responsibility, depending on the traditions of a state. We do not call for a set of mandatory, federally prescribed standards but welcome the savings and

Box 9.1

The National Goals of P. L.103–227:
Goals 2000 (1994)

1. By the year 2000, all children in America will start school ready to learn.

2. By the year 2000, the high school graduation rate will increase to at least 90 percent.

3. By the year 2000, all students will leave grades 4, 8, and 12 having demonstrated competency over challenging subject matter including English, mathematics, science, foreign languages, civics and government, economics, arts, history, and geography, and every school in America will ensure that all students learn to use their minds well, so they may be prepared for responsible citizenship, further learning, and productive employment in our Nation's modern economy.

4. By the year 2000, the Nation's teaching force will have access to programs for the continued improvement of their professional skills and the opportunity to acquire the knowledge and skills needed to instruct and prepare all American students for the next century.

5. By the year 2000, US students will be first in the world in mathematics and science achievement.

6. By the year 2000, every adult American will be literate and will possess the knowledge and skills necessary to compete in a global economy and exercise the rights and responsibilities of citizenship.

7. By the year 2000, every school in the United States will be free of drugs, violence, and the unauthorized presence of firearms and alcohol and will offer a disciplined environment conducive to learning.

8. By the year 2000, every school will promote partnerships that will increase parental involvement and participation in promoting the social, emotional, and academic growth of children.

other benefits offered by cooperation between states and school districts and the opportunities provided by a national clearinghouse of effective practices to improve achievement. But in whatever way is chosen, standards must be in place in all of our schools and must be in place quickly. (*American Educator*, 1996: 13)

Standards have come and are here to stay – at least temporarily, and they now constitute the central element in governmental agendas for currently reforming public schools.

The role of standards in postmodern society

Despite continued objection to their institution, indications are that a growing number of educators and the public feel that standards have a viable role in reforming public schools and are receiving them with varying degrees of enthusiasm. For example, the American Federation of Teachers (AFT), in the Spring of 1996, devoted an entire issue of their journal, *American Educator*, in support of standards. In several articles, including that of the editor, standards were advanced as a valid means to address the "disconnects" and the "enormous inequities of the current system" (1996: 7). In that same issue, the findings of two national surveys of parents and teachers were reported. One found that 82 percent of the general public, 87 percent of White parents and 92 percent of African-American parents wanted clear guidelines on what their children should learn and their teachers should teach (ibid.: 17). The other survey found that teachers favored standards as a means to address academic discontinuity caused by a highly mobile student body (53 percent), as well as constitute a means to reduce disruption in schools caused by educational fads (84 percent) (ibid.: 18–21). And in 1994, the annual Gallup Polls on education indicated that 83 percent of the nation's population surveyed responded that the establishment of a basic curriculum of subject matter or program for courses was important (Elam *et al.*, 1994).

Coupled with their endorsement of content and performance standards, the AFT also endorsed the use of state administered standardized assessment. They reasoned that "because these exams, and the rewards they elicit, will be tied to the classroom curriculum, students will know that they must study hard – not only in the year they take the exam but also in the grades leading up to that point" (*American Educator*, 1996: 24).

With such strong endorsements from both parents and within educational institutions, standards are becoming the centerpiece of the public's and the school's agenda for reform. Yet despite many educators' belief that the standards movement has the potential to greatly assist in reforming the public schools, they are only part of the answer. It is important to realize that standards are not synonymous with second-order change and will not necessarily bring these changes about. For example, the institution of standards will not automatically lead to the deconstruction of the psychological walls separating teachers, invert or flatten the schools' hierarchical structure, nor alter teachers' beliefs in all students' ability to learn. Their primary benefit is to help policymakers and school-based personnel clarify their purposes and set the direction in which schools and instruction should move. Standards prescribe the "what" of instruction; they do not prescribe the process of how schools should get there. For their optimum realization, second-order changes are needed as the means for schools to attain the standards. Thus, to bring about the desired levels of literacy, higher order thinking, and problem-solving skills sought by governmental authorities, child-centered instruction and joint teacher planning are by far the best means to these ends.

Ideally, schools and local agencies should be allowed to find the most effective ways of achieving these ends, however, in the real world, time is a factor and educational organizations differ markedly in their capacities and motivation to develop the most advantageous processes to ensure equity and excellence for all children.

Achieving School Success

For all schools and students to achieve the ends laid out in our national, state, or local standards a number of pieces must be put into place consistent with the current restructuring effort. In this section we offer some recommendations and guidelines on how to facilitate the creation of some of the most significant second order changes. We start this section with a discussion of the beliefs and assumptions that have traditionally maintained and condoned these outcomes. As stated throughout this text, attitudinal change cannot be mandated, but some timely comments are, nonetheless, offered to set a tone and provide a context for the recommendations that follow. We then move to the artifactual level, discussing the school's organization and instruction. In the last section of this chapter, we discuss how to facilitate the school change process, in general. The last two chapters of this book continue this discussion.

Placing children first

Probably the most significant lesson to be learned from the longitudinal case study of reform efforts at Professions Institute is the need to place students first – a motive at times lost amidst the presentism of teachers' daily lives. Where children are placed first, everyone involved with the schooling process has as their guiding concern the educational advancement of all the school's students. Sergiovanni (1994) calls this the development of a "community of mind," which he defines as the establishment of a core value that is so significant that it permeates every aspect of the organization. In schools where this exists, every decision that is made reflects stakeholders' commitment to this principle, coupled with a firm belief that all children can learn to high levels of proficiency.

If, as has been claimed by American politicians, that to ensure America's continued world pre-eminence and high standard of living, all children must be educated to levels of excellence, then the adoption of this attitude and this belief is essential. Currently, those students traditionally written off as "at risk" of poor academic performance or dropping out altogether – those primarily drawn from poor and minority backgrounds – represent not only an increasingly large share of the school population but of the future workforce as well. While the speculated date varies, it is assumed that sometime within the first half of this century, ethnic "minorities" will become the "majority" (Neiser, 2000; Pallas et al., 1989). This is already the case for public school systems in many of our largest states and cities (e.g., California, Texas, Arizona, New York, and Chicago) (Reyes et al., 1999). The challenge, therefore, is to teach successfully all children, including the burgeoning numbers of previously labeled "at-risk" students, whom the system has historically failed to educate (Grubb, 1995: 4).

If we are ever to achieve these ends, schools, teachers and the larger society, can no longer use poverty, ethnicity, and disability as reasons for under-educating these students nor continue to turn a blind eye to their failure. Familial circumstance would have to cease to be perceived as an excuse for failure, but rather viewed as an obstacle that must be overcome. Accomplishing this task may be difficult, but it is not novel or unheard of – as attested to by the effective schools literature, and the work of Jaime Escalante, Marva Collins and Kay Tolliver.

To the extent that educators at the local level continue to maintain Darwinistic conceptions is the extent to which they will fail to motivate low achieving students in general, and ethnic minority students in particular. For, as previously noted, where teachers lower academic demands and reward students for minimal effort, based on beliefs of their inability to learn or as a means to protect their self-esteem and increase school graduation rates, these actions only further serve to signal these beliefs to students – setting the stage for less effort and later failure on students' part (Bempechat, 1998; Tomlinson, 1992). As the criterion for judging school success increasingly becomes dependent on the academic performance of all its students, continued adherence to these beliefs can only undermine reform efforts to motivate poorly performing students. Although individuals cannot be forced to change their beliefs, state and local authorities can require that teachers give all students more rigorous work. Hopefully, in problem-solving efforts to meet these standards, and in demanding and helping all students achieve these ends, educators themselves will see the necessity of changing their beliefs.

Facilitating change at the artifactual level

To bring about these ends, the artifacts of the schooling process that maintain and support the current outcomes of public schooling must also be changed. The artifactual supports most frequently targeted by the current restructuring effort are the school's governance structures, the organization of students and its pedagogical practices. Below we discuss how their change might best be effected, based on our own and others' work in the field.

School organization

The current organization of schools and public schooling is, as we have repeatedly stated, a reflection of the vision of its founding fathers. If we are now to achieve a different set of ends, a number of organizational changes are strongly recommended. The organizational changes currently proposed by second wave reform are a good place to start, although all are not equally effective in attaining excellence with equity.

New governance structures As a means to encourage greater ownership of the schooling process and its outcomes, state and local policy-makers are increasingly shifting authority for the direct governance of schools to school councils or SBM/SDMTs. While the research finds little direct connection between the establishment of these bodies and discussions of, or changes in, instruction and student outcomes, ways to facilitate their more effective functioning have been identified.

Despite legislation outlining the composition and responsibilities of SBM/SDMTs and councils, there is still a great deal of gray area. It still is not always clear who should do what at what level. Schools instituting SBM/SDMTs should, therefore, be prepared to address issues of expertise, and confusion and dissension over authority. It is, therefore, important that early on, district representatives, principals and team members work together on delineating aegis over particular tasks and responsibilities. Holmes (1993) suggests that these deliberations consider:

- Which decisions the principal or staff members can make without approval of the council and which should be reviewed and approved by the council.
- What information should be provided to the council on a periodic basis.
- Which decisions having to do with day-to-day operations of the school should be made by the council.
- Who sets the agenda for council meetings, and how members of the school staff can place items on the agenda.
- How questions and complaints from parents and community residents will be handled.

To this list we would add how conflicts among council members and between the council and the school administration will be handled.

Infinitely more complex than these matters of procedure are problems and decisions faced by these teams related to instruction and learning, staff hiring, the inquiry process, familial distress, and group management, for example. While all politics may be local, sometimes a larger perspective and an in-depth knowledge of issues and ramifications are needed. To make wise and timely decisions in these regards, these bodies need knowledge and expertise of a fairly sophisticated order. Too often, however, when these groups are established, inadequate attention may be given to matters of the types of short- and long-term training needed to fulfill their new functions successfully (Tye, 1992). Fortunately, help is often near at hand in the potential for partnerships between local schools or school districts and the faculties of neighboring colleges and schools of education. These faculties can serve as non-voting team members, consultants, or coaches, providing expertise to various schools' and districts' governance and decision-making bodies on a range of subject matters including research on new practices, the inquiry process, valid data collection techniques, data interpretation and the sociological and psychological implications of particular actions.

Moreover, as these bodies increasingly assume decision-making responsibility for matters related to instruction and the outcomes of student education, it is incongruous for LEAs to continue to hold principals solely responsible for the achievement of students (Hallinger and Hausman, 1994). Such incongruities exacerbate conflicts within schools and retard the development of collaborative and supportive relationships between administrators and their faculties. The achievement of content and performance standards must be perceived and treated by local and state officials, as well as by the schools, as a group effort. Thus, when monitoring agencies have concerns with schools regarding capacity and problem-solving ability, they must be taken to and discussed directly with these teams. Such actions not only signal respect and legitimacy for these teams, they also convey messages about their necessary topical focus and the seriousness these agencies place on these teams successfully solving these problems.

Restructuring time As shown in Chapter 5, time is a key ingredient vital to the success of any school improvement effort. Its provision is essential for governance deliberations, the disaggregation of data, training and mentoring, the inquiry process, the diagnosis of students' needs, and the development of individualized and/or group educational plans for students. As greater governance responsibilities are placed on local school faculty, more time for collaborative deliberation will be needed. This cannot be done well, or even satisfactorily, in the context of the current school day and yearly calendar. The USA is no longer a largely rural nation where children must be home to do evening chores during the academic year and to harvest crops during the summer. Nonetheless, our school calendar continues to be based on the needs of an agrarian economy. As a nation, we continue to cram governance and school improvement tasks into a 9–3 o'clock workday, nudging out valuable instructional time. A clear example comes from New York City, where teachers are now given one day a month for professional development. This is an admirable acknowledgement of the time needed for professional development in fulfilling mandates and voluntary school reforms, but it comes at the expense of pupil instruction.

We see no other choice but that the workday and year be extended, as there just is not enough time otherwise. Students need the entire 9 to 3 o'clock instructional day for just that – instruction. And students who are behind or with special needs may require even more time for instruction each day. Vacations need to be shortened, as research shows that children lose academic ground in the long interim.

Similarly, teachers and other school personnel need time dedicated solely for conferencing, instructional planning, and other forms of professional development. According to the National Commission on Teaching and America's Future (1996: 14):

> Most U.S. teachers have only three to five hours each week for planning. This leaves them with almost no regular time to consult together or learn about new teaching strategies, unlike their peers in many European and Asian countries where teachers spend between 15 to 20 hours per week working jointly on refining lessons, coaching one another, and learning about new methods.

This averages out to three to four hours per day, fully half of the current school day! The most logical way to institutionalize the provision of this type and amount of time for needed joint and individual planning is to extend the regular workday for teachers and to permanently structure it in their schedules for after regular student dismissal. Rotating shifts of teachers might also use this time block to staff after-school extracurricular activities for students.

Detracking Probably one of the most problematic artifacts of the schools' current organization, and certainly the one most closely associated with the failure of large segments of the school population, particularly of poor and minority students, is the system of tracking. Mindful that there are many students who do, in fact, need targeted services, some of which cannot be well addressed in regular classroom settings, the system, as it exists, must be undone if students placed in "problem" special education categories are ever to attain the new standards. The primary problem with this system, as it exists, is that behind closed doors it is easier to throw away these children, rarely giving them opportunity to talk about scholarly content, to read real books, to write persuasive or argumentative essays, or to encounter and solve higher order and critical thinking problems, in short, the types of knowledge that are increasingly being required by the new standards and needed in the future economy (Oakes, 1986). This is particularly true at the elementary and middle school levels, as between 1965 and 1975 the vast majority of American secondary schools dismantled the procedures for assigning students to overarching curricular programs that determined students' courses for the duration of their high school years, substituting, instead, course stratifications within subject areas (Lucas, 1999).

Notwithstanding, how this innovation is done is crucial; for in the inconsiderate detracking of students, the risk is that many regular education classes may be thrown into turmoil; unprepared teachers would become immediately further overburdened; the learning of all students would suffer; and parents of regular, and "gifted" or "honors" students would become aggrieved. Consequently, the potential significance and risks of this reform make it not only one of the most crucial, but probably one of the easiest innovations to undermine by merely doing it badly.

One suggestion has been the creation of *multi-age classes* that include students of different ages and grades taught by skillful teachers. According to Darling-Hammond and Falk (1997: 194), this organization provides structures that do not penalize students for their natural variations in pace, learning style, and performance. Students would stay with the same teacher and classmates for more than one year, ensuring that they get more sustained support from teachers and peers. Research on multi-age classes indicate that children in these classrooms do show academic progress over time that equals or exceeds that of their peers in same-age classrooms. They also have better self-concepts, improved attitudes toward school, and better social ability (French *et al.*, 1986; Pratt, 1986). In many schools, the use of multi-age classrooms has totally eliminated the need for grade retention, as teachers have learned to teach in ways that support student development over the long term.

For elementary and middle schools to accomplish this task effectively, detracking must be accompanied by forethought and planning. All schools and districts must devise reasonable and considerate strategies to phase in special needs children. At the same time, teachers of mainstream classes must be re-schooled in meeting their needs, while "push-in" support from specialists is provided that is real, helpful, and available in a timely fashion. Assessment must be improved so as to provide real information on recommended resources and instructional approaches needed to use to facilitate these students' learning. Collaborative planning time must also to be provided for regular and special education faculty to meet (perhaps in grade or subject level meetings) to arrange instructional strategies for individualized, small and whole group instruction so that the needs of all children in the classroom setting are met. Moreover, as Oakes (1981) has shown that middle-class parents and those of "gifted" and "honors" students are the staunchest protectors of the existing in-school stratification system, equally as important, a plan must be designed to allay the fears of these parents, to help them to see the benefits not only to society, but to their children as well.

Class size Public school classrooms are becoming much, much more diverse. In many systems, it is not unusual for schools to have students variously speaking a total or 10 or more different languages (Sachs, 1999). Add to this, special needs children being mainstreamed and you have teachers faced with a range of complexity, the likes of which have seldom been seen before. To bring a cohort of students with such broad academic needs to the cognitive levels called for by current state and local standards will require a different type of teaching. For these ends greater use of constructivist techniques are recommended. As this approach to instruction cannot be advantageously done with large classes, it will necessitate smaller class size.

Class size does make a difference. Newer research is finding that class size does affect achievement, particularly in the early elementary grades. A study just released by the US Department of Education (2000) concludes that smaller classes, i.e., no more than 15–20 students, promote student achievement in the early grades; move the average child from the 50th to the 60th percentile, and for disadvantaged and minority children the increase is even larger. Parents and teachers also perceive positive effects on the quality of classroom activity when class size is reduced. In response to this new literature, 25 states have already started to or are considering some sort of class size reduction initiative for the early elementary grades (US Dept of Education, 2000). This trend should be extended through the secondary school grades, where smaller class size allows students to make stronger links with their teachers and their peers.

Instruction   In addition to organizational restructuring, efforts to attain new state and district standards will also require an intense rethinking of instructional practices, curricular offerings and assessment. To achieve excellence and equity, as called for by the new standards, a systematic questioning of all current instructional practices and a willingness to modify basic tenets (Lieberman and Miller, 1990) should ensue. With the ever growing diversity of the nation's student population, educators need to understand that there is no one best practice that can optimally be used to educate all children, irrespective of the immediate goals of instruction and without consideration of the learner's cognitive strengths and challenges. Adherence to any instructional ideology should not take priority over learners' practical needs. When adherents to constructivist approaches resist or feel no need to be constrained by the lower order skills and factual knowledge students are supposed to learn at a particular grade level, their failure to impart this information may doom these students to failure, as these requirements may constitute the content upon which crucial tests are based. Similarly, when users of more programmed approaches take false pride in these students' burgeoning wealth of factual knowledge, they fail to realize that these forms of knowledge, at best, prepare these children for low-level jobs as the employees of others, and that self-direction, inquiry, and critical thinking are becoming the coin of the realm. All students must be variously exposed to both methodological approaches. The issue is how best to use them. Students need both depth and breadth; process is hollow without content. The

---

Box 9.2

The Barclay School in Baltimore, Maryland

Maryland, where virtually all of the students qualify for a free lunch, teachers use a very specific, challenging curriculum. (It is the same curriculum used by the prestigious private Calvert School, whose students come from much wealthier families.) After four years of using this curriculum, reading scores, which had been under the thirtieth percentile, are now at or above the fiftieth. Research indicates that the basis for the terrific improvement is the very specific curriculum. As in Japan, the specific curriculum makes it possible to quickly identify students who need extra help. Plus, it enables teachers to devise, share, and institutionalize the most effective ways of teaching each part of the curriculum.

Source: *American Educator* (1996)

---

key is not in the substitution of one approach for the other, but rather both must be employed in combination. Teachers must, therefore, have a range of instructional techniques in their arsenal and knowledge of their strengths and weaknesses. In the artful combination of these tools, tailored to the unique needs of students and students' desired educational outcomes, teachers will find the heart of their role as professionals. Each teacher must find his/her own balance as to what works best for different groups and even individual students in these regards (see Box 9.2).

Curriculum and the opportunity to learn   Another major concern for teachers, schools and districts must be their capacity to provide all their students with equal access to curricular subjects and support materials that will enable them to reach state and district content and performance standards. Schools in under-funded communities and with large populations of English Language Learners (ELLs), poor, and minority students typically lack both the human and the financial resources to offer the range of necessary subjects and support experiences (e.g., well-equipped computer and science laboratories) to prepare these students adequately to compete with those from more advantaged schools and communities. States and local agencies bear the brunt of the responsibility for remedying this situation. (See Chapter 11 for a more complete discussion of school funding reform.) However, local schools and teachers can assist in this effort in two specific ways.

First, local school personnel can and must insist that all children, including ELLs and mainstreamed students receive access to higher-level subject area instruction and the guidance and encouragement to take them. They must be provided with the full range of academic courses necessary to meet the standards and participate in post-secondary education. This can be done in creative ways, e.g., increased opportunities to engage in laboratory and other hands-on activities, as well as games and films that present higher order concepts in meaningful ways. Students should be involved in group projects and problem-solving tasks that require them to reflect upon their own or other's observed actions. And the criteria for meeting state and district standards and other gatekeeping requirements, e.g., college entrance, need to be made explicit and meaningfully explained early and clarified often (Lacelle-Peterson and Rivera, 1994).

Second, schools can seek supplemental funds from government grants and private foundations. In some schools in which we have worked, their SBM/SDMTs have a subcommittee that assumed the task of ferreting out appropriate professional development and materials grants for which to apply.

Assessment and teacher practice   The results of standardized tests can and have been used for a range of purposes – good and bad. Despite the furor over their validity in providing true assessments of children's knowledge, they continue to function as gatekeepers, historically blocking the access of poor and special needs students from advanced levels of schooling (e.g., SATs and GREs) and professional training (e.g., LSATs and MSATs). With no immediate end in sight, educators have a professional and moral obligation to prepare their students for these examinations, in spite of their own personal beliefs and abhorrence, particularly where they are these children's only source of such cultural capital.

Fortunately these tests also have a formative function. When assessment results are disaggregated, they may inform schools and teachers of their students' cognitive strengths and weaknesses in specific subject and skill areas. School personnel need to focus on this diagnostic capacity. This information can be an invaluable tool. In aggregate, i.e., when patterns of skill and subject area weakness appear across classes and grades, it must signal to schools of their need for staff development or curricular modifications in those areas. If schools are piloting the use of innovative instructional procedures, they provide a source of significant evaluative data. Similarly, a student's disaggregated test results must be used to identify important cognitive gaps that must be addressed. These are group problem-solving tasks; and groups of teachers and site staff developers must variously come together with these data to identify need patterns and to plan prescriptive actions. In addition to curricular and instructional modifications, further in-house testing and investigation may also be planned. Such joint problem-solving efforts heighten school staff investment in and bring greater staff ownership to future test results.

Staffing   Research findings show that the single most important factor accounting for differences among students in learning is teacher expertise (Ferguson, 1991). For example, Armour-Thomas (1989) found that 90 percent of the variance in the reading and mathematics scores of students in New York City was attributable to teacher qualifications and experience. This should strongly signal to all schools, particularly, poorly performing schools, that quality staffing is essential. Unfortunately, a district's ability to pay competitive salaries constitutes a major problem for urban schools, which tend to be under-funded relative to suburban schools. However, there are things that can be changed at the local site level to improve staff expertise.

First, local schools must have the ability to make their own hiring determinations. Teachers are not interchangeable pieces, and should not be hired at the district level and placed in schools sight-unseen by a school's staff. In their hiring determinations, local school staffs or their SBM/SDMTs should variously consider a candidate's academic preparation, i.e., the possession of state certification; their past record of success; their proficiency in the use of a range of instructional techniques or their openness to innovation and growth; their beliefs concerning factors associated with underperforming students' ability to learn; their willingness to work collaboratively, and if schools have a theme or driving mission, the candidate's understanding or ability to facilitate these efforts. Schools should also have candidates give a demonstration lesson to a real class. The more a school staff invests in the outcomes of their students' performance, the more likely they are to desire input in the selection of new staff members to their team.

Similar criteria should also be used in the selection of principals. The "good ole boy club" mentality can no longer be used. At this level, it is vital that principals be able to forge positive working relationships with their staffs. While not all principals can be charismatic or instructional leaders, they must be able to show (e.g., in the capacity of assistant principal or program or mini-school director) a history of fairness and objectivity in working with staff; the ability to identify and support strengths in others that facilitate the functioning of the school as a whole; the ability to compromise and seek consensus; good communication skills; and the capacity to win the trust and allegiance of others.

Accountability With the increasing ability of local site level personnel to make decisions regarding hiring, budget, instruction and curriculum comes the responsibility to urge fellow staff to make an earnest effort to embrace and implement sincere school improvement efforts. We are not advocating "groupthink," (Fullan, 1991), but rather the creation of an internal peer review process in which teachers engage in reciprocal instructional facilitation. This may involve inter-classroom visitations, collaborative problem solving regarding students, and joint instructional planning on units and lessons. And similar to the optimal use of standardized assessments of students, this reciprocal assistance should also involve the use of criteria that can be used to identify strengths and challenges, tied to appropriate professional development. The goal of these assessments should not be punitive, but rather to create and nurture an atmosphere of community support and growth, on the order of the effective schools. As was mentioned previously, these types of activity run counter to the current school culture; however, if all schools have as their central focus the academic excellence of all their pupils, then objective and fair determinations can and will be made. However, where individuals refuse or cannot profit from such assistance, the system should be intolerant of ineptitude and mediocrity for inordinate periods of time, and ways must be devised at the local level to identify individuals who have been unable to profit from sincere support and assistance so as to minimize the harm done to children. According to Reyes, *et al.* (1999: 198): "Teaching and learning for all children in environments that liberate their thinking and develop their potential should be the force that shapes the educational policy for our schools as we approach the twenty-first century."

Reforming School Reform

Transforming public schools so as to achieve these ends is no simple matter. Throughout this text we have discussed and illustrated the difficulties inherent in the process of improving poorly performing schools. Presently it is all too easy for schools and teachers to resist change merely by closing their doors. In order truly to change our schools, educators at all levels need to understand that to continue along our present path may mean the demise of public schooling, in general. For there are strong and vocal factions in our government, business and public sectors seeking the privatization and/or the opening of the system to market forces. And if our system of public schooling is to be maintained, not only must the schools' counter-productive arti-factual and belief system change, but so too must the process of reform.

In the following section, we address reforming the process of school reform, specifically at the local school level. Here we briefly explore how this process might change so as to increase the likelihood of achieving positive ends. Process changes that relate to governmental or agency reform practices, e.g., top-down mandates, are addressed in Chapter 11. In advance, we state that, in general, we endorse the reform guidelines suggested by Fullan (1993; 1999), shown in Box 5.5. To this list we add the following recommendations, caveats, and warnings.

Reforming the change initiation process

Making informed decisions about school reform

A first step in reforming the schools must be in making informed decisions about what innovations to impose upon or invite into the schools. In these rapidly changing times, it is important for educational decision-makers at the district and local school levels to know what programs and issues to embrace and which, justifiably, to resist. Consider for a moment that each year, hundred and hundreds of changes are sought in our public school systems, and a surprisingly large number of these proposals actually reach the schoolhouse doors. Most of these innovations are not neutral and unbiased in their benefits, as there are many reasons other than educational merit that influence decisions to initiate change (Fullan, 1991). Many of the reforms imposed upon the school, coming as they do from often distant and sometimes opportunistic and selfish sources are biased, poorly thought out, and unconnected to the stated purposes of education (Fullan, 1982: 6). They should rightly be resisted. No matter how well intended are these change forces, caution is advised if their quality or appropriateness is not fully considered, if the main sponsors of the programs do not remain on the scene for more than a couple of years (Fullan, 1991: 20), or if the ends benefit the few at the expense of the many. Where this is the case, the innovation will do more harm than good, unduly burdening teachers and raising expectations that can only be dashed. Change is not necessarily progress (ibid.: 6); and a balance must be found "on the edge of chaos," i.e., between changing in response to every new fad or idea that comes along and blindly preserving the status quo.

Faced with the need to bring an increasingly diverse student population to unprecedented standards of excellence, the pressure is on local schools to make wise choices among the plethora of programs and projects to assist them in this effort. In these deliberations, educational decision-makers should know the assumptions underlying various programs and projects, hidden work requirements, and have some idea of how much work would be needed to adapt a given program to the unique needs of the school, its staff and its students.

Interfacing new and existing programs

Consistent with the above considerations, the links among new and existing programs must also be a factor. Care must be taken not only to ensure program compatibility but also to anticipate what a particular innovation will add to a specific operation or to the total functioning of the school. Districts and local schools also need to have some plan for the addition of improvement programs, as the opportunistic, *ad hoc* proliferation of programs and projects usually does little more than overload, frustrate and depress the momentum of faculty. A school's mission, theme, and/or problem-solving efforts related to attaining state and local standards should guide these plans. A perceived and defined need or goal should first exist, and decision-makers should have a clear picture of how the innovation, ideally, is intended to address this need or goal. Care and consideration also need to be given to the potential dynamics of program combinations. Remember, programs and projects may have philosophies and strategies that work toward advancing different purposes. While this does not mean that they cannot be combined advantageously, it does suggest that decision-makers should intend for these varied objectives to be met, so as not to conflict with each other.

In all this, it is important to ascertain the degree to which any innovation, in fact, does or does not solve the problem, as well as to discern the effects of program combinations. Research and inquiry, thus, need to be conducted to learn from each addition. This strategy serves not only to inform and improve practice, but also to advance the goals of local public school teachers as researchers, something often talked about in the literature but seldom found in reality. Where local schools and districts lack expertise in research design and implementation, assistance can be obtained through collaboration with local universities and colleges. This provides a golden opportunity for the creation of local school–university partnerships. Such efforts might best be co-ordinated at the district level where other district schools with similar populations may serve as control groups. The potential of this strategy to produce field-based knowledge on learning and instruction is enormous.

Reforming reform implementation

Reform models as guides not road maps

The dialogue between linear and non-linear approaches to organizational change can be confusing. Certainly it seems easier to follow maps and menus, but the reality of schools is dynamic complexity, and the change process is chaotic. Consistent with Fullan (1993), we have found that change is a journey not a blueprint, and no reform project can, in advance, prescribe in a linear fashion the steps that must be taken to reach success. Still, blueprints or menus are helpful! Granted that school innovation is a creative process, there are still basic or essential elements that must be brought to bear. Comprehensive reform projects can provide vital schooling in these elements and principles, set a general direction, and placed in the back of one's mind, can serve as benchmarks or milestones. We don't believe that an external change agent or a school about to embark upon a transformation can go about this process with no general plan whatsoever. Notwithstanding, we agree with Fullan (1993; 1999) that no plan can be followed religiously. Change agents must be sensitive and use their feel of the school culture to know when and where to deviate from or to adjust models, sometimes significantly. For example, with Professions Institute, at the start of the process, the faculty was not ready to construct a meaningful vision statement. Their opposition should have signaled this to the coach. Forcing them to engage in this activity was useless and may have done more to alienate them and set the process backward than move it forward.

Sergiovanni (1989: 3) gives the analogy of school reform as surfing. The idea, he states, is to ride the wave of the reform pattern as it unfolds, adjusting to shifting circumstances. The pattern is made up of goals and circumstances that must be handled in a balanced way. Crucial to success in both surfing and school reform are the successive, interrelated decisions the surfing reformer makes as he or she responds to unique and ever-changing situations. This analogy is a good one; still, even in surfing there are general principles, conditions that one looks for, and things that one does given these conditions to avoid wiping out. School improvement is neither free fall nor lock step, and as with surfing, one's skills, knowledge, instincts, and sensitivity improve with practice. It is the balance in this creative process that Fullan (1993; 1999) refers to in his concept of "living on the edge of chaos."

Small successes are important

Success can rally, unite and motivate a sleepy and cynical faculty. Many troubled schools are in their plight not because staff don't try, but because they are in a downward spiral of constant "firefighting," which leaves them little time nor room to develop a change plan, to implement it, and to experience the gratification of its efficacy. These kinds of schools, early on, need to experience success. Staff at such schools should, therefore, early on in the process be urged to identify a needy challenge area that is significant, yet doable, to develop an action plan, to implement it, and to engage in ongoing problem solving to make it work. Long delays, based on road maps, are counter-indicated. This process can be a cohesive force, better than any team-building workshop. In fact, we have found it to be the most effective team-building experience that we know of. At Professions the coach sensed this, but was too green to know the true significance and need for the plan to succeed.

The importance of affect

Change is a very emotion-laden process. As indicated in the case study discussion in Chapter 6, there is a tendency to avoid the "messiness" of affectivity. This tendency, itself, must be avoided as indicated in Fullan's (1993) Lesson 3: Problems are our friends. It took us, the first author in particular, a long time to figure this one out. Change does bring about feelings of disquiet, tension, and uncertainty. Once having adapted to and internalized traditional ways of being, feeling, and knowing the environment, threats of change to this known world, particularly when imposed from the outside, can engender feelings of confusion, dismay, hostility and resistance in school staff. In these circumstances, conflict, anxiety and hostility are very natural and very human by-products. These and other problems must be treated with respect, valuing them for what they can tell us about the school and what needs to be addressed. While this content may not surface in neat and readily manageable ways, they must be embraced "as our friends."

Problems must be addressed, for they carry within them significant issues that often prevent a school from moving forward. This was clearly the case at Professions Institute. Although the external coach made some effort to "show awareness and sensitivity in relation to the problems and concerns of the practitioner" (Gunter, 1997: 89). But when these "bandages" did not hold, and fearful of the looming chaos, she abandoned these efforts and sought to retreat to the order and seeming certainty of the reform model. She attempted to quiet the voices, but could not. The chaos within the imposed order ultimately rose to undermine the project. And the order within the chaos, i.e., the underlying meaning and significance of the faculty's discontent were never heard, understood, nor resolved. The lesson here is that the task truly is to function on the "edge of chaos," to respond and address the problems without their overwhelming and destroying the process.

In summary, change is afoot in the nation's public schools. Despite protestations, federal and state governments are moving to change public schooling as we know it. The challenge is not whether school reform is to take place, this decision has already been made. Nor is it to determine how it will occur. Based on an assumed societal consensus, state governments are setting content and performance standards for all their schools and students, and using standardized tests to determine and publicize their systems' relative success in meeting these standards. At the same time, greater decision-making power is being shifted to local level teams to determine how best to attain these standards. Within this reality, the question becomes how to make this work not only for educators, but more importantly for all students. If the system is not to be given over to an open market, which can only further disenfranchise those already pushed into society's margins, educators must read the writing on the wall and understand that traditional excuses for the system's failure to educate "non-traditional" students must be abandoned. Responsibility must be assumed, for with it comes the full power of being a professional.

Study Questions

1. The school change plan being promulgated by federal and state authorities is one involving simultaneous moves toward centralization and decentralization. Explain the feasibility or unfeasibility of this strategy.
2. Consistent with this bi-polar school reform pattern, what would be the role of LEAs?
3. From your knowledge of standards, how can they be made more user-friendly and practically meaningful to teachers and to parents?
4. In your mind, can the combination of a principal and an SBM/SDMT work? What are the obstacles to this marriage, and what types of reconceptualizations are necessary on the part of the principal and faculty members?
5. What additional elements would you add to facilitate effective school reform particularly as relates to:
   (a) the affective component?

(b) the organizational or governance component?

(c) the instructional or pedagogic component?

6. In what additional ways can testing and assessment be altered to make them more sensitive to the realities of special needs children and provide a more accurate picture of the work of individual schools, that would not be prohibitively costly?

7. Do you think the current recommendations and efforts are adequate to alter the deep structure of schooling? Explain.

References

American Educator (1996) A system of high standards: what we mean and why we need it. Spring, pp. 22–28.

Armour-Thomas, E. *et al.* (1989) *An Outlier Study of Elementary and Middle Schools in New York City: Final Report*. New York: New York City Board of Education.

Bempechat, J. (1998) *Against the Odds: How "At-Risk" Students Exceed Expectations*. San Francisco: Jossey-Bass.

Cohen, D. (1990) Policy and practice: an overview. *Educational Evaluation and Policy Analysis*, vol. 13, no. 3, pp. 327–345.

Darling-Hammond, L. and Falk, B. (1997) Using standards and assessments to support student learning. *Phi Delta Kappan*, November, pp. 190–199.

Elam, S., Rose, L. and Gallup, A. (1994) The 26th annual Phi Delta Kappan/Gallup poll of the public's attitudes toward the public schools. *Phi Delta Kappan*, vol. 76, September, pp. 41–59.

Ferguson, R. F. (1991) Paying for public education: new evidence on how and why money matters. *Harvard Journal on Legislation*, summer, pp. 465–498.

French, D. *et al.* (1986) Leadership asymmetries in mixed-age children's groups. *Child Development*, vol. 57, pp. 1277–1283.

Fullan, M. (1982) *The Meaning of Educational Change*. New York: Teachers College Press, Columbia University.

Fullan, M., with Stiegelbauer, S. (1991) *The New Meaning of Educational Change*. New York: Teachers College Press, Columbia University.

Fullan, M. (1993) *Change Forces: Probing the Depth of Educational Reform*. London: Falmer Press.

Fullan, M. (1999) *Change Forces: The Sequel*. London: Falmer Press.

Goodman, K. S. (1994) Standards. *NOT*. September 7, p. 39.

Grubb, W. N. (1995) The old problem of "new students," purpose, content and pedagogy. In E. Flaxman and A. H. Passow (eds) *Changing Populations Changing Schools: Mometu Fourth Yearbook of the National Society for the Study of Education*, Part II, pp. 4–29.

Gunter, H. (1997) Chaotic reflexivity. In M. Fullan (ed.) *The Challenge of School Change*. Arlington Hts, ILL: Skylight.

Hallinger, P., and Hausman, C. (1994) From Attila the Hun to Mary had a little lamb: principal role ambiguity in restructured schools. In J. Murphy and K. S. Louis (eds) *Reshaping the Principalship: Insight from Transformational Reform Efforts*. Thousand Oaks, CA: Corwin, pp. 154–176.

Hanushek, E. A. (1994). *Making Schools Work: Improving Performance and Controlling Costs*. Washington, DC: Brookings Institute.

Hill, H. D. (1989) *Effective Strategies for Teaching Minority Students*. Bloomington, IN: National Educational Service.

Hillard, A. G. III. (2000) Excellence in education versus high stakes standardized testing. *Journal of Teacher Education*, Sept/Oct, vol. 51, no. 4, pp. 293–304.

Holmes, G. (1993) *Essential School Leadership: Developing Vision and Purpose in Management*. London: Kogan Page.

House, E. R. (1998) *Schools for Sale: Why Free Market Policies Won't Improve America's Schools and What Will*. New York: Teachers College Press, Columbia University.

Lacelle-Peterson, M. W. and Rivera, C. (1994) Is it real for all kids? A framework for equitable assessment policies for English Language Learners. *Harvard Educational Review*, vol. 64, no. 1, pp. 55–75.

Lieberman, A. and Miller, L. (1990) Restructuring schools: what matters and what works. *Phi Delta Kappan*, June, pp. 759–765.

Lucas, S. R. (1999) *Tracking Inequalities: Stratification and Mobility in America's High Schools*. New York: Teachers College Press, Columbia University.

National Commission on Teaching and America's Future (1996) *What Matters Most: Teaching for America's Future*. New York: Carnegie Corporation of New York.

Natriello, G., McDill, E. J. and Pallas, A. M. (1990) *School Disadvantaged Children: Racing Against Catastrophe*. New York: Crown Publishers.

Neiser, O. J. (2000) How does teacher education need to change to meet the needs of America's schools at the start of the 21st century? *Journal of Teacher Education*, vol. 51, no. 3, May/June, pp. 248–255.

Oakes, J. (1981) A question of access: tracking and curriculum differentiation in a national sample of English and math. *Study of Schooling* (Technical Report No. 26). Los Angeles: I/D/E/A and C. F.: Sage.

Oakes, J. (1986) Tracking in secondary schools: a contextual perspective. *Educational Psychologist*. vol. 22, no. 19, pp. 129–154.

Pallas, A. M., Natriello, G. and McDill, E. L. (1989). The changing nature of the disadvantaged population: current dimensions and future trends. *Educational Researcher*, vol. 18, no. 5, pp. 16–22.

Pratt, D. (1986) On the merits of multi-age classrooms. *Research in Rural Education*, vol. 3, pp. 111–115.

Ravitch, D. (1994) Forgetting the questions: the problem of educational reform. In A. R. Sadovnik, P. W. Cookson and S. F. Semel (eds) *Exploring Education: An Introduction to the Foundations of Education*. Boston: Allyn and Bacon.

Reyes, P., Wagstaff, L. and Fusarelli, L. (1999) Delta forces: the changing fabric of American society and education. In J. Murphy and K. Seashore Louis (eds) *Handbook of Research on Educational Administration*. San Francisco: Jossey-Bass.

Sachs, S. (1999) Advocates for immigrant students protest new English exams. *New York Times*, June 18, Section B. pp. 1 and 6.

Sergiovanni, T. J. (1989) What really counts in improving schools? In T. J. Sergiovanni and J. H. Moore (eds) *Schooling for Tomorrow: Directing Reform to Issues that Count*. Boston: Allyn and Bacon.

Sergiovanni, T. J. (1994) *Building Community in Schools*. San Francisco: Jossey-Bass.

Tomlinson, T. (1992) *Hard Work and High Expectations: Motivating Students to Learn*. Washington, DC: Office of Research and Improvement, US Department of Education.

Tye, B. B. (2000) *Hard Truths: Uncovering the Deep Structure of Schooling*. New York: Teachers College Press, Columbia University.

Tye, K. (1992) Restructuring our schools: beyond the rhetoric. *Phi Delta Kappan*, September, pp. 9–15.

US Department of Education (2000) website.

10

Preparing Educators for the Twenty-first Century

> By the standards of other professions and other countries, U.S. teacher education has historically been thin, uneven, and poorly financed. Teacher recruitment and hiring are distressingly ad hoc, and salaries lag significantly behind those of all other professions. This produces chronic shortages of qualified teachers in fields like mathematics and science, and the continual hiring of large numbers of people as teachers who are unprepared for their jobs. Furthermore, in contrast with other countries that invest most of their education dollars in well-prepared and well-supported teachers, half of the educational dollars in the United States are spent on staff and activities outside of the classroom. (National Commission on Teaching and America's Future, 1996: 5)

Ever complex and often thankless jobs, the challenge of a career in education has increased exponentially. With the exponential increase in information that must be taught to students and in the amount of diversity found among students in schools, the resultant expansion in learner needs has progressively rendered traditional modes of and assumptions about instruction obsolete. These new conditions require that principals and teachers perform tasks that most have never done before in these contexts. Further complicating these tasks, all these transformations must be made in a societal environment that has become increasingly hostile and critical. Considering the total picture, most sane individuals might logically ask: "Who would want such careers?" and "How should those few hardy or foolish souls be prepared to assume such positions?" Factors relating to these questions are the focus of this chapter. Before beginning this chapter, the reader is asked to answer the following questions:

1. How are the jobs and tasks of teachers and administrators changing as a result of the new demands of the twenty-first century?
2. How, if at all, should the current demands on teachers and administrators change the entry criteria for occupations in these positions?
3. In what ways should teacher and administrator preparatory programs be changed better to meet the challenges of this century?

Transforming School Staff

The new demands of the twenty-first century

Good schools, teachers and administrators are more essential now than ever before in our nation's history. Due to sweeping economic and technological changes, today's world has little room for workers who cannot read, write, and compute proficiently; find and use resources; frame and solve problems with other people; and continually learn new technologies and occupations (National Commission on Teaching and America's Future, 1996). Accomplishing this task is infinitely complicated by the extreme diversity of the nation's student population. In 1992, 50 of the largest 99 school districts in the United States had enrollments that were more than 50 percent students of color (National Center for Educational Statistics, 1994). New immigration has drastically increased diversity in the schools, as between 1981 and 1990, more than 7,300,000 people immigrated to the United States (US Bureau of the Census, 1994), more varied in their countries of origin than in previous generations. In fact, it is not uncommon in today's schools to have students who, combined, speak ten or more different languages (Sachs 1999). These students also have widely disparate academic histories, such that immigrant students in the same age cohort may range in their amount of previous formal academic instruction from a number of years corresponding to our own system to no formal education at all! Add to this, mainstreamed students from detracked special education classes and the magnitude of these students' instructional needs become gravely apparent.

Facing these students is a teaching force that has become more monolithic, monocultural, and monolingual in the past century (Nieto, 2000). According to the National Education Association (1997), the percentage of White teachers grew from 88 percent in 1971 to 90.7 percent in 1996, whereas the number of Black teachers decreased from 8.1 percent to 7.3 percent, and those classified as "other" have decreased from 3.6 percent to 2.0 percent during the same time. And for the most part, these teachers have had neither extensive personal experience nor professional training in cross-cultural studies, and would prefer to work in suburban settings, teaching White, middle-class youths (Zeichner and Hoeft, 1996 in Nieto, 2000).

The challenge of today's teaching and administrative workforce, therefore, is to bring this diverse population of students, the likes of which the system has never seen before, to levels of academic achievement never before attempted. However, this must be done by a system that, as it currently exists, may lack the capacity to do so. Consider the follow facts published by the National Commission on Teaching and America's Future (1996):

- In the nation's poorest schools where hiring is most lax and teacher turnover is constant, thousands of children are taught throughout their school careers by a parade of teachers without preparation in the fields they teach, inexperienced beginners with little training and no mentoring, and short-term substitutes.
- In recent years, more than 50,000 people who lack the training required for their jobs have entered teaching annually on emergency or substandard licenses.
- Nearly one-fourth (23 percent) of all secondary teachers do not have even a minor in their main teaching field. This is true for more than 30 percent of mathematics teachers.
- Among teachers who teach a second subject, 36 percent are unlicensed in the field and 50 percent lack a minor.
- Fifty-six percent of high school students taking physical science are taught by out-of-field teachers, as are 27 percent of those taking mathematics and 21 percent of those taking English. The proportions are much higher in high-poverty schools and in lower track classes.
- In schools with the highest minority enrollments, students have a less than 50 percent chance of getting science or

mathematics teachers who hold a license and a degree in the fields they teach.

There is one ray of light. According to this report, this immense challenge is accompanied by an equally great opportunity: In the next decade, the nation will have to recruit and hire more than 2 million teachers for America's schools. How then should these "new professionals" be prepared and the schools' existing staff be retooled? A first step is in better understanding the new requirements, tasks and conditions being placed on educators today.

The new teacher

Teachers of the twenty-first century have the task of instructing an extremely diverse student population that resists pat solutions. The exponential rise in the range of instructional needs alone defies the use of scripted programs developed by distant educators, normed on populations grossly different from those in our schools. These demographic changes also increasingly render traditional whole class instruction less practical as a dominant mode of teaching, as the situation demands the flexible and skilled use of an arsenal of instructional and organizational approaches (Darling-Hammond and Cobb, 1996: 16). To perform their tasks, teachers of the twenty-first century will need to be proficient in their ability to interpret diagnostic and student profile data from varied sources, including disaggregated standardized test scores, Individualized Educational Plans (IEPs), informal and "authentic" assessments, and to construct academic plans to meet their students' varied educational needs. They must also be able to select from an ever widening range of organizational techniques, instructional strategies, learning materials, and support services as is appropriate to implement their varied individual, small and occasional whole class lessons, and to bring all these entities into an integrated, cohesive whole.

State and local standards and mandates for second-order reforms demand a host of additional skills. In these regards, Lytle (2000) states that teachers need to do the following:

- be conversant with national, state, and local curriculum standards for reading, English, language arts, mathematics, science, and social studies, and able to address those standards in daily instruction;

- know state and local testing and assessment programs and be able to ensure student success on the tests;
- know their school's chosen Comprehensive School Reform (CSR) model and be deeply involved in implementing it;
- be familiar with new technologies and incorporate them into classroom instruction;
- be able to govern the school as part of a school management team (and therefore be knowledgeable about budgeting, policy, planning, etc.);
- be able to maintain contact with parents; and
- be able to conduct critical inquiry into one's practices and on the conditions of schooling as these affect various groups of students.

Although by sociological definition, teaching cannot now be regarded as a true profession, these new demands not only increase the complexity of teaching, they increase the uncertainty in problems presented and their possible solutions, fulfilling one of the criteria posited by Bacharach and Conley (1989), for the job's status as a profession (see Box 1.1 on p. 20). This may be both a blessing and a curse, for with the expansion of teachers' decision-making capacity – both in regards to instruction and school governance – there are concomitant calls for their greater accountability, commensurate with that of other professions.

According to Sergiovanni (1989: 6), empowerment and accountability are inseparable. If teaching is to emerge as an independent profession, beholden only to the norms of what the profession believes to be best practice and not become a civil service profession, the practitioner must have discretion over both the "whats" and the "hows" of their field. The "whats" of schooling, Sergiovanni states, have to do with issues of purpose, substance, and broad outcomes. In our society, the "whats" are decided externally to the system, by the policy process in response to the wishes of the people, directly and through government. The "hows" are synonymous with best practice, which include how the curriculum is best arranged and taught in given situations and how classrooms are to be organized. According to Sergiovanni: "The professsion of teaching should rightly be held accountable to these 'whats' but only if the profession is given responsibility for deciding the hows. In the absence of this discretion, one must look to where decisions are actually made in order to place accountability properly."

The new administrator

Accompanying new views of teachers and teaching is a plethora of new conceptualizations of the principalship. While principals are still largely conceived as instructional leaders, managers, and political leaders, the priorities given to these roles have variously changed; new roles have been added, along with new considerations and constraints. As with teachers, the most formidable factors associated with these shifts have been the demands for improved student achievement amidst greater diversity and the expectations of shared decision-making.

Whereas principals previously regarded themselves and were regarded as individuals using formal authority to control and direct the activities of subordinates, now their role as leader is being reconceptualized as facilitators and professional peers, who, though still central in the decision-making process, collaborate with teachers to make decisions (Seyfarth, 1999: 75). This is not to say that principals are no longer the heads of their schools, for truly they are, perhaps even more so. The task, however, has become subtler. This reconceptualization is perhaps best understood as a shift in some significant respects from that of authority to influence. Authority refers to the power to make final decisions on a matter, and influence is the ability to shape decisions through informal and nonauthoritative means (Seyfarth, 1999: 77). Principals still have the authority to make final decisions on certain matters, but must increasingly exert influence on other matters. For example, with the institutionalization of SBM/SDMTs, or school councils, many of the responsibilities and decisions formerly made by the principal as well as at the district level have been ceded to these teams. This means that principals must now make things happen through being well organized and focused on aims of the organization. They must have human relation skills and be able to motivate people to work together in teams, as they work toward goals agreed upon by all.

As a consequence of these changes, an essential part of the new role of school leader is the ability to take "right action," i.e., pursuing organizational goals and objectives in such a way that the growth and integrity of people are respected (Seyfarth, 1999: 76). Principals now must delegate responsibility to others in the school community and ensure the fair and even-handed distribution of the potential or opportunities for leadership widely throughout the organization. Increasingly, they become the prime individuals responsible for recognizing teachers' expertise and facilitating the restructuring of their schools to allow these individuals to make important decisions that capitalize upon these strengths.

In addition, principals are being projected, more and more, as cultural and moral leaders, and as visionaries. School cultures are mutable, and principals are viewed as individuals who play a significant part in establishing these cultures or in (re)shaping the perceptions, thoughts, feelings and actions of their members (Schein, 1997). As visionaries, they must identify a clear sense of what the school can become and facilitate the school's movement in that direction (Deal and Peterson, 2000; Sergiovanni, 1994). Consistent with this view, principals need to understand how people's values and attitudes toward symbolic activities affect the operation of the organization. Whatever decisions are made in these regards, principals need to know that values that run counter to the prevailing community can engender strong resistance and must be prepared to negotiate them. Principals must, therefore, have political savvy, and be able to work with parents, superintendents, and political leaders (Moore-Johnson, 1996). This carries the administrators' work into the realm of moral activity, by challenging them to consider the implications for human beings of a proposed course of action. In this reconceptualization, greater weight must be given to human values and interpersonal considerations, rather than focusing exclusively on the goals of efficiency and rationality (Seyfarth, 1999).

And last but not least, the trend toward demanding student attainment of high standards has resulted in yet another focal need for principals – i.e., simultaneous emphasis on results. This focus necessitates that instructional objectives be clearly identified and that teachers be charged with achieving these outcomes.

To establish a set of goals and responsibilities for the new administrator the Interstate School Leaders Licensure Consortium developed a set of standards adopted by 44 states (McCarthy, 1999). These standards are compatible with those developed by the National Council for the Accreditation of Teacher Education (NCATE) and the American Association of School Administrators (AASA). While these standards reflect recognition that there are many ways to excel, many kinds of leaders, and that every leadership style has both a downside as well as positive attributes (Evans, 1996), these standards call for a new kind of leader, one who can transform schools into collaborative research centers, where principals work with parents and teachers in providing the best education for all children (see Box 10.1).

The transformations called for in both the roles of teacher and school administrator are enormous. To meet these challenges changes are concomitantly being called for in teacher and administrator preparation programs.

Preparing Educators for the Twenty-first Century

Historically, the substance and quality of programs preparing educators for our school systems have been a source of criticism and targets of reform. It has long been questioned whether a specialized body of knowledge that all practitioners must master even exists as well as how field-related knowledge should be taught. According to Britzman (2000: 200):

> as the new century unfolds, there is still little agreement in our field of teacher education as to which knowledge matters or even what might be the matter with knowledge . . . We cannot agree on the length of the practicum, on whether the 19th century apprentice model is still relevant, or even the future of schooling itself . . . It is difficult then to even find the subject of teacher education.

With the field "inundated with the romance of cognitive styles, the idealization of information and standards, and the parade of new diagnoses of learning failures," e.g., attention deficit disorders, overstimulation, understimulation, no wonder that research on teacher preparation programs finds wide variation in the curricula and quality of programs, with excellent programs operating alongside those that are out of touch with current knowledge or are inadequately funded to do the job (National Commission on Teaching and America's Future, 1996).

To ensure that professionals learn and adhere to a knowledge base, governmental agencies have a set of safeguards: (a) program accreditation; (b) initial teacher licensing; and (c) advanced professional certification. However, unlike other professions, where groups of professionals in the field come together to determine this knowledge base and set the standards, in education, often these same legislative agencies set standards, curriculum, and policies that govern the work of these programs (Darling-

Box 10.1

Standards for School Leaders

Standard 1

A school administrator is an educational leader who promotes the success of all students by facilitating the development, articulation, implementation, and stewardship of a vision of learning that is shared and supported in the school community.

Standard 2

A school administrator is an educational leader who promotes the success of all students by advocating, nurturing, and sustaining a school culture and instructional program conducive to student learning and staff professional growth.

Standard 3

A school administrator is an educational leader who promotes the success of all students by ensuring management of the organization, operations and resources for a safe, efficient and effective learning environment.

Standard 4

A school administrator is an educational leader who promotes the success of all students by collaborating with families and community members, responding to diverse community interests and needs, and mobilizing community resources.

Standard 5

A school administrator is an educational leader who promotes the success of all students by acting with integrity, fairness and in an ethical manner.

Standard 6

A school administrator is an educational leader who promotes the success of all students by understanding, responding to, and influencing the larger political, social, economic, legal, and cultural context.

Source: Interstate School Leaders Licensure Consortium (2000)

Hammond, 1997). For example, several states including Florida and New York have mandated that colleges can require no more than 120 credits for a bachelor's degree and have further limited the maximum number of credits professional programs can consume of these total credits. Undergraduate teacher training programs in New York are limited to one quarter of this amount, or 30 credits. In Maryland, teacher preparation programs now are required to have 12 credit hours in the teaching of reading alone. Notwithstanding, other competencies are added via statute (e.g., the provision of drug and child abuse information), with little regard for existing content requirements and thought to what might have to be eliminated in order to accommodate this new content. Professional organizations have tried to intervene by setting their own standards for the preparation of educators; and many teacher preparation programs voluntarily integrate these standards into their training sequence. These kinds of actions have led some to assert that teacher education programs are the servant of too many masters, both outside and inside the academy, resulting in their being heavily regulated and constrained in their offering (Sindelar and Rosenberg, 2000).

Despite attempts to comply with these legislative guidelines, these programs still tend to be held in low regard. Evidence of this is abundant both outside and inside the academic community. At the state level, there is a proliferation of alternate routes to certification and licensure that may waive or postpone instructional requirements, and some top-level government representatives have suggested they be eliminated altogether. In more than 40 states, policy-makers have enacted alternate routes to teacher certification to create pathways into teaching other than those provided by traditional four-year undergraduate teacher education programs. Whereas some of these alternate routes are carefully structured post-baccalaureate programs, others are little more than emergency hiring options (Darling-Hammond, 2000: 166). Especially in times of teacher shortages, schools are forced to hire, and states feel compelled to allow, less than fully qualified personnel to hold positions of full responsibility in the classrooms – waiving or temporarily postponing the attainment of these requirements! Some key government officials e.g. Newt Gingrich in 1995, and Chester Finn and the Thomas B. Fordham Foundation in 1999, proposed the elimination of teacher certification rules asserting that they created "barriers" to entering teaching (Darling-Hammond, 2000: 166). Probably most distressing is the low regard in which teacher preparation programs are held in their own academic community. These programs have been called the "cash cows" of institutions of higher education, i.e., sources of significant revenue but unworthy of equal regard and treatment. And probably most damaging, teaching preparation programs are perceived by teacher candidates more as a perfunctory requirement than as a necessary and vital step.

Like teachers and the schools, college-based, pre-service teacher and administrator preparation programs face the awesome task of meeting these new challenges in reaction to public outcries for change, legislative mandates and constraining requirements. Having to struggle to maintain their viability, teacher educators characteristically feel, but are never quite sure, that they make a difference. Research strongly suggests that these programs do make a significant difference, but more needs to be done. They need to be brought to levels such that states would no sooner allow an uncertified teacher in front of a classroom than allow an unlicensed doctor to operate on a patient. How might this be done? We organize our discussion in terms of teachers' and administrators' programs. Within each, we discuss pre- and in-service preparation.

Preparing teachers

Pre-service preparation

The major challenge to public perceptions of teachers and teacher preparation is that it is an enormously difficult job that looks easy (Labaree, 2000). Consequently, many people believe that almost anyone who knows a subject, or how content area knowledge, is adequately equipped to be a teacher. But how true is this? Research on successful new teachers strongly supports the necessity of rigorous pre-service teacher training programs. Darling-Hammond (2000) argues that whereas knowledge of subject matter is often found to be an important factor in teaching effectiveness, it appears that its relationship to teaching is curvilinear; that is, it exerts a positive effect up to a threshold level and then tapers off in influence. On the other hand, pedagogical knowledge, e.g., knowledge of learning theory, teaching methods, curriculum, and classroom management, is more frequently found to influence teaching performance and often exerts even stronger effects than subject-matter knowledge. Moreover, teachers who have less than full preparation perceive this loss and it is reflected in their work. Studies of teachers with less than full preparation found that recruits tended to be less satisfied with their training and have greater difficulty planning curriculum, teaching, managing the classroom, and diagnosing students' learning needs. They were less able to adapt their instruction to promote student learning and less likely to see it as their job to do so, blaming students if their teaching proved ineffective. Most important, their students learned less!

As evidence, Darling-Hammond cites an extensive body of research including findings based on teachers from alternative certification routes (e.g., Gomez and Grobe, 1990), as well as research on the most well-publicized of these efforts: Teachers for America (TFA), created to recruit the "best and the brightest" college graduates to teach in disadvantaged areas (e.g., Grady *et al.*, 1991; Popkewitz, 1995). This research found that teachers who come through these alternate routes have much higher attrition and much lower job satisfaction rates. For example, of the graduates from the TFA program who started teaching in 1990, 58 percent had left before the third year, a two-year attrition rate nearly three times the national average for new teachers. The Maryland State Department of Education found that 62 percent of corps members who started in Baltimore in 1992 left within two years. And studies of short-term alternative programs also note that their teachers report less satisfaction with their preparation (Darling-Hammond *et al.*, 1989).

Still criticized with each new wave of reform, teacher preparation programs are now being told to remake themselves. Current bureaucratic solutions call for raising admission criteria, increasing the academic rigor of instruction, and extending the practical, or field, component. Programs respond, as they must, with little protest concerning the negative implications and contradictory findings related to these solutions.

Recruiting the best and the brightest   A common complaint voiced in several of the first wave of national reports was the poor quality of inductees into teacher preparation programs. Reports urged these programs to recruit and admit a better teacher applicant, the best and the brightest (e.g., National Commission on Teaching and America's Future, 1996). But how valid is this claim of poor quality?

Teachers are not totally monolithic. Gitomer and Latham

(2000), for example, found significant differences among teacher candidates for elementary versus those for secondary education programs. Candidates who applied for and passed licensure tests for elementary, special education and physical education tended to have lower SAT scores than the average college graduate, whereas candidates who passed the Praxis tests in secondary- and specialized-subject areas such as math, social studies, art and music, science, foreign languages, and English all had mean SAT scores that were comparable to or higher than those of all college graduates.

Also, the implications of raising admission requirements may be a case of the remedy being worse than the disease. Thus in response to state demands, many teacher preparation programs have variously instituted a number of prerequisites as screening mechanisms for program entry including (1) increasing the minimum overall G.P.A. for applicants; (2) mandating the satisfaction of all college entrance requirements, i.e., remediation; the passing of certain critical gate-keeping courses (e.g. basic college writing and mathematics courses); (3) instituting screening interviews and writing exams; (4) the declaration of and passing grades in certain liberal arts and science majors; and (5) the taking, if not the passing, of standardized national exams, assessing a students' general knowledge.

Successful in raising the mean academic performance of the prospective teaching population, these types of programmatic changes do more than just bring in a "better" quality student. As most candidates are unaffected by these changes due to their relatively high passing rates, their primary effect is to deny access to those with lower scores. For minority students, this is a classic example of double jeopardy, i.e., first being underprepared due to inadequacies in the public schools, and then being denied the opportunity to prepare for a career in the system, because of these weaknesses.Thus, it tends to lower the supply of minority candidates much more drastically than the supply of majority candidates, and hit some licensure areas harder as well (e.g., elementary and special education). The effect is, therefore, to exacerbate the racial homogeneity of the teaching population, already over 90 percent White. In light of the increasing diversity of students within the public schools this is cause for concern, particularly in the context of Delpit's (1995: 151) warning that: "We all interpret behaviors, information, and situations through our own cultural lenses; these lenses operate involuntarily, below the level of conscious awareness, making it seem that our own view is simply 'the way it is.'" If diversity of the teaching force is a socially desirable outcome, raising academic requirements for teacher candidates is not the answer. Rather, means must be sought to increase the pool of qualified individuals through very targeted policy initiatives (Gitomer and Latham, 2000: 217).

Imposing higher entrance standards would also substantially limit the supply of teachers. There is no unlimited pool of academically prepared individuals waiting to get into teacher education programs. As a field, education seldom attracted bright and ambitious males. Now with more attractive fields opening their doors to females, many of the "best" females have begun to turn their backs on the profession as well (Brandt, 1990: 10), preferring more status-oriented and lucrative careers. By raising admission requirements, the existing pool would be further shrunk. Already, teacher-training programs are finding that there are inadequate numbers of strong applicants. Without other interventions, these programs will be unable to produce sufficient numbers of teachers to fulfill the anticipated needs of the twenty-first century; and the supply of minority candidates would be hit the most severely. Ironically, the probable result will be recourse to alternate routes, sending more unprepared individuals to teach our most needy students – ultimately thwarting policy-makers' own goal for getting the best and the brightest.

One final point; there is an assumption underlying all this that Darling-Hammond (2000) calls the "bright person myth." People presume that anyone can teach what he or she knows to anyone else. However, people who have never studied teaching or learning often have a very difficult time understanding how to convey material that they themselves learned effortlessly and almost subconsciously. Such teachers also tend to maintain a single cognitive perspective that makes it difficult for them to understand the experiences, perceptions, and knowledge bases of students who are different from themselves. We, therefore agree with Gitomer and Latham (2000: 219) when they state that:

> blindly raising testing standards in an effort to make the teaching for ce more academically talented may well do more harm than good. Where will all these individuals come from and why haven't they shown up already? If, as a country, we are going to be more discriminating about who

enters the teaching force, we must also increase the supply of qualified applicants or be faced with intense shortages. One way to increase the supply of strong teacher candidates is to create pay and work conditions similar to competing professional employment opportunities. Raising standards is a wonderful idea, but it cannot be done in isolation. Unless high standards are coupled with aggressive steps to entice and retain top quality candidates, the result will be a small, but insufficient pool of highly qualified teacher candidates.

Greater academic rigor and relevance   The second reform wave renews previous calls to advance teacher professionalization through more rigorous and relevant teacher preparation. States have responded by mandating the inclusion of additional curricula content into preparatory programs as a condition for their re-registration. These content areas include: teaching the ESL learner, teaching students with disabilities in inclusive classrooms, formal and informal assessment, using technology in instruction, classroom management, health promotion, drug abuse, child abuse and working with parents. This solution of adding content courses is solid in terms of its face validity, i.e., it sounds good, but there are three problems here. First, it is a quick and simplistic bureaucratic fix to a difficult problem; second, it equates rigor and relevance to the mere addition of course content. And, third, it continues and increases the states' regulation of university practices and programs.

In perfunctorily mandating additional courses, this solution fails to extend the analysis beyond the question of what subject content do teachers need to possess to ask how must this knowledge be held by teacher candidates so as to impart it successfully to others or to use it in the process of instruction. Not to engage again in a discussion of the relative merits of content knowledge versus pedagogical knowledge, the issue here is that content knowledge alone will not suffice. Simply adding and disseminating additional content knowledge to teacher candidates does not solve the problem of application and instruction. That is, teachers with content knowledge, often, do not know it in ways that help students learn. According to Ball (2000), it is not what teachers know, but rather how they know it and how they are able to mobilize it in the course of teaching. We need to probe not only what teachers need to know, but also how this information must be held in their minds, how best to impart it, i.e., what *sort* of content understanding and insight about this information matters in the practice of teaching?

Most essentially, teachers must possess the content in such a way as to deconstruct it into its inchoate form, where critical components are accessible and visible. That is, teachers must be able to recall contents in their growing unfinished state, i.e., to work backward from mature and compressed understanding of the information to unpack its constituent elements (Ball, 2000). Only then is the teacher able to problem solve about how best to impart or recreate these constituent components for students.

The other side of this coin is that teachers must have ways to integrate this knowledge with practice. Shulman and his colleagues (1977) term this "pedagogical content knowledge," i.e., a special amalgam of knowledge that links content and pedagogy. It may be conceived of as mental representations of things that are typically difficult for students to understand. Like an algorithm, pedagogical knowledge is useful for conveying a specific idea or procedure, e.g., the best way to teach the concept of the division of fractions.

To contend effectively with the challenges of a diverse classroom teachers require not only knowledge of the subject matter, but also the ability to respond differentially to the varied needs of learners in the flexible use of these content-based pedagogical representations. Pre-service programs must, therefore, help teacher candidates represent ideas in multiple ways, to connect to contexts effectively, and to think about things in ways other than their own. Where teacher programs are unable to do this, it makes hollow any claims of preparing high-quality teachers who can teach all students, teach in multicultural settings, and work in environments where teaching and learning are difficult.

Characteristically, the search for such ways of knowing and imparting knowledge is omitted as preparation programs scramble to innovate almost solely on the basis of state prescriptions. Interestingly, in the states' defining of both the problem and the solution there has been little input on the part of teacher educators. One result of this reactive approach to innovation is program fragmentation. Content knowledge is added with little thought as to how this knowledge should be translated into pedagogical content knowledge in the context of teachers' work. Ball says this assumes that the integration process is simple and will happen automatically in the course of experience. In fact, however, this does not happen at all. It is in bridging the gap between content and pedagogy that is the essence of making pre-service teacher training more rigorous and relevant, not in the mere addition of courses. Field experience is one route, but only if done properly.

Field experiences Almost all states require some type of pre-service field experience or tutoring for state certification. Its significance is frequently reported in studies of student teachers who view their school-based experiences as the central piece in their pre-service teacher preparation. (e.g., Eltis and Cairns, 1982; Zeichner, 1980), often regarding it as the only *real* learning of their teacher education program (Amarel and Feiman-Nemser, 1988). As recognition grows of the general value teacher candidates and education researchers place on the clinical experience, some states are increasing the minimum number of hours that teacher candidates must devote to the field. The rationale behind these actions is a commonly held belief in the relationship between the quantity of field experience and candidates' amount of learning: the more pre-service experience one has in the classroom, the more one will automatically learn about teaching. However, surprisingly little is known about how field experiences contribute to the process of learning to teach. When an inquisitive eye is turned to teacher candidates' perceptions of the field experience and what and how they learn from it, the findings reveal complexities that have significant implications for possible ways to revise and renew field experience (Johnston, 1994).

In general, it appears from the research that pre-service field experiences may not be providing adequate opportunities to link content and practice, and may be limiting possible links to only a specific kind of knowledge. In a longitudinal study of teacher candidates in both Australia and the USA in various phases of their teacher preparation, Johnston (1994) explored their perceptions on how they learned and the perceived value of their various field experiences. Teacher candidates indicated primary use of observational learning modeled upon their co-operating teachers; active involvement in teaching activities; and a great deal of, often painful, trial and error as the mechanisms through which they developed their own style and sense of teaching. Most teacher candidates had a rather passive attitude toward their learning. They had few explicit expectations, and rather, waited to see and take whatever came out of it – leaving much to chance placement and the role of the supervising teacher. Most subjects reported that their early learning involved just getting by after being "thrown to the dogs" (ibid.: 203) by these programs. Curiously, in the context of supervised field experiences, few felt that they had been helped in their construction of pedagogical content knowledge. The high value they placed on the clinical experience was due to their equating increased time spent in field activities with increased confidence and exposure to the routines and the types of challenges they would face as teachers. Johnston uses a banking analogy, in which candidates viewed themselves as building a stock of skills and ideas through actually carrying out the tasks. The more situations they experience, the more they feel prepared for varied situations. However, most candidates could not maximize the lessons learned from these experiences, as they were limited in both their ability and the inclination to transfer skills and knowledge learned in one situation to another. Thus, not ever being able to encounter all possible situations, teacher candidates tend to feel that they always need more time in the field.

Ironically, there was also a definite sense of doubt among students that they were learning what they needed to learn in the field setting. Candidates complained about not being able to do or see the *kinds* of teaching they felt they needed to be the most effective teachers themselves. Often, they were constrained by their co-operating teachers to handling routines and by the curriculum to manual-guided instruction. These experiences were not regarded as "learning experiences." Candidates typically did not regard time spent in the classroom, observing teaching, interacting with children, preparing and implementing lessons as part of the learning process because it did not conform to their acquired images of what teaching should be.

> The images of what teaching should be like usually revolved around working independently, using innovative approaches, and creating new materials and resources. If student teaching did not provide the student teachers with the opportunity to prepare and teach in this way, it was not perceived as giving them the right kind of experience. (Johnston, 1994: 204–205)

This perception is quite pervasive and problematic. When teacher educators limit possible links between content and pedagogy to only one narrow approach to instruction, they waste valuable time and experiences by ignoring the possible contribution to candidates' learning provided by other approaches to instruction.

While more time in the field may be desirable, as candidates cannot be provided with an infinite amount of field experience, the time that students spend in the field is too dear for such a narrow view of the types of experiences from which they will and will not learn. Moreover, as most teacher education programs cannot place all student teachers in model classrooms, they must acknowledge this fact to students and help them to learn from the range of experiences in which they will become involved. Ball and Feiman-Nemser (1988) encourage use of these experiences as a scaffold upon which to undertake the more complex tasks of teaching. Ultimately, experience alone is not enough; it is the contemplation process and subsequent action associated with reflecting on these experiences that will determine their value to candidates' learning process. Students need to develop a perspective that recognizes the possibility and the importance of being attentive to all experiences and the opportunity to learn from them.

> Experience may well be the best teacher, but only if student teachers use the full range of experiences they encounter as contributors to their learning process. Moreover, this learning process must be one of actively seeking specific experiences from which to learn and then actively processing the learning from those experiences. (Johnston, 1994: 207)

In addition, field experiences must also be a means to help teacher candidates better understand the needs and the most advantageous ways of teaching students from diverse backgrounds. To teach the rapidly increasing population of heavily minority students content standards to levels set by new performance standards, new teachers must have an understanding of their students' ways of knowing and how to build upon these varied foundations. As indicated in Chapter 3, how teachers and teacher candidates conceptualize student learning and failure is integral to what they do as teachers. If teachers are to help these children to learn, teacher candidates must be aware of the cultural contexts that shape their students' ways of knowing and their own as well. As a first step, candidates need to own the historical and cultural roots of who and what we are as a nation and a people. They need to recognize common, taken for granted assumptions that are a reflection of those historical and cultural roots (Harrington, 1994: 194). Field experiences can be the opportunity to revise long-held assumptions, but only if guided. For inadequately guided field experiences in diverse settings can teach harmful, unintended lessons by socializing pre-service teachers into existing school cultures or cementing preconceived, stereotypical notions about others (Burant, 1999: 209; Sleeter, 1993).

These experiences must be reframed and reconceptualized so that from them all prospective teachers are able to develop meaningful and accurate understandings about how people adapt to their complex realities and what it means to come to know in these contexts. This will require a shift in focus from the "what" of teacher preparation to the "how." To accomplish this task, field experiences must become educative practicum (in which fieldwork is tied to each didactic course) and clinical reframing (in which candidates engage in guided reflection upon their student teaching experiences). Teacher educators must work to move teacher candidates beyond trial and error knowledge gleaned from individual classroom placements to focus on the full scope of teachers' complex roles within schools and communities, stressing that all students can learn, elucidating how varied students know and best be helped to learn, at the same time preparing them for the process of lifelong learning and professional development that is ahead.

These tasks cannot be accomplished in the current constrained and prescribed contexts of traditional undergraduate and graduate teacher preparation programs. To maximize the usefulness of field experiences and to ensure the quality of supervision by cooperating teachers and college-based teacher educators, some programs have broken with the traditional model to embrace extended five-year programs, bachelor's programs that move into one- and two-year graduate programs, and partnerships with local school districts (Fullan, 1993; Goodlad, 1991; Darling-Hammond, 2000). Some of these programs structure opportunities to weave together course work on subject content with school-based clinical experiences that focus on pedagogy, other programs have embraced the use of intensive reflection and dialogue on how teacher candidates know and understand learning in themselves and others (e.g., Fountain and Evans, 1994; Ladson-Billings, 2000).

Still other programs and schools of education have begun to develop partnerships with local schools and districts. One manifestation has been in the establishment of professional development schools (PDSs), where novices' clinical experiences can be more purposefully structured. While public schools have traditionally co-operated in providing apprentice experiences for pre-service students, partnerships should, ideally, expand the nature of these relationships to function with greater reciprocity. Benefits to the college must extend beyond field placement and candidate supervision to include learning from local school and district staff about the changes occurring in the schools today, and how instruction needs to be adapted for differing student needs. This will require the joint development of action research between local school staff and teacher educators. In this process, the partnership also gives back to and informs the schools and districts. District and site staffs that have become masters in action research can teach teacher candidates at these colleges. To encourage college faculty to work in local schools, college reward structures must also change by acknowledging and supporting the work of faculty in the field.

In the "sacred stories" of teachers, i.e., stories told of their passage in the profession, seldom is there mention of their pre-service preparation. Despite research attesting to its usefulness, few teachers or educational administrators perceive the learning obtained from these programs as particularly vital, rigorous and relevant. Those currently in these programs or those with these programs behind them, too often, feel that they acquired their skill through trial and error, being "thrown to the dogs" to either "sink or swim." The way to make these programs more rigorous and relevant is not through simplistic bureaucratic solutions, but rather, through helping teacher candidates build true cognitive bridges connecting their content knowledge, pedagogical knowledge and students' academic needs. Instead of throwing more content and unguided field experiences at candidates in the same ways that we always have, the nature of the courses and experiences must shift in three regards: (1) to dispensing content in ways that will be properly held by the learner; (2) transforming this subject knowledge into flexible pedagogical content knowledge; and (3) helping candidates understand the learning process in students so as to adapt their pedagogical knowledge variously to the unique needs of their learners. This is what will make these programs more rigorous and relevant, and further move the field toward greater professionalization – not the bureaucratic solutions sought by government, which often tend to exert a powerful, conservative force. Rather, teacher educators in pre-service programs must become proactive in the development of curricula and course content based on desired outcomes in teachers (e.g., teacher retention, leadership in school governance, flexible use of instructional methodologies, sensitivity to issues of diverse learners, and demonstrated "value added" in the knowledge-base of their pupils). If we can do this, our programs will become part of teachers' sacred stories.

In-service staff development

Districts and schools should similarly adopt a focus on the how of knowing in both their new teacher induction process and in existing teachers' professional development.

Induction

One of the major criticisms of the field has been its sink or swim indoctrination for beginning teachers. An enormously difficult task, teaching cannot be learned neatly in two years of pre-service instruction (Labaree, 2000; Shulman, 1997). Nonetheless, it is not uncommon for novice instructors to assume full and lone responsibility for large, and sometimes problematic, classes from the very first day they begin their formal teaching career. This is bad practice, if not cruel and inhuman treatment, and may be a contributory factor to the field's high turnover rates among novices.

A more gradual induction process is needed on the order of that provided to doctors, in the form of paid internships and residences. Like any true profession, teachers need time to learn their craft, aided and supervised by experienced master teachers. Pedagogues need to take a leaf from their own book on the use of "scaffolding." Here, a more knowledgeable other erects a cognitive scaffold around the novice, assuming primary decision-making responsibility, while the learner executes the tasks and in collaboration with the mentor, jointly reflects upon the outcomes. As the learner gains expertise and skill, the scaffold is gradually withdrawn. In this reflective process, the mentor can guide the inductee in deconstructing and reorganizing inflexible and ill-conceived content and pedagogical knowledge. The collaborative process should be developmental, reflecting first upon acquiring needed procedures and routines, then, rapidly moving to the reflective development of pedagogic content knowledge. Mentors would, therefore, have to be master teachers, staff developers, or college-affiliated teacher educators.

What, in essence, is needed is to establish a continuum in the process of teacher learning, operating from recruitment and pre-service education through licensing, hiring and induction to advanced certification. Such a plan has been advocated by the National Commission on Teaching and America's Future (1996). An offshoot of this practice would be the creation of a natural career ladder and/or the strengthening of partnerships between public schools and colleges. Fountain and Evans (1994) describe such a partnership where there is a continuum from college-based teacher preparation to partnership-supported beginning teacher experiences. The institution of such practices would certainly go a long way toward enhancing student outcomes in classes staffed by novices, as well as begin their socialization into a new teacher culture of collaboration and knowledge sharing.

Professional development

Staff development is and must be a central component for change in the schools. As new knowledge and problems serve as the impetus to further study and learning (Fullan, 1999; Sagor, 1997; Shulman, 1997; Zederayko and Ward, 1999), ongoing pro-fessional development must be part of this teacher-learning con-tinuum. Currently the vast majority of professional development is done through "spray and pray," i.e., one shot or a mini-series of workshops housed at the local school or district office. The literature is replete with condemnations of this approach, as teachers seldom extend or apply content dispensed in these settings to their classrooms. The problem, again, is the provision of content knowledge without the necessary pedagogical sup-ports. Even when provided as methodological workshops, a guided reflection process after initial implementation is still, very much, needed. Whether organized as school, district or union-sponsored mini-courses, and even with the best of intentions, staff development without the necessary practical and reflective follow-up becomes static isolated knowledge, which practitioners are often unable or disinclined to implement.

Creative and proactive support networks need to be developed at the school and district levels. These support networks need to facilitate, encourage and guide teachers in the implementation and reflection processes. One possibility is locating (union or district) staff developers at local school sites. These individuals would be masters not only of pedagogical knowledge, but also in facilitating the reflective process in others. They would be responsible for co-ordinating all staff development at a site; monitoring the implementation of innovations; leading some instructional workshops; and conducting group and individual reflective sessions. Where they lack the expertise or where an innovation is being brought to the school, outside staff developers would give the initial presentations. However, the in-house staff developer, working at times in collaboration with an innovation's project personnel, would then be responsible for implementation follow-up at the school. He or she would make appropriate classroom visits to observe and hone teachers' use and hold reflective sessions on the implementation process. Another possibility is in the use of ongoing or topic-specific staff development partnerships with colleges. Such partnerships would involve joint planning, action research, and reflection. Allen *et al.* (1995) provide a good example of this in their work with a local high school. With students from over 100 different countries, their collaboration focussed on issues of increased conflict due to diversity. Essentially, any serious staff development must provide teachers with specific rehearsal time, periodic observations of use, and follow-up activities that allow teachers to reflect upon these experiences with those engaging in similar activities. The focus of these discussions would be on how the new procedures "fit" both the school and its students, looking specifically for possible conflicts and variations in the outcomes that seem to be the result of differences in students' varied ways of knowing. Such sessions also provide an opportunity to deconstruct teacher isolationism.

Finally, professional development works best when it is relevant to the needs of staff. Teachers frequently complain that much of their staff development is decided at the district level, with little regard for distinctions between novice and veteran teachers or the unique needs of individual schools. Consistent with the trend toward site-based management, the professional development agenda should largely be the responsibility of staff at local schools. Several advisory lists have been developed identifying the key characteristics of good professional development (e.g., Hawley and Valli, 1996). We like Seyfarth's (1999: 263) adaptation of the work of Fenstermacher and Berliner for the Rand Corporation, duplicated in Box 10.2.

Box 10.2

Criteria of Effectiveness of Professional Development Activities

Relevance
Workshop addresses an identified need or a topic of interest to teachers

Clear Objectives
Presenter and participants understand objectives of workshop

Attractive Incentives
Participants receive incentives for participating and trying new techniques

Application
Content sufficiently clear that participants understand how to apply it in the classroom

Maintenance
Teachers who implement new ideas receive support

Instructor Knowledge
Instructor is knowledgeable of workshop content and able to present it clearly and engagingly

Classroom Fit
Content fits teachers' instructional style and classroom circumstances

Duration
Time allowed for participants to practice new techniques

Source: From Seyfarth (1999) which was an adaptation of *A Conceptual Framework for the Analysis of Staff Development N-2046 NIE* by G. Fenstermacher and D. Berliner (1983), Santa Monica: Rand. Adapted by permission of RAND Corporation.

Preparing school administrators

At the same time that principals' jobs are becoming increasingly more complex and constrained (Fullan, 2000), more and more is expected of them. The new tasks require qualities of disposition and nature rather than of skill and knowledge. Principals are being challenged to distinguish themselves not by their techniques or styles, but by their integrity and their savvy. Integrity, as defined by Evans (1996: 228), is a fundamental consistency between personal beliefs, organizational aims, and working behavior; and savvy as practical competence, a hard to quantify cluster of qualities that includes craft knowledge, life experience, native intelligence, common sense, intuition, courage and the capacity to "handle things." This combination of genuineness and effectiveness is said to make a leader "authentic," a person who inspires trust and confidence, someone worth following into the uncertainties of change. These qualities also are embodied in the concept of principals as visionaries, moral and cultural leaders, transformationists, and those living on the edge of chaos. In preparing principals for these roles, one must wonder if these are qualities that can be instilled through training in college programs. Evans (1996) believes they cannot be taught:

> a blunt truth: not everyone can. Despite the popularity of technical notions of leadership, most of us believe that good leaders must have the "right stuff," the right personal qualities to lead, and that these, like savvy or charisma, are to some extent innate: you either have what it takes or you don't.

Yet college-based administration and supervision programs, nonetheless, have just this responsibility. In this subsection we discuss how this preparation might best be done considering the constraints.

Pre-service leadership preparation

Starting with the best   To achieve the ends of the current wave of reform efforts, principals are needed who can effectively facilitate their staffs' and students' functioning at high levels of excellence (Wagner, 1998). Recruitment of quality candidates who have the potential to succeed as leaders is, therefore, crucial. Unfortunately, in the field of education, there are no "head hunters" or employment agencies screening individuals for the possession of the requisite personal attributes. The National Association of Secondary School Principals developed a screening instrument that uses simulations and structured interviews to discern skills in 12 key areas (McCarthy, 1999). Not in general use, programs in school administration continue to rely on undergraduate GPAs, essays and interviews, which may still be poor identifiers and predictors of the desired attributes in individuals. By default, self-selection remains the major determiner, and individuals wanting to advance in the field, take the step to enroll in administration programs.

To improve the selection process, public school/university partnerships can plan a major role by being a primary conduit for these programs. Program or other college faculty working in the local schools can make recommendations, as can school administrators and district personnel, based on observations of these individuals in the context of their schools. Individuals who work tirelessly and productively on their leadership teams and are able to engender the trust and respect of others would be identified. Similarly, individuals who exhibit good communication skills, collaboration, the quality of placing children first, persuasiveness, a meaningful understanding of instruction, ethics and an other-orientedness would be encouraged to enter these programs.

Course and fieldwork Similar doubts raised about the effectiveness of college-based pre-service teacher training programs have been raised about college-based administrator training programs. Interviews with school administrators have not found these programs or the course work leading to their licensing to be highly valued or regarded as useful (McCarthy, 1999). This same research did, however, find that an experimental program that included field-based projects, research, extensive practice under mentor guidance, collaboration with school districts, and a co-ordinated curriculum across courses was perceived as making them better leaders.

These findings further emphasize the need to make coursework meaningful through bridging activities in the field, combined with mentoring and reflective dialogue in the knowledge internalization process. Again, the focus must not be on merely dispensing information on the various organizational and leadership models; new curricula, instruction and assessment techniques; or implementing new reforms and standards, it must also focus on how this knowledge is held in mind. For example, many administrators know the various leadership models, in theory, but have neither seen them in action nor know how to use them themselves. Coursework needs to be accompanied by field opportunities or action research so as to develop appropriate pedagogical content knowledge in these regards. Candidates as part of their course assignments may have to take leadership roles in their schools' SBM/SDMTs, sit on subcommittees, engage in the inquiry process, and assume responsibility for implementing a subcommittee's action plan or part of their school's comprehensive plan. Each such course would also provide opportunities to reflect upon these experiences. These discussions would focus on how best to hold, or understand the information, and to facilitate its flexible application in working with different populations. An integral part of any candidate's grade for a course would be performance assessments highlighting their ability to work in teams, to assume responsibility, to communicate and show respect, to be fair and equitable, and to engender a sense of trust from others. These assessments also should be used to provide candidates with ongoing feedback on their strengths and challenges in these regards. The goals should be to help them know themselves, their strengths and weaknesses, and to provide them with useful strategies for developing and using skills needed in the schools today.

Although fieldwork in administration programs is analogous to student teaching in teacher training programs, in practice, it ironically encompasses far less time. Moreover, many, if not most, administrative candidates do their fieldwork at their home-school setting. Where home-school administrators do not employ newer administrative models or are poor examples of a model's use, desired knowledge tends to remain an abstraction, which hinders candidates' personal ownership and its translation into usable pedagogical knowledge. Ideally the fieldwork year should be transformed into a subsidized apprenticeship, where candidates can "shadow" and observe "master" administrators in action. This experience needs to be combined with opportunities for reflective dialogue, not only with their mentors, but also with others in their preparatory cohort, who may be apprenticing with administrators exemplifying different schools of thought. This way, candidates can begin to learn, in a meaningful fashion, the differential implications of the various models. This necessitates the need to identify good school administrators and model fieldwork sites.

Ultimately, like teachers, administrators need to learn that there is probably no one best leadership model under all circumstances. Moreover, schools being chaotic and spontaneous environments, like pre-service teachers, administrative candidates can never be presented with all possible situations to know which tool from any model to use at any particular time. Therefore, reflective sessions must help candidates identify key contextual factors and the conditions that signal their various uses. They would provide opportunities to reframe problematic situations, so as to elucidate the applied science versus the attitude and art of being an administrator (Schein, 1973), i.e., a type of "reflection-in-action" (Schon, 1989). Making the distinction between leadership and management, Hughes (1999) states that administration is a complex operation embracing both. Ultimately, the administrator must learn to apply the "craft" of administration (Blumberg, 1989) by judiciously balancing the art of leadership and the science of management to improve school climate, curriculum, instruction, and student performance.

Finally, college-based administration programs must also make these programs more rigorous and relevant. Research shows little or no relationship between the amount of graduate preparation and the perceived effectiveness of principals as instructional leaders (Zheng, 1996). Many states have, thus, expressed dissatisfaction with traditional administration programs and some are considering alternatives (McCarthy, 1999). If such college programs shift in their focus from dispensing knowledge to the development of appropriate ways of knowing and advancing pedagogical content knowledge, these programs too would advance in both rigor and relevance.

In-service leadership development

The transition from administrator in training to full administrator can be a daunting experience. School administrators, like teachers, tend to be isolated, seldom interacting with administrators from other schools to share ideas and resources, or to collaborate in the process of mutual problem solving. In fact, the opposite is true. The competition for high scores on standardized tests, and the comparisons made between schools on the basis of test scores, makes principals secretive, niggardly, and defensive with their peers. The trend toward punitive accountability further undermines qualities and habits needed for their professional growth as it limits their willingness to take risks. The task of in-service professional development must be that of reversing administrator isolationism and nurturing the qualities needed to be successful leaders in a changing postmodern world.

Internships and residencies   Easing and facilitating this transition should be the prime objective for the first three years of an administrator's functioning. Time and timing are crucial. Ideally, this transition should be a guided, gradual process through a series of positions each requiring and involving ever-greater responsibility and task complexity. Again, based on the medical model, an internship and residency seem advisable. The internship might take the form of a directorship of a program or mini school. Intern/Directors would meet periodically with their similar status peers under the aegis of a master administrator to problem solve and come to a better understanding of the impact of their actions on others. Informational needs evolving from these sessions would become the topics for ongoing developmental workshops. To further nurture a culture of administrative collaboration, periodic observations of each other, as well as performance assessments with structured opportunities for reflective feedback provided by the mentor/supervisor are recommended. Upon completion of the internship, the trainee would be granted a provisional certificate.

The residency would involve a natural progression to the position of assistant principal. This phase might last two or more years. At this level, as a means to constantly extend and nurture administrative collaboration, principals would engage in guided peer meetings and performance assessments on the order discussed for interns. Upon completion of minimally three successful years as an assistant principal, the leadership trainees would be eligible for a principal's license and application for a school leader position.

Developing master administrators   Attaining the position of school principal should not be the end of the administrator's growth and development. As is now the case in many states, first year principals need the assistance of a mentor, who spends at least one day a week with the trainee on the school site. Ideally, the mentor's primary role is to continue the administrator's collaborative reflection on his/her activities and on the complexities of educational leadership. Periodic collaborative problem-solving sessions for new principals at the district or a local college should assist in their initial adjustment.

Another resource in the development of principals is principal centers. Here, principals can be exposed to new conceptions of school leadership, meet with other principals, learn about promising new practice, or discover better ways to accomplish goals. At these sites, principals can discuss promising school practices, share problems, and where there are no solutions, they can collaborate on designing action research and experiment with different strategies in different settings without fear and worry of appearing inadequate (Barth, 1990). As neither staff nor principals at the centers evaluate or are evaluated by each other, less is at stake. The potential for learning is unlimited! According to Barth (1990: 155):

> If ways can be devised to help principals reflect thoughtfully about the work they do, analyze that work, clarify and reveal their thinking through spoken and written articulation, and engage in conversation with others about that work, both they and their colleagues will better understand their complex schools, the tasks confronting them, and their own styles as leaders. And understanding schools is the single most important pre-condition for improving them.

Study Questions

1. Why or why not would giving teachers greater decision-making authority and responsibility over student instruction lead to the enhanced professionalization of the field?
2. Give at least two arguments both for and against the elimination or significant abbreviation of college-based teacher and administrator preparatory programs.
3. If we grant that there is a need to enhance the caliber of the teaching force, what other means can be used to achieve this end without raising salaries or pre-service entrance requirements?
4. In what other ways would you recommend improving college-based teacher preparation programs so as to prepare them to meet the educational demands of today's society?

5. It is very hard to change an individual's attitudes. How might teacher preparation programs help teacher candidates develop facilitative attitudes, other than those mentioned?

6. Do you feel that the qualities sought in leaders today are primarily innate or can they be taught? Based on this view, how should course content be restructured in administration programs?

7. What would be the major benefits and obstacles of using a medical model in the preparation of teachers and administrators? Is it practical? Why?

8. What in your mind would be an optimum accountability plan? Be specific and explain the rationale behind each component.

References

Allen, K. W., Hutchinson, C. J. and Johnson, J. (1995) A new vision for staff development: hearing from the upstaged voices. *Journal of Teacher Education*, vol. 46, no. 4, pp. 312–318.

Amarel, M. and Feiman-Nemser, S. (1988) Prospective teachers' views of teaching and learning to teach. Paper presented at the AERA annual conference, New Orleans.

Bacharach, S. B. and Conley, S. C. (1989) Uncertainty and decision-making in teaching: implications for managing line professionals. In T. J. Sergiovanni and J. H. Moore (eds) *Schooling for Tomorrow: Directing Reforms to Issues that Count*. Boston: Allyn and Bacon, pp. 301–311.

Ball, D. and Feiman-Nemser, S. (1988) Using textbooks and teachers' guides: a dilemma for beginning teachers and teacher educators. *Curriculum Inquiry*, vol. 18, no. 4, pp. 401–423.

Ball, D. L. (2000) Bridging practices: intertwining content and pedagogy in teaching and learning to teach. *Journal of Teacher Education*, vol. 51, no. 3, May/June, pp. 241–247.

Barth, R. (1990) *Improving Schools from Within: Teachers, Parents and Principals can Make the Difference*. San Francisco: Jossey-Bass.

Barth, R. (2000) Learning to lead. In *The Jossey-Bass Reader on Educational Leadership*. San Francisco: Jossey-Bass, pp. 146–155.

Blumberg, A. (1989) *Administration as a Craft*. Boston: Allyn and Bacon.

Brandt, R. M. (1990) *Incentive Pay and Career Leaders for Today's Teachers*. New York: State University of New York Press.

Britzman, D. P. (2000) Teacher education in the confusion of our times. *Journal of Teacher Education*, vol. 51, no. 3, May/June, pp. 166–173.

Burant, T. (1999) Finding, using and losing (?) voice: a preservice teacher's experiences in an urban educative practicum. *Journal of Teacher Education*, vol. 50, no. 3, pp. 209–219.

Darling-Hammond, L. (1997) *The Right to Learn: A Blueprint for Creating Schools that Work*. San Francisco: Jossey-Bass.

Darling-Hammond, L. (2000) How teacher education matters. *Journal of Teacher Education*, vol. 51, no. 3, May/June, pp. 166–173.

Darling-Hammond, L. and Cobb, V. L. (1996) The changing context of teacher education. In F. B. Murray (ed.) *Teacher Educators' Handbook: Building a Knowledge Base for the Preparation of Teachers*. American Association of Colleges for Teacher Education, San Francisco: Jossey-Bass, pp. 14–62.

Darling-Hammond. L. and Falk, B. (1997) Using standards and assessment to support student learning. *Phi Delta Kappan*, November, pp. 190–199.

Darling-Hammond, L., Hudson, V. and Kirby, S. N. (1989) *Redesigning Teacher Education: Opening the Door to New Recruits to Mathematics and Science Teaching*. Santa Monica, CA: Rand.

Deal, T. E. and Peterson, K. D. (2000) Eight roles of symbolic leaders. In *The Jossey-Bass Reader on Educational Leadership*. San Francisco: Jossey-Bass, pp. 202–216.

Delpit, L. (1995) *Other People's Children: Cultural Conflict in the Classroom*. New York: The New Press.

Doyle, W. (1986) Classroom organization and management. In M. C. Wittrock (ed.) *Handbook of Research on Teaching*. 3rd edn. New York: Macmillan, pp. 392–431.

Elmore, R. (2000) Building a new structure for school leadership. *American Educator*, Winter 1999–2000, vol. 23, no. 4, pp. 6–13, 42–44.

Eltis, K. and Cairns, L. (1982) Perceived effectiveness of supervisors of the practicum. *The Australian Journal of Teaching Students*, vol. 2, no. 2, pp. 101–110.

Evans, R. (1996) *The Human Side of School Change*. San Francisco: Jossey-Bass.

Fountain, C. A. and Evans, D. B. (1994) Beyond shared rhetoric: a collaborative change model for integrating preservice and inservice urban educational systems. *Journal of Teacher Education*, vol. 45, no. 3, pp. 218–228.

Fullan, M. (1990) Staff development, innovation and institutional development. In B. Joyce (ed.) *Changing School Culture Through Staff Development*. Alexandria, VA: ASCD, pp. 3–25.

Fullan, M. (1993) *Change Forces, Probing the Depths of Educational Reform*. London: Falmer Press.

Fullan, M. (1999) *Change Forces: The Sequel*. London: Falmer Press.

Fullan, M. (2000) Leadership for the twenty-first century. In *The Jossey-Bass Reader on Educational Leadership*. San Francisco: Jossey-Bass.

Gitomer, D. H. and Latham, A. S. (2000) Generalizations in teacher education: seductive and misleading. *Journal of Teacher Education*, vol. 51, no. 3, pp. 215–220.

Gomez, D. L. and Grobe, R. P. (1990) Three years of alternative certification in Dallas: where are we? Paper presented at the meeting of the American Educational Research Association, Boston.

Goodlad, J. (1990) *Teachers for our Nation's Schools*. San Francisco: Jossey-Bass.

Goodlad, J. (1991) Why we need a complete re-design of teacher education. *Educational Leadership*, vol. 43, no. 3, pp. 4–10.

Grady, M. P., Collins, P. and Grady, E. L. (1991) Teach for America 1991. Summer Institute Evaluation Report. Unpublished manuscript.

Harrington, H. (1994) Teaching and knowing. *Journal of Teacher Education*, vol. 45, no. 3, pp. 190–198.

Hawley, W. and Valli, L. (1996) The essentials to effective professional development: a new consensus. Paper presented to the AERA Invitational Conference on Teacher Development and School Reform, Washington, DC.

Hughes, L. W. (1999) *The Principal as Leader*. Upper Saddle River, NJ: Prentice-Hall.

Interstate School Leaders Licensure Consortium (2000) "Standards for School Leaders." In M. Fullan (ed.) *The Jossey-Bass Reader on Educational Leadership*. San Francisco: Jossey-Bass, pp. 97–113.

Johnson, S. M. (1996) *Leading to Change: The Challenge of the New Superintendency*. San Francisco: Jossey-Bass.

Johnston, S. (1994) Experience is the best teacher – or is it? *Journal of Teacher Education*, vol. 45, no. 3, pp. 199–208.

Labaree, D. F. (2000) On the nature of teaching and teacher education: difficult practices that look easy. *Journal of Teacher Education*, vol. 51, no. 3, pp. 228–233.

Ladson-Billings, G. (2000) Fighting for our lives: preparing teachers to teach African American students. *Journal of Teacher Education*, vol. 51, no. 3, pp. 206–214.

Lytle, J. H. (2000) Teacher education at the millennium: a view from the cafeteria. *Journal of Teacher Education*, vol. 51, no. 3, pp. 174–179.

McCarthy, M. (1999) The evolution of educational leadership preparation programs. In J. Murphy and K. Seashore Louis (eds) *Handbook of Research in Educational Administration*. San Francisco: Jossey-Bass.

National Commission on Teaching and America's Future (1996) *What Matters Most: Teaching for America's Future, Summary Report*. New York: Carnegie Corporation of New York.

Nieto, S. (2000) Placing equity front and center: some thoughts on transferring teacher education for a new century. *Journal of Teacher Education*, vol. 51, no. 3, pp. 180–187.

Popkewitz, T. S. (1995) Policy, knowledge and power: some issues for the study of educational reform. In P. Cookson and B. Sneider (eds) *Transforming Schools: Trends, Dilemmas and Prospects*. New York: Garland, pp. 414–455.

Sachs, S. (1999) Advocates for immigration students protest new English exams. *The New York Times*, June 18. B1 and 6.

Sagor, R. (1997) Collaborative action research for educational change. In A. Hargreaves (ed.) *Rethinking Educational Change with Heart and Mind*. Alexandria, VA: ASCD.

Schein, E. H. (1997) *Organizational Culture and Leadership*. San Francisco: Jossey-Bass.

Schon, D. A. (1989) Professional knowledge and reflective practice. In T. J. Sergiovanni and J. H. Moore (eds) *Schooling for Tomorrow: Directing Reforms to Issues that Count*. Boston: Allyn and Bacon.

Sergiovanni, T. J. (1989) What really counts in improving schools? In T. J. Sergiovanni and J. H. Moore (eds) *Schooling for Tomorrow: Directing Reforms to Issues that Count*. Boston: Allyn and Bacon, pp. 1–8.

Sergiovanni, T. J. (1994) *Building Community in Schools*. San Francisco: Jossey-Bass.

Seyfarth, J. T. (1999) *The Principal: New Leadership for New Challenges*. Upper Saddle River, NJ: Prentice-Hall.

Shulman, L. S. (1997) Professional development: learning from experience. In B. S. Kogan (ed.) *Common Schools, Uncommon Futures: A Working Consensus for School Renewal*. New York: Teachers College Press, pp. 89–106.

Sindelar, P. T. and Rosenberg, M. S. (2000) Serving too many masters: the proliferation of ill-conceived and contradictory policies and practices in teacher education. *Journal of Teacher Education*, vol. 51, no. 3, pp. 188–193.

Sleeter, C. (1993) How White teachers construct race. In C. M. McCarthy and W. Crichlow (eds) *Race, Identity and Representation in Education*. London: Routledge, pp. 157–171.

Tozer, S. E., Violese, P. C. and Senese, G. (1998) *School and Society*. 3rd edn. New York: McGraw-Hill.

Wagner, T. (1998) From compliance to collaboration. *Education Week*, April 22, pp. 36, 40.

Zederayko, G. E. and Ward, K. (1999) Schools as learning organizations: how can the work of teachers be both teaching and learning? *NASSP Bulletin*, February, pp. 35–45.

Zeichner, K. M. and Hoeft, R. (1996) Teacher socialization for cultural diversity. In J. Sikula, T. Buttery and E. Guyton (eds) *Handbook of Research on Teacher Education*. 2nd edn. New York: Macmillan, pp. 525–547.

Zheng, H. (1996) School contexts, principal characteristics, and instructional leadership effectiveness: a statistical analysis. Paper presented at the Annual Meeting of the American Educational Research Association, New York.

11

It Takes a Village

Improving a nation's school system is no easy matter. It is simplistic to assume that uni- or even multi-dimensional solutions focused solely on the school system are sufficient to address long-standing problems rooted not only in decades of systemic neglect but which reflect the cultural beliefs of the larger society as well. The fact that each year tens of thousands of children drop out of school or are passed onto the next grade unable to demonstrate academic competence appropriate for their grade and age levels with only sporadic or opportunistic societal outcry is indicative of the context in which current reform efforts are being made. Significantly ameliorating, much less transforming, deep-rooted culturally based institutional problems cannot be accomplished merely by the setting of higher standards, allowing school choice, restructuring, and offering a plethora of professional development workshops for teachers and administrators. Those societal beliefs and assumptions that support these structures and outcome patterns in the schools must also be deconstructed, as we now know them to be counter-productive not only to the academic achievement of many children but to the welfare of the nation as a whole. The schools' larger support structures must also change.

In this concluding chapter we discuss how the agencies and stakeholder groups that support our school system need to change to facilitate and sustain second-order reform. We, therefore, revisit several of the major groups discussed in Chapter 2, this time from the perspective of what they can do to facilitate the school change process. If the current reform wave is not to go the way of previous efforts, these groups and the larger society need to "scaffold" the schools, i.e., provide the necessary support until the schools are able to function independently. Sacrifices are called for at all levels. What they are and the problems surrounding them are unpacked. Before reading this chapter, consider the following questions:

1. What should be the role of the federal government in respect to the public schools?
2. What should be the role of the state governments?
3. What, if any, should be the role of the nation's citizenry in school reform?

Putting School Reform in Context

Throughout this treatise, we have tried to convey the message that reform to and improvement in the nation's public schools are a matter best conceived not as a problem facing our educational system but rather as a dilemma facing our society today. It is estimated that one out of every four children in the United States fails to complete school with adequate literacy abilities (Allington and Walmsley, 1995: 255; Cohen, 1990: 256–257). The majority of these poorly performing students can be predicted, in advance, based on demographic information alone. It is quite telling about the true nature of our society when sociological and economic factors, like low SES, ethnic minority status, and English as a second language are those most correlated with school failure. Whether by design or benign neglect, our school systems have always been ineffectual in successfully educating children who begin school with few academic and economic advantages. Granted that the system has made great strides improving the academic performance of students from these groups since the 1960s (Berliner and Biddle, 1995), we can still predict with devastating accuracy what lifestyles different six-year-olds who begin with comparable ability levels will attain when they reach adulthood based on these factors alone. As long as schools perpetuate or do little to alter these patterns of circumstance, they, minimally, may be indicted as benign contributors to our nation's massive loss of human potential.

Curiously, in the face of this loss, we, as a society, have adopted a callous complacency to the fact that our schools have become "sorting machines" (Spring, 1996). We have, in fact, developed a conventional wisdom that explains and excuses it, passively condoning institutional procedures that literally work to deliver the school's stratified outcomes (Allington and Walmsley,

1995: 2). Despite sound evidence that the vast majority of children can become literate alongside their peers (McGill-Franzen and Allington, 1991), teachers, parents, communities, and interest groups that traditionally have fared well in the system desperately adhere to the belief that these children cannot do better, and have strenuously opposed various efforts to integrate, detrack, or channel adequate resources to needy schools and student groups – lest any redistribution jeopardize the benefits they or their children receive from the status quo (Oakes *et al.*, 1997: 43). Indeed:

> parents of students in high track classes exude a strong sense of entitlement. According to these parents, their children are entitled to more – resources, teacher time, challenging curriculums, and better instructional strategies – because they are more intelligent and talented than other students. (ibid.: 57)

So deep-rooted and prevalent are these societal beliefs that those who have reaped the benefits of the system's inequities can, without guilt, turn a blind eye to children who start life less advantaged, receive lesser resources in their schools, more watered-down and slower-paced curricula, and less proficient teachers. In fact, society, as a whole, tends to view these patterns of success and failure as proper and part of the "natural" order of things.

One major benefit of the publication of *A Nation at Risk* (National Commission on Excellence in Education, 1983) is that it has focused prolonged media attention on the influential role played by our public schools both in determining the nation's standard of living and in maintaining its pre-eminent world position. Recognizing that those students traditionally written off as "at risk" – those primarily drawn from poor and minority backgrounds – represent not only an increasingly large share of the school population but of the future workforce as well, government officials are increasingly declaring the necessity of altering these outcome patterns. Based ostensibly on claims of increased international economic competition, a shrinking pool of new workers, and the sheer desire to have an educated population, many educators and politicians believe that society can no longer productively continue to ignore the plight of this quarter of the population and to maintain institutionalized practices that virtually guarantee their academic and societal failure. As these reports warn, the future well-being of this country more and more depends upon the educational success of this population (Cohen, 1990: 253, 257).

Regardless of disagreements in labor market projections, to ensure continued international competitiveness with other nations the United States will increasingly have to open up its workforce. Needed is a greater pool of viable workers broadly distributed throughout the workforce, some unknown portion of which will need greater intellectual competence and flexibility. According to Allington and Walmsley (1995), the recent "Back to Basics" movement was a first step. It focused attention on developing minimal competency in reading and writing in all children and seems to have reduced the number of functionally illiterate children as well as narrowed the achievement gap between more and less advantaged students. However, they and others find little evidence that all children are reading and writing as well as they need to if they are to become productive and contributing members of American society. The present minimal competency levels are simply insufficient in today's world.

A great deal more effort and commitment from all stakeholders is required, for the schools cannot accomplish this task alone. As with any significant change, the cultural transformations called for by second wave reforms require a supportive environment if they are to be achieved and maintained. This means that we need to explore the types of supports that are needed to help create and sustain the current restructuring reforms. We focus on these types of reforms, rather than on some of the choice proposals as most types of alternate schools are currently being contested in the courts, and the indications are that their existence may become moot. In the first part of this section we discuss creating a supportive governmental and economic environment, and in the last part, we explore public support.

Creating Contextual Support for Public Schooling

The nation's school system is an integral part of the very fabric of our society. Jane David (1990) makes the analogy of an interlocking jigsaw puzzle with students and teachers in the center, surrounded by rings of interlocking pieces representing the demands of local, state, and federal agencies. "Trying to change one piece of an interlocking set of pieces is not possible unless the other pieces are flexible enough to yield when the shape of a neighboring piece is changed" (ibid.: 210). Previous reforms, she states, have either added another piece to the puzzle or have tried to change one piece without recognizing the need to change neighboring pieces. In this section, we discuss how the surrounding governmental agencies can create a multi-leveled scaffold around the schools, supporting the establishment of the types of changes that are needed to make current restructuring efforts work.

Creating a supportive institutional environment

Change is easier said than done. Momentarily setting aside affective change, improving schools cost money, e.g., to purchase new programs, train staff, and provide for ongoing support and assistance. The most needy schools, i.e., those with high proportions of underachieving students, also tend to have the most meager budgets and to lack the necessary resources to make the requisite improvements – irrespective of mandates or the setting of standards. Recognition of their plight is a first step in creating the political and economic climate necessary to bring these schools on par with other more advantaged schools. Capacity building, thus, needs to become the central focus of all actions directed at the school. This will require a paradigm shift for all governmental agencies, from a focus on procedural compliance to one on facilitation. Just as in construction, a scaffold is needed to support needy structures; these agencies must erect a scaffold around needy schools to provide the necessary assists, each at their own level.

District level support

At the district level such a paradigm shift would be manifest in altering their relationship to the schools from primarily monitoring and supervisory to that of resource provider. If at the heart of this redefinition is a reorientation toward the schools in terms of increased performance – rather than procedures – then the districts' role should most advantageously shift so as to assist the schools in acquiring the enabling tools and resources needed to meet content and performance standards as well as to become effective schools (Corcoran and Scovronick, 1998; Smith and Purkey, 1985).

Empowerment coupled with responsibility In making the shift toward empowerment of local schools, many functions affecting all schools that have typically been performed at the district level would be either delegated to or shared with the schools. For example, local schools need to have control over their instructional practices; the scheduling of classes; the various, but equitable grouping of students; professional development; and the budgetary resources needed to attain desired goals. District control and standardization of these practices for all schools, without regard to variations in local circumstances, are incompatible with the new views on discretion required by local schools to improve their productivity. Consequently, districts and schools need to sort out which responsibilities and authority can be assigned to the individual schools and which must remain at the central office level.

Districts and schools also need to engage in collaborative, cross-agency planning as part of the districts' efforts to help schools attain the current standards. Currently, many districts construct their own comprehensive educational plans without input from or discussion with their local schools. In turn, these schools receive and utilize district plans as a *fait accompli*. In combination with state standards they then serve as guidelines to develop the schools' local comprehensive educational plans. Structured in this way, these goals still carry the effects of top-down mandates. One possible way to alter this pattern is for districts to set goals and develop plans in co-operation with local school administrators. Local school personnel would then have a better understanding of their roles in the attainment of district goals and could then, more knowledgeably, establish their own goals within this context, tailoring their objectives to the unique needs of their school. Both district- and school-specific comprehensive education plans should also outline ways in which the district could and would assist the schools in meeting their goals. Districts would review and provide feedback to local schools on the perceived feasibility, possible challenges to these plans, as well as state the districts' ability to provide requested or proffered forms of assistance.

In return for greater empowerment, schools would have the responsibility of making sincere efforts to attain the stated goals and work toward the establishment of internal, as well as external, peer review mechanisms. In addition to establishing internal mechanisms for peer review, local schools should also participate in the development of district-wide intervention strategies for schools that fail to meet desired performance levels without prematurely punishing desirable risk taking and experimentation. The goal of schools and districts in these regards should not be punitive, but rather to create and nurture an atmosphere of community support and growth, on the order of the effective schools literature. Internal peer reviews should be a component of these plans, as well as a code of ethics that locate benefits or harm to students as the central consideration. In combination, such arrangements extend the decentralization process, reserving oversight and direction by the district only where necessary (Cohen, 1990).

Coupling top-down and bottom-up initiatives This plan, in essence, couples top-down and bottom-up change initiatives, and builds upon the finding that district advocacy is necessary to signal to stakeholders at the local level of their intent and seriousness not only in advancing a change initiative, but in their commitment to helping schools achieve the desired ends. Truly troubled schools still need the impetus of top-down mandates to signal the importance of a reform initiative and the necessity for change in their practices. However, prodding alone, even when combined with threats, will seldom suffice to move these schools. Truly troubled schools may need the help of an external coach or district monitor who can facilitate the school's bottom-up efforts. With loosely coupled organizations, individuals at the local level need to be given the responsibility to monitor their school's implementation, with foreknowledge that they will be held accountable for attaining these goals. In this way, these systems will learn the art of combining centralization and decentralization, lesson six in Fullan's (1993) Eight Basic Lessons on the New Paradigm for Change. The key is achieving control without controlling (Senge, 1990: 287):

> [L]earning organizations [need to] invest in improving the quality of thinking, the capacity for reflection and team learning, and the ability to develop shared visions and shared understandings of complex business issues. It is these capabilities that will allow learning organizations to be both more locally controlled and more well coordinated than their hierarchical predecessors.

Of babies and bath water Another vital role for districts is in helping schools to sort through the fragmentation, overload, and incoherence resulting from the uncritical and unco-ordinated acceptance of too many different innovations (Fullan, 1991). Local schools often lack the resources to research adequately and weed through the plethora of new innovations. Moreover, to test the usefulness and appropriateness of particular innovations, action or field-based research may be needed that might best be conducted at the district level, so that neighboring schools could serve as controls. With a district level shift to a focus on school capacity building and student achievement, then decisions concerning the institutionalization of a particular innovation would, of necessity, be evaluated primarily on the bases of the degree to which it advances local and district goals. Such collaboration between schools and districts would not only seriously reduce the incidence of the premature abandonment of projects based on a lack of funding or neglect occasioned by a shift of focus to other more trendy programs, it would also encourage research and discoveries on how best to match instructional strategies to particular populations. If schools are to become true sources of expertise and institutions are to learn in the process, this is the type of work that must be done.

State governments

The ultimate authority of the states over the schools gives them paramount significance in school change efforts. At the same time that local schools are being granted more control over their actions, states have a responsibility to ensure that at the local levels, excellence is being achieved with equity. Toward this end, states may have to take a more active role in promoting structural change through advocacy, direct support, and, finally, monitoring and review in co-operation with professional boards.

Advocacy Just as districts need to signal to local schools their serious commitment to an innovation, states can send similar messages. Through legislation, states can be powerful advocates for particular reform proposals by facilitating large numbers of stakeholders and schools in the adoption of particular innovations. They can also reinforce the goals and actions of restructuring districts, as well as inspiring and assisting restructuring efforts in districts that do not have the leadership or capacity of those which do (David, 1990). States can and are now sending strong messages to their districts about their curricular goals and learning objectives through the current changes in their accountability and assessment procedures, modifications in credentialing require-ments, and in their funding initiatives and patterns.

The essence of the advocacy role must be alignment coupled with diversity. While states seek the attainment of high levels of achievement in particular subject areas by all their schools and students, at the same time they must acknowledge and allow different schools and districts to attain these ends as they see fit. They must also support the schools in these efforts, both through advocacy and directly. If their actions are not consonant with their stated goals and proclaimed restructuring efforts, this will influence district and local school action far more than any verbiage.

Direct support   The primary way through which states support schools is through funding. The challenge, then, is to devise ways to ensure that schools have the capacity to achieve state standards as well as to effect current second wave reforms. Obviously this requires equitable school financing. The gross disparities resulting from the nation's system for financing public schools have been challenged in the courts since the 1970s. Although actual and threatened legal actions have been able to produce substantially revised or altogether new systems of school finance, many state legislatures remain unreceptive to committing new resources or reallocating existing funds, and have been reluctant to implement the decisions of courts that struck down the finance system in some states (Vandersall, 1998: 17).

Court challenges have, thus, continued contesting the use of foundation programs, seeking in their stead programs that will achieve equity in school financing. One proposal is tax base equalization, an approach that combines state and local revenues for school operation. Unlike flat grants, these plans stress local determination of a desired level of spending or taxation. Once local officials or voters set an expenditure goal, the state equalizes school districts' abilities to raise the necessary funds (Swanson and King, 1997: 203). According to Elmore and Fuhrman (1995: 437):

No longer did equalization schemes take the route of setting spending levels necessary to fund minimum standards ... Providing "adequate funding" in that manner had become a charade, since foundation levels over the years had increasingly been driven by the degree to which states were willing to tax themselves and appropriate money for education, rather than any substantive consideration of the costs of providing an "adequate" level of service. In response to the shortcomings of previous equalization, many states embraced the emerging doctrine of "fiscal neutrality," which permitted spending levels to vary within some limit as long as the differences were not wealth-related.

The cornerstone of many court challenges to the constitutionality of state policies for financing public schools, this plan maintains fiscal neutrality while demanding that resources for public education be a function of the wealth of the state as a whole rather than of localities. Currently six states use some form of tax base equalization while five others rely on this form of equalization either as an add-on within the basic formula or as a second tier of funding that builds on the base foundation program. However, as a whole, states seem reluctant to redistribute, or "recapture," locally raised property taxes, and some state courts have ruled that certain plans violated their respective state constitutions, e.g., in Wisconsin and Wyoming (Swanson and King, 1997).

Full state funding, therefore, seems the only answer, as complete state assumption of all reasonable school costs is needed to ensure uniformity or needs-based spending across school units. This proposal was made by Morrison in 1930 and again by the Fleischman Report in 1973. This report states:

> Full state funding makes possible, though it does not automatically provide, more effective controls over expenditures. It permits the state to invest in improvement in quality at a rate consonant with the growth of the over-all economy of the state. It eliminates the present competition among wealthy districts for the most elaborate schoolhouse and similar luxuries. (ibid.: 56)

Hawaii has a fully state-financed and a heavily state-controlled educational system, as is school spending in Washington. As a result of the school finance reform movement and subsequent movements to limit taxes and expenditures, California, New Mexico and a few other states are moving toward full state assumption (Swanson and King, 1997: 215–216). While these moves are in the right direction, it is important that funding be not equal, but needs-based; that it not be overly controlled, but allow local school personnel to make appropriate budget decisions consistent with the goals of second order school reform; and, finally, that it be adequate and not too little for everyone.

Accompanying tax equalization or full state funding should be the institution of opportunity-to-learn standards. Two specific strategies have been proposed: input-guarantee and performance-guarantee opportunity-to-learn standards. According to Elmore and Fuhrman (1995), the former seeks to guarantee that every student has equal access to high-quality learning by specifying key inputs (e.g., per-pupil spending, textbooks, and teacher training) in the form of binding standards. Although addressing resource inequalities, there are several problems with this approach. Not only do input-guarantee standards not provide any assurance that students will receive roughly the same "enacted curriculum," i.e. whether resources will actually be used in ways that promote student learning, they do not provide the right incentives for schools to improve, nor do they link educational inputs directly with student performance. Performance-guarantee standards, on the other hand, would reduce state input regulations of all kinds and focus policy primarily on school and student performance. Concern with low-achieving students would be addressed by formulating objectives in terms of the "value added" by schools to student learning, and rewarding and recognizing those schools that provide the greatest boost to low-achieving students. The weakness of this approach is that it continues to rely on and assume that tests and assessments actually measure what is worth knowing. Elmore and Fuhrman (1995: 449) conclude that:

> We know with some degree of certainty that past state policies, focused on the input side, have not come close to providing equal access to learning, judged either in terms of the distribution of inputs or the distribution of student learning. This conclusion would suggest that more emphasis on student performance in state policy and less on specifying inputs would at least send a signal to schools, students, and parents that results are important. But the uncertainty attached to performance-based policies suggests that state policy makers should be deliberate and skeptical about relying heavily on new performance measures as a basis for new policies. As a strategic matter, then states should probably be looking for mechanisms that nudge state policies

generally in the direction of greater reliance on performance, rather than input, controls, while looking for more effective and less obtrusive ways to engage input regulation.

Assessment   Mindful of both their responsibility and the problems associated with any type of performance measure, states are faced with the challenge of devising ways to ensure that schools and districts make honest efforts to bring all their students to levels of academic excellence. This requires assessment, i.e., some determination of what is being or has been done. Two things are crucial here, the validity of the data and the ends to which they are used. We previously discussed concern over whether current standardized tests accurately assess the full range of students' subject area knowledge as well as the higher order cognitive processes sought as part of the present reform wave. To achieve greater correspondence, several states have already begun broadening their test batteries to include items requiring use of these skills, as well as piloting the use of various types of authentic assessments, e.g., portfolios.

Currently, assessment data are used primarily for summative, rather than formative ends. With the former, data are used to make final determinations regarding program continuation and to mete out punishments and rewards. With formative assessment, data are used to identify challenge areas associated with local schools and student populations within schools as a means to provide help and assistance. The primary goal here is not to punish schools or students, but rather to support them. States, as well as districts, would use these data to disperse aide teams, comprised of former school administrators, master teachers and scholars in learning to help these schools devise plans to meet these challenges. For example, administrators may be helped to learn how to provide better support for their teaching staff, while teachers may need assistance in broadening their instructional repertoire so that students reach the same outcomes (Hill, 1989; Ladson-Billings, 2000).

States also need to become far more sophisticated in developing and using indicators and other information systems both to guide state policy development and to stimulate and inform local improvement efforts. Current reporting methods provide a very distorted picture of school performance. While standardized tests still provide one of the best means of comparing student performance among schools and states, scores must be adjusted for the demographic characteristics of the schools and provide some indication of "value added." Moreover, where innovations are involved, a realistic implementation time frame rather than an electoral schedule must be allowed before any valid determinations of progress can be made.

Like districts, states need to shift from a reward and sanction orientation to one that emphasizes enhancing school capabilities by providing technical assistance to local districts and schools, and by helping local educators define problems and devise imaginative solutions. According to Cohen (1990: 273):

> States face the challenge of creating an appropriate balance between central control and local autonomy – a balance between setting goals, standards, and expectations and providing districts with enough authority and flexibility to choose their own paths. States must avoid the trap of stifling change through shortsightedness, overly restrictive rules, and narrow measure of success.

Accountability States and districts are still wrestling with a range of proposals to determine the most effective one or combination thereof to hold schools and their staffs more responsible for students' outcome performance. Based on the belief that rewards and sanctions can impel schools to improve, the state of Kentucky, for example, enacted a policy in which schools that do not show each year specified percentage increases on students' standardized test scores automatically suffer sanctions, which include actions against the staff. Those that meet the standards, conversely, are financially rewarded (Darling-Hammond, 1994: 14). Research, however, indicates that such accountability measures do not tend to achieve the desired effect, and in fact, may do more to constrain the very processes schools need to bring about the sought after outcomes.

Newmann *et al.* (1997) explored the effects of several accountability methods in 24 schools undergoing reform. Of primary concern to these researchers was the issue of capacity, which they operationally defined in terms of teachers' professional knowledge and skills, shared commitment and collaboration toward a clear purpose for student learning, and school autonomy to act. They reasoned that to the extent that these factors reach high levels within a school, one would expect an increase in their ability to produce high quality student achievement (ibid.: 47). They found strong accountability was rare; organizational capacity was unrelated to accountability; schools with strong external accountability tended to have low organizational capacity; and strong internal accountability tended to be superior in reinforcing school capacity. What these findings imply is that the external forms of accountability used by states in this study may not be the best means to bring about increased student achievement. If organizational capacity is relatively unaffected, e.g., not significantly improved, by the imposition of external sanctions and incentives, they will do little to improve student achievement in any significant way. This finding is consistent with our case study, which showed that negative sanctions in the form of SURR status and being urged to adopt a school improvement model, in actuality, set a negative tone in the school toward the improvement effort and did little to spur the types of second changes desired. Seyfarth (1999), similarly, concluded that bureaucratic accountability has limited uses. Its exercise, through authoritative actions to direct the work of teachers, cannot be counted on to produce marked improvement in teacher performance, as the results depend as much on the teacher's desire to improve as on the actions of the authority.

Further adding to the argument against the use of external sanctions are problems associated with meting out equal punishments to schools with unequal challenges. Schools do not begin on a level playing field. Not only do schools differ in regard to the needs of their student populations, e.g., their initial distance from the goal standards, they also differ significantly in the available resources needed to facilitate students' attainment of the standards. As noted in the previous chapter, urban schools in poor neighborhoods tend to be under-funded, often lacking decent library and laboratory facilities, and have inadequate numbers of fully certified and experienced teachers – the single factor most associated with achievement differences between black and white students in several studies (Armour-Thomas, 1989; Ferguson, 1991). So great was the effect of this factor, that the wide disparities in achievement between black and white students in Ferguson's (1991) sample were almost entirely accounted for by differences in qualifications of teachers! The equal meting out of sanctions, thus, doubly penalizes poor schools and their students, first, by their inadequate funding, and then by punishing them for failing to perform as well as other students attending schools with greater resources and more capable teachers. Similarly problematic is the fairness and accuracy of public reporting of students' test scores. As not all schools are coming from the same starting point, the public needs to be informed of these initial disparities. Public rankings of schools' test scores should, therefore, include indicators of value added and follow ethical guidelines of the sort delineated by Myers and Goldstein (1997) shown in Box 11.1.

Moreover, strong external sanctions, by their very nature, often remove from schools the authority, mechanisms and resources that constitute the basis for reasonably holding them accountable. Where sanctions involve mandates and prescriptions related to their methods of comprehensive reform, impose close monitoring by district and/or state officials, assume external control over the school's budget and spending, centralize critical decisions related to the choice of curricula, texts and instructional methodology, and create contrived collegial planning bodies for the purpose of implementing decisions that are made elsewhere or that staff feel forced to make, they, in essence, remove from the schools the ownership of the change process. For under these circumstances, the schools are neither deciding the "what" nor the "how" of change. And to recall Sergiovanni's (1989) point, where schools do not have control over the "how" of instruction, one must look to where decisions are actually made to place accountability properly.

Similarly problematic are the use of incentives and threats of closure. Newmann *et al.* (1997) found that incentives for schools and teachers were rare and not significant enough to make a difference. Threats of closure and takeover, likewise, proved inconsequential. This was clearly seen in our case study, where the threat of the school's closing and subsequent Redesign status was actually welcomed by some staff members! Newmann *et al.* also found that the plethora of agencies to which schools are legally and bureaucratically accountable, e.g., local boards, district administrators, state and federal agencies, and parents, caused a great deal of confusion and conflict among staff as to whom they should respond. While some schools have improved under these conditions, these strategies are not magic bullets. As awareness grows of the nonlinear relationship between strong external accountability mechanisms and successful school improvement, policy-makers at the (federal) Office of Educational Research and Improvement are increasingly concluding that there is a need to "rethink their heavy reliance on legal and bureaucratic

Box 11.1

Myer and Goldstein's Ethical Guidelines for Performance Indicators

1. *The principle of unwarranted harm.* The fundamental guiding principle should be that publication, or communication by other means, should cause no unwarranted harm to those who are identified. The term "unwarranted" is used because under some legitimate circumstances it is in the public interest for genuinely poor performance to be made known.
2. *The principle of the right to information.* If acceptably accurate and unbiased information is available about the performance of public institutions, there should be a presumption that this will be made public.
3. *The principle of contextualization.* All performance indicators should endeavor to provide information that will allow the institutions involved to be judged in a fair manner. Indicators that are known to be affected largely by factors extrinsic to the institutions should not be used. No indicator should be published without a careful description of how it has been contextualized and how further contextualization could be achieved. This information should be presented prominently and in a manner that allows it readily to be understood.
4. *The principle of uncertainty estimation.* All performance indicators should be accompanied by estimates of statistical uncertainty. The presentation of uncertainty intervals or ranges should be as prominent as the presentation of the indicator values themselves.
5. *The principle of multiple indicators.* Where possible, multiple indicators relevant to each institution should be presented, rather than a single indicator or a summary over several. No single indicator should be more prominent than another.
6. *The principle of institutional response.* Any institution for which there is a set of indicators should have the opportunity to make a representation about the accuracy of the information presented. Further, the data for an institution should be available to that institution for scrutiny.

> 7. *The principle of the responsibilities of agencies publishing information.* Any agency involved in publicly providing performance indicators should assume responsibility for disseminating material about its procedures and their justifications. The agency should also publish the technical procedures used for data collection and analysis.
>
> *Source*: Myers and Goldstein (1997)

accountability, incentive systems – which remain problematic, and choice, as no one knows at this time if parents' knowledge that they have choice will be an important accountability technique" (Kirst, 1990: 28–29).

Similarly unsuccessful has been the use of holding students accountable, through grade retention and the withholding of diplomas for low achievement. There is a large body of research that demonstrates that grade retention typically does not help student learning and often has harmful effects on students in these regards, as well as on their graduation rates. Dozens of studies over the past two decades have found that retaining students contributes to academic failure and behavior difficulties, as students tend to interpret retention as proof of their personal inadequacy. It also has been found to increase dropout rates. More positive alternatives must be sought. Research suggests that effective alternatives are those that (1) ensure that teachers have the knowledge and skills they need to teach to the new standards; (2) provide school structures and targeted services that support intensive learning; and (3) create processes for school assessment that can evaluate opportunities to learn and leverage continuous change and improvement – which are, again, capacity issues. Until school systems address the dramatic inequalities in students' access to quality instruction, assessment policies and their consequences will prove ineffective in raising student achievement.

This does not mean that there are no effective means through which schools and their personnel may be held accountable. Research supports the use of internal forms of accountability. Newmann *et al.* found that where staff identified clear standards for student performance, collected information to inform themselves about their levels of success, and exerted strong peer pressure within the faculty to meet the goals that student achievement was greatest. Where schools had a commitment to monitor their progress and offer their own rewards and sanctions, there was greater consensus and skill development among staff. Seyfarth (1999), similarly, concludes that professional accountability is more promising. Improvement in practice and gains in student achievement may be achieved by helping teachers extend their professional expertise, providing opportunities for teachers to collaborate with colleagues, and helping teachers feel pride in their work. Clearly, the implication is that the school systems need to move toward the establishment and institutionalization of internal accountability mechanisms in the form of peer review boards, inside as well as outside the school.

At this point, however, exclusive use of internal and professional accountability, in our minds, appears premature. On the one hand, the incidence of schools with levels of internal accountability on the order reported by Newmann *et al.*, is probably small, for these appear to be sites possessing the attributes of effective schools. Where they do not already exist, achieving such levels of internal accountability may be as difficult as transforming these schools into effective schools. As for professional accountability systems, the creation of professional boards that ensure quality control over personnel, and not the delivery of service, is no guarantee that the needs of special needs children will be addressed. There are certified teachers in poorly performing schools whose professional behavior, save for their students' consistently low academic performance, would not cause them to appear before a professional review board. And at the present time, peer boards do not regard such behavior as warranting strenuous efforts at removal.

As a result of the problems associated with both external and internal forms of accountability, it appears that some combination of the two is advised. Consistent with our recommendation for districts, both top-down and bottom-up reforms are needed simultaneously. Top-down accountability systems will continue to involve the setting of clear content and performance standards for which schools should aim, as well as send clear signals to schools about the serious intent of SEAs and LEAs to support and monitor their implementation. Schools, principals and teachers must then be given the room to decide the "how" of attaining these standards. Internal systems must be put in place, including professional boards that will aggressively work to weed out incompetence at the same time that they nurture internal capacity building from the bottom-up. Once given true help and assistance, continued failure must meet with just consequences that have been spelled out in advance. One proposal is to alter the tenure system. Rather than grant tenure for life, administrators would sign periodically renewable contracts, e.g., every five to ten years, based on satisfactory performance – with one criterion among others being student performance.

Lessons from early restructuring efforts suggest that political will and organizational capacity for change at the local district level are critical preconditions for successful restructuring. States cannot create the will through legislation, nor bring about organizational capacity through the use of sanctions and incentives. Policy tools and strategies of influence are needed that are better suited to modifying the culture and capacity of local districts and the knowledge, skills and talents of individual educators (Cohen, 1990: 272). States must make use of these tools without relaxing civil rights protection. In fact, states have an obligation to ensure that districts not overlook the schools at the bottom – typically those serving disadvantaged students (David, 1990). In Box 11.2 David summarizes the types of assistance that school districts should provide.

The federal government

With the introduction of the federal government into the educational arena in 1965, through the passage of ESEA, one of its most significant roles has been as a bellwether, signaling to the nation's populace, its elected officials, and to educational authorities at the state and local levels, the importance of equity and excellence in our school systems. This symbolic role of the federal government should not be underestimated, as evidenced by the ways in which *A Nation at Risk* galvanized and indirectly spawned massive reform efforts across the United States (Fullan, 1991). In this document, the federal government set the tone and sent out a message that excellence was to be given paramount importance in the nation.

The very effectiveness of the office of the President to be used as a bully pulpit, necessitates that individuals serving in this capacity use their influence in rational and moral ways that support the realities, as well as the hopes, of school reform. Wishful thinking and hyper-rational declarations in the absence of knowing how or even whether something can be accomplished can and have only given reform a bad name (Fullan, 1991: 263). Our most recent example is George H. Bush, who in his State of the Union address on January 31, 1990 revealed to the nation his education goals for the year 2000, embodied in the Goals 2000 legislation (see Box 9.1). The hyperbole contained in these goals made them impossible to accomplish given the realities of the nation's school systems and the slow and plodding nature of the reform process. Naturally, by 1999, the National Education Goals Panel reported that the nation had made progress in only 12 of the 28 indicators (Hoff, 1999). In making sense of this failure, in characteristic style, elected officials blamed the victims, i.e., schools, teachers and society's disenfranchised for the seeming intractability of their plight, thereby perpetuating the larger society's cultural assumptions about poor and minority students. If this is not the intention or if true reform and the achievement of all children are the real goal, then in setting a tone and projecting a wish list for the public schools, the public needs simultaneously to be given a reasonable time frame and realistic expectations. They need to know that decades, if not a century, of neglect cannot be reversed in the course of a political term. It takes time for political wishes, or even enacted policy, to mature into changes in resource allocation, organizations and practice. Electoral time and implementation time are radically different. If the nation is ever to stop blaming the schools for a situation that is as much, if not more, the nation's responsibility, elected officials and policy-makers at all levels must help our citizenry become aware and sensitive to the true realities of the school change process.

In particular, the nation's changing demographics and the resultant economic need to educate previously disenfranchised populations require that the federal government, through the office of the President, signal to the nation that excellence must be achieved with equity. George W. Bush, the victor of a historic election in which the outcome was determined by the Electoral College contrary to the nation's popular vote, should take this election phenomenon and the fact that state after state passed ballot initiatives to increase support for public schools as an indication of a possible shift in public sentiment away from the nation's long-standing conservative ethic. According to Sandra Feldman (2001), President of the American Federation of Teachers, this election suggests that Americans are divided on many issues, but not on whether to support public schools and not on the quality of education we owe our children. Thus, the federal government, through this office, needs to take a strong and positive stand on equity and the public schools. The president must signal to the nation of the government's commitment to make sure that all children in our public schools receive the education that the world's greatest, wealthiest and most powerful nation owes to each of them (Feldman, 2001).

Creating a supportive societal environment

Parents and the larger societal community also have very significant roles to play in improving the nation's schools and student achievement. As our schools are a reflection of the beliefs and values of the larger society and the communities they serve, our school communities must want and support the changes made to the system. Similar to the question previously raised as to the ability of our nation's political elite to reach any consensus in the setting of national goals and state standards, is the question of whether public consensus can be reached. As people want different things for their children and from the schools, the signals they send to the nation's youths and to our politicians have been mixed, especially those about the significance of academic achievement. Compared to other developed societies, achievement in US schools often takes a backseat to the whirl of students' social lives and the demands of participation in intramural sports and part-time jobs. Most parents say they want their children to do well in school and get good grades; but they also want their children to have friends and to participate in after-school activities. Teenagers are encouraged not only to learn academic subjects but also to develop a social life, get a job, find romance, and pursue myriad other activities that compete with academic subjects for their time and interest. Indeed, in its quest for the well-rounded student, American society often steers the attention of students away from academic pursuits. According to Tomlinson (1992), so long as we, as a society, are ambivalent about the comparative importance of academic achievement, we shall continue to underwrite academic mediocrity. What needs, therefore, to be done?

Parent involvement

It's almost a truism that parent involvement with their children's education will facilitate their academic achievement. The work of Epstein (1988) who has conducted considerable research in the area strongly supports this conclusion. She states:

> There is consistent evidence that parents' encouragement, activities, interest at home and their participation at school affect their children's achievement, even after the student's ability and family socioeconomic status is taken into account. Students gain in personal and academic development if their families emphasize school, let their children know they do, and do so continually over the years.

Fullan (1991) cautions, however, that the term "parent involvement" is confusing and can mean several things. Based on Epstein and Dauber's (1988) work, he distinguishes four main forms of involvement: (1) parental involvement at school (e.g., volunteers, aides and assistants); (2) parent involvement in learning activities at home (e.g., tutoring); (3) home/community–school relations; and (4) governance (e.g., advisory councils). In reviewing the literature on these various forms, he concludes that the first two forms of involvement have a more direct impact on learning than do the other forms. Supporting the significance of the first form of parental involvement, Clark *et al.* (1980) found, in their research, that successful schools were more likely to have parents in the classroom as aides, visitors and as volunteers, and that involvement in the classroom rather than in the school in general, was related to academic success. The "carry-over effect" on students occurred as a result of parents' familiarity with the school and the instructional program, which helped students develop better attitudes toward their work (Fullan, 1991).

Fullan similarly endorses the facilitative effect of parent involvement in students' learning activities at home. However, research in the area of student motivation produces somewhat contradictory findings. Bempechat (1998), for example, finds that too much parental intervention at home can signal to children that their parents have low expectations of their ability. She gives greater weight to motivational support supplied by parents, particularly in regards to the school achievement of poor and minority children. Specifically, she supports parents providing unequivocal support for school and higher education, stressing

the importance of education in their children's future, and helping them complete applications (ibid.: 39–40).

Findings related to the participation of parents in school
government consistently reveal no significant relationship with
increased student performance. Despite state and district mandates for parental involvement in school governance, there is little
evidence to support any direct relationship between the two.
Moreover, most parents do not want to be involved in advisory
councils and SBM/SDMTs, and as a result of legislative mandates,
schools spend an inordinate amount of time in these efforts to
little avail. There may be many reasons to account for this
reluctance, not the least of which may be that such governance
groups do not have a clear focus and are not well implemented.
And parent groups can be effective in influencing decisions and
improving schools where they are provided with assistance in
gathering accurate information about the system, mastery of a
variety of intervention techniques, and the effective functioning
of their own group (Fullan, 1991: 239).

Similar to the above, the role of the home/community in
advancing student achievement is more one of potential than
actuality. Parents and community-based groups can (1) put pressure on schools and districts to do something about a problem; (2)
oppose specific innovations that have been adopted; or (3) do
nothing. In general, parent and community groups do not tend to
initiate or play a major role in bringing innovations to schools.
More often, they tend to "rise to the occasion to reject ill-
conceived innovations – what some have called the 'crap detector'
capacity of those on the receiving end of change" (Fullan, 1991:
244). Home/community groups can also play a vital role in
building political support for schools across constituencies and,
thereby, press for reform in school-based "service quality," i.e., in
monitoring and maintaining the structures necessary to ensure
the quality of education for all students (Moore et al., 1983;
Wilson and Corcoran, 1988: 116). However, this potential is not
evenly dispersed across parent groups and communities. According to Fullan (1991: 244):

> Communities in which parents are less educated are not as
> able to translate their doubts into concerted efforts to com-
> bat change for the sake of change. In other words, middle
> and upper class communities are more able to keep school
> districts honest.

Thus, while all parents' groups or mixed parent/teacher groups may need assistance and training to organize their efforts, those in poor and high minority neighborhoods may need particular assistance. Such help for parents and community groups is sometimes hard to find. In fact, Fullan states that parents are at a very great disadvantage if the school wants to keep them at a distance, as most do. He recommends that parents start with *Child Advocacy and the Schools*, a handbook put out by Designs for Change (Moore *et al.*, 1983).

Societal support

According to Davies, (1989: 15), without pressure from the outside, organizations like schools are not likely to overcome the built-in inertia that defeats change. As stated above and in Chapter 2, parents and the community, large voter groups, public sentiment and societal trends can exert strong forces for the initiation, the institution or the discontinuation of various school innovations. This may be particularly true for our public schools, as they are directly funded by public taxes. Public support, thus, seems to be a essential factor needed by the schools to sustain the reform efforts. If true, to what degree is society-at-large behind pivotal first and second wave reforms?

One way heuristically to assess the degree to which society is likely to support the major components of the current reform wave is to revisit the mission of public schooling to determine the extent to which key components of the first and second reform waves further various of these goals. If these reforms are consistent with the general values, aims, and underlying assumptions of the larger society and the various missions of public schooling, they will likely be condoned, if not supported. However, if they run counter to these forces, support is not likely and resistance may follow. Let us look first, in way of example, at the themes of equity and excellence, and then turn to the deconstruction of the school's hierarchy and teacher isolationism.

One way to gauge potential societal support for the reform theme of equity is to determine the degree to which society has condoned the reality of the system in advancing either functionalist or conflict theories on the key mission of the school. That is, what has been and seems to be societal reaction to the school's success or failure as a "vehicle through which countless individuals and groups of individuals have been able improve themselves socially, economically, morally, and politically" (Ravitch, 1994). The data are unequivocal regarding the reality of the system. Our schools have not, heretofore, been a vehicle through which the nation's poor and ethnic minorities, as a whole, have been able to attain this functionalist goal. Yet, societal reaction, in general, has been one of curious complacency with these outcomes. In fact, parents and the public have been found to be vociferous advocates for the maintenance of those public school practices that have been most instrumental in the educational disenfranchisement of the poor and many ethnic minorities (Oakes, 1985; Oakes et al., 1997). These findings strongly suggest that the dominant society largely continues to adhere to conventional wisdom about why people succeed and fail and/or seeks to maintain the "perks" that result from the current status quo. This does not bode well for this reform effort.

Similarly, in regard to issues of excellence and standardized testing, the larger society may not have "bought" the alarmist media and political hype about the "rising tide of mediocrity" in our schools today. Most parents, when asked about their own personal satisfaction with the schools their children attend, responded favourably (Rose and Gallup, 1998). Despite parents and the larger society's support for the setting of standards and the increased use of standardized testing (e.g., 71 percent of the parents in the Rose and Gallup (1998) survey indicated they support a voluntary national test program), societal dissatisfaction may be afoot concerning the additional pressure this puts on their children. For example, one third of parents in a wealthy New York suburb organized to keep their children home on the day scheduled for standardized tests to protest against the school's over-emphasis on test preparation, which they felt stifled creativity and the very programs that have made their schools excel (Zernike, 2001).

It is similarly doubtful whether the public will insist on the institution of second-wave reforms aimed at deconstructing the school hierarchy and teacher isolationism. Save for the presence of computers and Internet access, society as a whole does not appear to have changed its conceptions of what a "real school" looks like.

In aggregate it would, thus, seem that current public attitudes toward the schools' outcome patterns, extant curriculum, and their views on the right ways to structure and to teach do not strongly support the major components of first- and second-wave reforms. To achieve these changes, schools would have to adopt cultural features, promulgate a belief system, and revise curricula in ways that are currently inconsistent with the larger dominant society. The only other time in recent history when similar reform themes or approaches to instruction were adopted was during the 1960s, when they then reflected a concomitant change in societal thinking and national events. It is probable that if greater public support cannot be elicited, these first- and second-wave reforms will likely go the way of earlier reforms. It would also suggest that the schools' problem with sustaining earlier reforms may not be completely their own fault. The schools' seeming resistance to change and the reassertion of traditional modes and patterns may, in fact, be a manifestation of these institutions' continuous realignment with societal values. This may be the very backbone of the system's stability and at the heart of its seeming intransigence. If this is true, any effort to change the schools without the support of the larger society that they serve, whose culture and values they reflect and promulgate, would be a gargantuan task, if not impossible.

We feel, however, this situation is not without hope. Forces are currently impacting upon the schools and society that are pushing both toward the adoption of values consistent with current reforms, e.g., the loss of ground in international comparisons of students' academic performance, the increasing proportion of the nation's workforce filled by ethnic minorities, and the need for more higher-order thinkers to maintain world preeminence. To the extent that the dominant society has the ability and feels the necessity to maintain its privilege and a conservative ethic, second-order innovations will probably go the way of past efforts and excellence will be sought for the few. On the other hand, to the degree that society responds to these forces, they will see that excellence cannot be achieved without equity and will push the schools to embrace second-order change.

> In actuality, the only way public education will ever become excellent is through pursuing a plan of equity. The educational system must be improved for all children. Those who have espoused excellence without equity have only improved the system for a select few – hardly an acceptable result in a democratic society. To eliminate this historical struggle, priority must be placed on equity with the necessary financial support from the public to assure an excellent education for all students. (Gittell and McKenna, 1998: 4)

The Second Wave of School Reform

Themes revisited

The current reform wave, like its predecessors, reflects the themes that have historically been at issue in public schooling in these United States. Unique from previous reform waves and mirroring the ambivalence of the larger society, current proposals are a potpourri, offering plans and proposals at the same time that are consistent with the opposing forces that have traditionally vied for pre-eminence and control over the schools. In this final subsection we revisit these themes in light of the lessons learned throughout this text.

Control over the schools

Who should control the schools remains front and center with current reform efforts. Plans that would move the schools toward greater governmental control, or centralization, have been principally embodied in the concept of standards. The federal government, the states, and local districts have all promulgated their own list of content area knowledge that all children should acquire through public schooling, as well as set performance goals in their attainment. Standards have already been instituted, as have sanctions for schools failing to reach these goals.

On the other hand, plans that push the system in the opposite direction, toward greater decentralization, have sought to give teachers and parents greater voice. Those that seek to create alternate paths or options for parents include opening school selection to market forces, e.g., vouchers, tax credits, charter schools, and privatization. Those seeking to work within the current system advocate a flattening of the organizational hierarchy at the local level through the creation of school councils and SBM/SDMTs. Almost all these proposals have been or are variously being tried in the states, as well as in the courts. At this point it is impossible to determine which, if not all, of these reforms will go the way of previous efforts.

Lessons from previous reform waves have taught legislatures that with loosely coupled institutions, like the schools, control works best when it comes from the bottom. Reason and reality indicate that state governments may well retain control over the "what" of public schooling; however, local schools must be empowered and given control over the "how" of instruction. In essence, centralization must be combined with decentralization if the nation's larger goals are to be achieved.

Best practices: instructional methodology

Similarly, debate continues on the issue of the best method for educating youths. However, forces both inside and outside the system are greatly influencing decisions in this area. The imposition of state content and performance standards would, in some ways, encourage a more teacher-centered approach, as teachers and schools must introduce to students particular bodies of knowledge and skill areas at each grade level. On the other hand, the rapidly increasing diversity of the schools' student populations, and the states' new emphasis on students' acquiring higher order and critical thinking skills suggest the use of more child-centered approaches to instruction.

For all children to achieve these standards of excellence it is important that educators realize that there is no one best practice under all circumstances. All practices and approaches to learning and instruction have their strengths and weaknesses. They are merely tools to be variously used toward an end. Practices should be chosen to match students' needs, the type of knowledge to be learned, and the desired outcome of instruction. It is in the wise and expert use of these approaches by teachers that excellence will be attained for all.

Teaching as a profession

According to sociological definitions, teaching is still not yet a true profession. There are several criteria which the occupation is said to be lacking. Most often mentioned are the existence of a body of knowledge necessary for professional practice; the functioning of a system for professional accountability in the form of a peer review board that monitors and ensures quality of preparation and practice; the existence of a code of ethics that orients practice within the profession toward the greatest good; and a large degree of uncertainty encountered in the problems faced and in the possible solutions to these problems. In the past twenty years, forces for change have tended to operate most on the last of these criteria. That is, with the increasing diversity of the schools' student population, the uncertainty in and the expertise required for practice are increasing exponentially. The circumstances under which all teachers now must practice necessitate problem solving and higher order thinking, which would thus, move the field toward greater professionalization.

However, challenges to the field's professionalization remain relative to the other criteria. For teaching to become a profession, educators at all levels must embrace these criteria as opportunities to achieve greater self-determination in the professionalization of the field. Through action research on the teaching and learning of diverse populations as well as on optimal ways to develop both pedagogical and pedagogical content knowledge, educators can create and advance the body of knowledge needed for the practice of the profession. Practitioners in the field must also embrace the concept of empowerment with responsibility. They can no longer continue to turn a blind eye or close their doors to incompetence. Means must be devised to establish internal accountability mechanisms and to develop a code of ethics and quality in practice that will ensure excellence and equity in practice.

Accountability

In the current reform era, different forms of accountability have variously been tried. Most efforts have utilized bureaucratic, market and legal forms. As indicated above, bureaucratic forms of accountability, including public reporting, punitive designations, close monitoring coupled with the imposition of constraints, threats of closure, sanctions on students, and incentives have been found to be relatively ineffectual in raising student achievement at poorly performing schools. Their use is further complicated by problems associated with their validity and fairness. The effect of the use of market forces remains an open and hotly contested issue. On the one hand, disparities in parents' access to information and their wherewithal to pursue alternatives run the serious risk of further exacerbating the chasm separating SES groups. On the other hand, the use of public funds to pay children's tuition at parochial schools, which tends to be the primary alternate path taken by most parents in urban areas, violates the separation of church and state. Legal contestations are rife. Similarly, state funding formulas are being challenged on the basis of the resulting inequities in schools' and districts' capacity to meet the standards and winning cases in these regards. However, it is an open question as to how many states will follow the lead of states like Kentucky, California, Texas, Arkansas, Washington, Ohio, Montana and Florida in their efforts to equalize the spending capacity of rich and poor districts. For example, New York State's Governor has promised to challenge the recent court ruling against his state's funding formula.

Research, on the other hand, supports the use of internal, or professional, accountability systems. However, the lack of existence of a formal peer review board and the rarity of in-house peer review mechanisms at the local school level pose a serious challenge to their use at this time. Thus, until and while peer review boards and committees can be established in and outside the schools that are guided by a code of ethics and a paramount concern for the greatest good, education authorities must help in their establishment and continue to signal their serious intent to bring about excellence with equity in all schools through their support and guidance.

Change and stability

What are we to conclude from all this about reforming schools, in general, and the probability for success of the current reform wave? It is difficult to say, several things may happen. Elmore (1990) presents three options that seem apt: co-optation, adaptive realignment and true transformation. With co-optation, states and localities embrace school restructuring as a label for what they are already doing and discard the substance. However, as second-wave reforms currently being strenuously pushed by the states run counter to traditional school cultures, it is unlikely that schools can adopt the rhetoric of school restructuring without some of the substance.

With adaptive realignment, shifts in alignment of key interests occur in response to changes in the political and social environment of schooling. For example, ever larger concentrations of the extremely poor and affluent, accompanied by the erosion of the middle class will produce pressure for urban and suburban school systems to become more responsive to differences among student populations. Such forces combine to push schools in the direction of needed reforms, but only as is necessary. As these forces are not evenly distributed, Elmore predicts a significant number of states and school districts will embrace major school restructuring initiatives as a response to pressing social and political problems and will pursue the initiative as long as the pressure persists. How much restructuring occurs will be a function of how pressing are the problems. School restructuring would then become a series of strategic responses to a set of pressing problems, organized around a certain set of themes, rather than a comprehensive template for the transformation of school. The risk here is that reform will become a scattered collection of isolated experiments without any coherence; and there is no guarantee that the restructuring it produces will change the conditions of teaching and learning for teachers and students.

The third option is true transformation. It depends on schools and teachers developing clear strategies for dealing with student diversity, changes in the organization of authority and the responsibilities of the school, and the substitution of process controls for standardized output measures. Elmore gives little hope for this possibility as it implies the presence of certain political and social conditions, e.g., the alignment of state and local reform policies around a common conception of what schools should do, interest groups reaching consensus on a common set of purposes, adequate training and support for school personnel, and outreach to parents. Elmore questions the nation's ability to align political and institutional interests necessary to produce the required changes in policy and practice.

We, on the other hand, do feel some hope. The presidential election in the year 2000 was unique and historical. The nation seemed split down the middle between those wanting to maintain the status quo and further the society's conservative ethic and those desirous of societal change and a better quality of life for all. This signals a possible turning point for society at large. In addition, the rapid increase in the nation's "minority" populations, such that they will soon constitute the majority – as they already are in some localities – will change the character of the nation. These demographic changes will enable these groups to use the politics of education both to effect legislation and to exert societal support for measures that will create more egalitarian ends in public schooling or engender forces against this threat. According to Fullan (1999: 84):

> we are on the brink of a new age. The future could go in two opposite directions. It could march down the path of self-interest, with greater gaps between the haves and have

Box 11.2

What Restructuring School Districts Do

Provide leadership
Make long-term commitment to comprehensive change:
- guided by goals not prescriptions
- characterized by many reinforcing strategies and steps

Communicate goals, guiding images, and information:
- create a language for change and a focus on student learning
- have direct communication between schools and district leaders

Encourage experimentation and risk taking:
- begin with schools that volunteer
- support experimentation with waivers from constraining rules

Demonstrate and promote shared decision-making:
- involve all staff in developing educational goals and values
- limit faculty meetings to items that require immediate action

Create new organizational structures
Participate actively in building new alliances:
- make co-operative agreements with teachers' unions
- create new joint ventures with foundations, advocacy groups, businesses and universities

Devolve authority to schools and to teachers:
- give schools authority over staffing and materials budgets
- provide incentives for principals to involve teachers in school-site decisions

Promote creation of new roles, for example:
- teachers as leaders, evaluators, curriculum developers, and facilitators of student learning

- administrators as facilitators of teachers and as instructional leaders

Develop and demonstrate during the summer new models of:
- restructured programs for staff and students
- support for teachers to develop curriculum and educational materials

Create new forms of accountability that:
- match the comprehensive nature and time line of restructuring
- use many measures, including those defined by schools

Provide support and assistance
Provide a broad range of opportunities for professional development such as:
- on- and off-site assistance for teachers and administrators
- development sessions that include techniques in management, clinical supervision, instruction, and content

Provide time for staff to assume new roles and responsibilities:
- time for planning, working with colleagues, and school decision-making
- release time for professional development activities

Seek supplementary sources of funding and assistance from
- state and federal governments
- local businesses, private foundations, and individuals

Source: David (1990)

---

nots and a continuing deterioration of democracy and the common good. Or the negative forces of postmodernity could play themselves out. We could, in evolutionary terms, not so much reclaim higher ground but move toward it.

It is our hope that these events will serve as a catalyst for change and advancement, not only in the schools but also in the nation as a whole.

Study Questions

1. Outline a plan for reforming schools that shows the responsibilities of each of the major stakeholders. Include the school, i.e., teachers and parents; the district; the state; and the federal government.
2. Imagine that you are a member of a school creating an internal peer review committee, establish a set of criteria and state what data or information you would seek.
3. Should and can schools and their staffs be held reasonably accountable for the academic performance of their students? Explain.
4. How do current proposed accountability systems compare with those employed over the last decade? Have the nation's notions of accountability progressed or regressed? Why?
5. It has been said that a balance is needed between top-down and bottom-up efforts, particularly regarding the issue of accountability. Devise an accountability system of external and internal supports and sanctions for the interface between local schools and districts, as well as with the state.
6. What system for school funding do you support, and why?
7. Create a code of ethics for a teacher peer review board. How would it change for an administrator peer review board?
8. What factors do you feel are necessary to bring the larger society vigorously to support the values and outcome ends of the current reform wave? What factors would mitigate for or against their occurrence?
9. What is your belief about the probable fate of the current reform wave? Which of Elmore's consequences do you feel is more likely to occur and why?

References

Allington, R. L. and Walmsley, S. A. (1995) *No Quick Fix: Rethinking Literacy Programs in America's Elementary Schools*. New York: Teachers College Press, Columbia University.

Armour-Thomas, E. *et al.* (1989) *An Outlier Study of Elementary and Middle Schools in New York City: Final Report.* New York: New York City Board of Education.

Bempechat, J. (1998) *Against the Odds: How "At-Risk" Students Exceed Expectations.* San Francisco: Jossey-Bass.

Berliner, D. C. and Biddle, B. J. (1995) *The Manufactured Crisis: Myths, Fraud, and the Attack on America's Public Schools.* New York: Longman Publishers.

Clark, D., Lotto, S. and MacCarthy, M. (1980) Factors associated with success in urban elementary schools. *Phi Delta Kappan,* vol. 61, no. 7, pp. 467–470.

Cocoran, T. and Scovronick, N. (1998) More than just equal: New Jersey's quality education act. In M. Gittell (ed.) *Strategies for School Equality.* New Haven, CT: Yale University Press, pp. 53–59.

Cohen, M. (1990) Key issues confronting state policymakers. In R. F. Elmore and Associates (eds) *Restructuring Schools: The Next Generation of Educational Reform.* San Francisco: Jossey-Bass, pp. 251–288.

Darling-Hammond, L. (1994) Performance-based assessment and educational equity. *Harvard Educational Review,* vol. 64, no. 1, Spring, pp. 5–30.

Darling-Hammond, L. and Falk, B. (1997) Using standards and assessments to support student learning. *Phi Delta Kappan,* November, pp. 190–199.

David, J. L. (1990) Restructuring in progress: lessons from pioneering districts. In R. F. Elmore and Associates (eds) *Restructuring Schools: The Next Generation of Educational Reform.* San Francisco: Jossey-Bass, pp. 209–250.

Davies, D. (1989) Poor parents, teachers and the schools: comments about practice, policy and research. Paper presented at the American Educational Research Association annual meeting.

Dewey, J. (1900) *The School and Society.* Chicago: Chicago University Press.

Elmore, R. F. (1990) Conclusion: toward a transformation of public schooling. In R. F. Elmore and Associates (eds) *Restructuring Schools: The Next Generation of Educational Reform.* San Francisco: Jossey-Bass, pp. 289–297.

Elmore, R. F. and Fuhrman, S. H. (1995) Opportunity-to-learn standards and the state role in education. *Teachers College Record,* vol. 96, no. 3, Spring, pp. 432–457.

Epstein, J. L. (1988) Effects on student achievement of teachers' practices for parent involvement. In L. Silvern (ed.) *Literacy through Family, Community, and School Interaction.* Greenwich, CT: JAI Press.

Epstein, J. L. and Dauber, S. L. (1988) Teacher attitudes and practices of parent involvement in inner-city elementary and middle schools. Paper presented at the American Sociological Association annual meeting.

Feldman, S. (2001) Voters agreed that no child should be "left behind." *On Campus*, vol. 20, no. 5. p. 5.

Ferguson, R. F. (1991) Paying for public education: new evidence on how and why money matters. *Harvard Journal on Legislation*, Summer, pp. 465–498.

Fullan, M. (1993) *Change Forces: Probing the Depth of Educational Reform*. London: Falmer Press.

Fullan, M. with Stiegelbauer, S. (1991) *The New Meaning of Educational Change*. New York: Teachers College Press, Columbia University.

Fleishmann, M. (1973) *The Fleishmann Report on the Quality, Cost, and Financing of Elementary and Secondary Education in New York State*, vol. 1. New York: Viking Press.

Hill, H. D. (1989) *Effective Strategies for Teaching Minority Students*. Bloomington, IN: National Education Service.

Hoff, D. J. (199) Goals push for 2000 falls short. *Education Week*, vol. xix, no. 15, December 8, pp. 1, 10–11.

Kirst, M. (1990) *Accountability: Implications for State and Local Policymakers*. Policy Perspectives Series. Washington, DC: US Department of Education, Office of Educational Research and Improvement.

Labaree, D. F. (2000) On the nature of teaching and teacher education: difficult practices that look easy. *Journal of Teacher Education*, vol. 51, no. 3, pp. 228–233.

Ladson-Billings, G. (2000) Fighting for our lives: preparing teachers to teach African-American students. *Journal of Teacher Education*, vol. 51, no. 3, pp. 206–214.

McGill-Franzen, A. and Allington, R. L. (1991) Every child's right: literacy. *Reading Teacher*, vol. 45, pp. 86–90.

Metz, M. H. (1990) Real school: a universal drama amidst disparate experiences. In D. E. Mitchell and M. E. Goetz (eds) *Educational Policies for the New Century*. London: Falmer Press, pp. 75–92.

Moore, D., Soltman, S., Steinberg, L., Manar, U. and Fogel, D. (1983) *Child Advocacy and the Schools*. Chicago: Design for Change.

Myers, K. and Goldstein, H. (1997) Failing schools or failing systems? In A. Hargreaves (ed.) *Rethinking Educational Change with Heart and Mind*. Alexandria, VA: ASCD.

National Commission on Excellence in Education (1983) *A Nation at Risk*. Washington, DC: US Department of Education.

Newmann, F. M., King, M. B. and Rigdon, M. (1997) Accountability and school performance: implications from restructuring schools. *Harvard Educational Review*, vol. 67, no. 1, pp. 41–74.

Oakes, J. (1985) *Keeping Track: How Schools Structure Inequality*. New Haven, CT: Yale University Press.

Oakes, J., Wells, A. S., Yonezawa, S. and Ray, K. (1997) Equity lessons from detracking schools. In A. Hargreaves (ed.) *Rethinking Educational Change with Heart and Mind*. Alexandria, VA: Association for Supervision and Curriculum Development (ASCD), pp. 43–72.

Ravitch, D. (1994) Forgetting the questions: the problem of educational change. In A. R. Sodovnik, P. W. Cookson and S. F. Semel (eds) *Exploring Education: An Introduction to the Foundations of Education*. Boston: Allyn nad Bacon, pp. 123–131.

Rose, L. C. and Gallup, A. M. (1998) The 30th Annual Phi Delta Kappan/Gallup Poll of the public's attitudes toward public schools. *Phi Delta Kappan*, September, pp. 41–56.

Sadovnik, A. R., Cookson, P. W. and Semel, S. F. (1994) *Exploring Education: An Introduction to the Foundations of Education*. Boston: Allyn and Bacon.

Senge, P. (1990) *The Fifth Discipline: The Art and Practice of the learning organization*. New York: Doubleday.

Sergiovanni, T. (1989) What really counts in improving schools? In T. J. Sergiovanni and J. H. Moore (eds) *School for Tomorrow: Directing Reform to Issues that Count*. Boston: Allyn and Bacon.

Sergiovanni, T. J. (1979) *Building Community in Schools*. San Francisco: Jossey-Bass.

Seyfarth, J. T. (1999) *The Principal: New Leadership for New Challenges*. Upper Saddle River, NJ: Prentice-Hall.

Smith, M. S. and Purkey, S. C. (1985) School reform: the district policy implications of the effective schools literature. *Elementary School Journal*, vol. 85, no. 3, pp. 353–390.

Spring, J. (1996) *American Education*. New York: McGraw-Hill.

Swanson, A. D. and King, R. A. (1997) *School Finance: Its Economics and Politics*. New York: Longman Publishers.

Tomlinson, T. (1992) *Hard Work and Higher Expectations: Motivating Students to Learn*. Office of Educational Research and Development, Washington, DC: US Department of Education.

Vandersall, K. (1998) Post-Brown school finance reform. In M. J. Gittell (ed.) *Strategies for School Equity*. New Haven, CT: Yale University Press, pp. 11–23.

Wilson, B. and Corcoran, T. (1988) *Successful Secondary Schools: Visions of Excellence in American Public Education*. Philadelphia: Falmer Press.

Zernike, K. (2001) In high scoring Scarsdale, a revolt against state tests. *New York Times*, April 13, pp. A1 and B6.

Index